How time flies! *Black Cat* is now in its 15th volume. Three years have passed since I started this series. At first, I thought, "If it goes ten volumes, I'll be happy." I never imagined that it would continue this long. This is all due to the support all of you have given me. Thank you so much!! The story of the battle against Creed, which was first introduced in Volume 2, will soon reach its culmination. What happens thereafter is, frankly, uncertain even in my mind. (laugh) However, I will continue to do my very best, so I ask for your continued support!!

—Kentaro Yabuki, 2003

Kentaro Yabuki made his manga debut with *Yamato Gensoki*, a short series about a young empress destined to unite the warring states of ancient Japan and the boy sworn to protect her. His next series, *Black Cat*, commenced serialization in the pages of *Weekly Shonen Jump* in 2000 and quickly developed a loyal fan following. *Black Cat* has also become an animated TV series, first hitting Japan's airwaves in the fall of 2005.

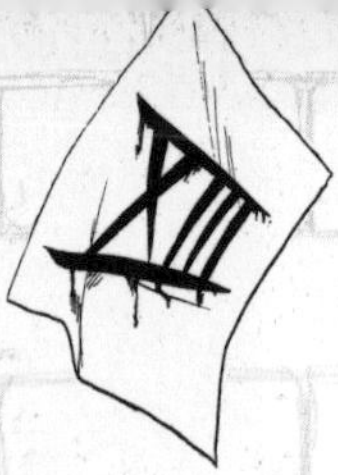

BLACK CAT VOL. 15
The SHONEN JUMP Manga Edition

STORY AND ART BY
KENTARO YABUKI

English Adaptation/Kelly Sue DeConnick
Translation/JN Productions
Touch-up Art & Lettering/Gia Cam Luc
Design/Courtney Utt
Editor/Jonathan Tarbox

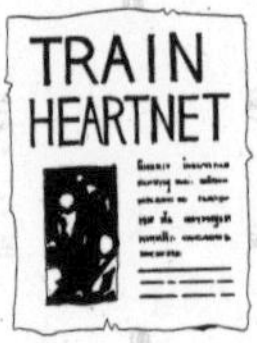
TRAIN
HEARTNET

Editor in Chief, Books/Alvin Lu
Editor in Chief, Magazines/Marc Weidenbaum
VP of Publishing Licensing/Rika Inouye
VP of Sales/Gonzalo Ferreyra
Sr. VP of Marketing/Liza Coppola
Publisher/Hyoe Narita

A CIP catalogue record for this book is available from the British Library.

Printed in the U.S.A.

Published by VIZ Media, LLC
P.O. Box 77010
San Francisco, CA 94107

SHONEN JUMP Manga Edition
10 9 8 7 6 5 4 3 2 1
First printing, July 2008

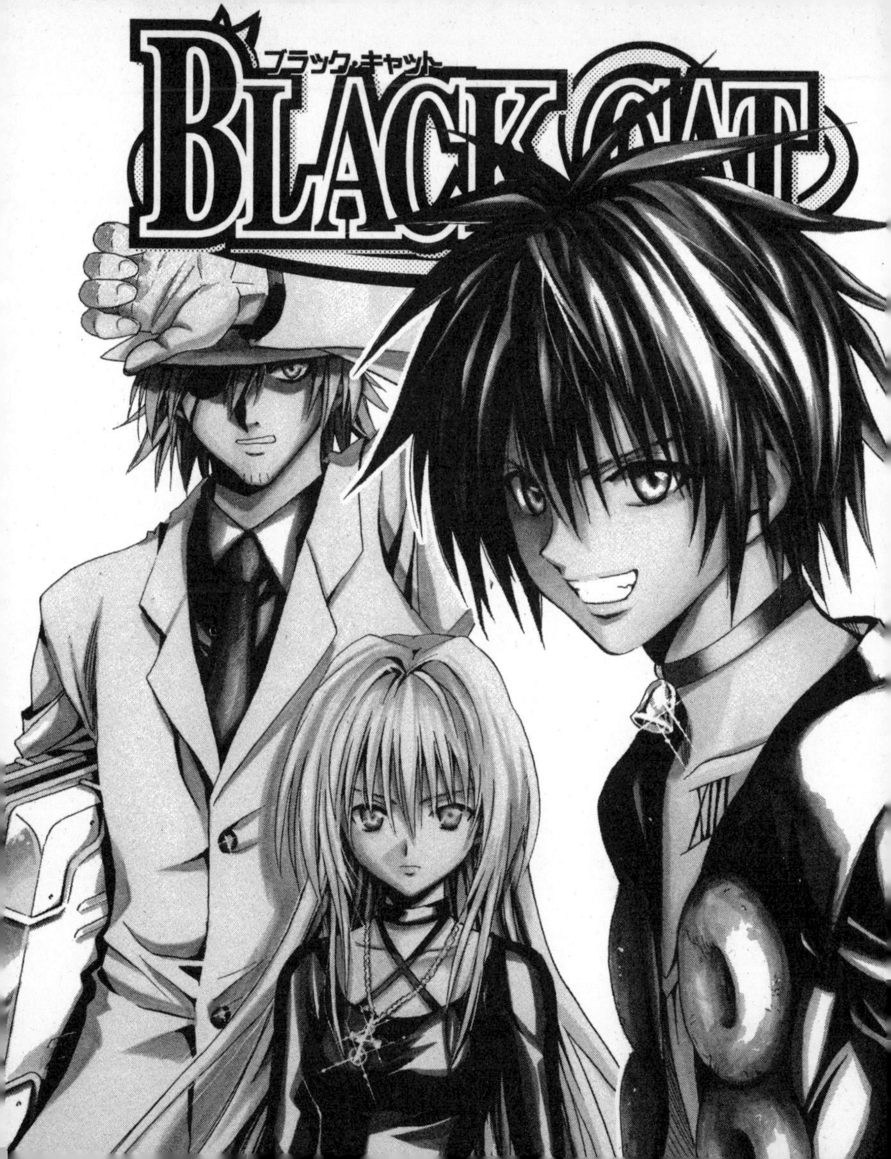
ブラック・キャット
BLACK CAT

TRAIN HEARTNET

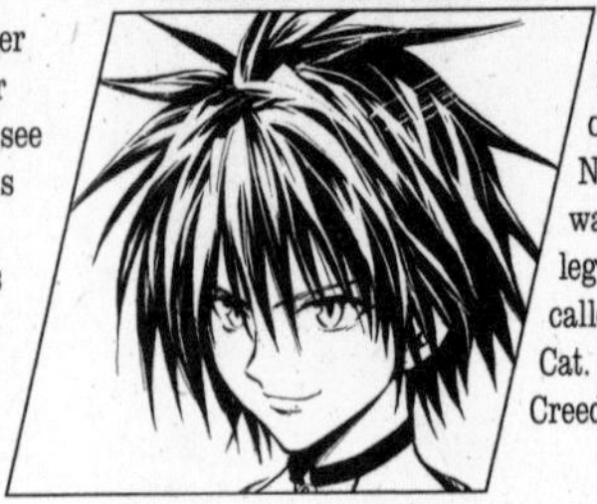

Formerly Number XIII of the Chrono Numbers, Train was once a legendary eraser called the Black Cat. He now pursues Creed as a sweeper.

SVEN VOLLFIED

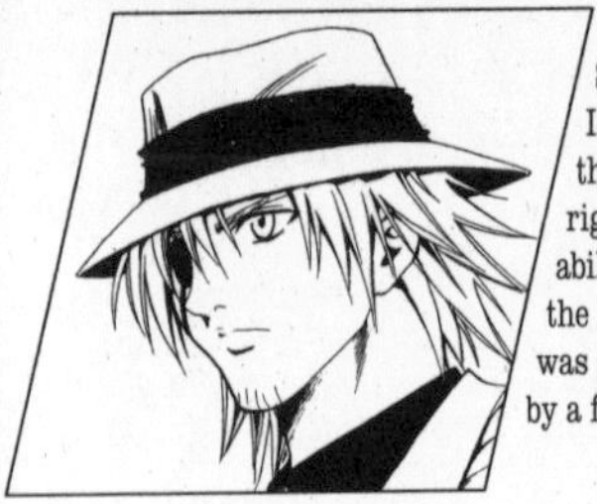

Train's partner Sven, a former IBI agent, can see the future in his right eye. This ability, known as the Vision Eye, was given to him by a friend.

EVE

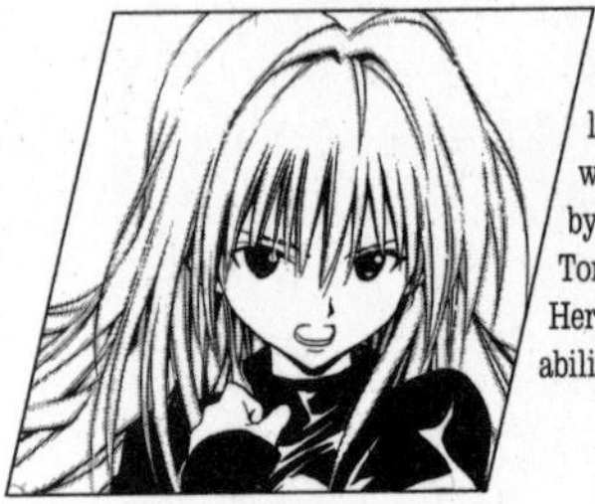

Part bio-weapon and part little girl, Eve was manufactured by weapons dealer Torneo Rudman. Her power lies in her ability to transform.

SEPHIRIA ARKS

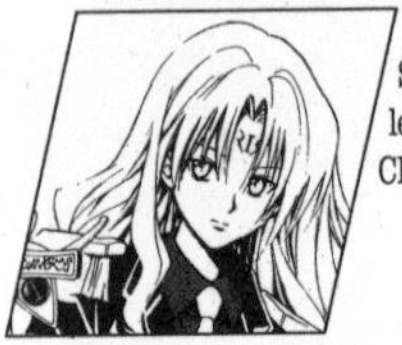

As Number I, Sephiria is the leader of the Chrono Numbers.

BELZE ROCHEFORT

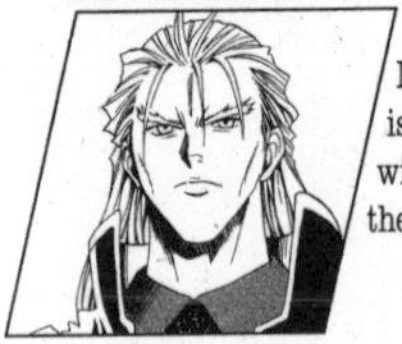

As Chrono Number II, Belze is equally adept with the pen and the sword.

RINSLET WALKER

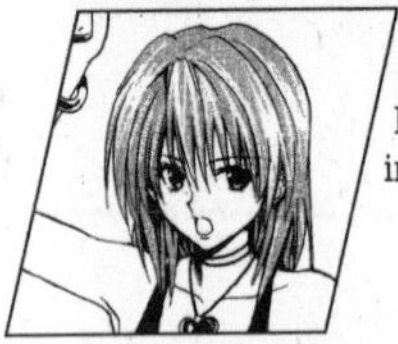

A self-styled thief-for-hire, Rinslet is fiercely independent.

JENOS HAZARD

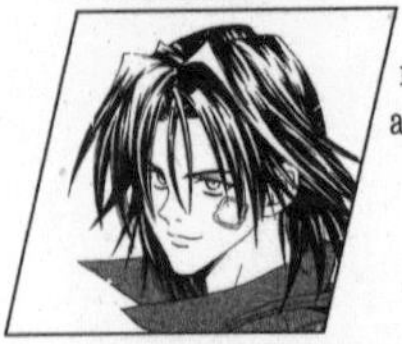

Chrono Number VII manipulates wires... and women.

RIVER ZASTORY

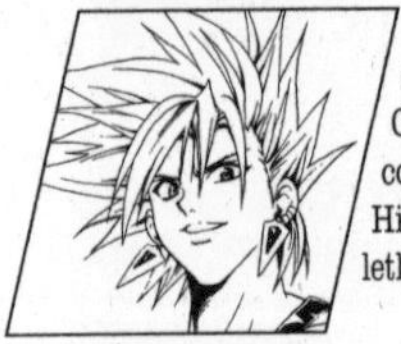

River is a sweeper and a master of the Garbell Commando combat technique. His fists are lethal weapons.

LIN SHAOLEE

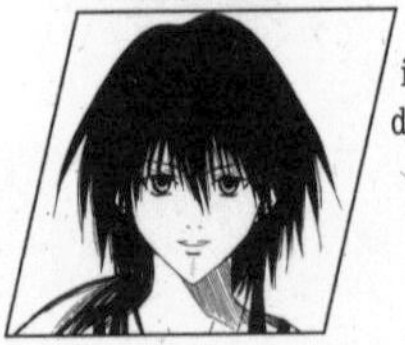

Chrono Number X is a master of disguise.

SAYA MINATSUKI

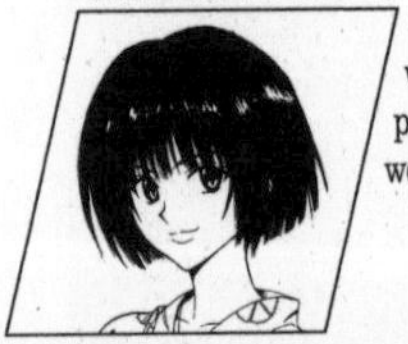

Saya is an important woman from Train's past who was fatally wounded by Creed.

A fearless "eraser" responsible for the deaths of countless powerful men, Train "Black Cat" Heartnet was formerly an assassin for the crime syndicate Chronos. Train betrayed Chronos and was supposedly executed for it, but two years later he lives a carefree life, working with his partner Sven as a bounty hunter ("sweeper") while pursuing Creed Diskenth, the man who murdered Train's beloved friend Saya. The two sweepers are allied with sexy thief-for-hire Rinslet Walker and Eve, a young girl (and experimental living weapon) whom they rescued from a nanotech lab.

Creed finally turns up, determined to lead a revolution against Chronos. He tries to convince Train to join his "Apostles of the Stars," but fails and escapes once again.

Train decides Creed must be stopped, and for the first time, he tells his friends the story behind Creed and Saya.

Train, Sven and their littlest partner, Eve, then head out to find Creed and stop at a Sweepers' Café to gather intel. They meet a man named Glin who offers them information, but only if they complete a video game. Train and his team master the game and show up at the meeting place for the information they've been promised. There they find other formidable sweepers with whom they form an alliance. The group sets out for Creed's hideout, but Creed's Apostles of the Stars attack them at sea and the sweepers are scattered.

CREED DISKENTH

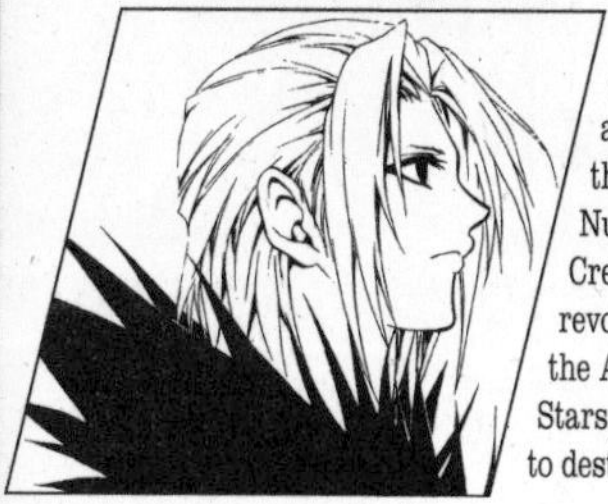

Though he and Train were associates in their Chrono Numbers days, Creed now heads the revolutionary group the Apostles of the Stars, whose goal is to destroy the world.

SHIKI

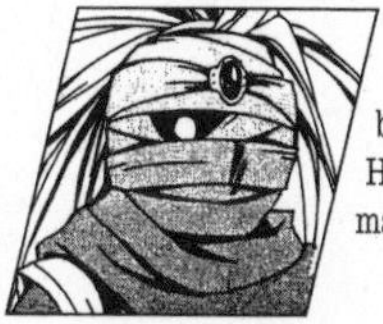

Shiki hails from Itairiku, the birthplace of the Tao. He has the power to manipulate insects.

MARO

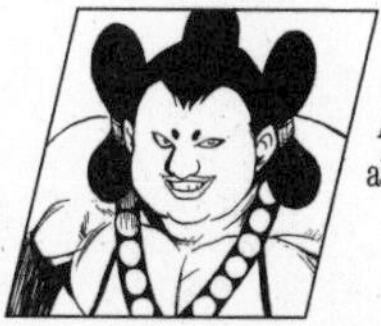

This larger-than-life member of the Apostles of the Stars is able to control gravity.

LEON ELLIOT

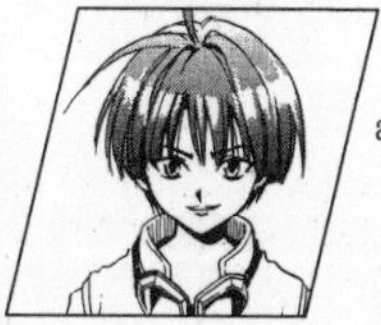

Young Leon Elliot wields the wind as a weapon.

BLACK CAT

VOLUME 15 EVE ATTACKS

CONTENTS

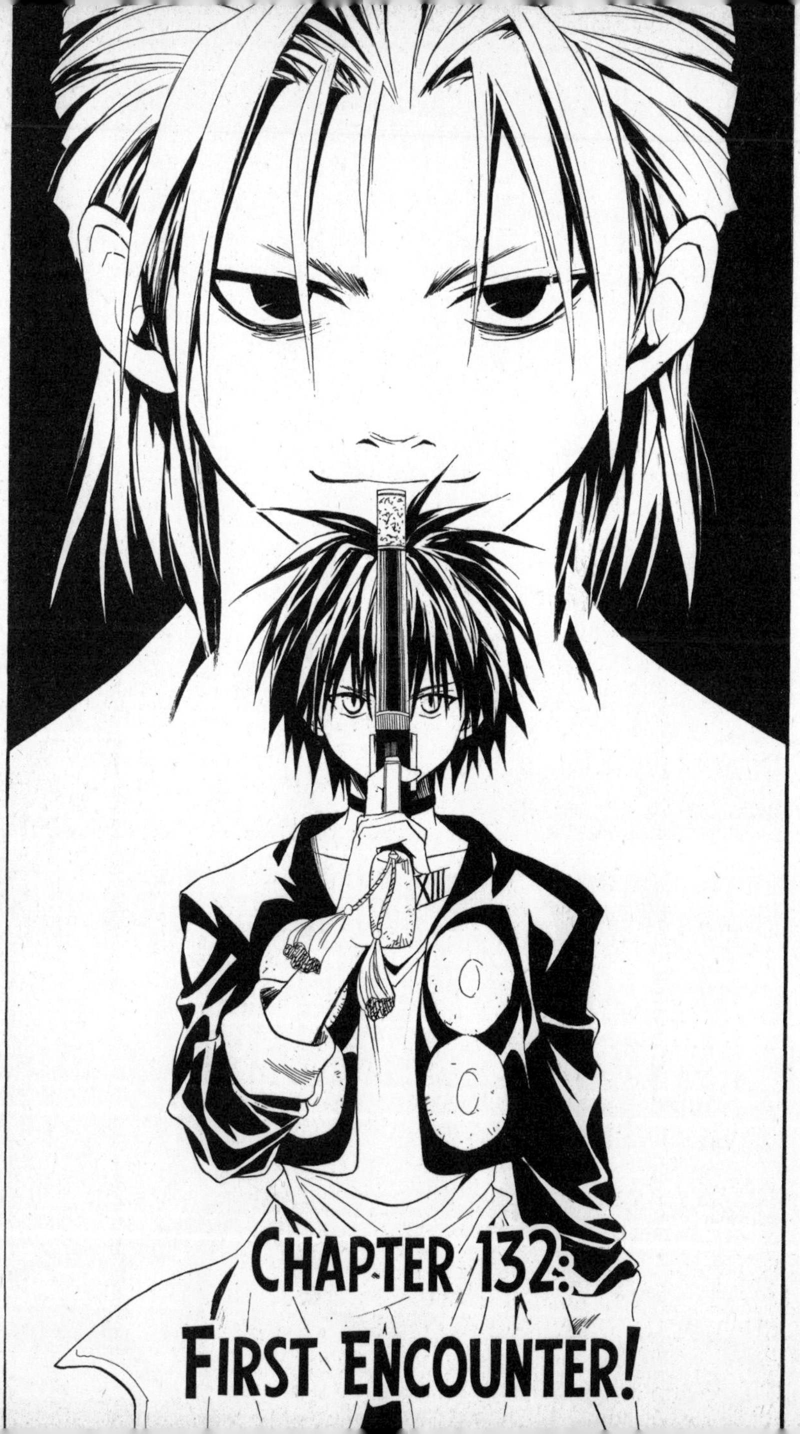

Chapter 132: First Encounter!

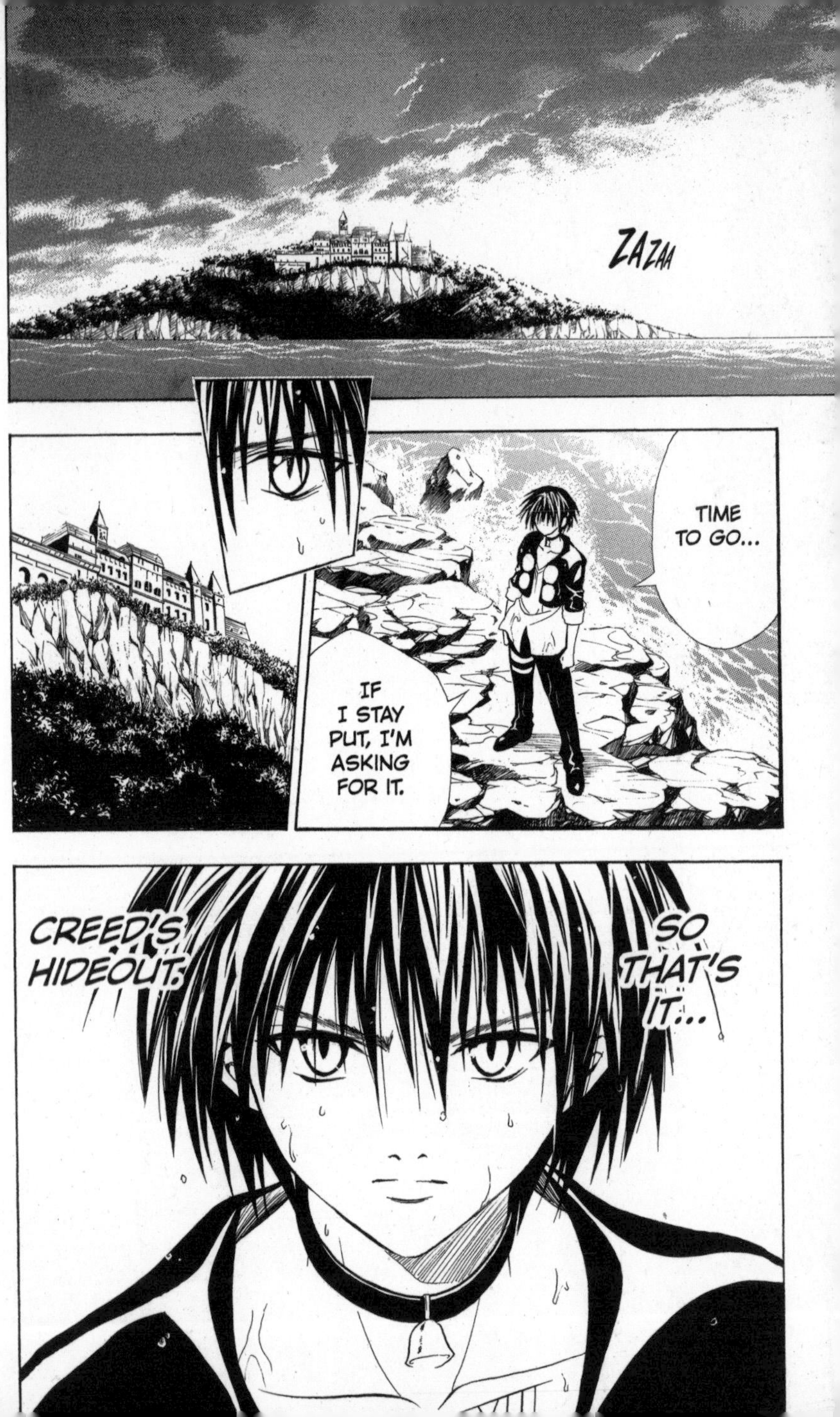
ZAZAA
TIME TO GO...
IF I STAY PUT, I'M ASKING FOR IT.
SO THAT'S IT...
CREED'S HIDEOUT.

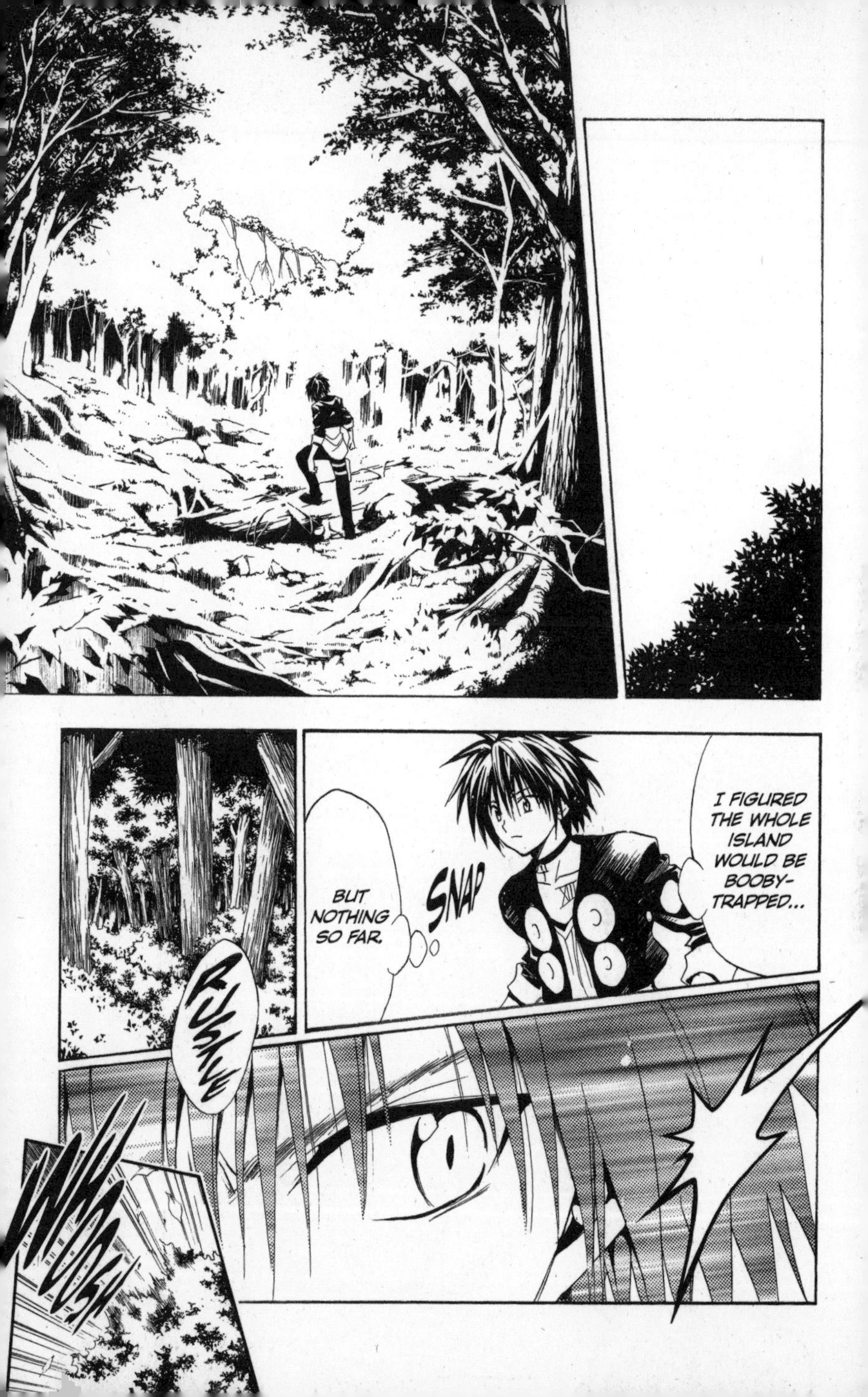
I FIGURED THE WHOLE ISLAND WOULD BE BOOBY-TRAPPED...
SNAP
BUT NOTHING SO FAR.
WHOOSH

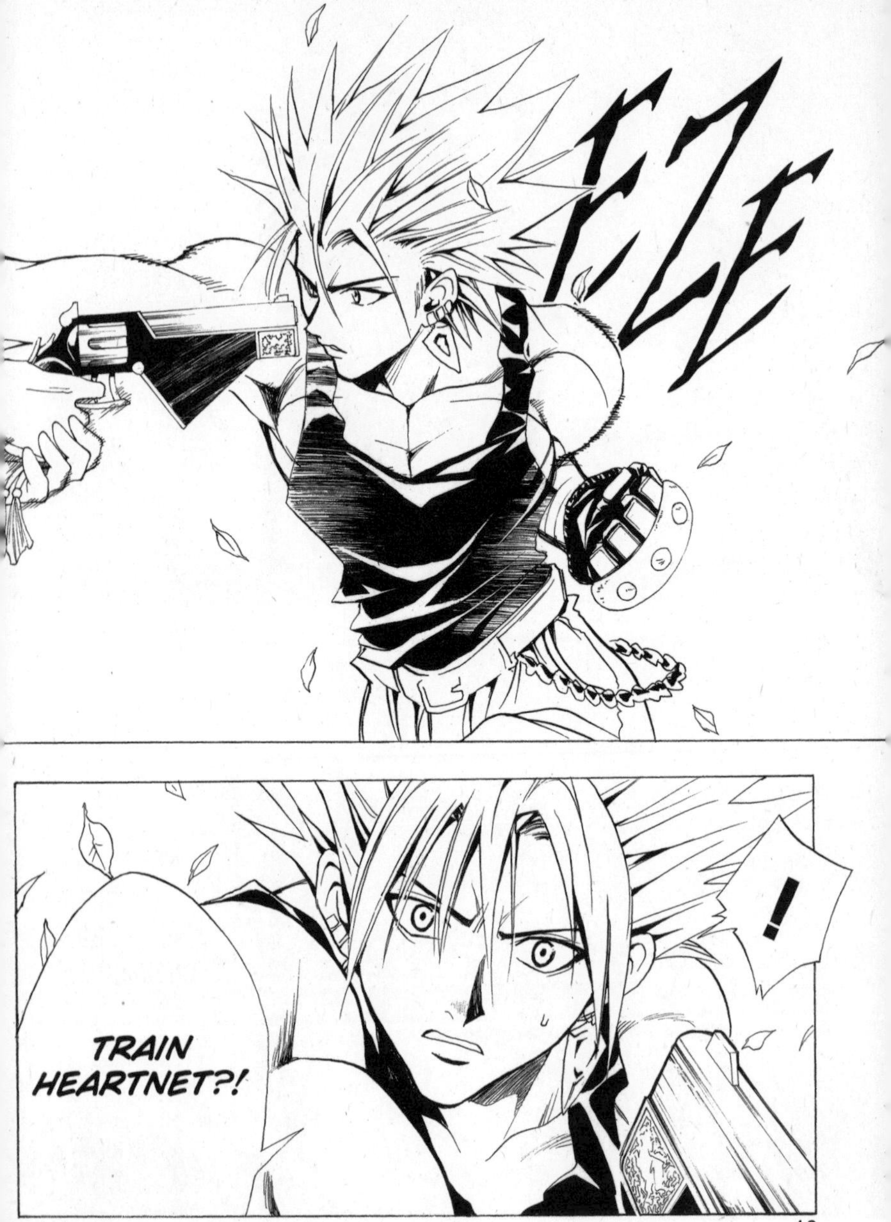
!
TRAIN HEARTNET?!

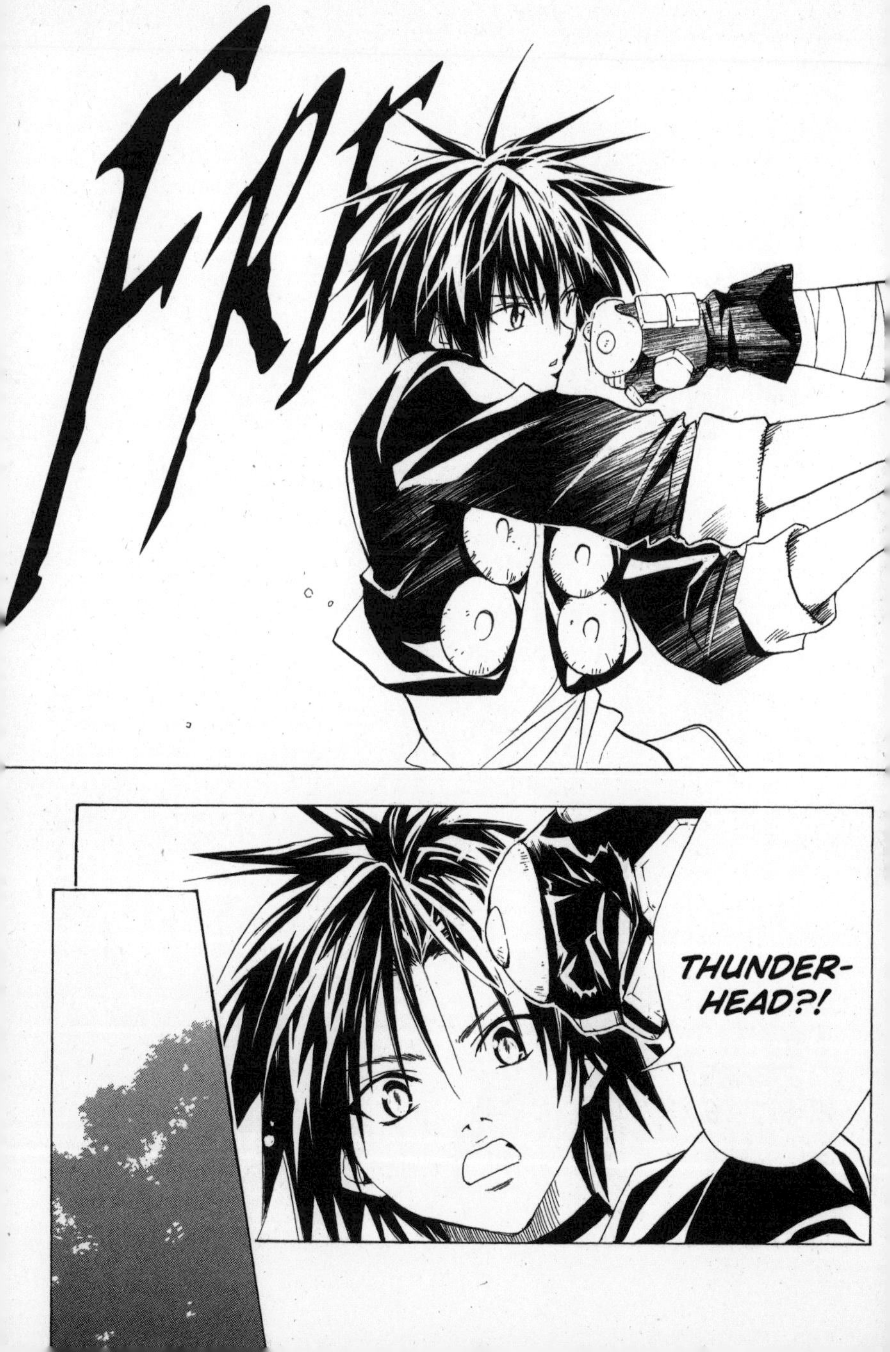
THUNDER-
HEAD?!

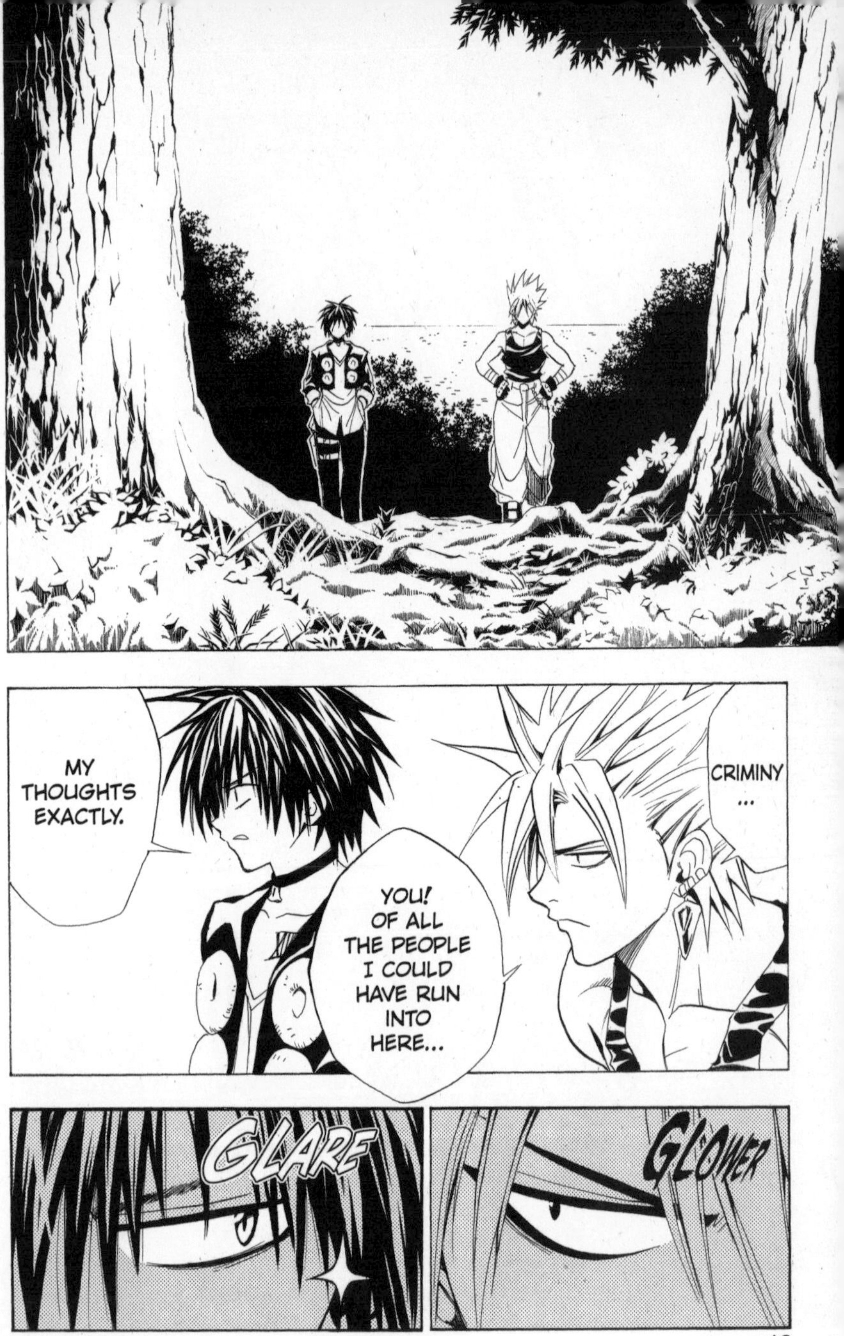
CRIMINY ...
YOU! OF ALL THE PEOPLE I COULD HAVE RUN INTO HERE...
MY THOUGHTS EXACTLY.
GLOWER
GLARE

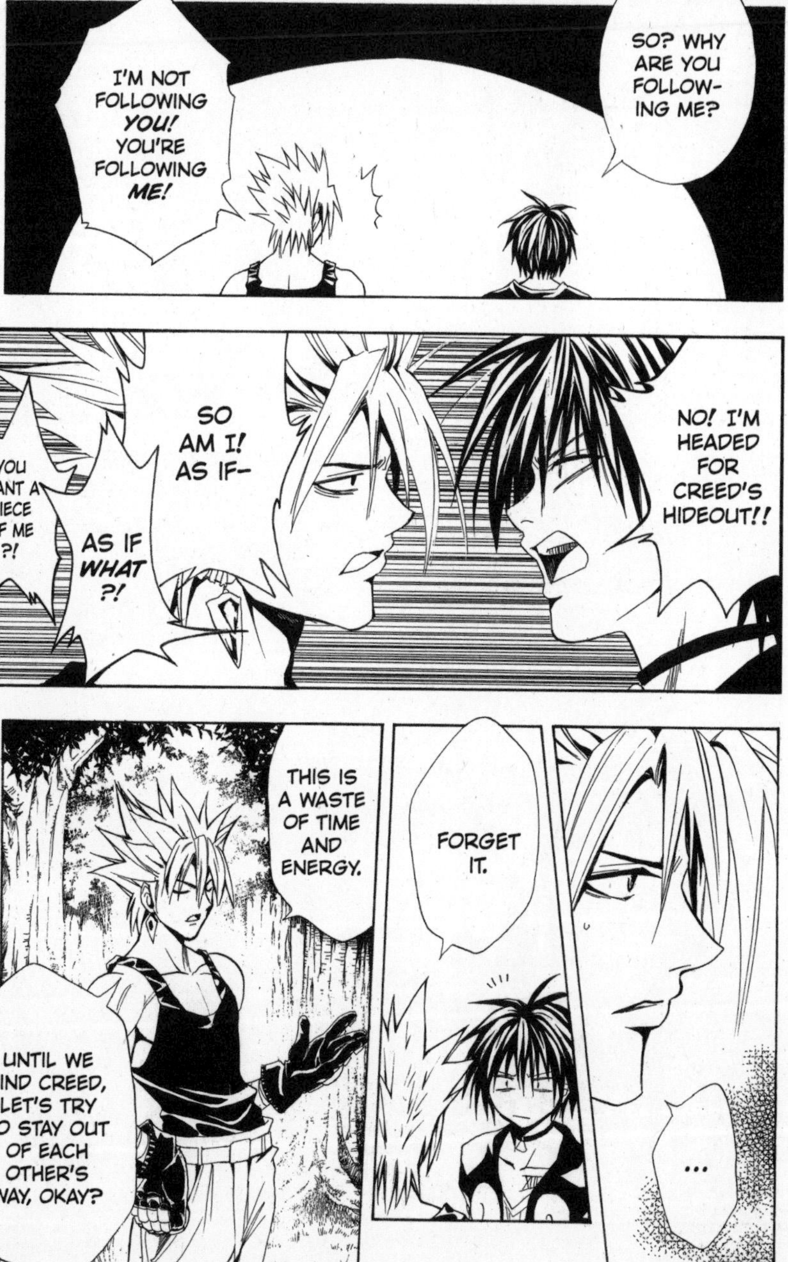
SO? WHY ARE YOU FOLLOWING ME?
I'M NOT FOLLOWING *YOU!* YOU'RE FOLLOWING *ME!*
NO! I'M HEADED FOR CREED'S HIDEOUT!!
SO AM I! AS IF-
AS IF *WHAT*?!
YOU WANT A PIECE OF ME?!
...
FORGET IT.
THIS IS A WASTE OF TIME AND ENERGY.
UNTIL WE FIND CREED, LET'S TRY TO STAY OUT OF EACH OTHER'S WAY, OKAY?

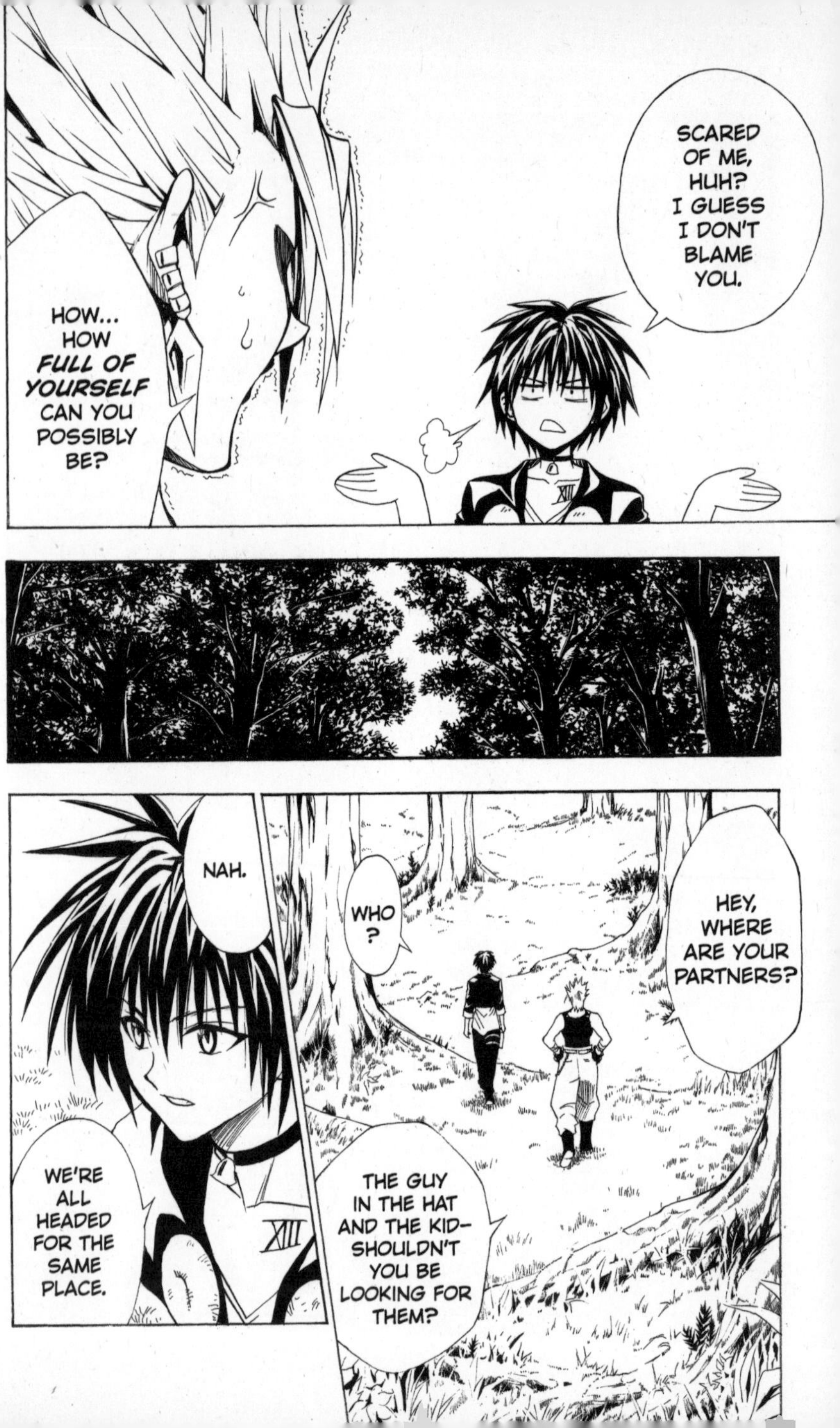
SCARED OF ME, HUH? I GUESS I DON'T BLAME YOU.
HOW... HOW *FULL OF YOURSELF* CAN YOU POSSIBLY BE?
HEY, WHERE ARE YOUR PARTNERS?
WHO?
THE GUY IN THE HAT AND THE KID- SHOULDN'T YOU BE LOOKING FOR THEM?
NAH.
WE'RE ALL HEADED FOR THE SAME PLACE.

READ THIS WAY

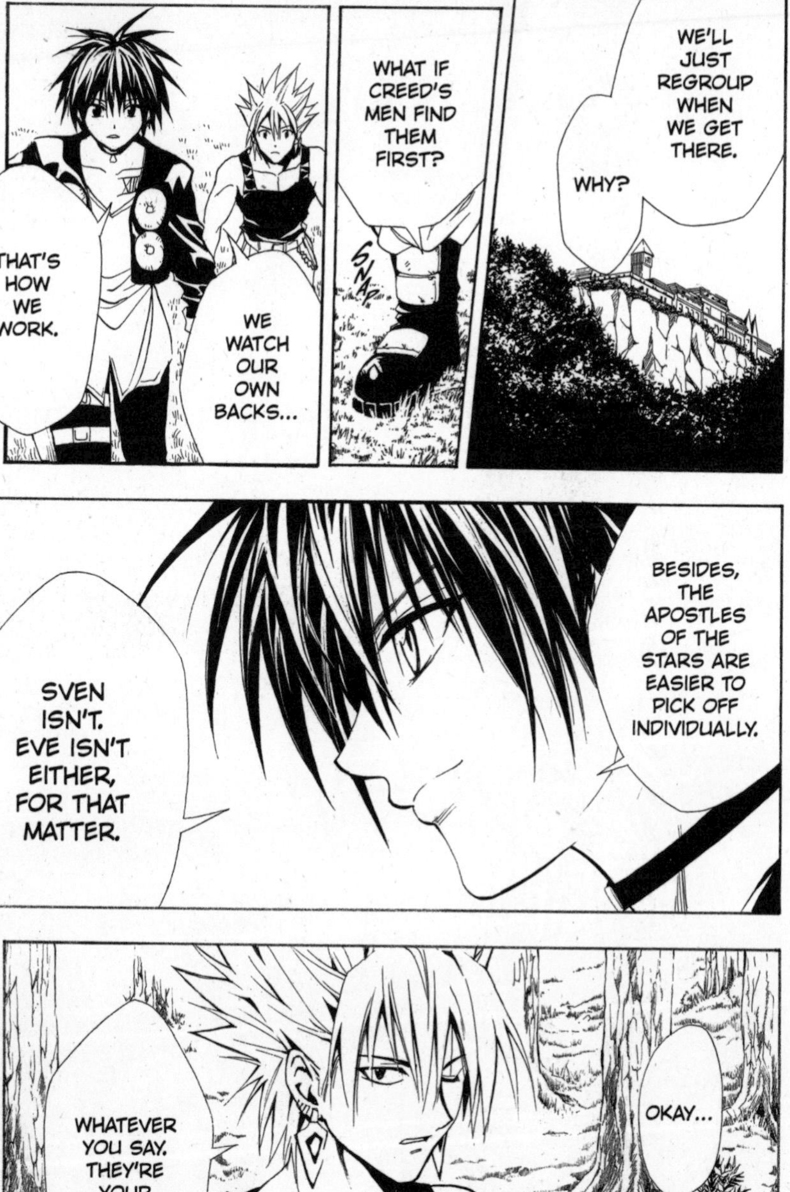
WE'LL JUST REGROUP WHEN WE GET THERE.
WHY?
WHAT IF CREED'S MEN FIND THEM FIRST?
SNAP
WE WATCH OUR OWN BACKS...
THAT'S HOW WE WORK.
BESIDES, THE APOSTLES OF THE STARS ARE EASIER TO PICK OFF INDIVIDUALLY.
SVEN ISN'T. EVE ISN'T EITHER, FOR THAT MATTER.
OKAY...
WHATEVER YOU SAY. THEY'RE YOUR PARTNERS.

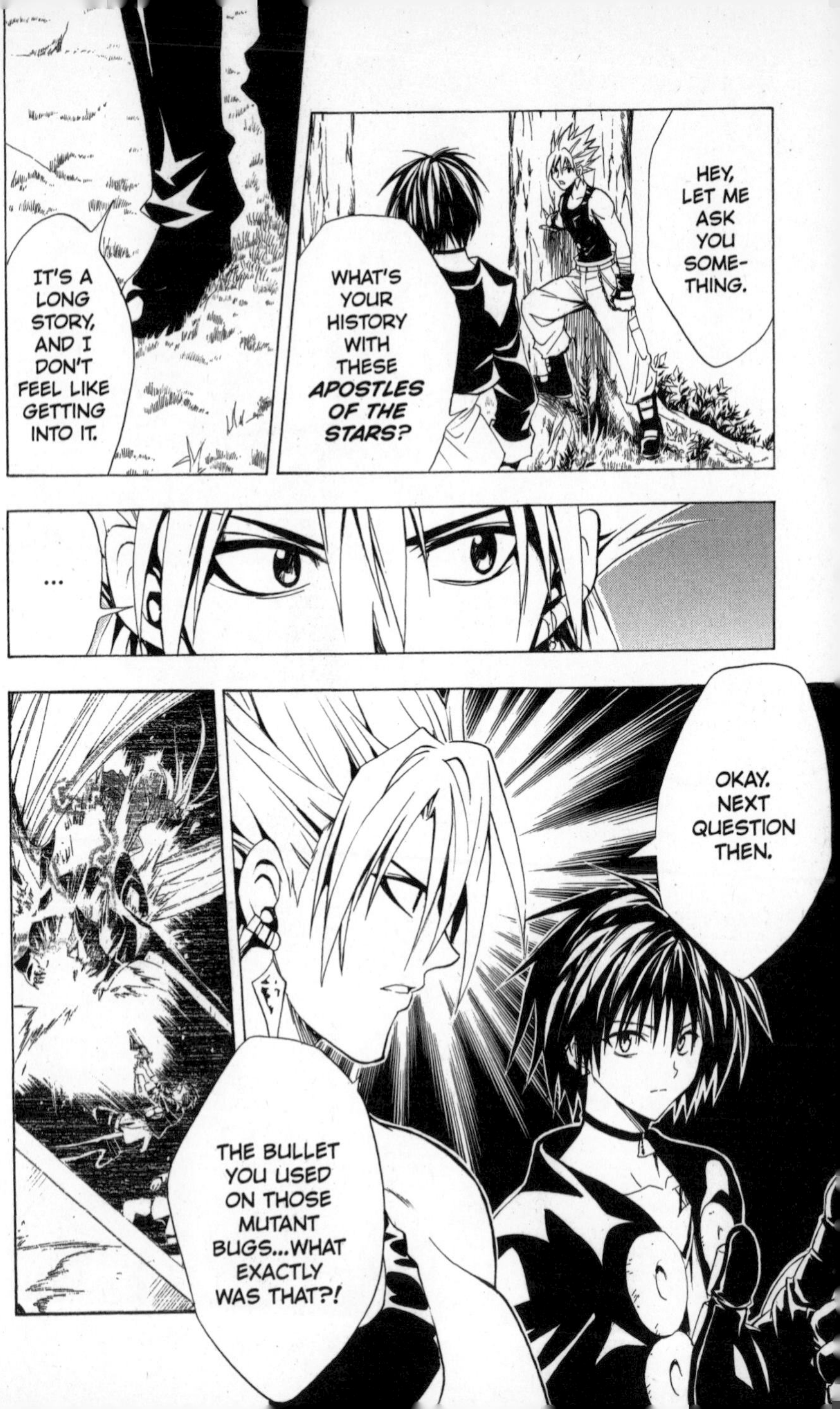
HEY, LET ME ASK YOU SOMETHING.
WHAT'S YOUR HISTORY WITH THESE *APOSTLES OF THE STARS?*
IT'S A LONG STORY, AND I DON'T FEEL LIKE GETTING INTO IT.
...
OKAY. NEXT QUESTION THEN.
THE BULLET YOU USED ON THOSE MUTANT BUGS...WHAT EXACTLY WAS THAT?!

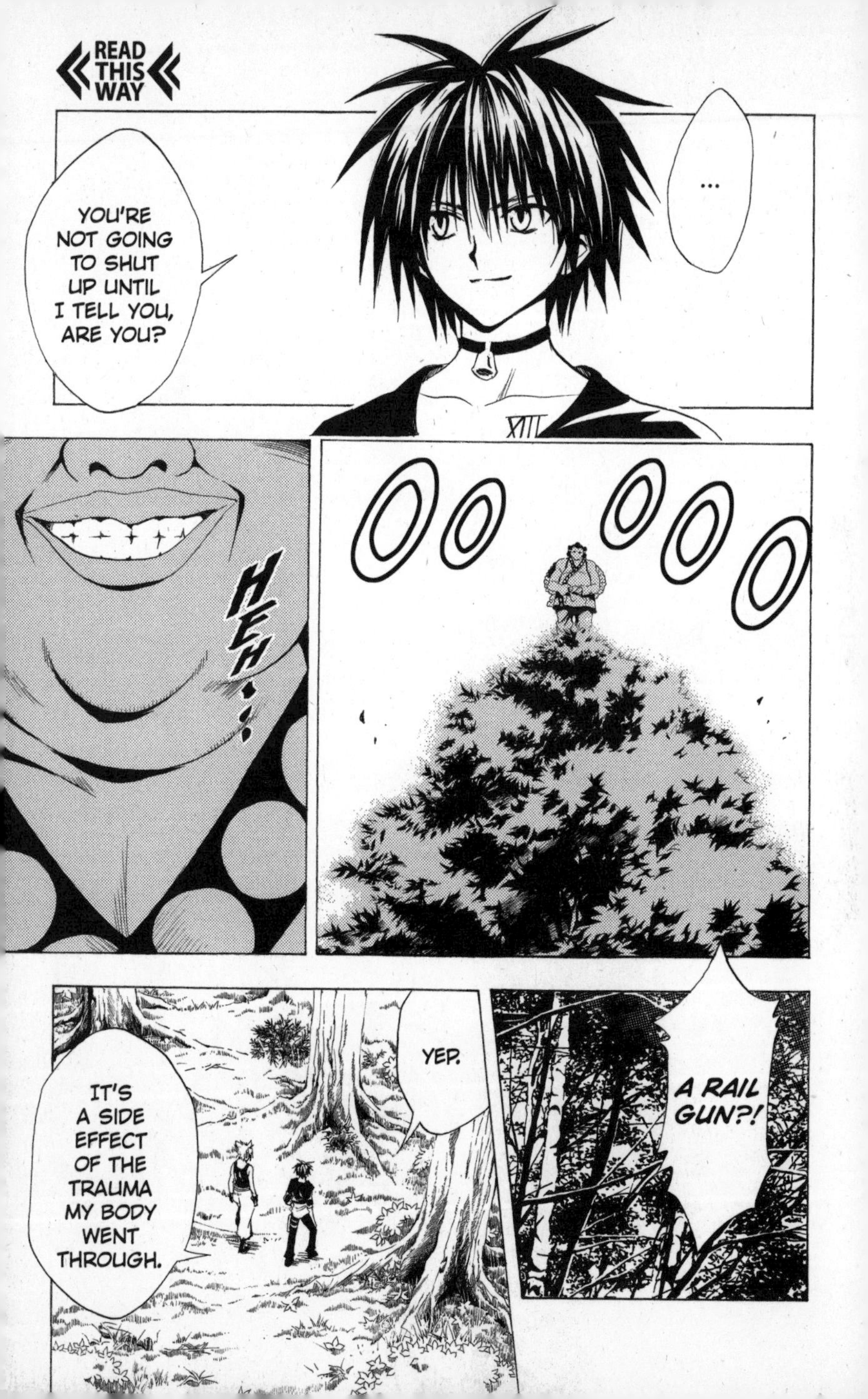
READ THIS WAY
...
YOU'RE NOT GOING TO SHUT UP UNTIL I TELL YOU, ARE YOU?
HEH...
A RAIL GUN?!
YEP.
IT'S A SIDE EFFECT OF THE TRAUMA MY BODY WENT THROUGH.

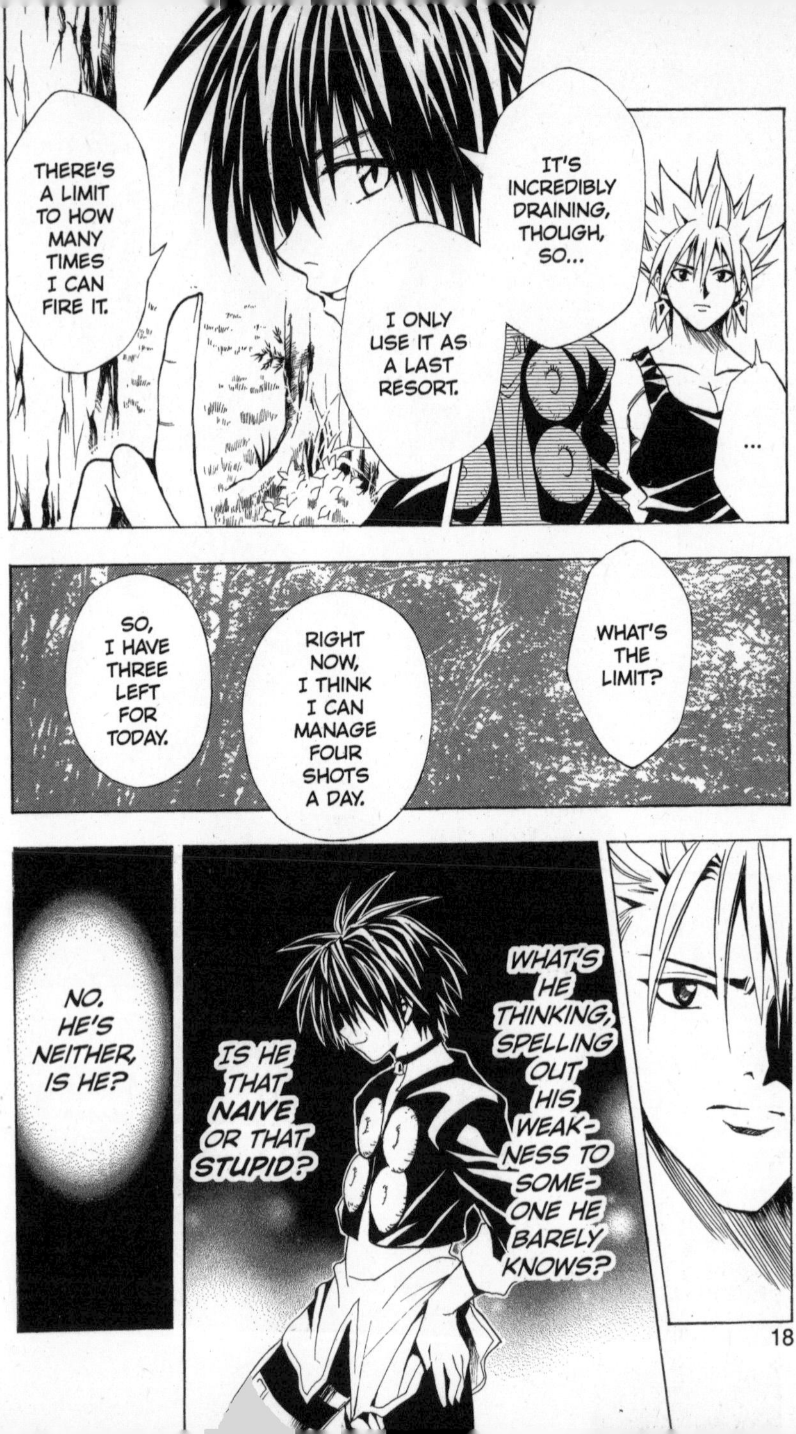
IT'S INCREDIBLY DRAINING, THOUGH, SO...
I ONLY USE IT AS A LAST RESORT.
...
THERE'S A LIMIT TO HOW MANY TIMES I CAN FIRE IT.
WHAT'S THE LIMIT?
RIGHT NOW, I THINK I CAN MANAGE FOUR SHOTS A DAY.
SO, I HAVE THREE LEFT FOR TODAY.
WHAT'S HE THINKING, SPELLING OUT HIS WEAK-NESS TO SOME-ONE HE BARELY KNOWS?
IS HE THAT NAIVE OR THAT STUPID?
NO. HE'S NEITHER, IS HE?

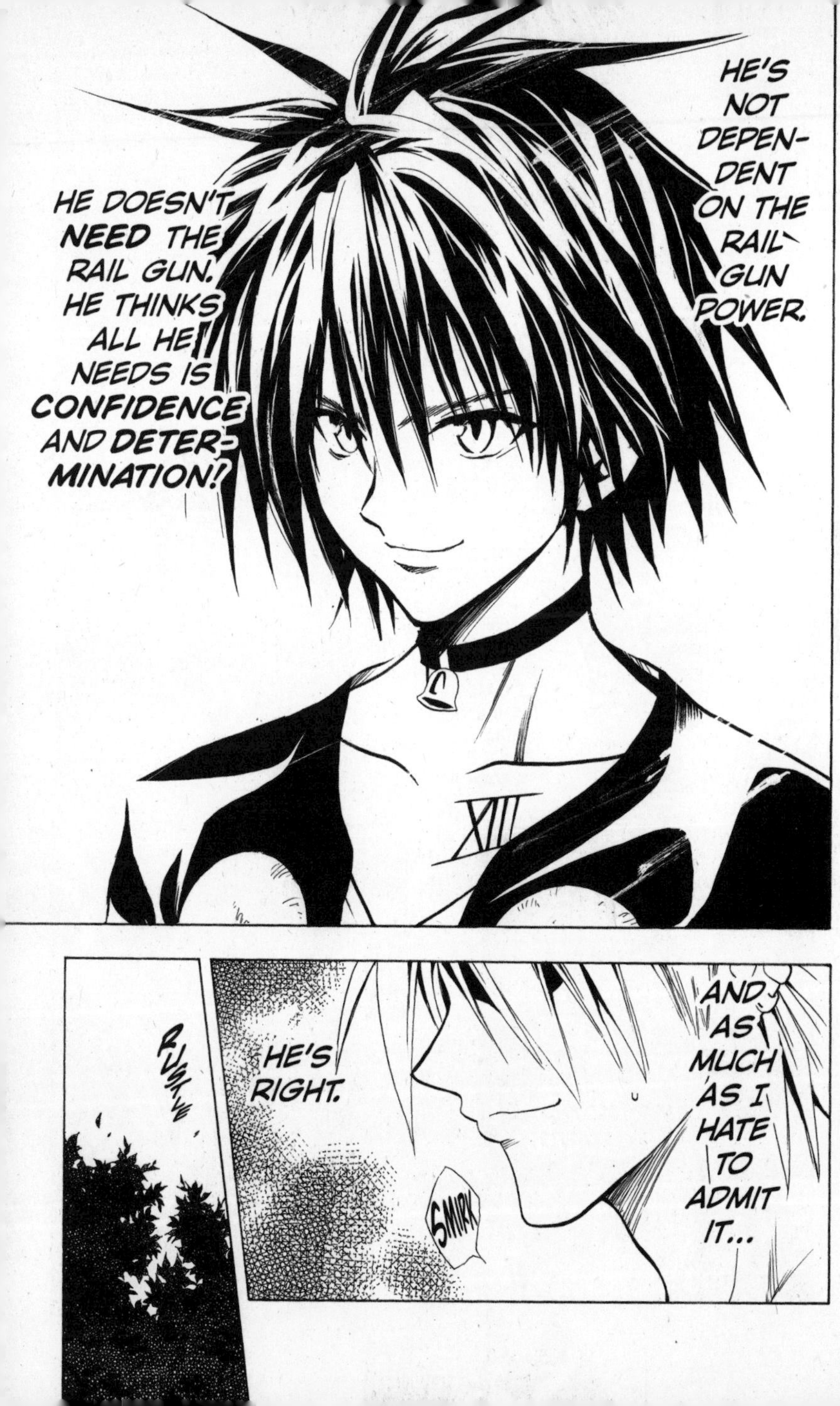
HE'S NOT DEPENDENT ON THE RAIL GUN POWER.
HE DOESN'T **NEED** THE RAIL GUN. HE THINKS ALL HE NEEDS IS **CONFIDENCE** AND **DETERMINATION**!
AND AS MUCH AS I HATE TO ADMIT IT...
HE'S RIGHT.
SMIRK
RUSTLE

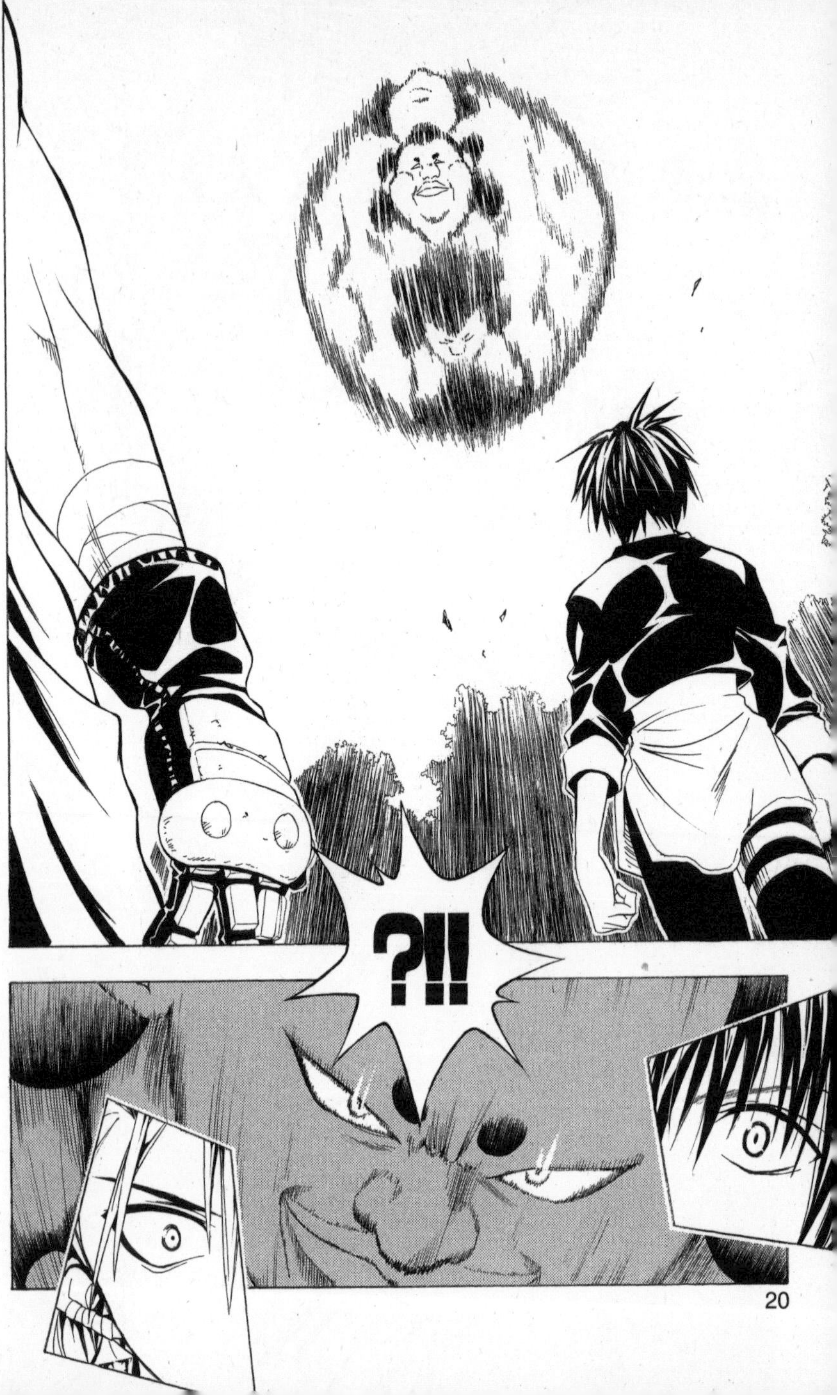
?!!

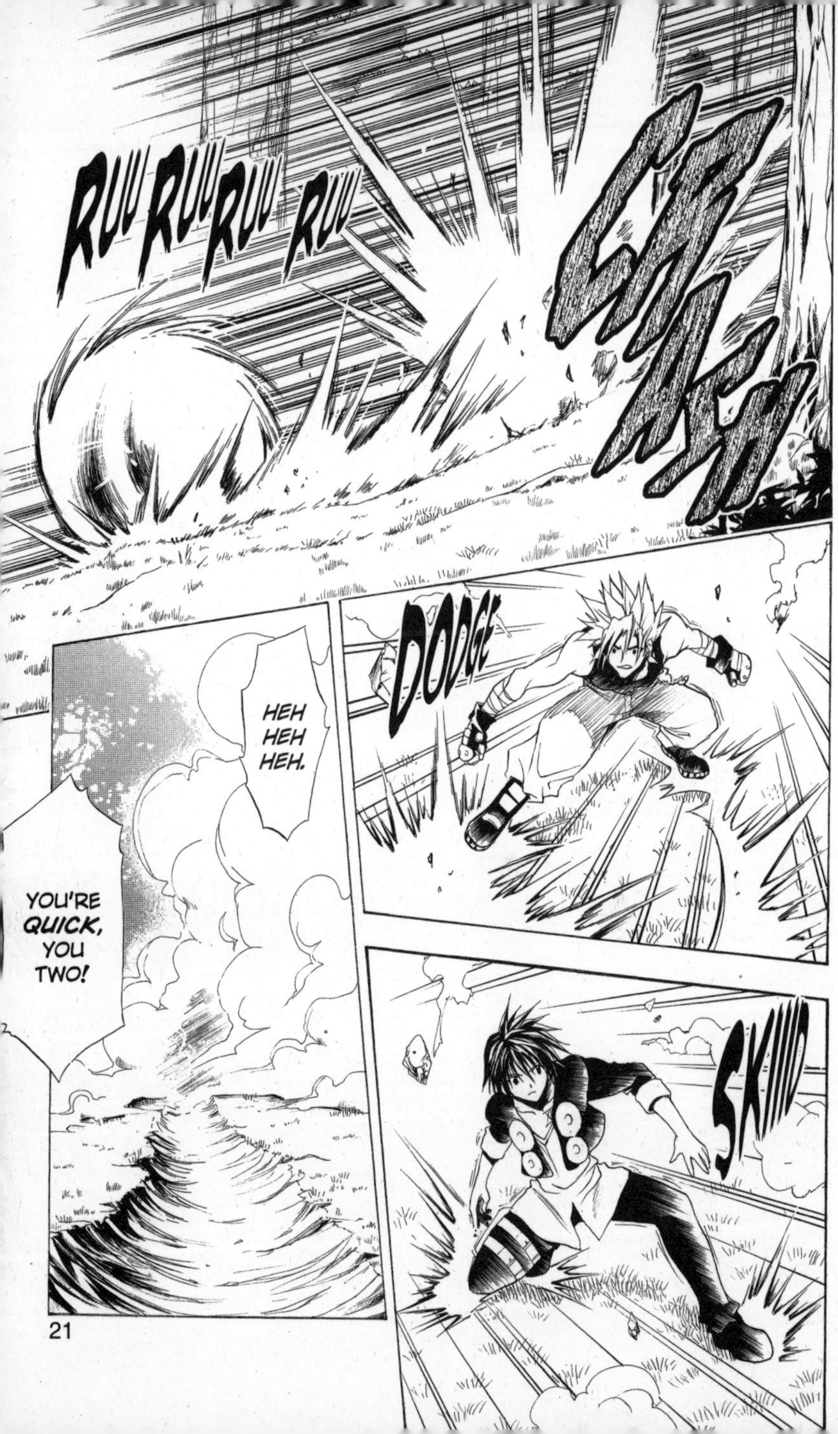
RUU RUU RUU RUU
DODGE
SKID
HEH HEH HEH.
YOU'RE QUICK, YOU TWO!

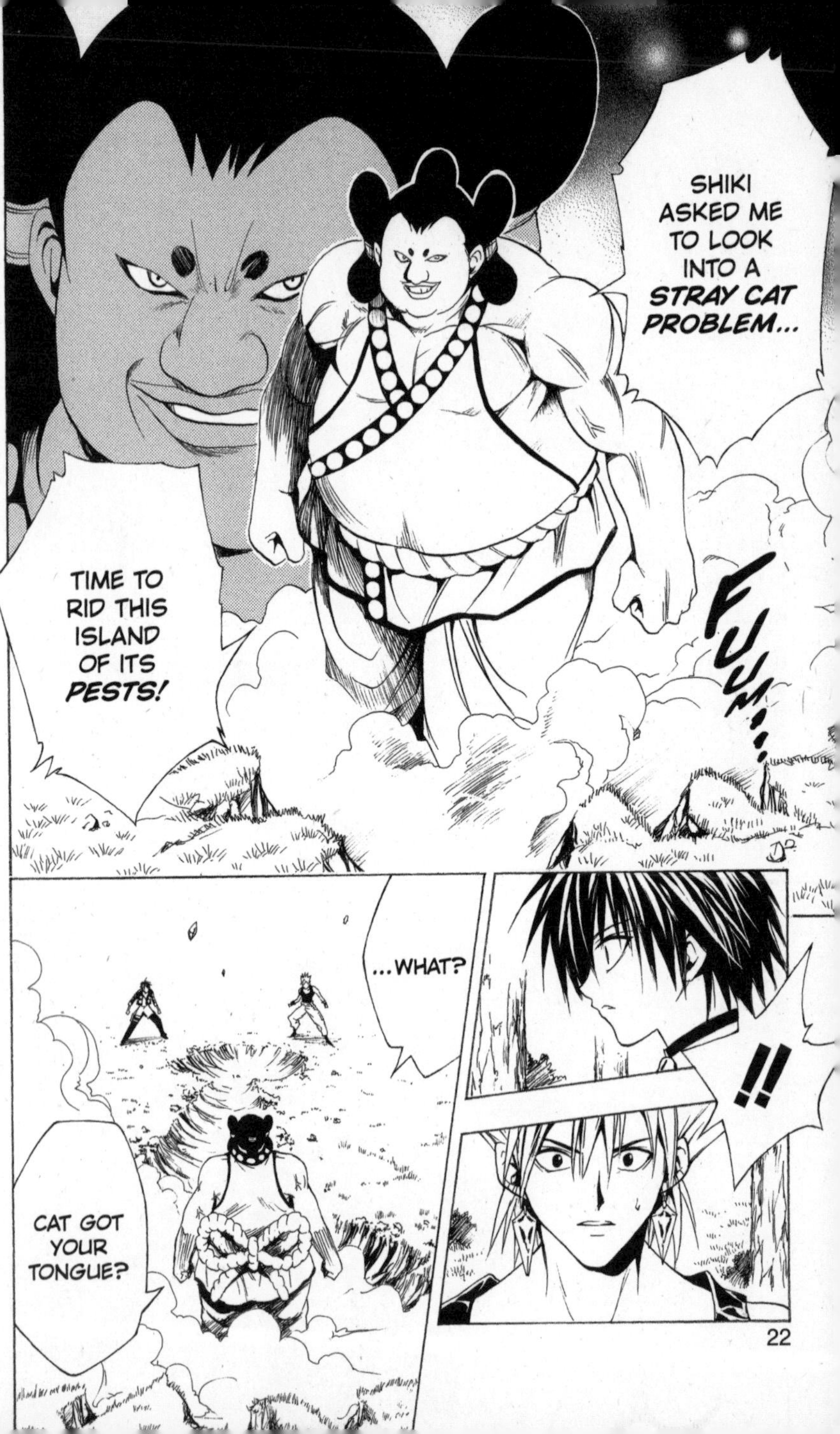
SHIKI ASKED ME TO LOOK INTO A *STRAY CAT PROBLEM...*
FUUM...
TIME TO RID THIS ISLAND OF ITS *PESTS!*
!!
...WHAT?
CAT GOT YOUR TONGUE?

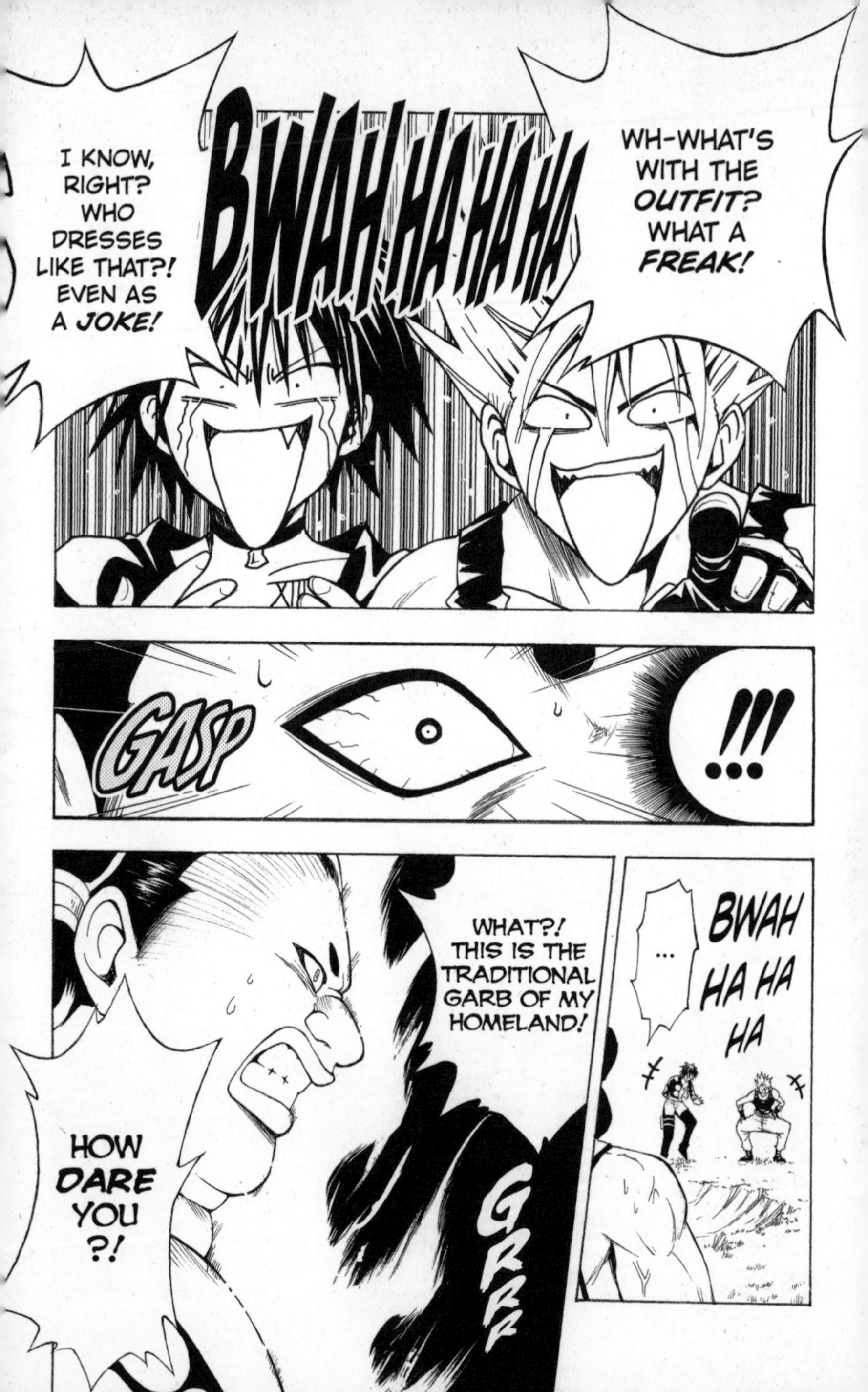

WH-WHAT'S WITH THE *OUTFIT?* WHAT A *FREAK!*
BWAHHAHAHA
I KNOW, RIGHT? WHO DRESSES LIKE THAT?! EVEN AS A *JOKE!*
!!!
GASP
BWAH HA HA HA
...
WHAT?! THIS IS THE TRADITIONAL GARB OF MY HOMELAND!
GRRR
HOW *DARE* YOU?!

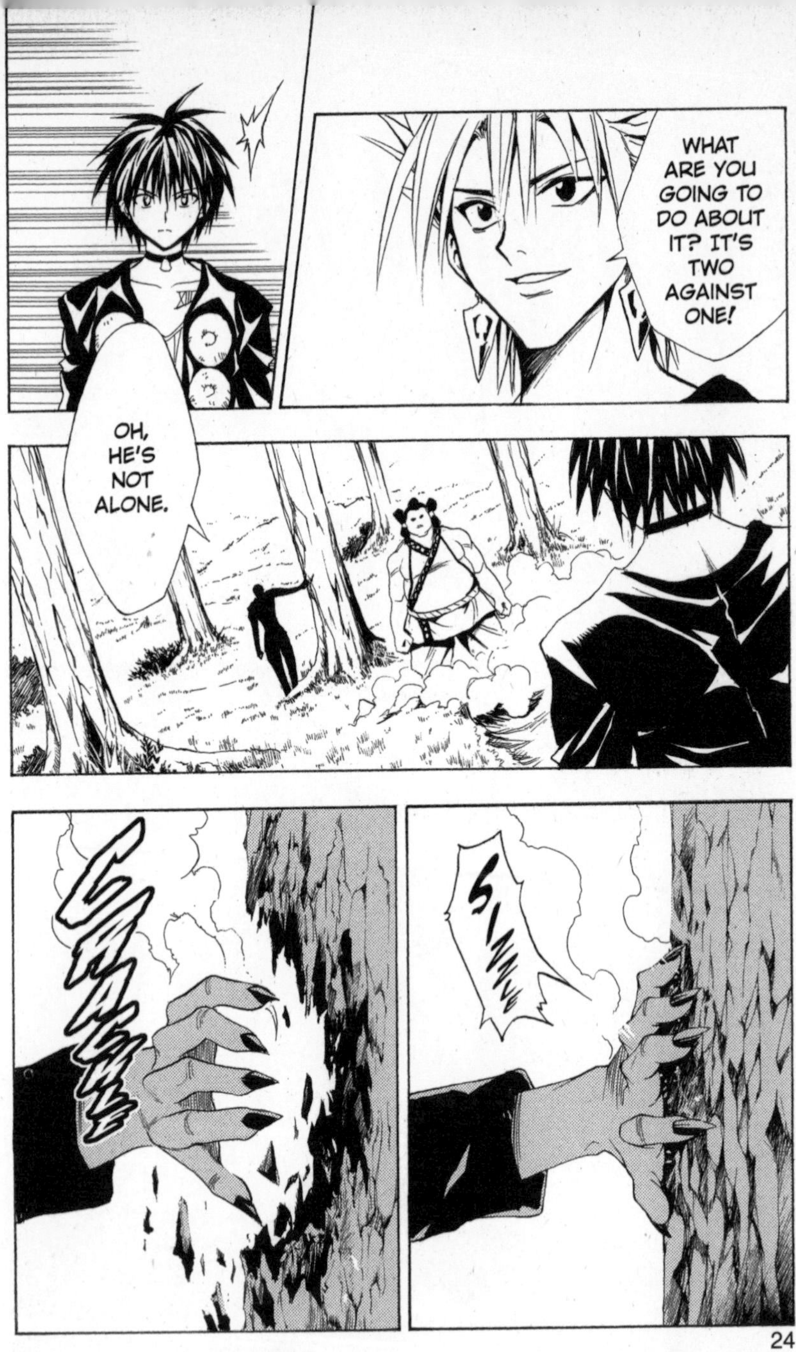
WHAT ARE YOU GOING TO DO ABOUT IT? IT'S TWO AGAINST ONE!
OH, HE'S NOT ALONE.

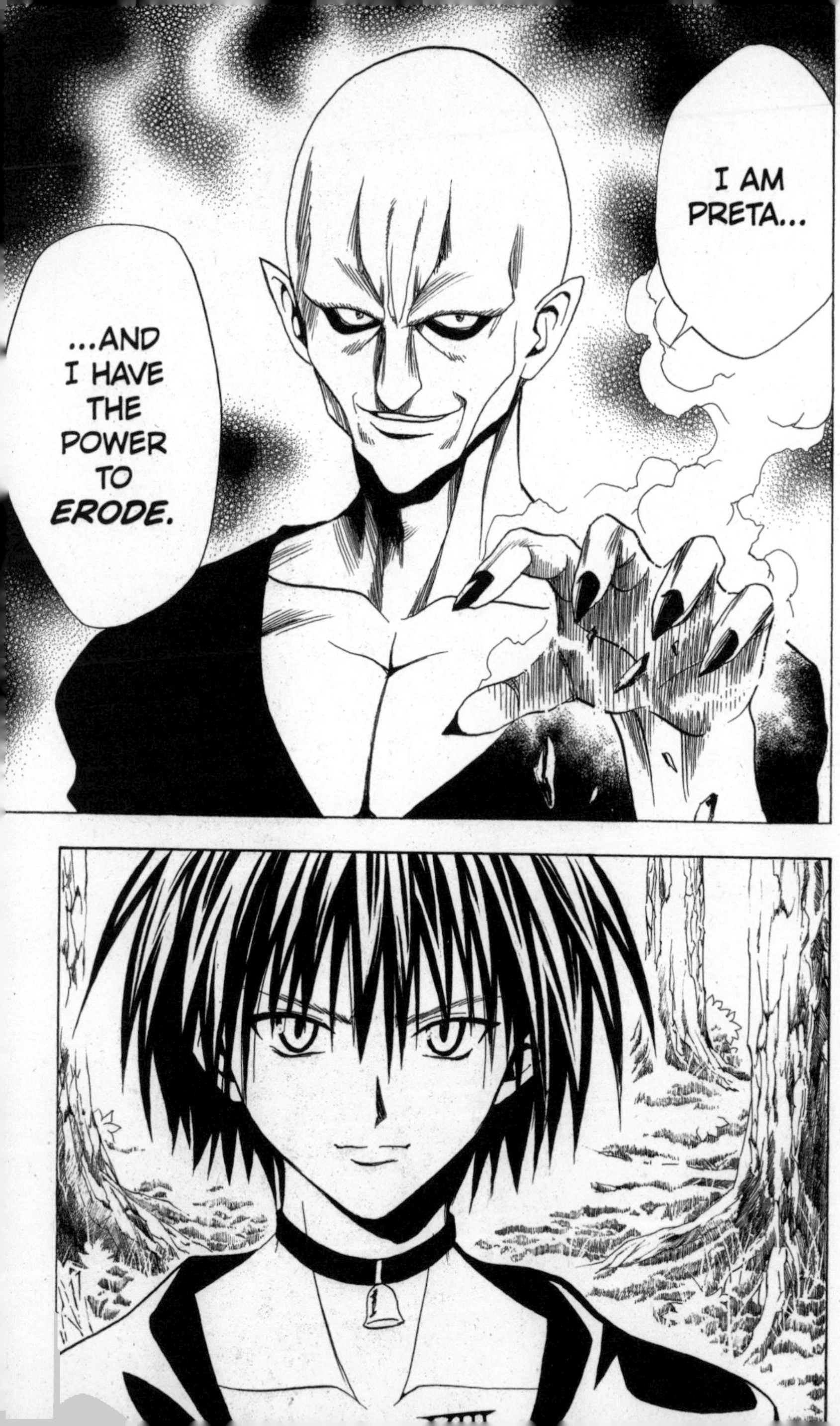
I AM PRETA...
...AND I HAVE THE POWER TO *ERODE.*

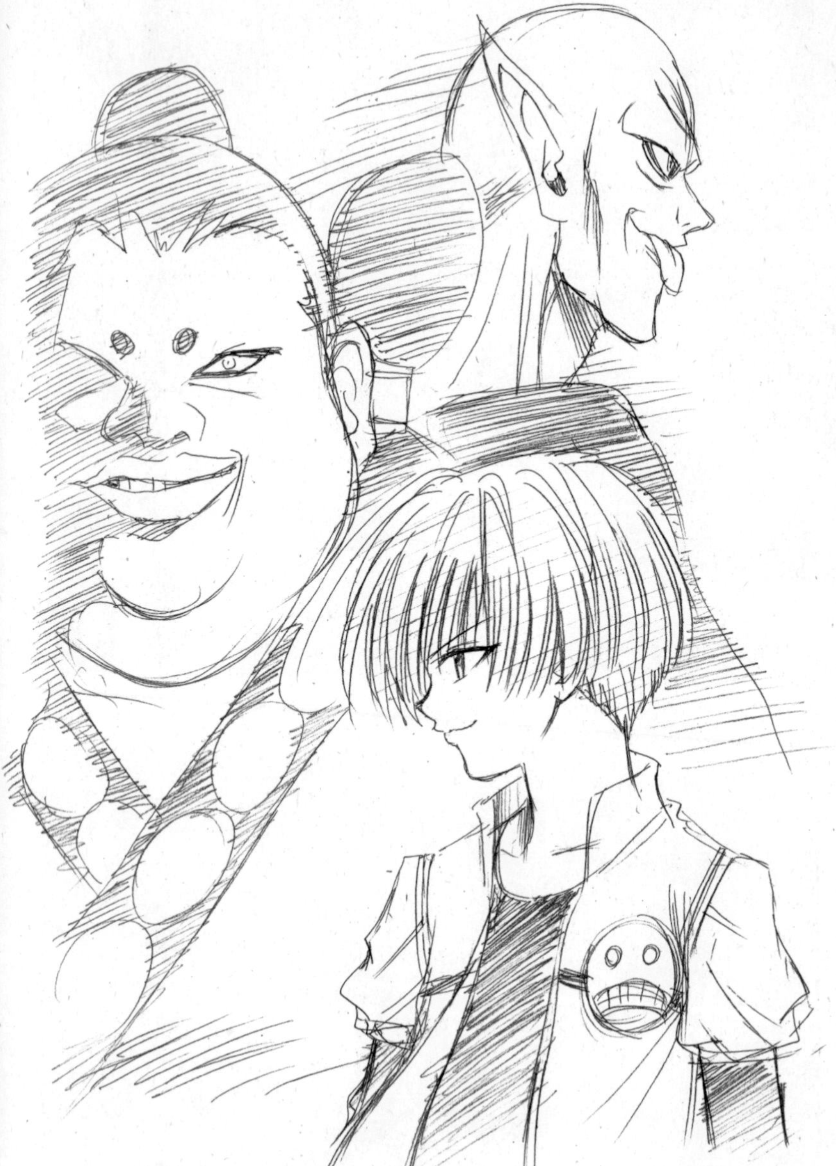

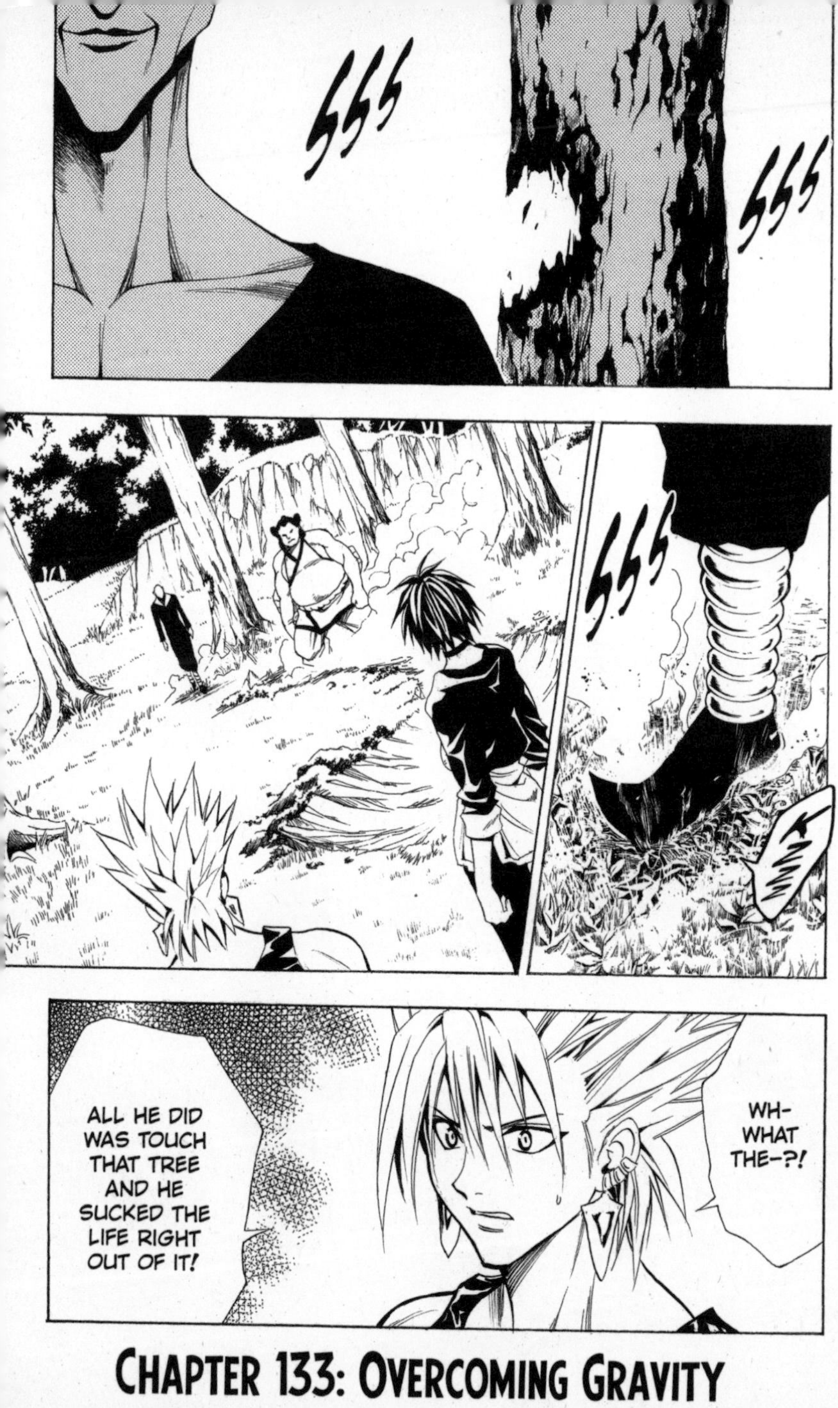
SSS
SSS
SSS
WH- WHAT THE-?!
ALL HE DID WAS TOUCH THAT TREE AND HE SUCKED THE LIFE RIGHT OUT OF IT!

Chapter 133: Overcoming Gravity

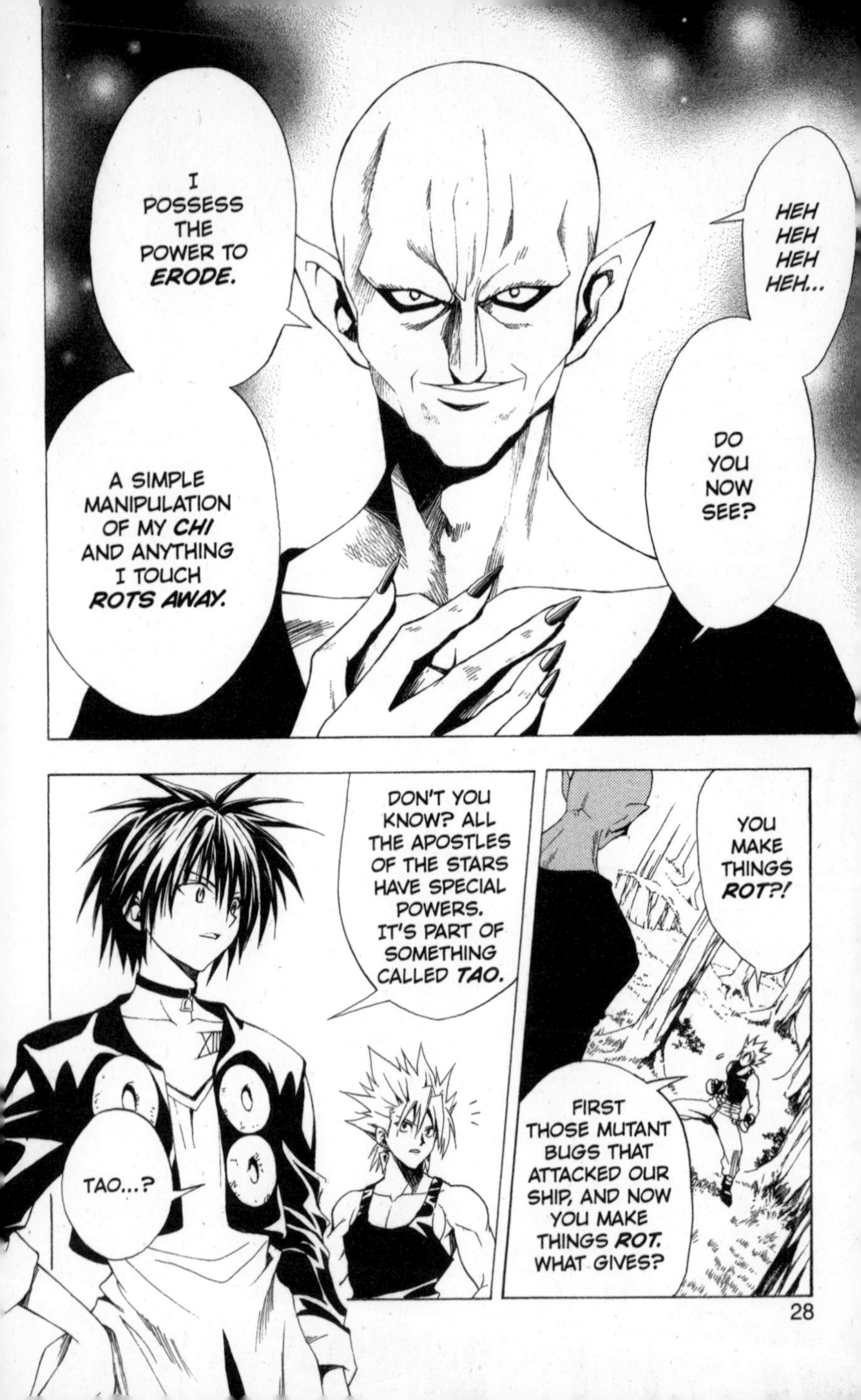
HEH HEH HEH HEH...
I POSSESS THE POWER TO *ERODE.*
DO YOU NOW SEE?
A SIMPLE MANIPULATION OF MY *CHI* AND ANYTHING I TOUCH *ROTS AWAY.*
YOU MAKE THINGS *ROT?!*
FIRST THOSE MUTANT BUGS THAT ATTACKED OUR SHIP, AND NOW YOU MAKE THINGS *ROT.* WHAT GIVES?
DON'T YOU KNOW? ALL THE APOSTLES OF THE STARS HAVE SPECIAL POWERS. IT'S PART OF SOMETHING CALLED *TAO.*
TAO...?

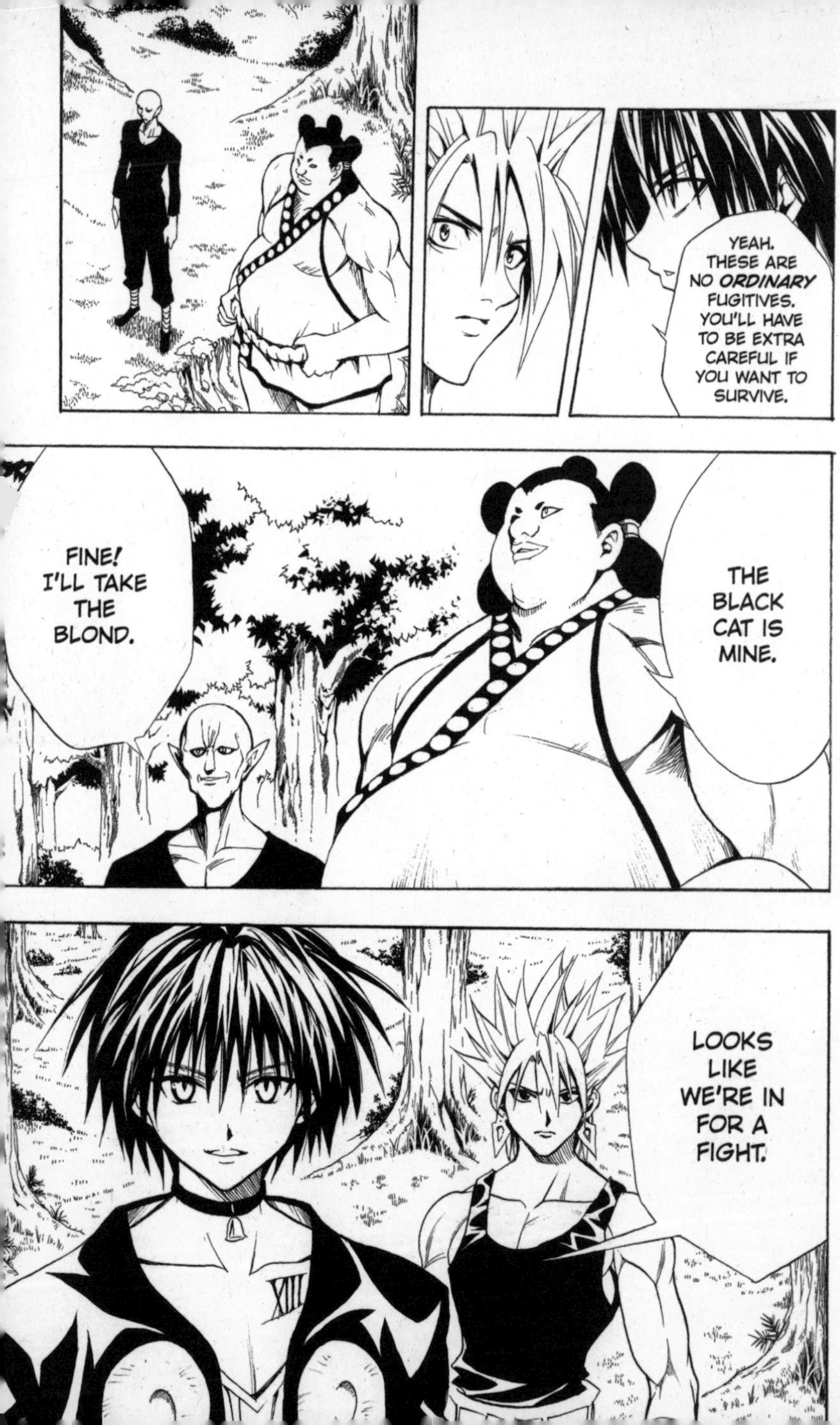
YEAH. THESE ARE NO *ORDINARY* FUGITIVES. YOU'LL HAVE TO BE EXTRA CAREFUL IF YOU WANT TO SURVIVE.
THE BLACK CAT IS MINE.
FINE! I'LL TAKE THE BLOND.
LOOKS LIKE WE'RE IN FOR A FIGHT.

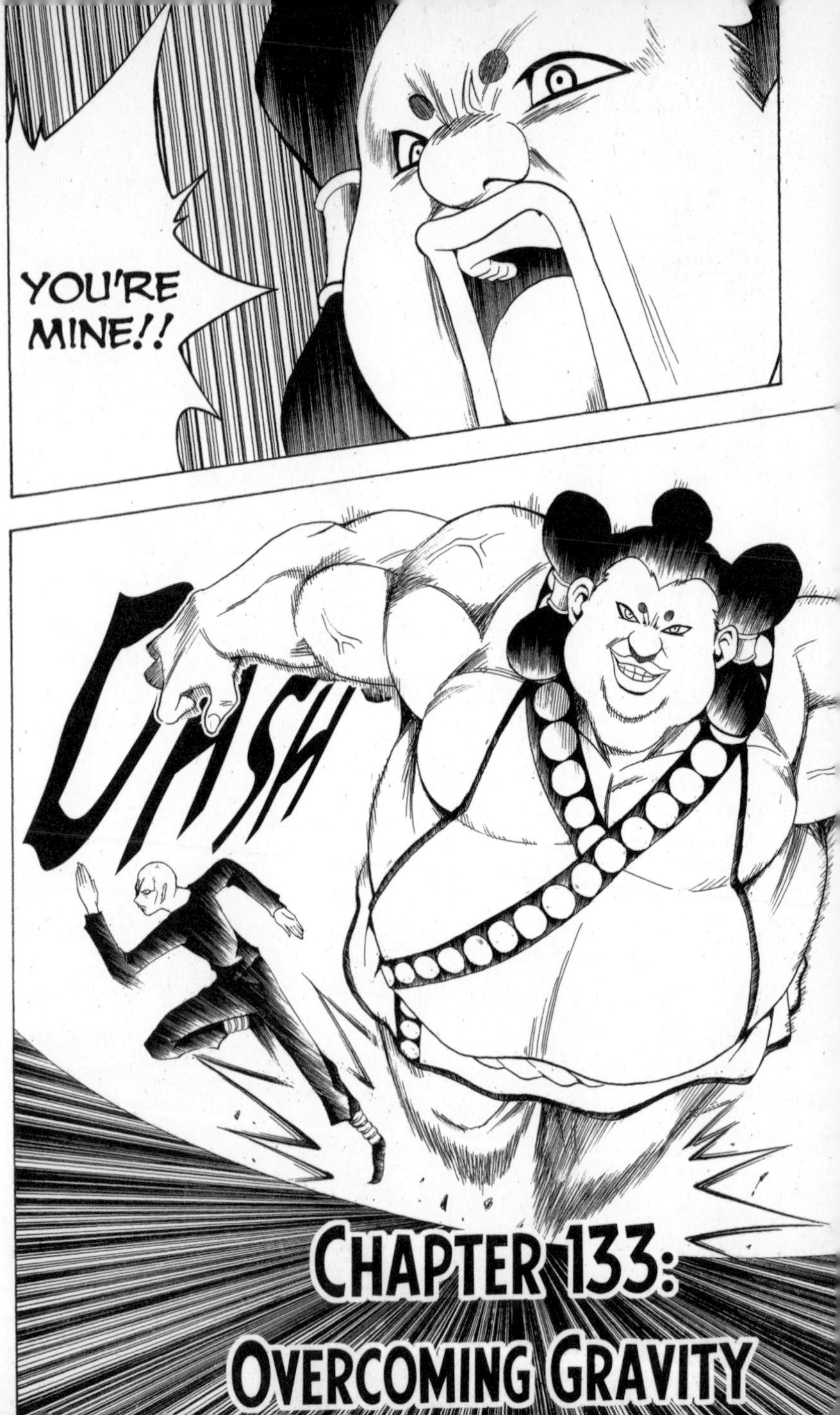
YOU'RE MINE!!
DASH

Chapter 133: Overcoming Gravity

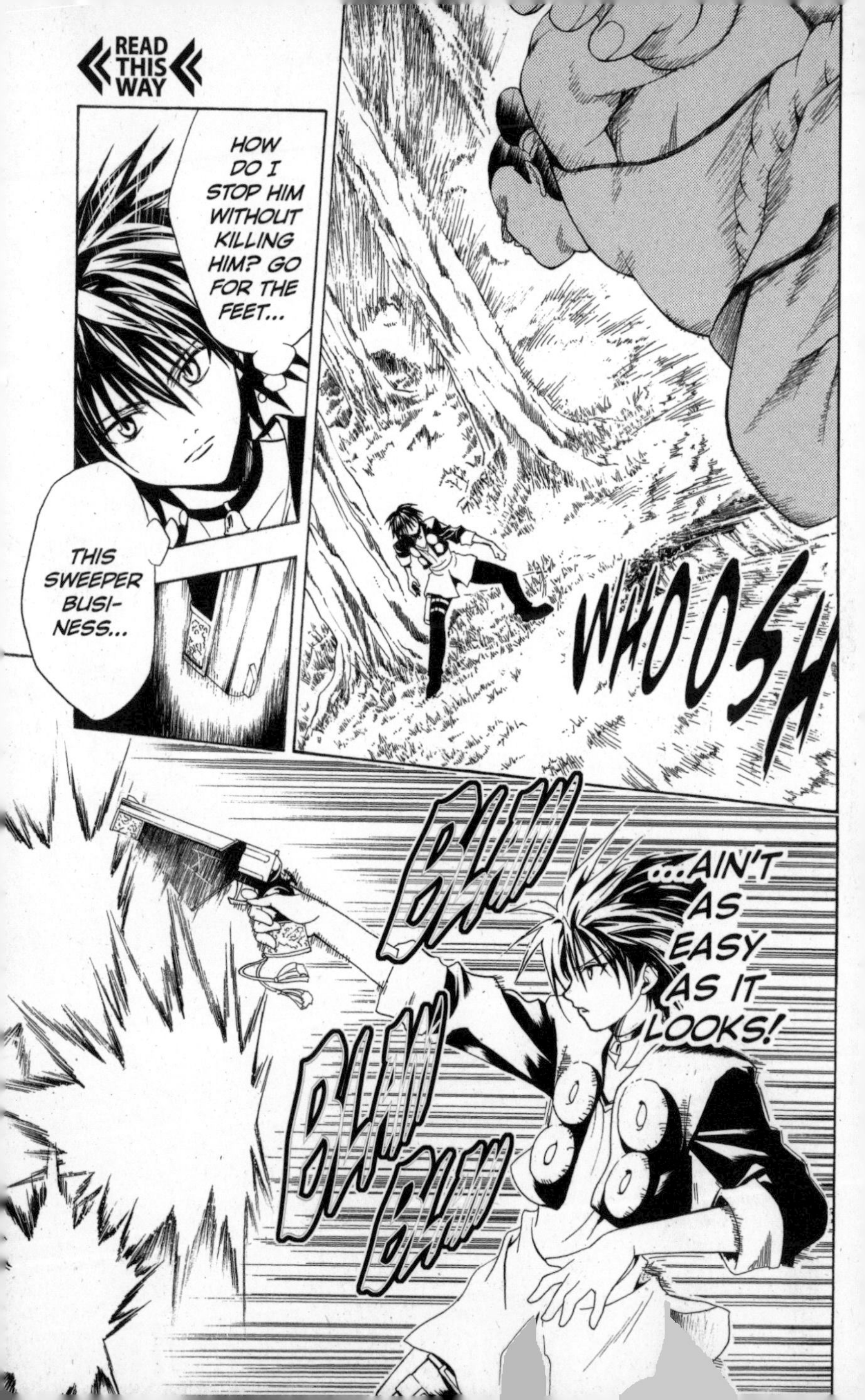
READ THIS WAY
WHOOSH
HOW DO I STOP HIM WITHOUT KILLING HIM? GO FOR THE FEET...
THIS SWEEPER BUSI-NESS...
BLAM
...AIN'T AS EASY AS IT LOOKS!
BLAM
BLAM
BLAM

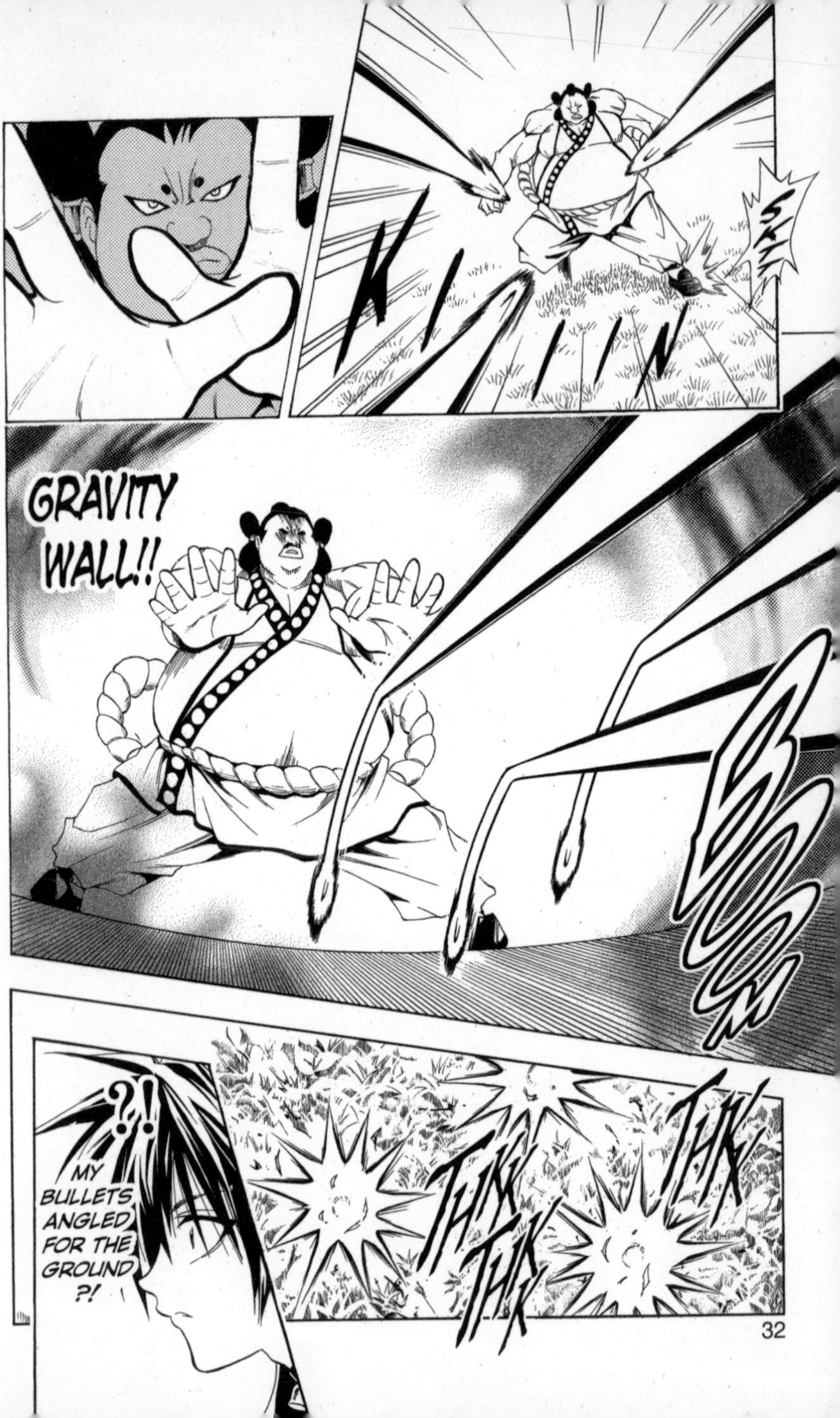
SKKK
KIIIN
GRAVITY WALL!!
BOOOM
THK THK THK THK
?!
MY BULLETS ANGLED FOR THE GROUND?!

READ THIS WAY

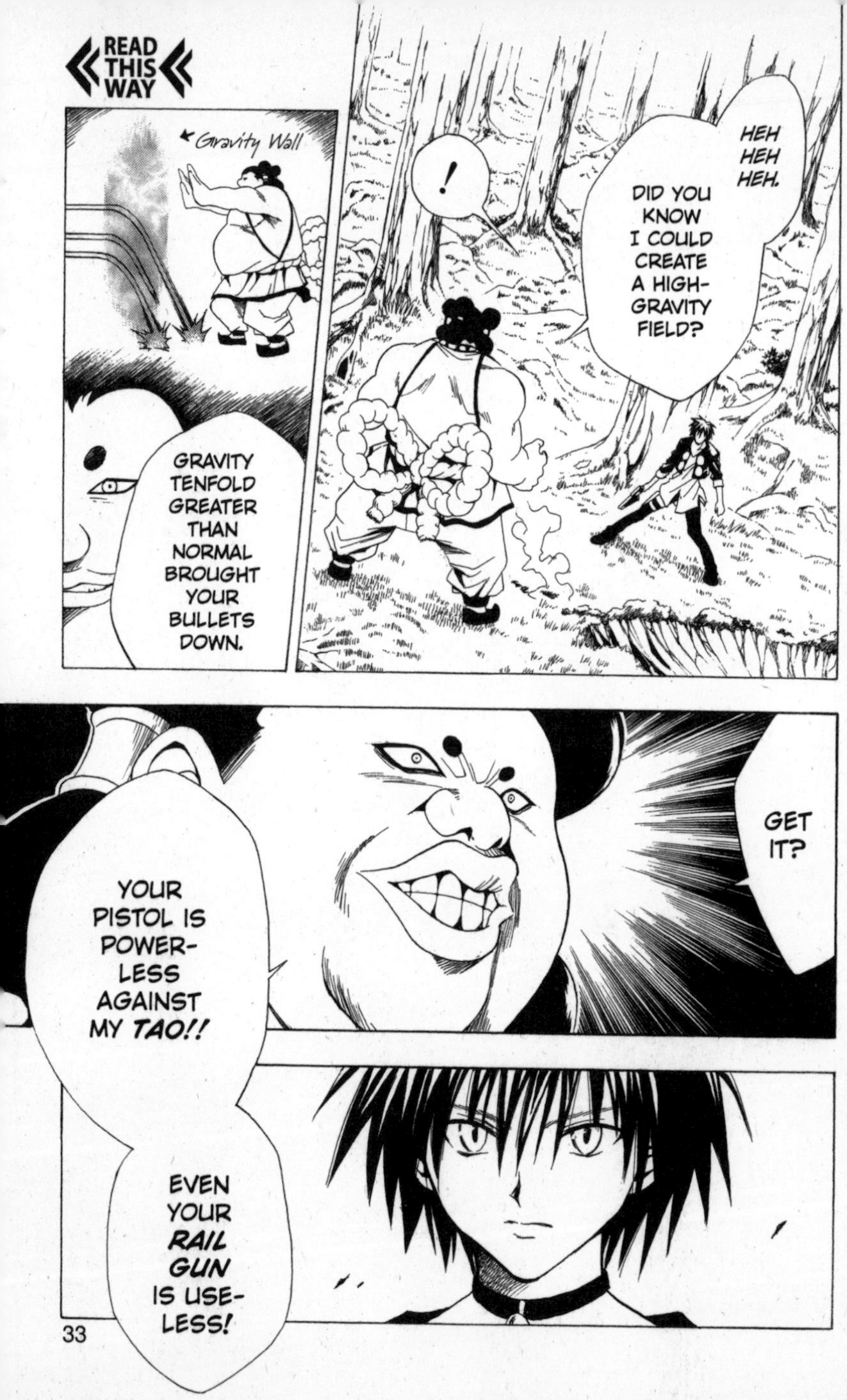
HEH HEH HEH.
DID YOU KNOW I COULD CREATE A HIGH-GRAVITY FIELD?
!
Gravity Wall
GRAVITY TENFOLD GREATER THAN NORMAL BROUGHT YOUR BULLETS DOWN.
GET IT?
YOUR PISTOL IS POWERLESS AGAINST MY *TAO!!*
EVEN YOUR ***RAIL GUN*** IS USELESS!

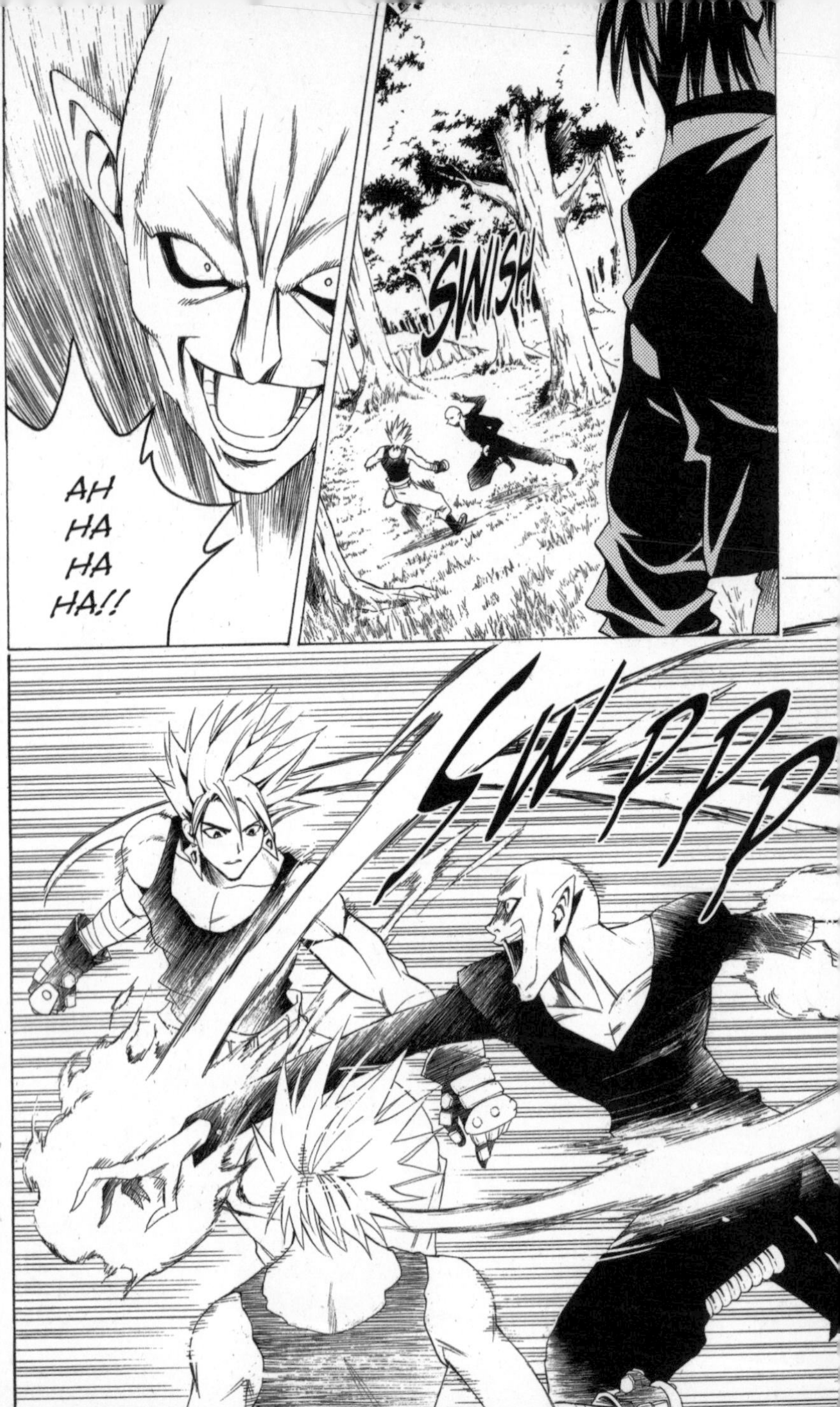
SWISH
AH
HA
HA
HA!!
SWIPPP

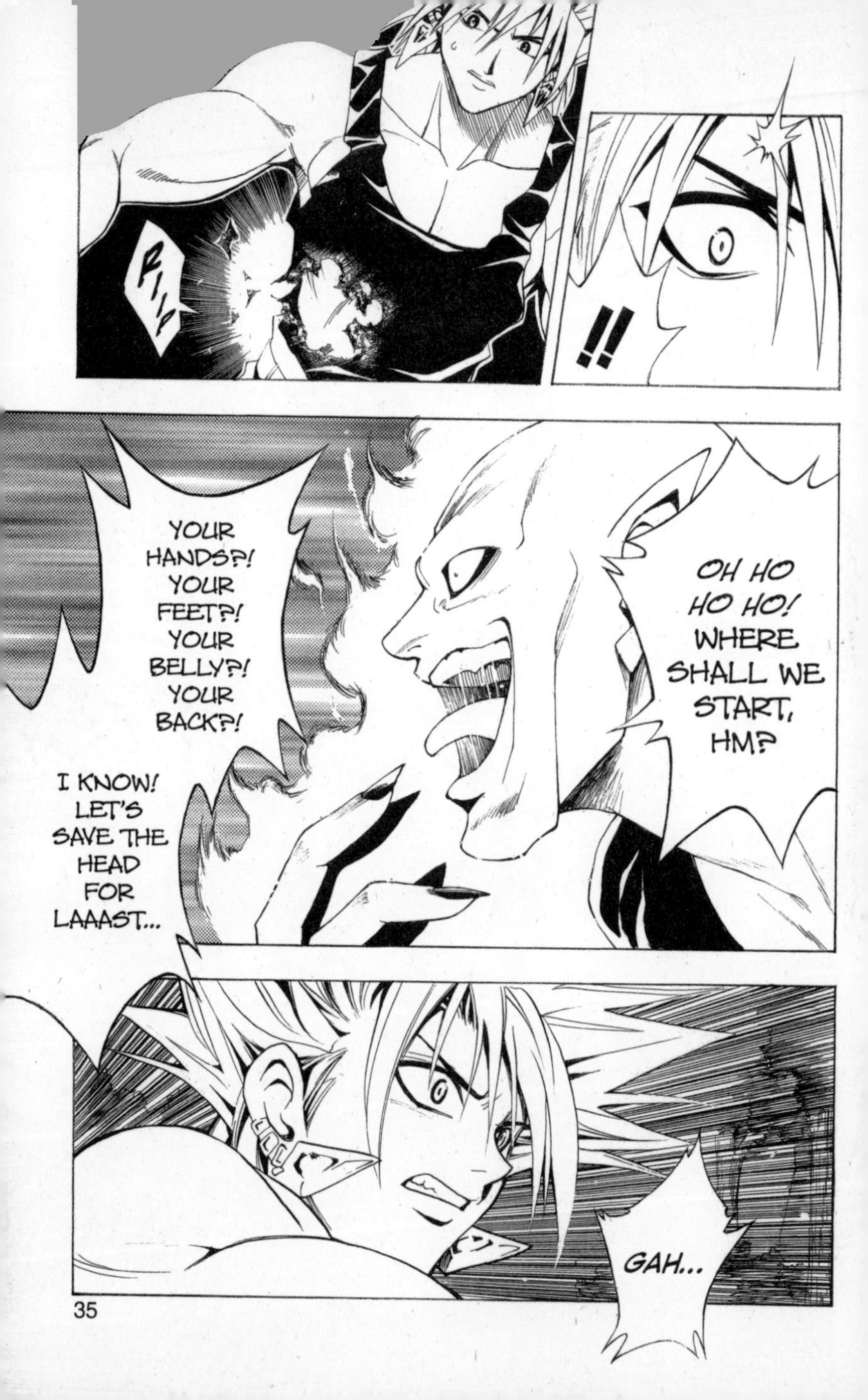
!!
RIP
OH HO HO HO! WHERE SHALL WE START, HM?
YOUR HANDS?! YOUR FEET?! YOUR BELLY?! YOUR BACK?!
I KNOW! LET'S SAVE THE HEAD FOR LAAAST...
GAH...

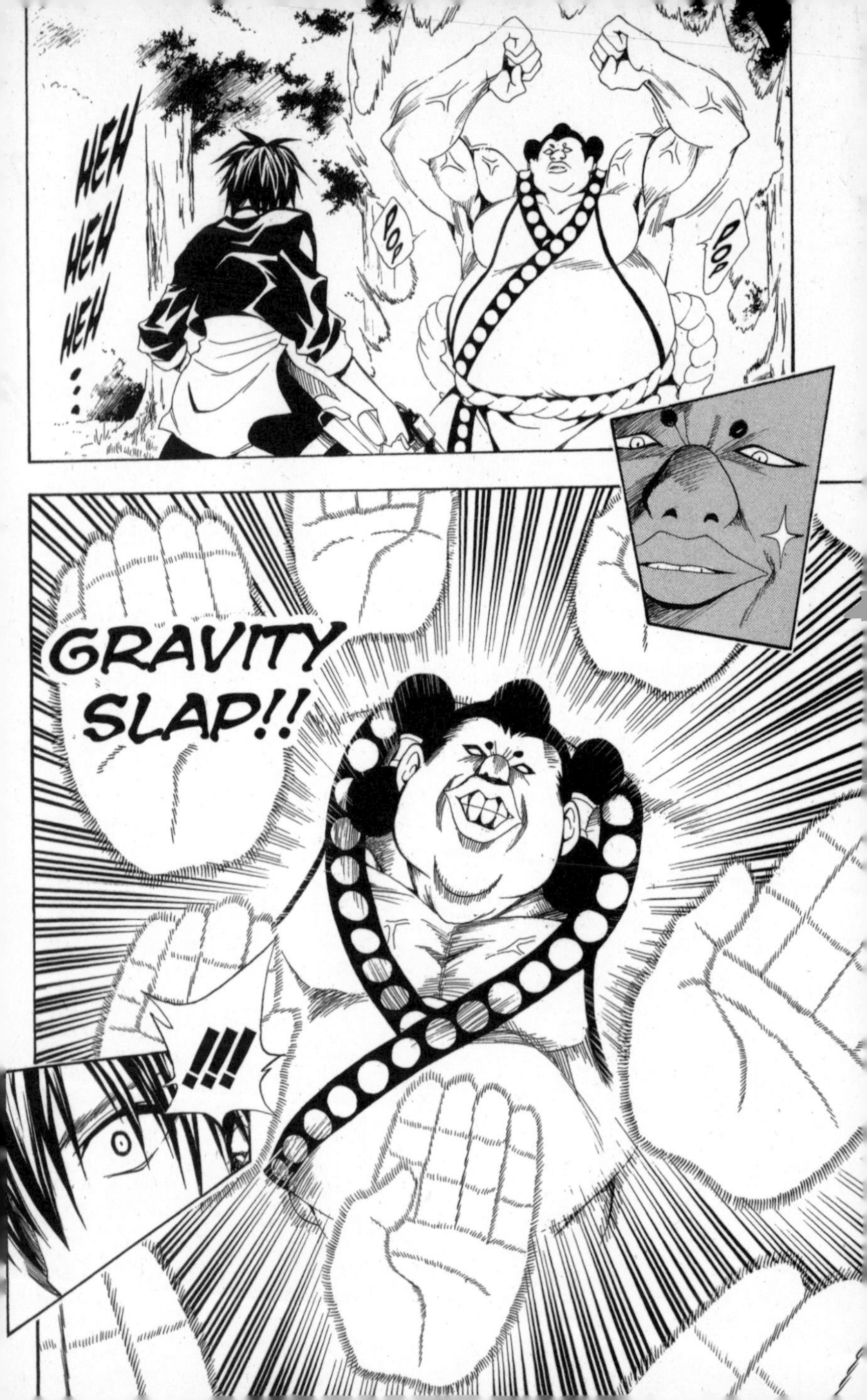
DOP
DOP
HEH HEH HEH HEH...
GRAVITY SLAP!!
!!!

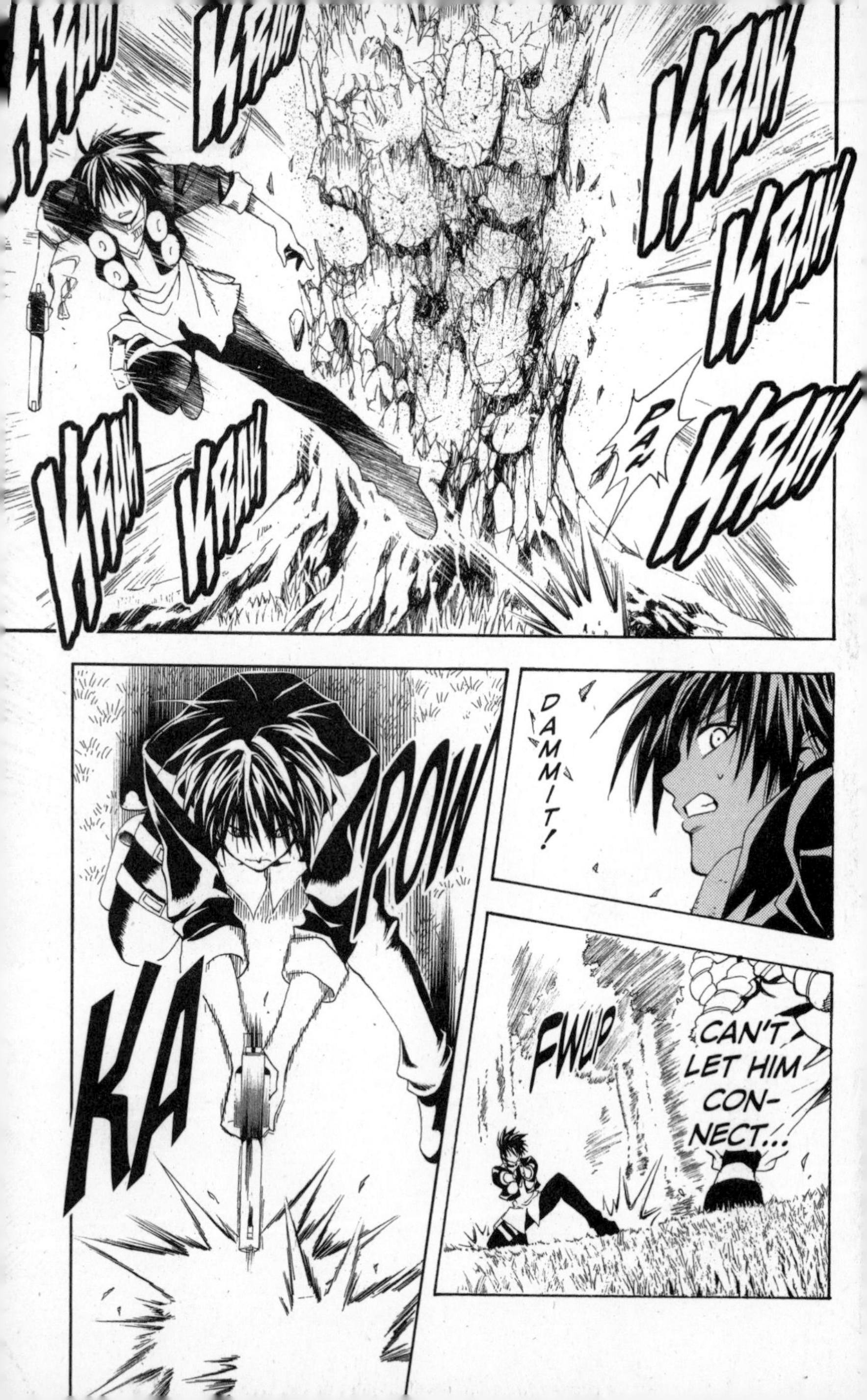
DAH
DAMMIT!
CAN'T LET HIM CON-NECT...
FWUP
KA
POW

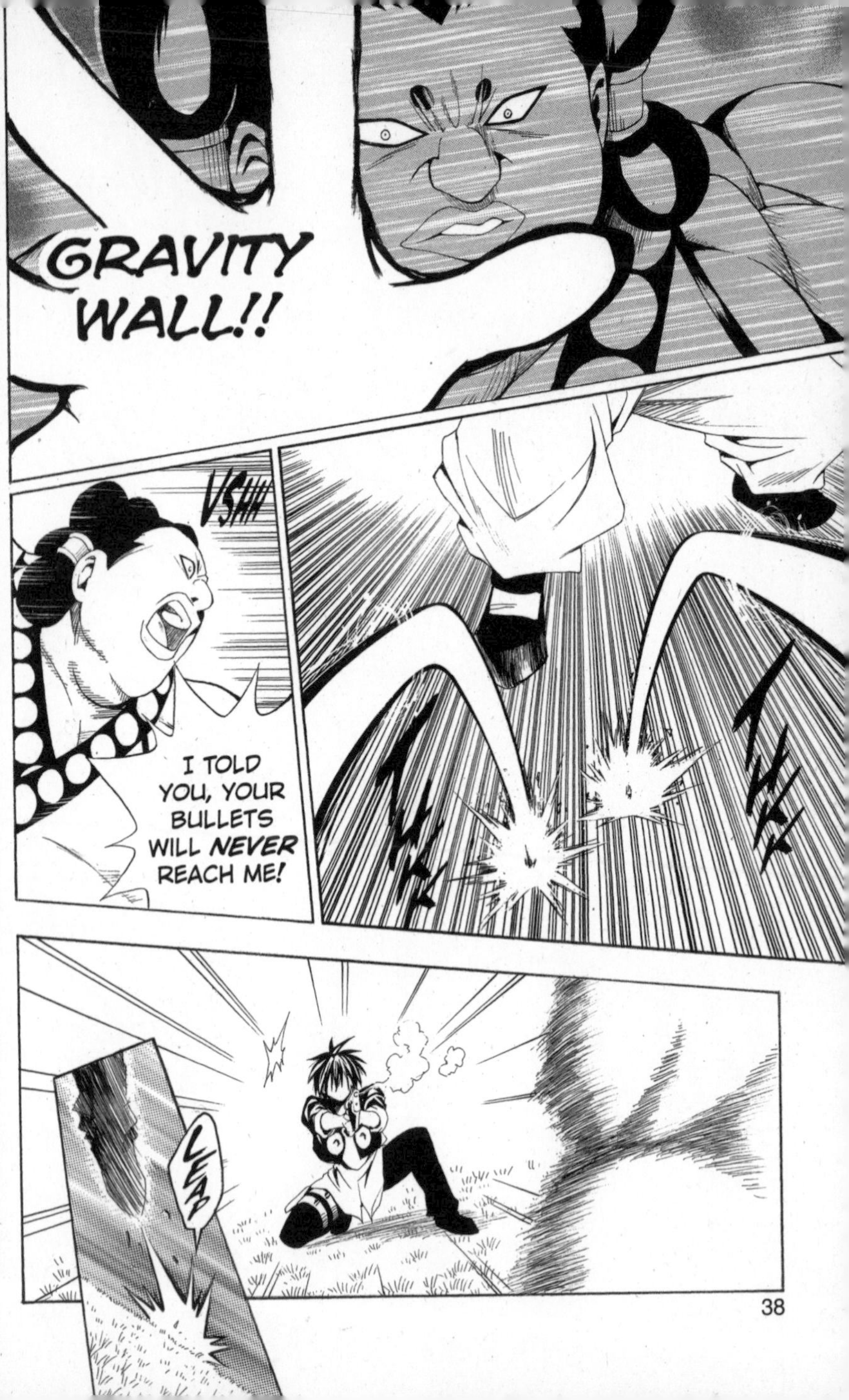
GRAVITY WALL!!
VSHH
I TOLD YOU, YOUR BULLETS WILL NEVER REACH ME!
LEAP

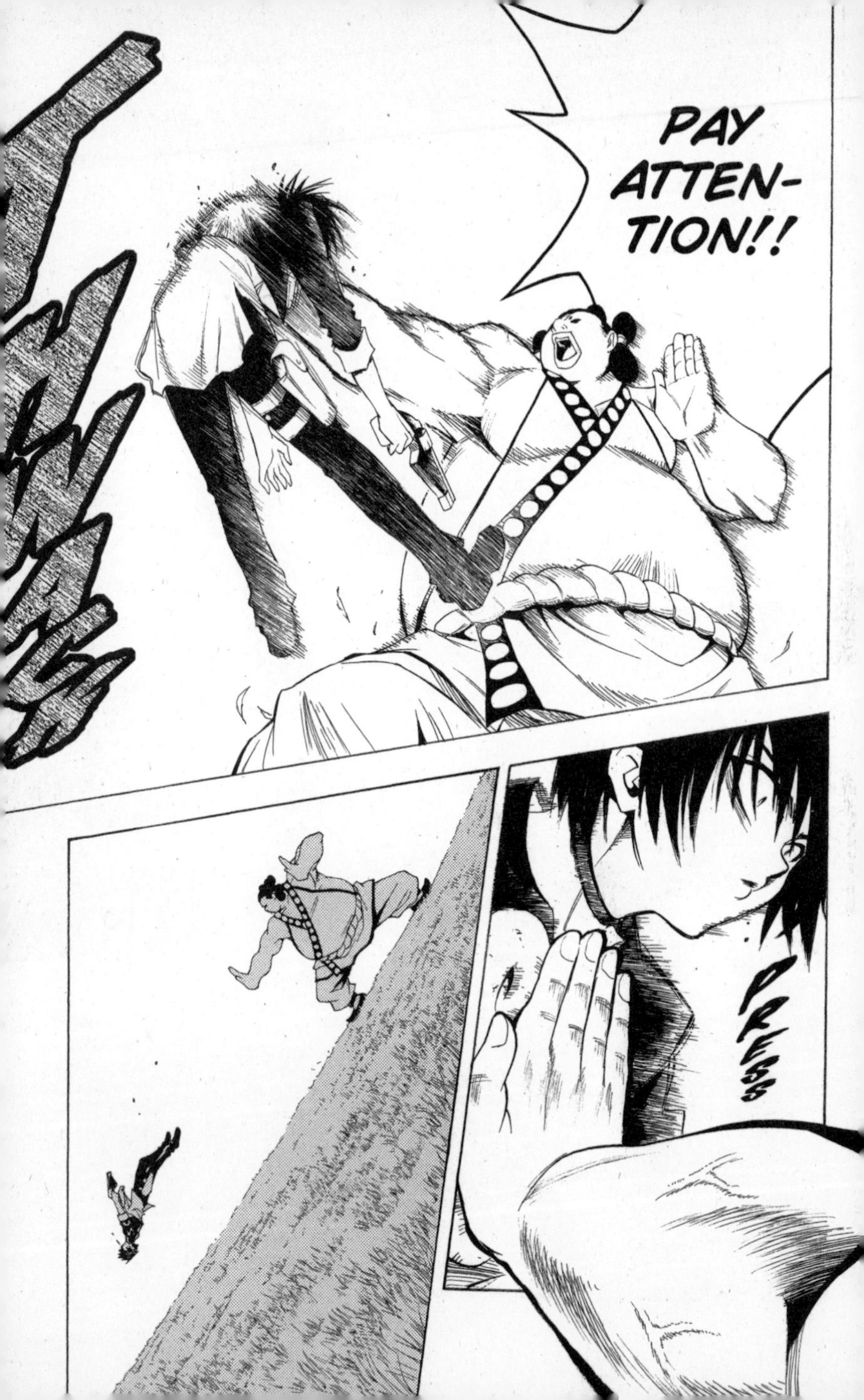
PAY ATTEN-TION!!
PRESS

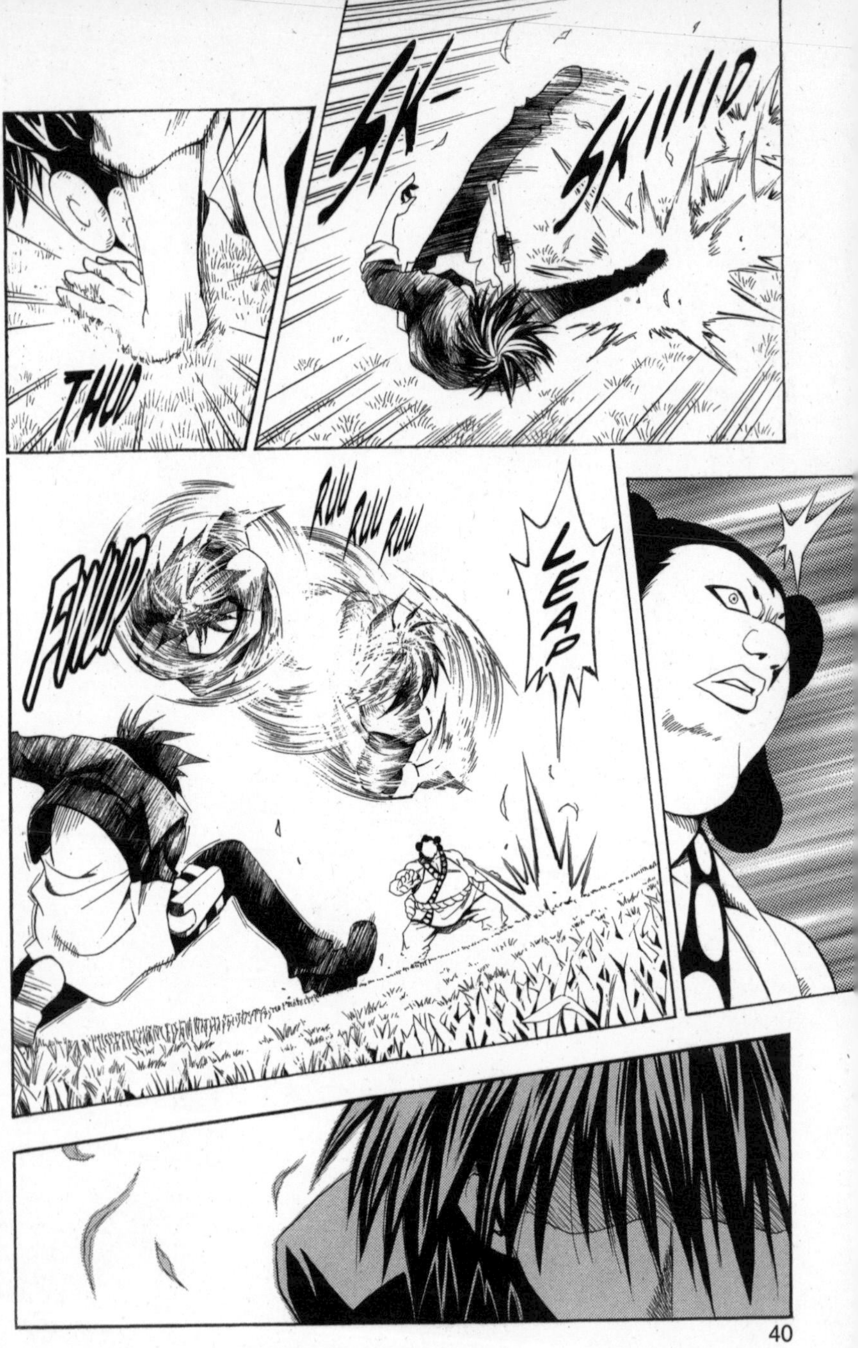
SK-
SKIIIID
THUD
LEAP
RUU RUU RUU

READ THIS WAY

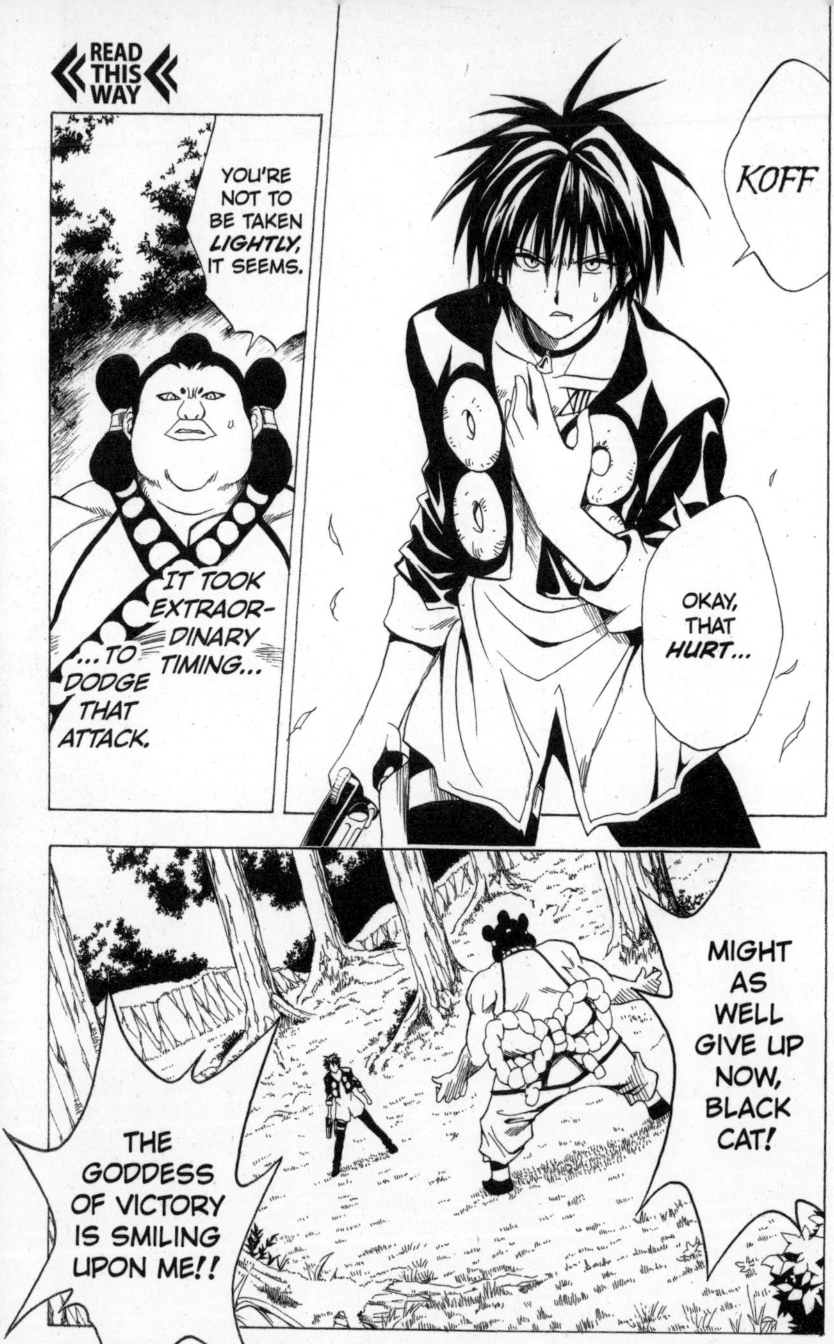
KOFF
OKAY, THAT HURT...
YOU'RE NOT TO BE TAKEN LIGHTLY, IT SEEMS.
IT TOOK EXTRAORDINARY TIMING...
...TO DODGE THAT ATTACK.
MIGHT AS WELL GIVE UP NOW, BLACK CAT!
THE GODDESS OF VICTORY IS SMILING UPON ME!!

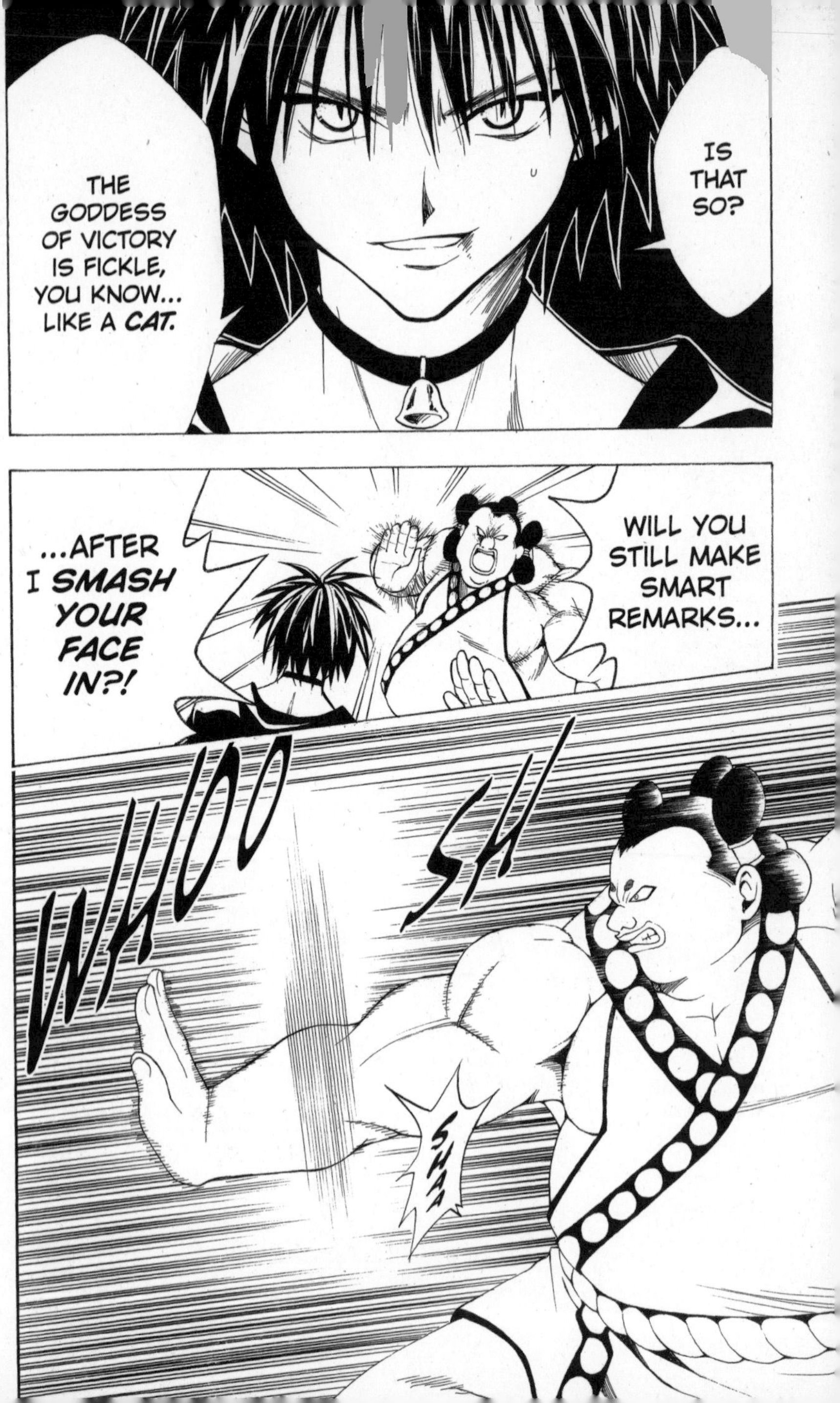
IS THAT SO?
THE GODDESS OF VICTORY IS FICKLE, YOU KNOW... LIKE A *CAT.*
WILL YOU STILL MAKE SMART REMARKS...
...AFTER I *SMASH YOUR FACE IN?!*
WHOOSH
SHAA

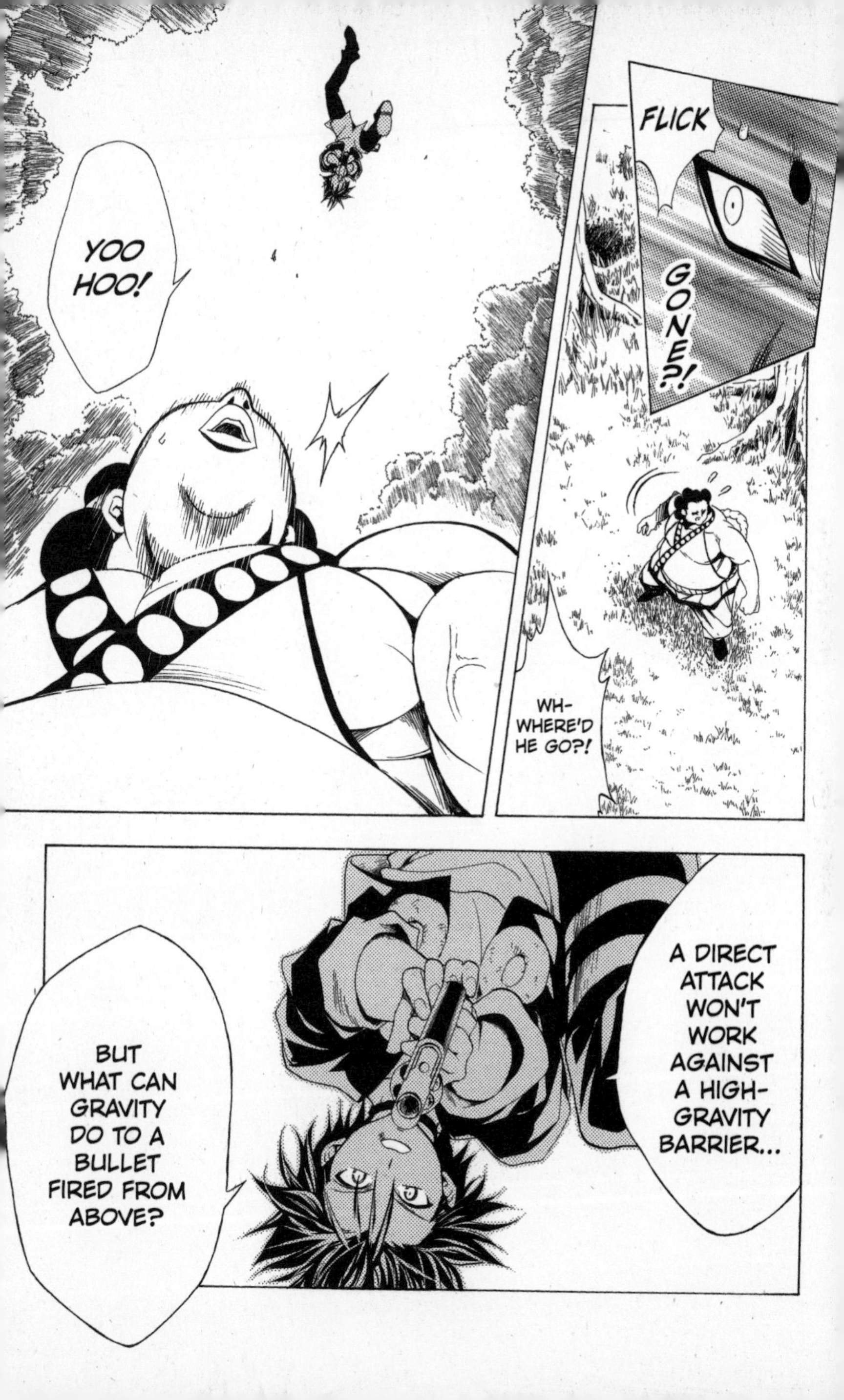
FLICK
GONE?!
WH-WHERE'D HE GO?!
YOO HOO!
A DIRECT ATTACK WON'T WORK AGAINST A HIGH-GRAVITY BARRIER...
BUT WHAT CAN GRAVITY DO TO A BULLET FIRED FROM ABOVE?

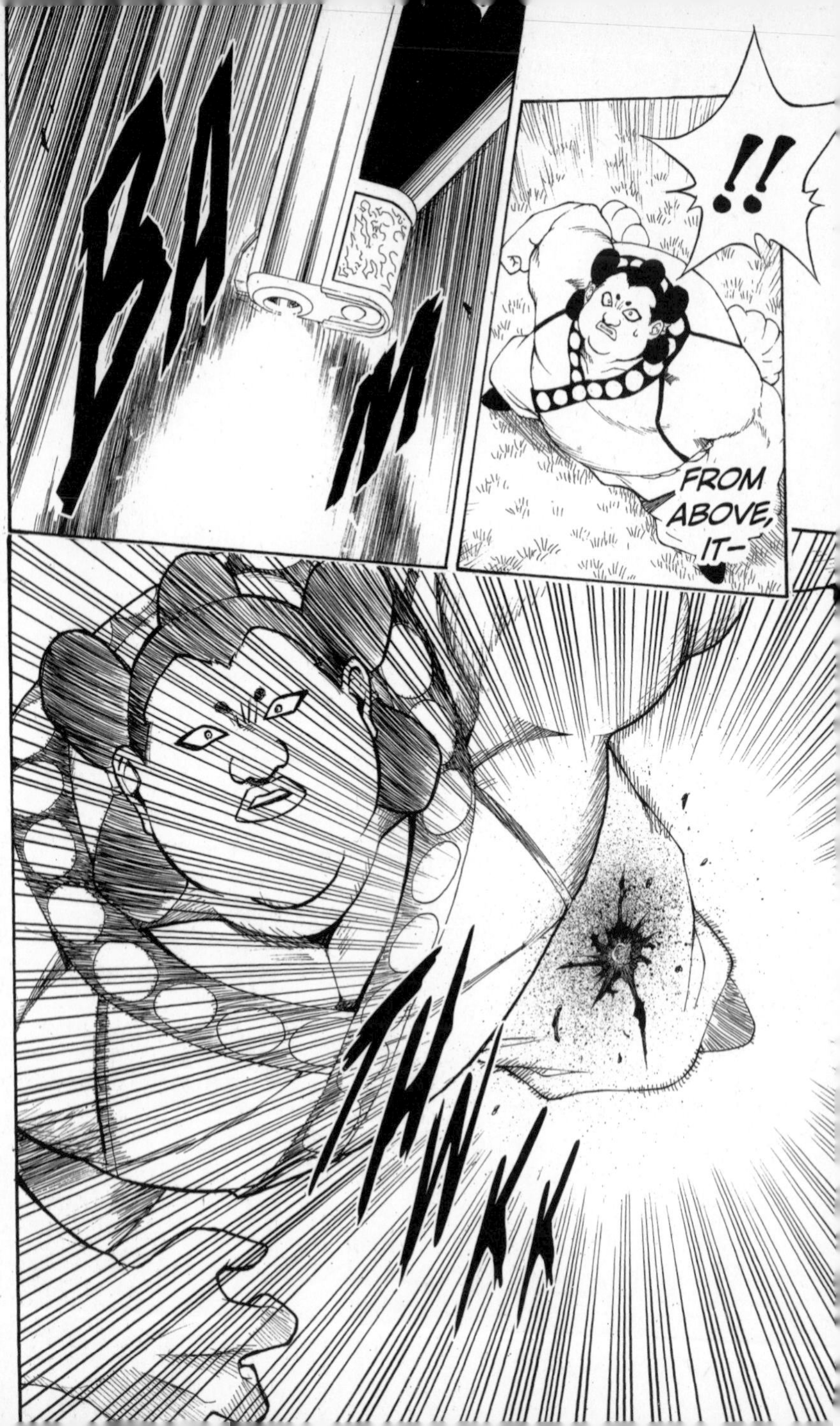
!!
FROM ABOVE, IT–
BAM
THWAKK

READ THIS WAY

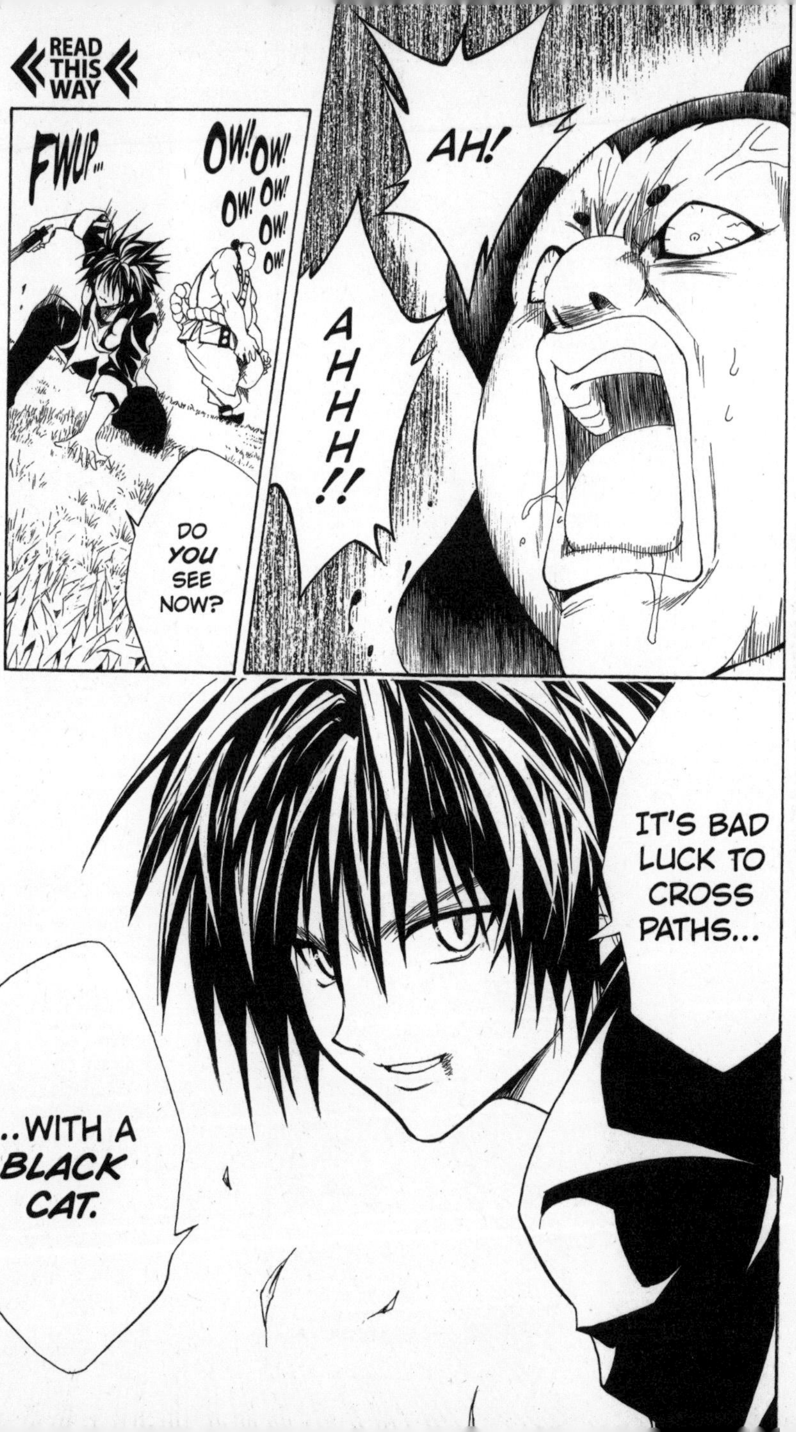
AH!
AHHHH!!
OW! OW! OW! OW! OW! OW!
FWUP...
DO YOU SEE NOW?
IT'S BAD LUCK TO CROSS PATHS...
...WITH A BLACK CAT.

TO THE HIDE-OUT

EVEN A WATER-MELON CAN BE A BOMB ...

...
THAT WATER-MELON LOOKS TASTY.
WHERE'D YOU GET IT, PRINCESS?
SOMEONE LEFT IT HERE.
OH YEAH?
YOINK
WELL THEN, I CALL DIBS!!
EH?
BOOM
HEY EVE, HAVE YOU SEEN MY LATEST BOMB? IT LOOKS LIKE A WATERMELON.

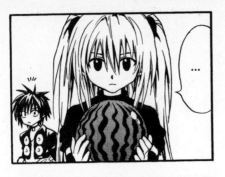

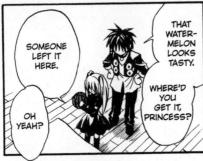

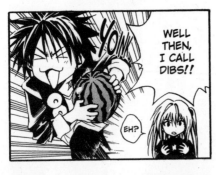

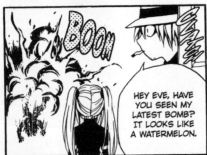

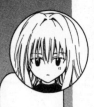

Chapter 134: There is a Way

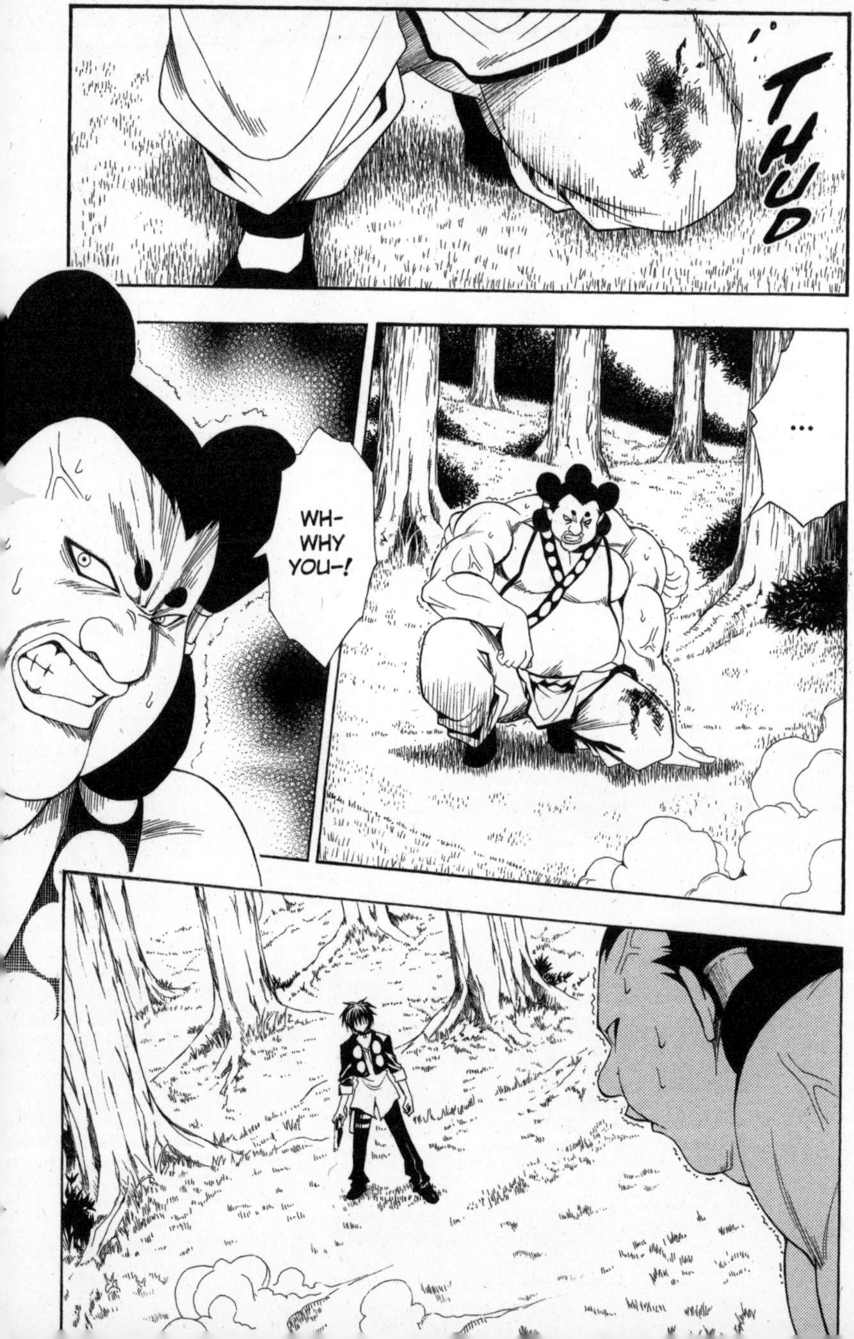
THUD
...
WH-
WHY
YOU-!

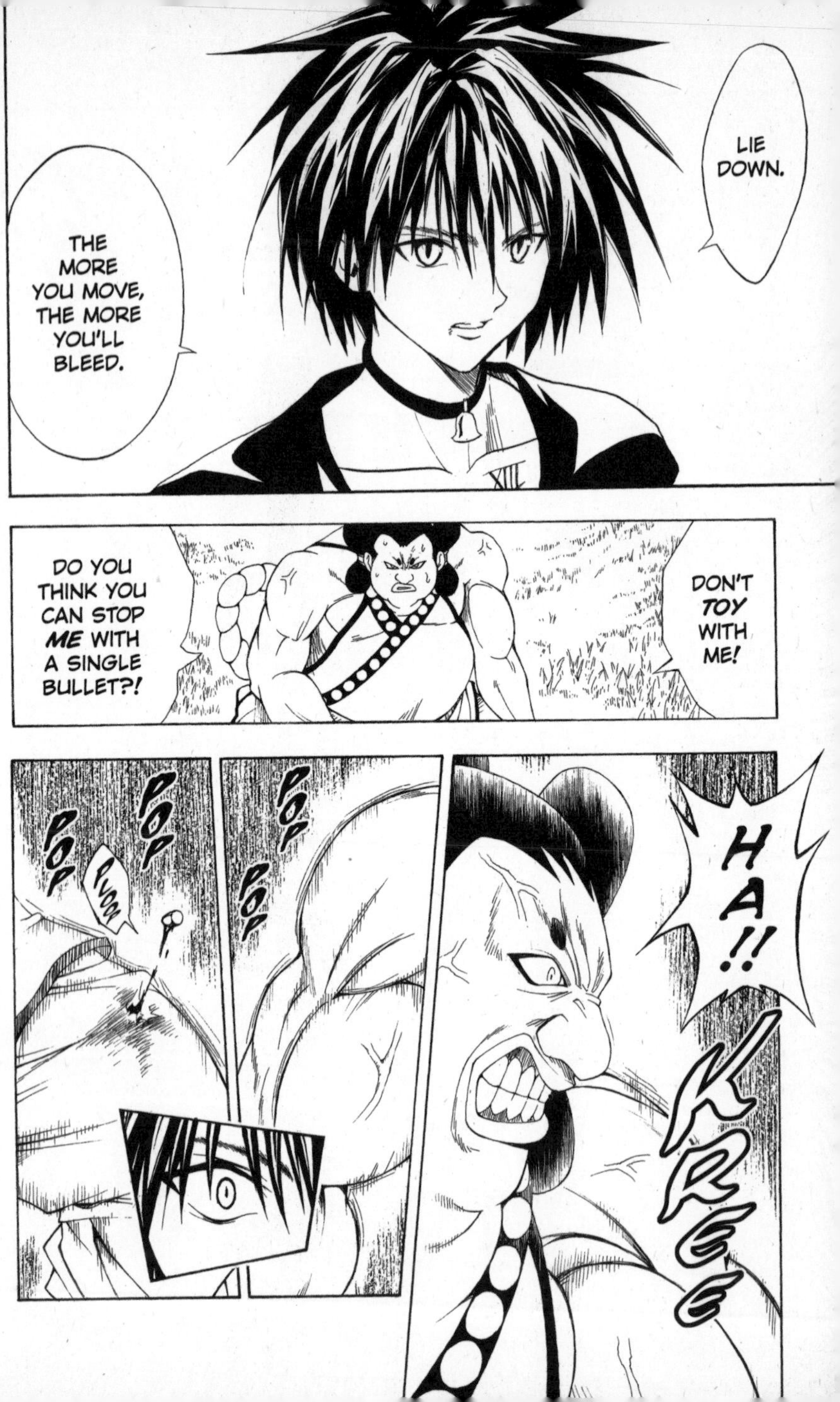
LIE DOWN.
THE MORE YOU MOVE, THE MORE YOU'LL BLEED.
DON'T *TOY* WITH ME!
DO YOU THINK YOU CAN STOP *ME* WITH A SINGLE BULLET?!
HA!!
KRGG
POP
POP
POP
PUOOO
POP

READ THIS WAY

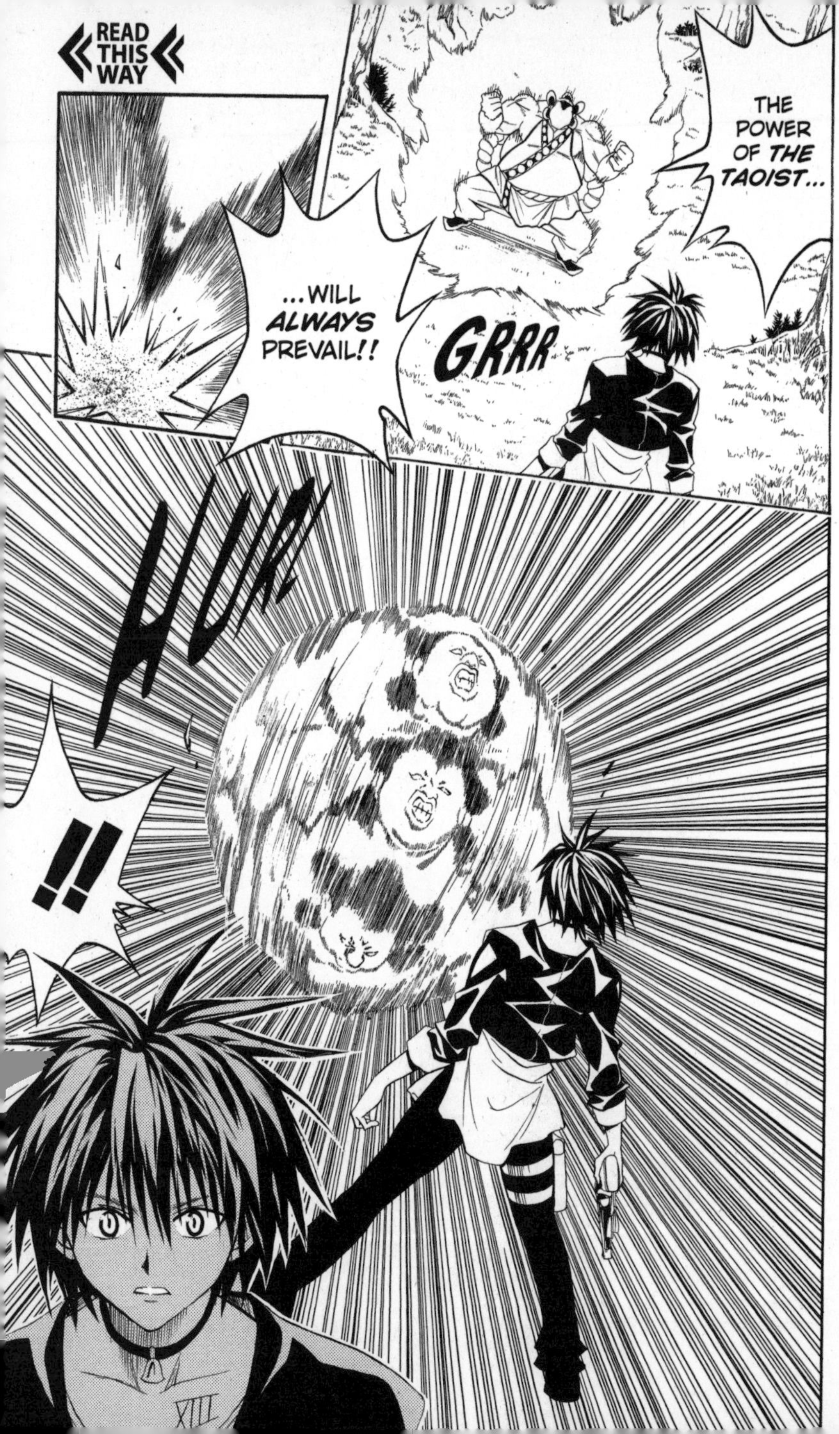
THE POWER OF THE TAOIST...
...WILL ALWAYS PREVAIL!!
GRRR
HUR
!!

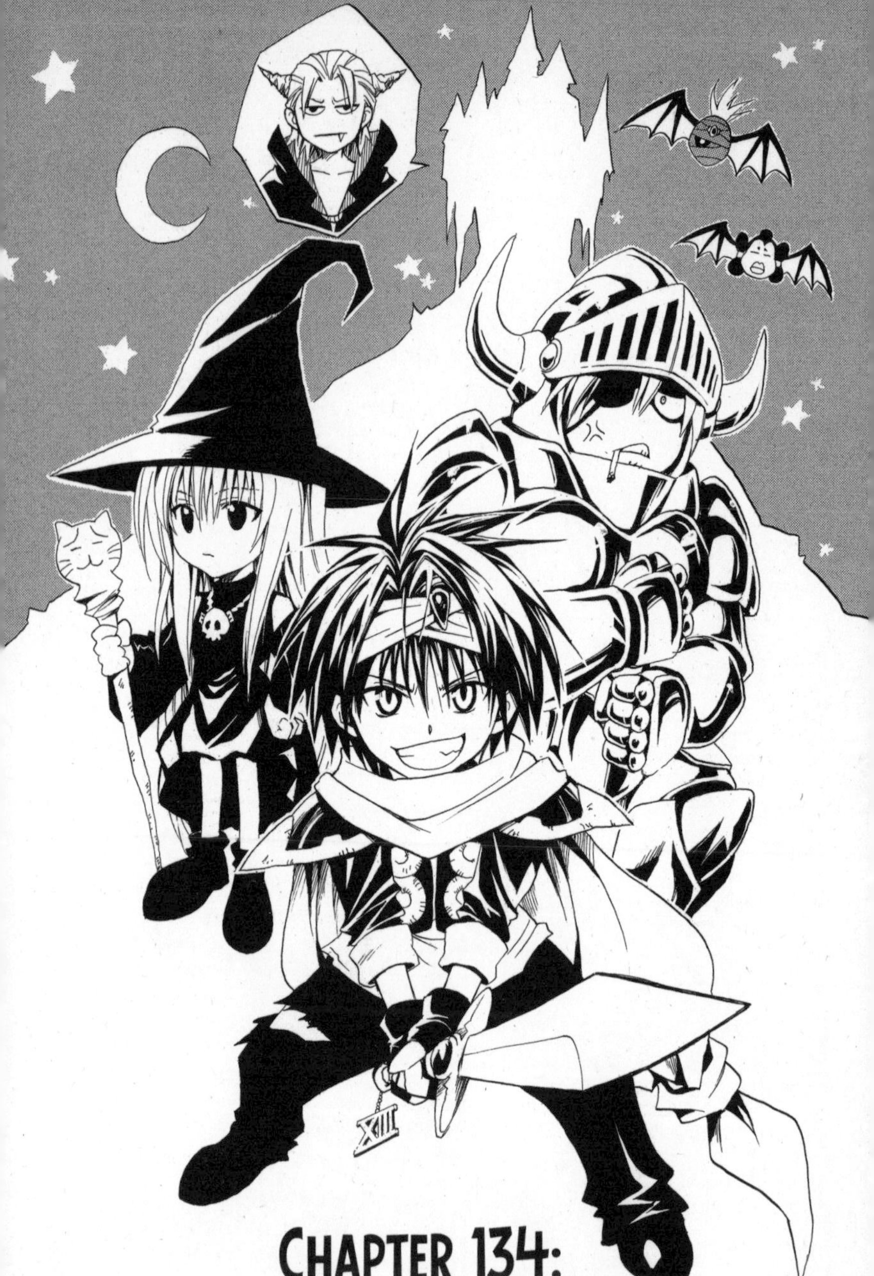
XIII

CHAPTER 134:
THERE IS A WAY

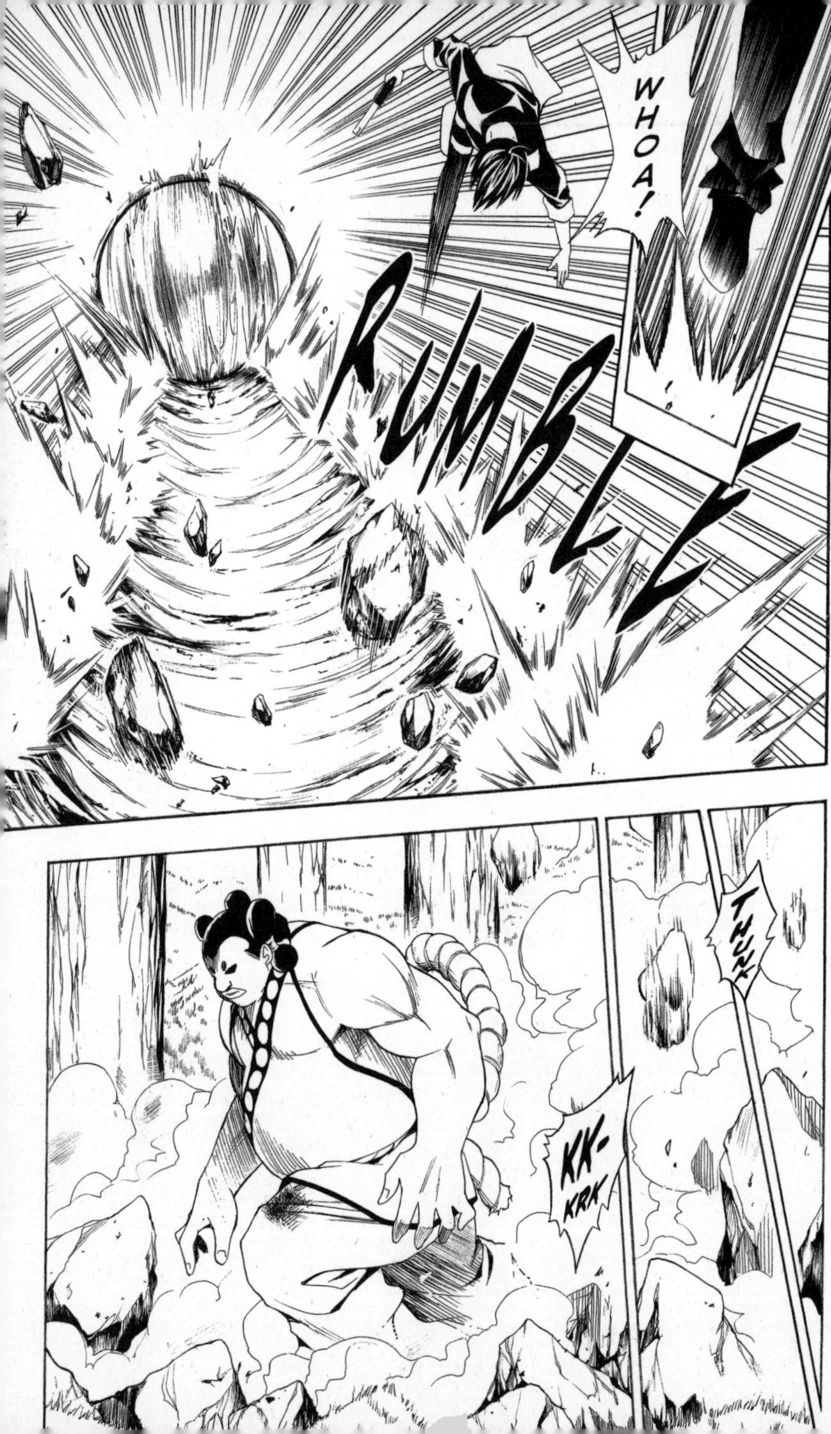
WHOA!
RUMBLE
THUNK
KK-KRK

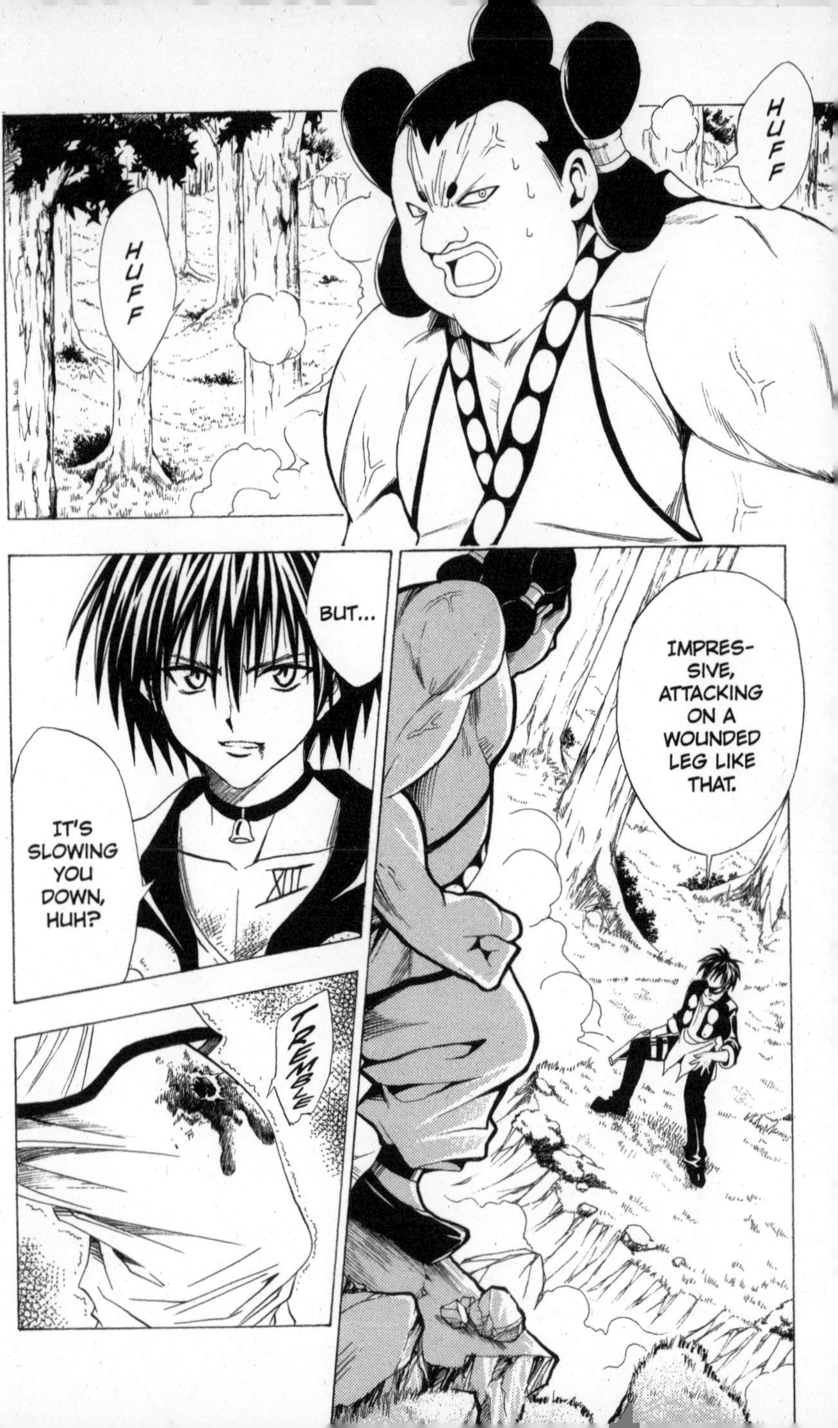
HUFF
HUFF
IMPRESSIVE, ATTACKING ON A WOUNDED LEG LIKE THAT.
BUT...
IT'S SLOWING YOU DOWN, HUH?
TREMBLE

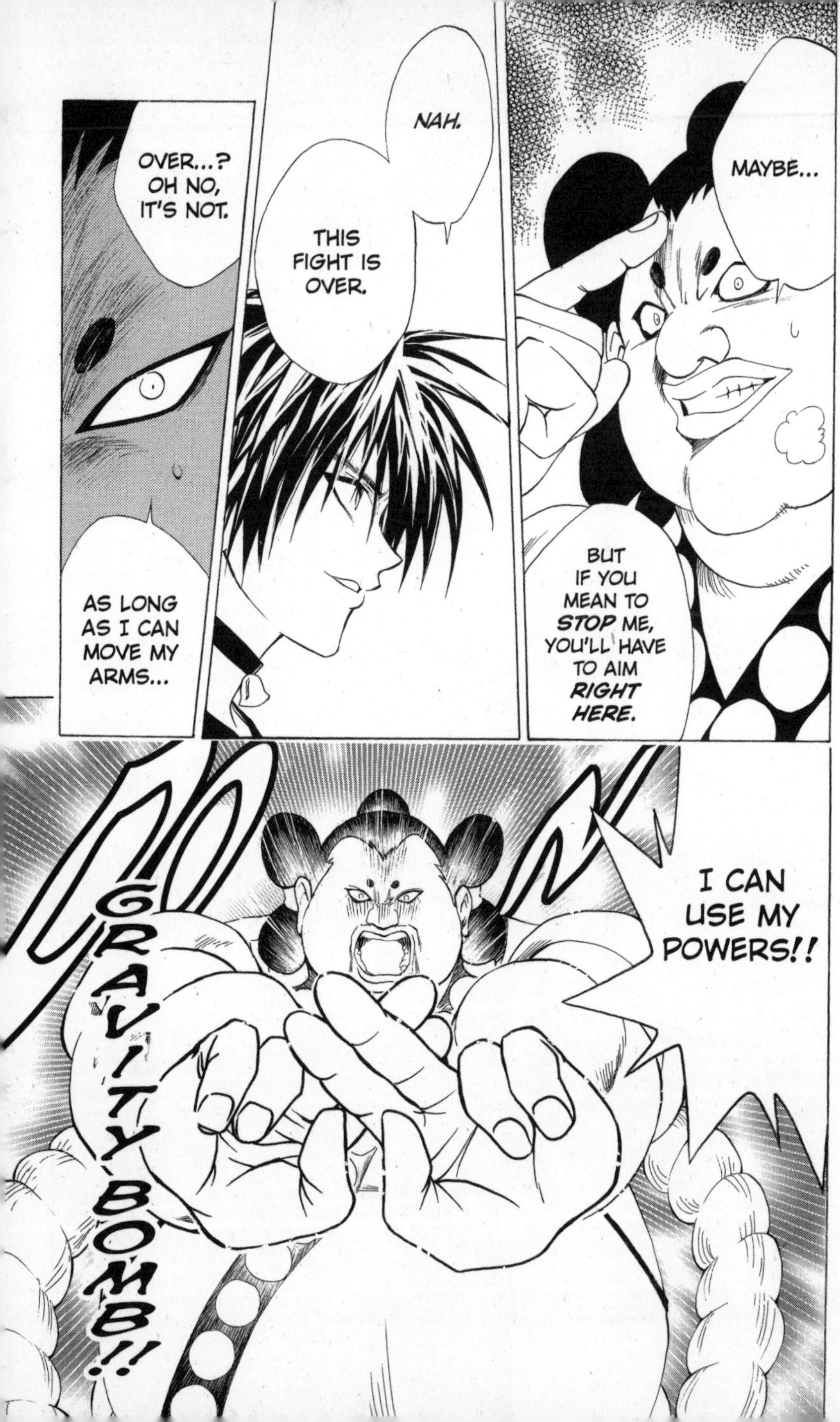
MAYBE...
BUT IF YOU MEAN TO STOP ME, YOU'LL HAVE TO AIM RIGHT HERE.
NAH.
THIS FIGHT IS OVER.
OVER...? OH NO, IT'S NOT.
AS LONG AS I CAN MOVE MY ARMS...
I CAN USE MY POWERS!!
GRAVITY BOMB!!

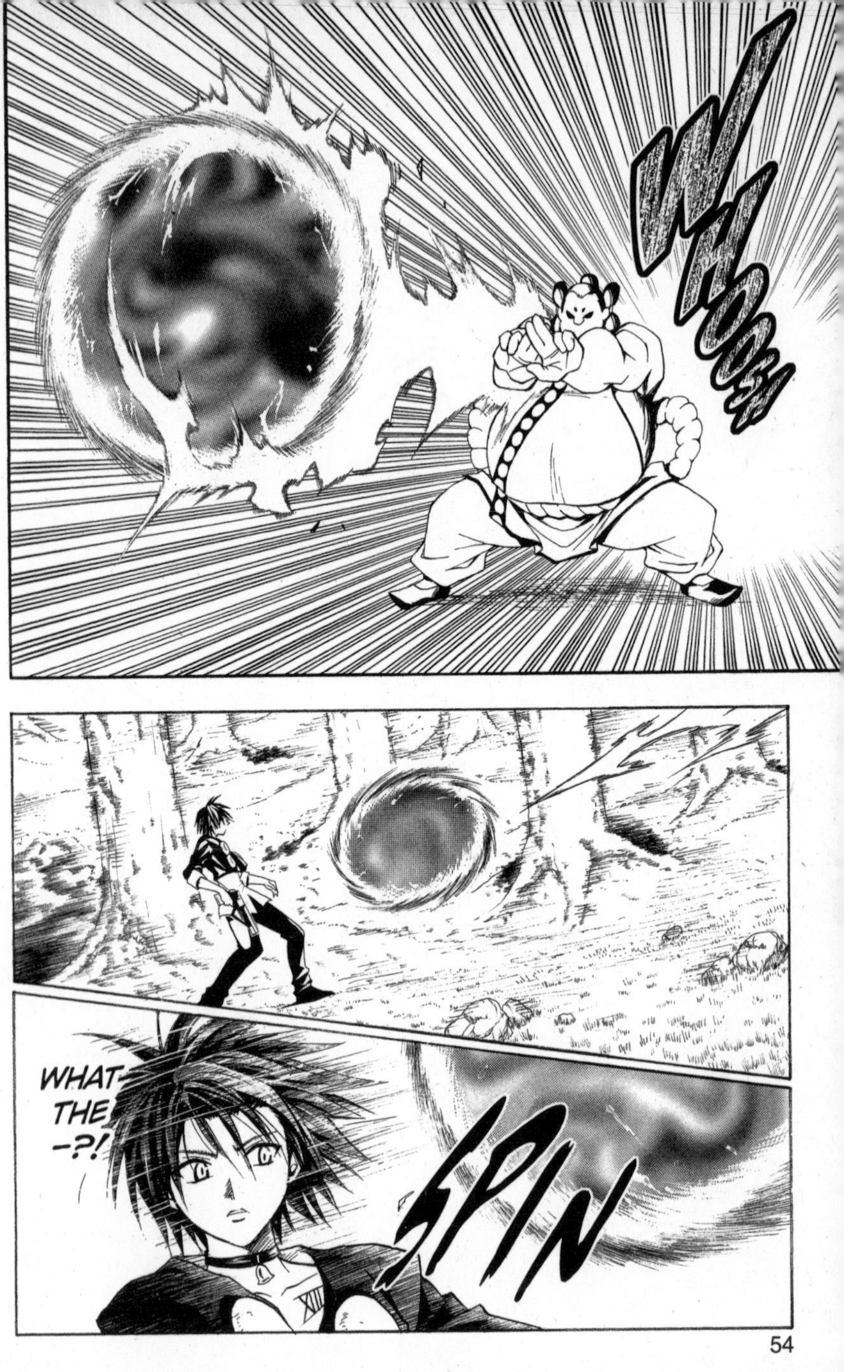
WHOOOM
SPIN
WHAT THE-?!

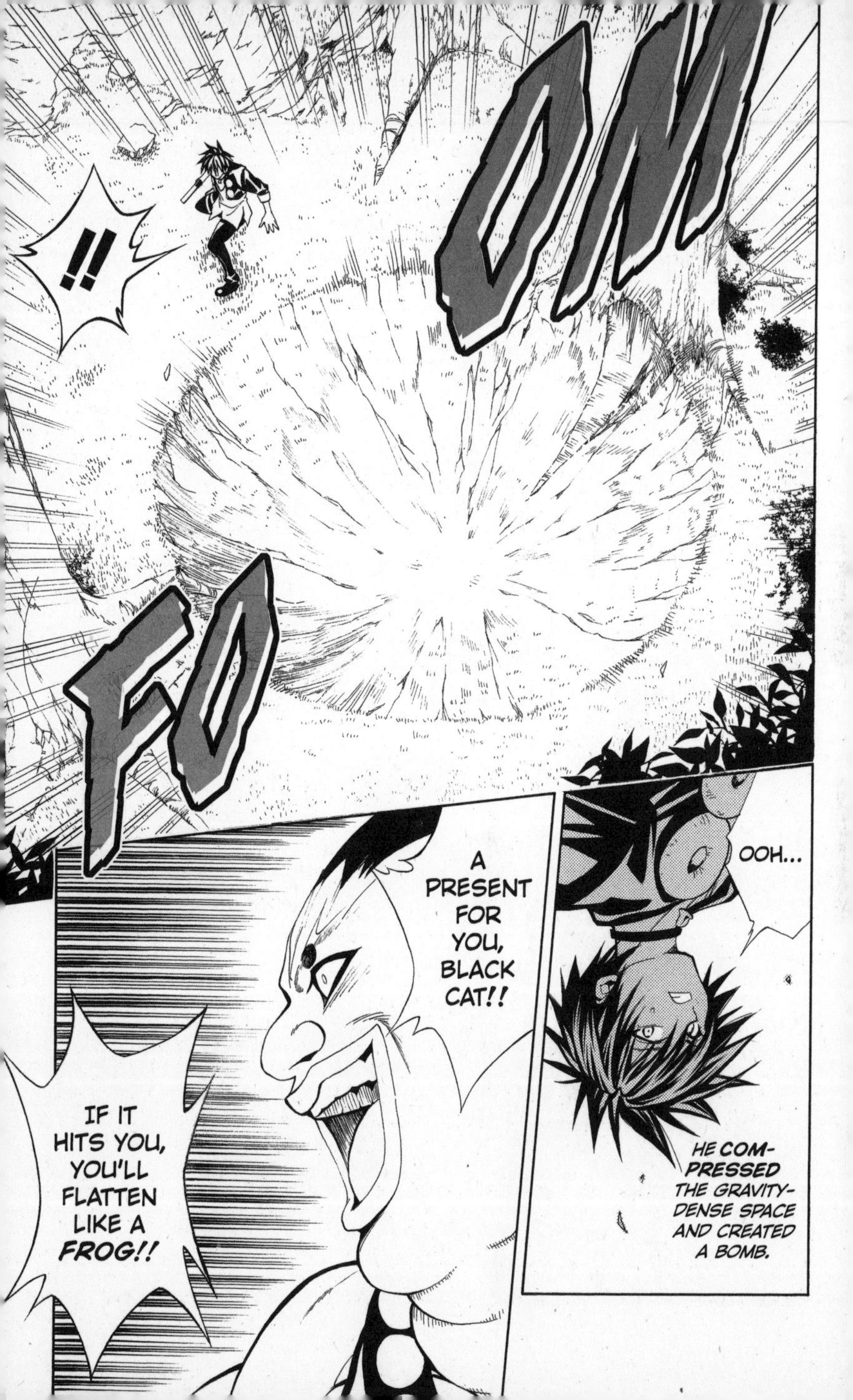
OM
!!
FO
OOH...
HE COMPRESSED THE GRAVITY-DENSE SPACE AND CREATED A BOMB.
A PRESENT FOR YOU, BLACK CAT!!
IF IT HITS YOU, YOU'LL FLATTEN LIKE A FROG!!

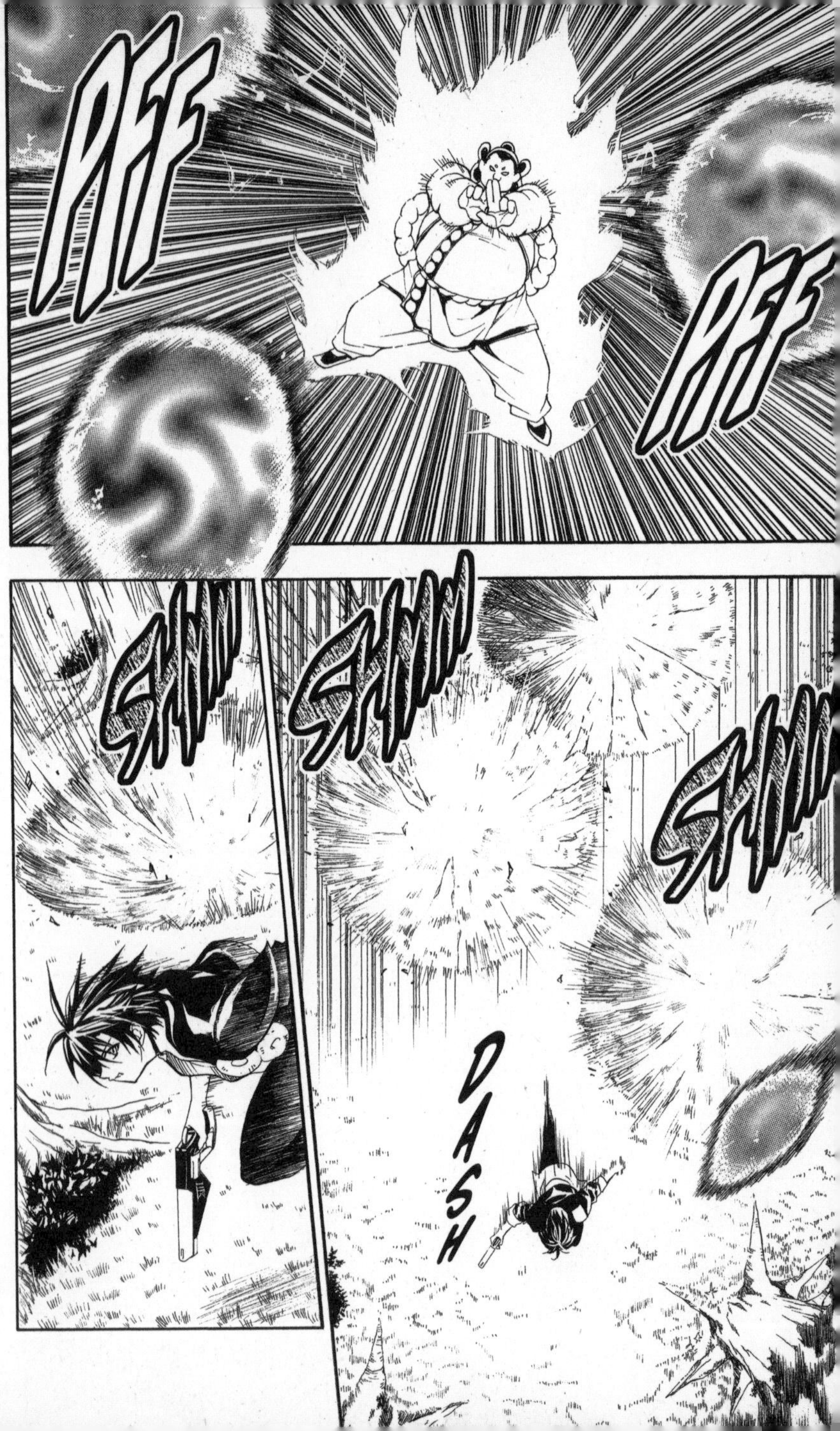
PFF
PFF
SHHH
SHHH
DASH
SHHH

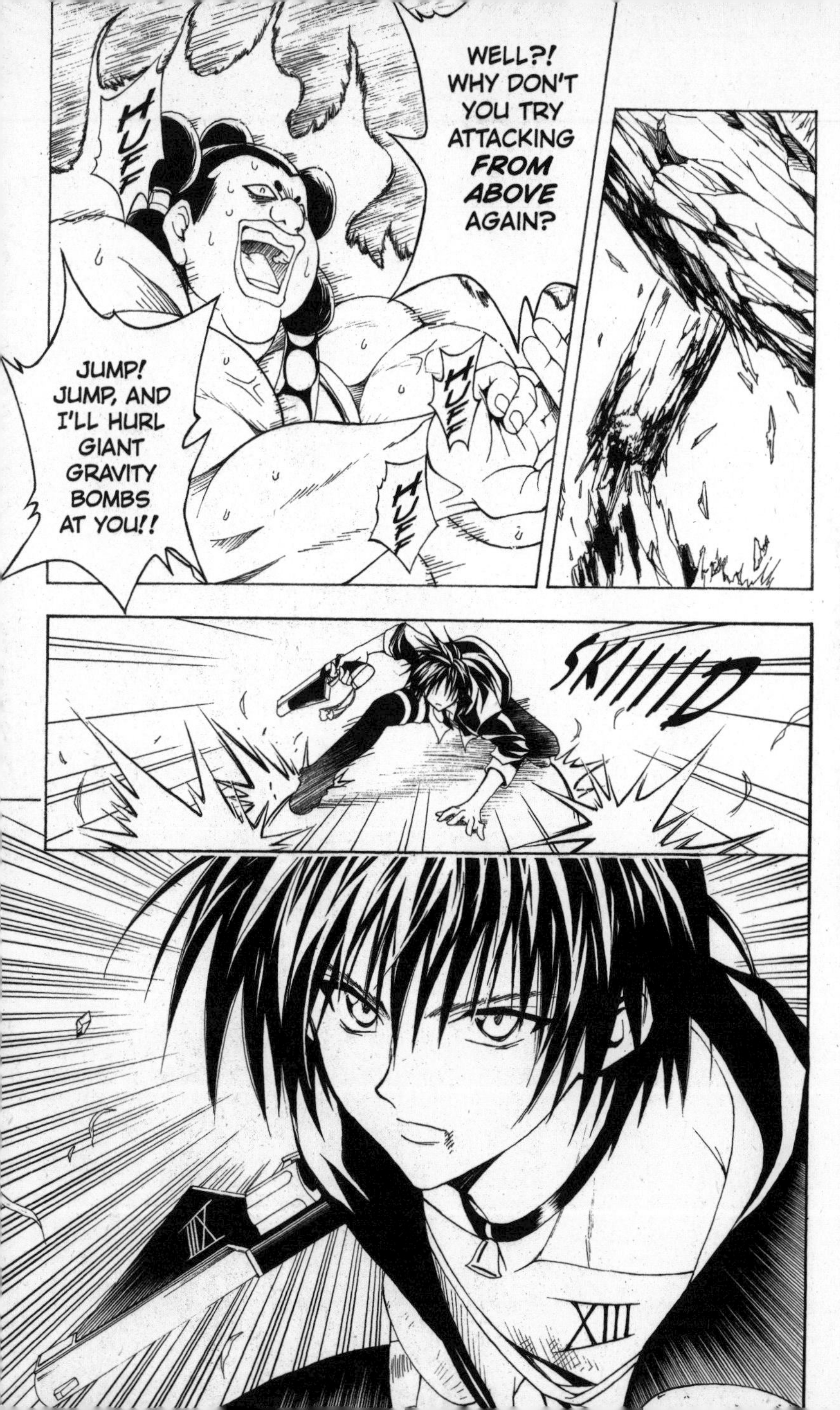
WELL?! WHY DON'T YOU TRY ATTACKING FROM ABOVE AGAIN?
HUFF
HUFF
HUFF
JUMP! JUMP, AND I'LL HURL GIANT GRAVITY BOMBS AT YOU!!
SKIIIID
XIII

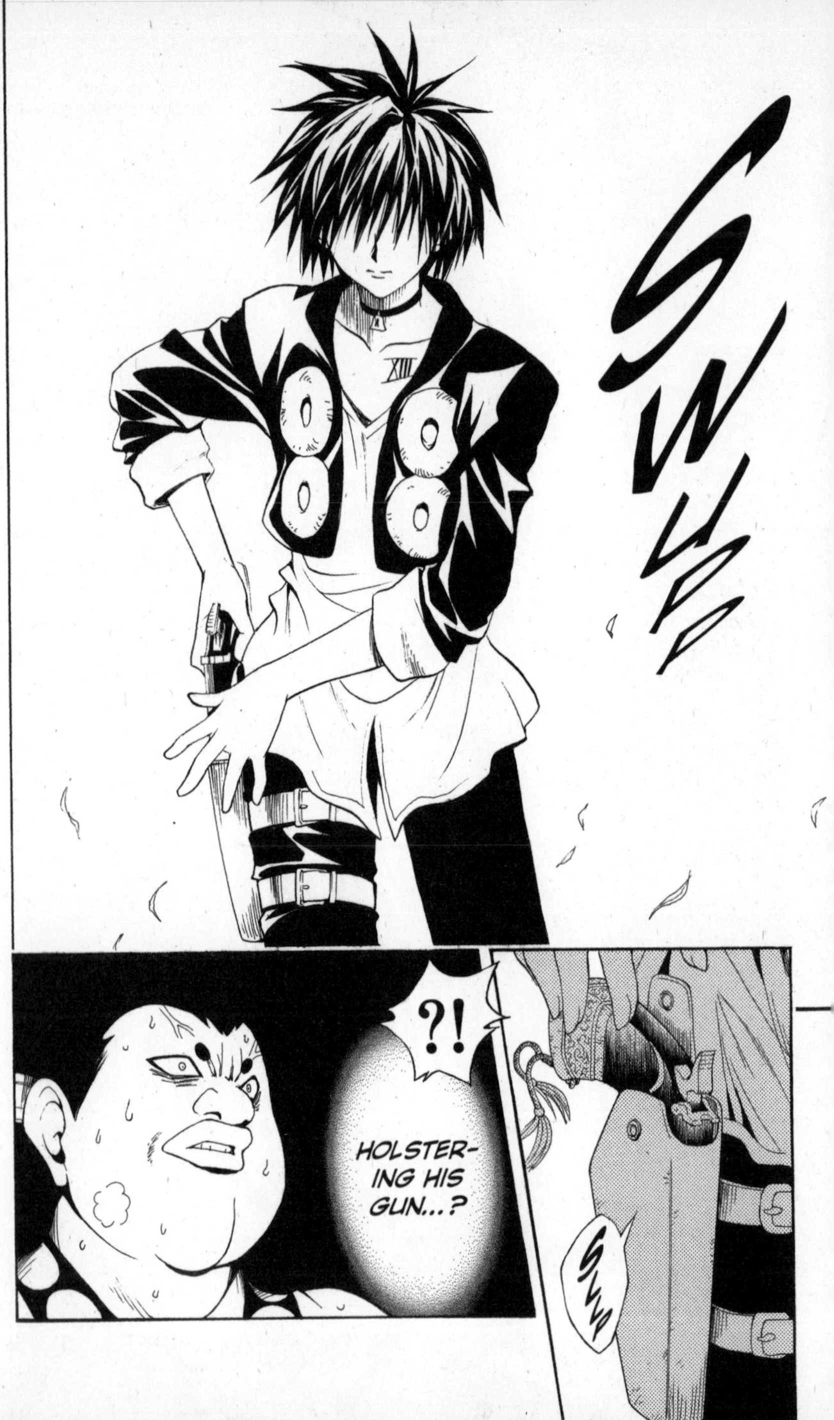
?!
HOLSTER-
ING HIS
GUN...?

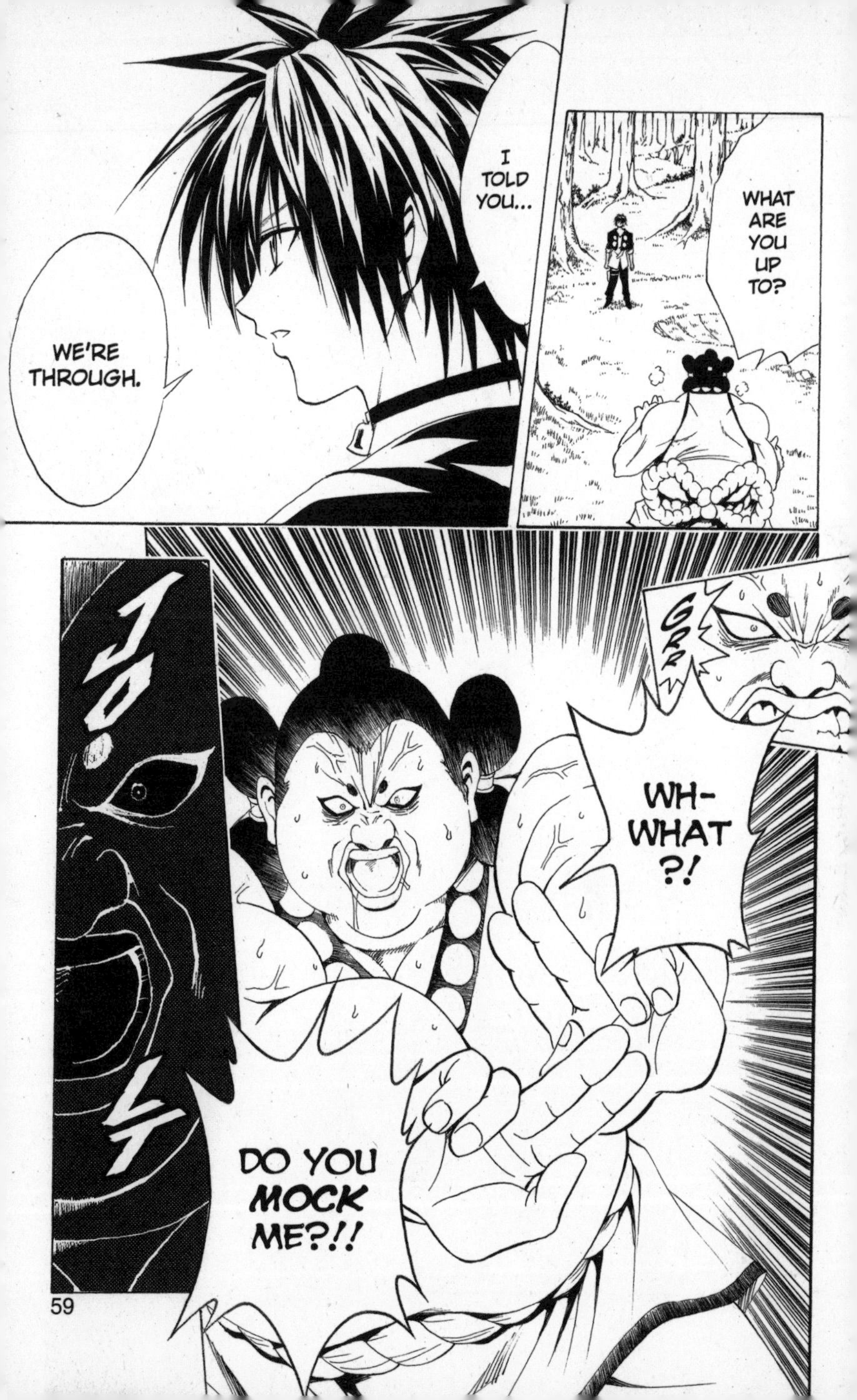
WHAT ARE YOU UP TO?
I TOLD YOU...
WE'RE THROUGH.
GRR
WH-WHAT?!
DO YOU MOCK ME?!!

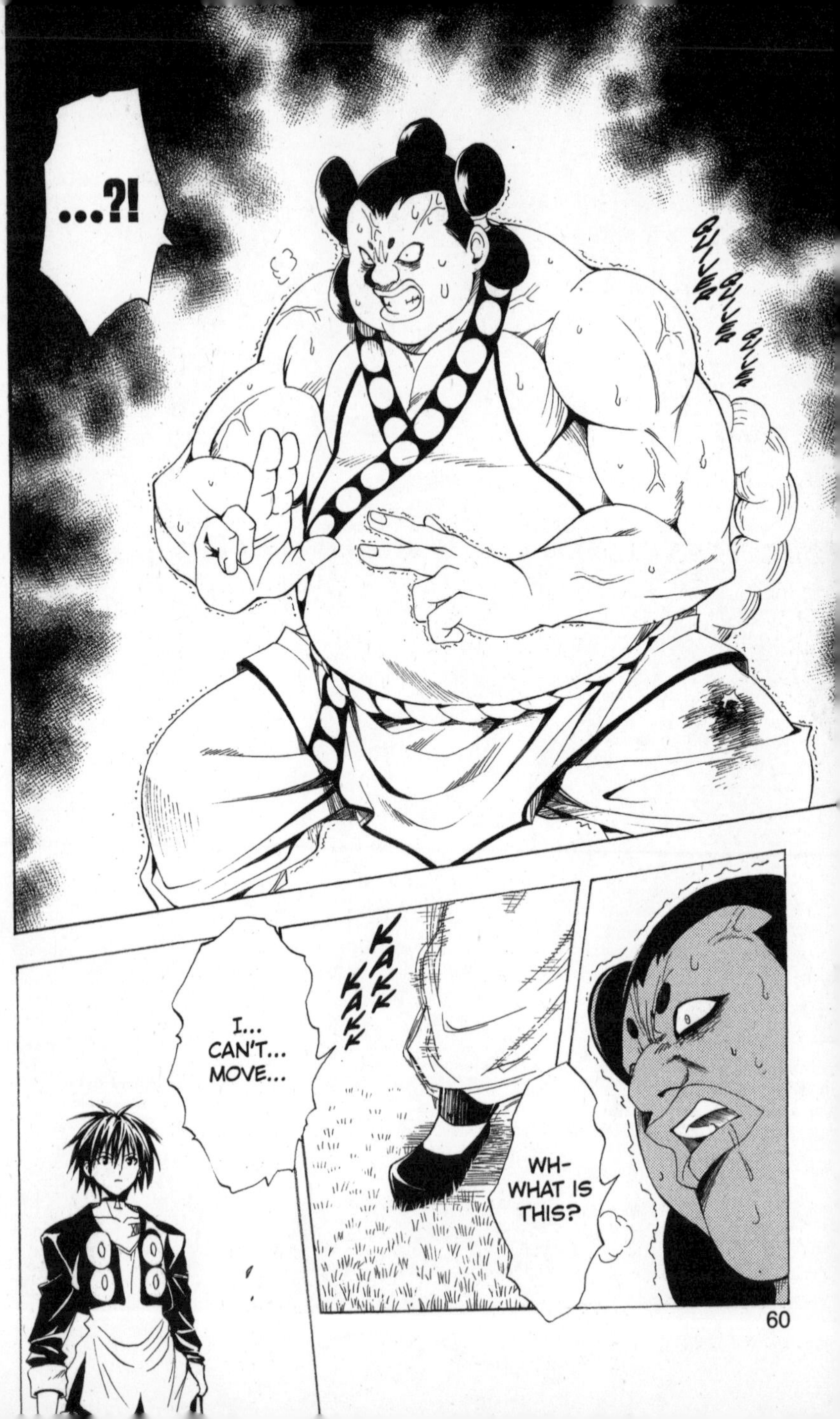
...?!
QUIVER QUIVER QUIVER
WH- WHAT IS THIS?
KAKK KAKK
I... CAN'T... MOVE...

READ THIS WAY

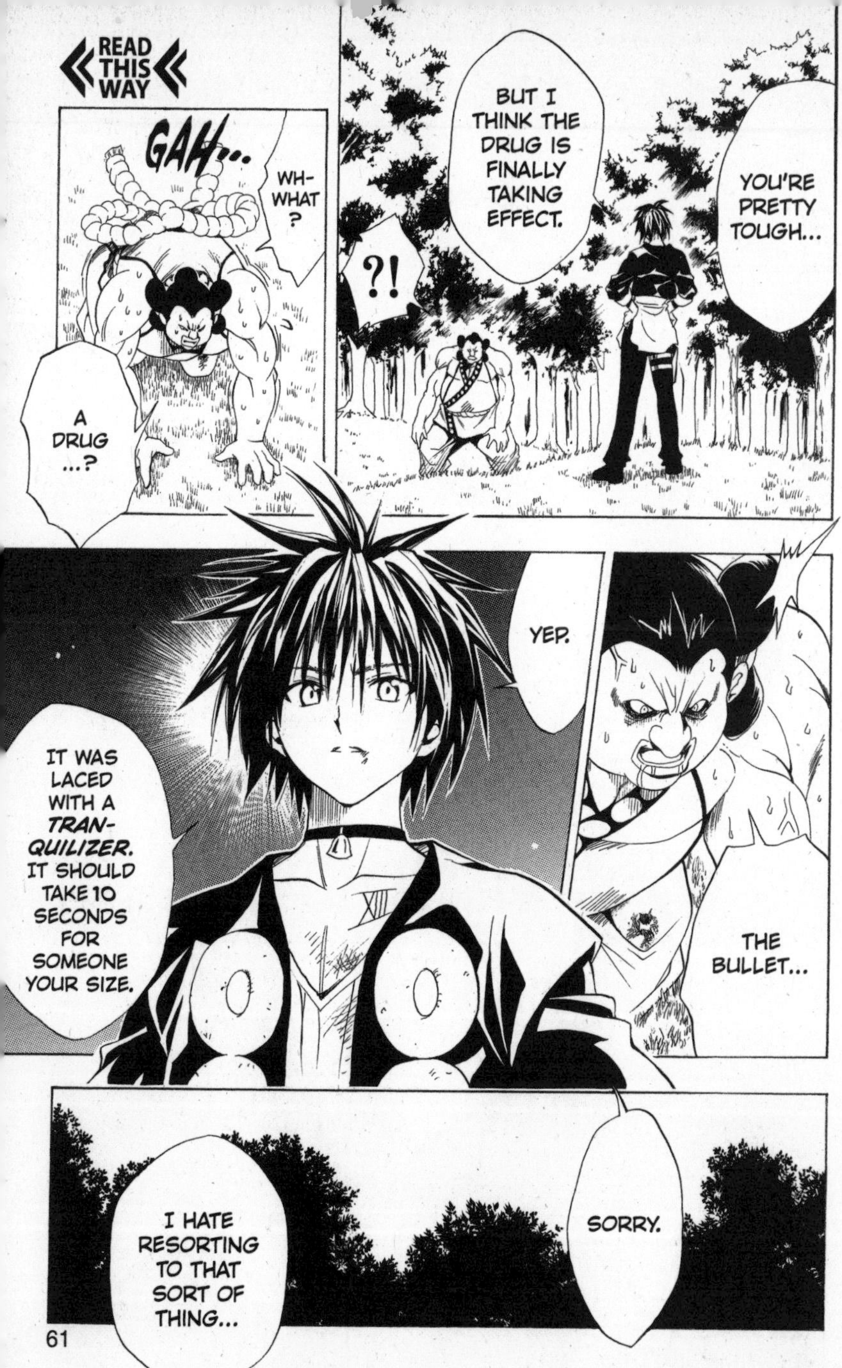
YOU'RE PRETTY TOUGH...
BUT I THINK THE DRUG IS FINALLY TAKING EFFECT.
?!
GAH...
WH-WHAT?
A DRUG...?
THE BULLET...
YEP.
IT WAS LACED WITH A *TRANQUILIZER*. IT SHOULD TAKE 10 SECONDS FOR SOMEONE YOUR SIZE.
SORRY.
I HATE RESORTING TO THAT SORT OF THING...

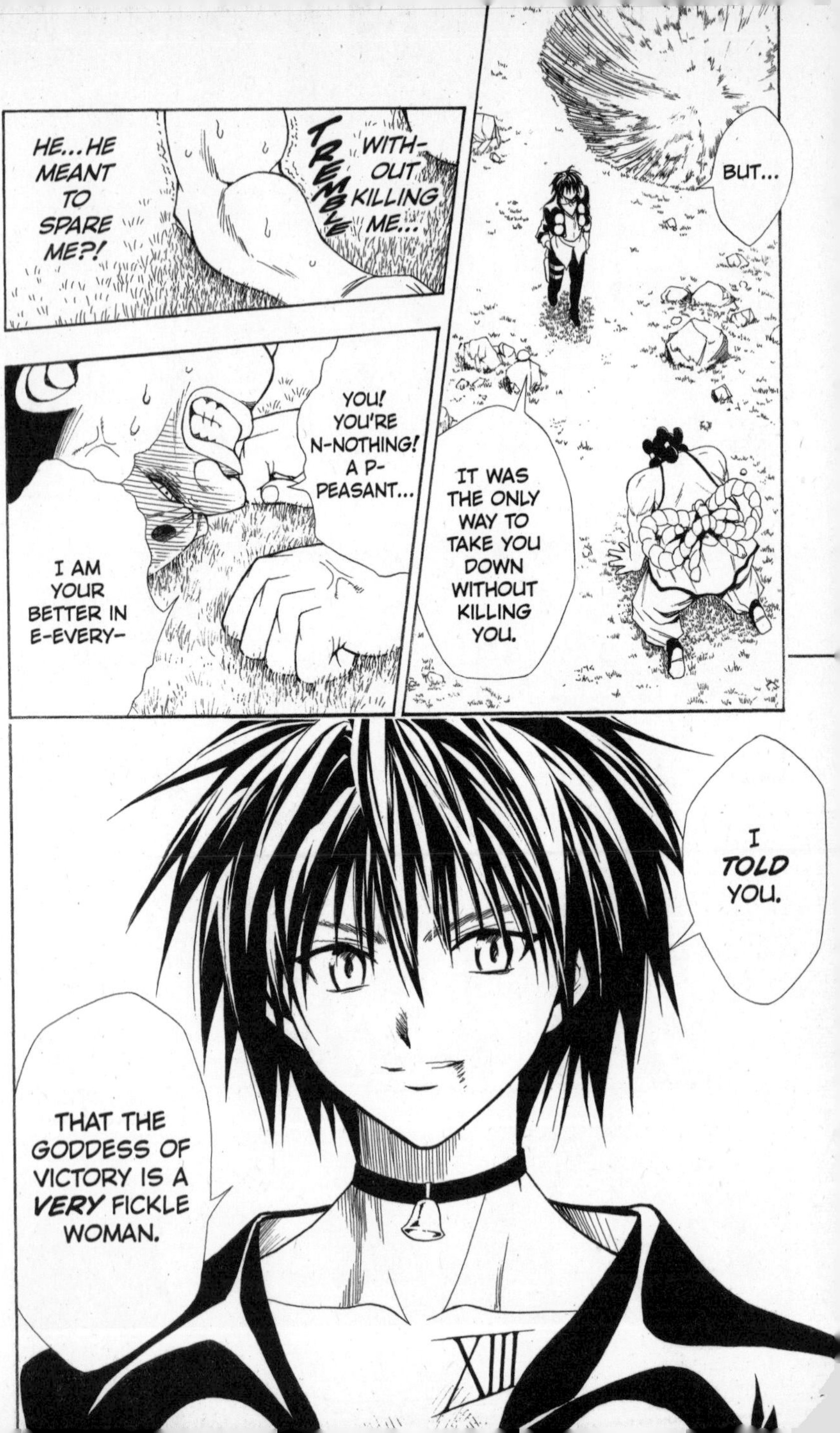
BUT...
IT WAS THE ONLY WAY TO TAKE YOU DOWN WITHOUT KILLING YOU.
WITH-OUT KILLING ME...
TREMBLE
HE...HE MEANT TO SPARE ME?!
YOU! YOU'RE N-NOTHING! A P-PEASANT...
I AM YOUR BETTER IN E-EVERY-
I *TOLD* YOU.
THAT THE GODDESS OF VICTORY IS A *VERY* FICKLE WOMAN.
XIII

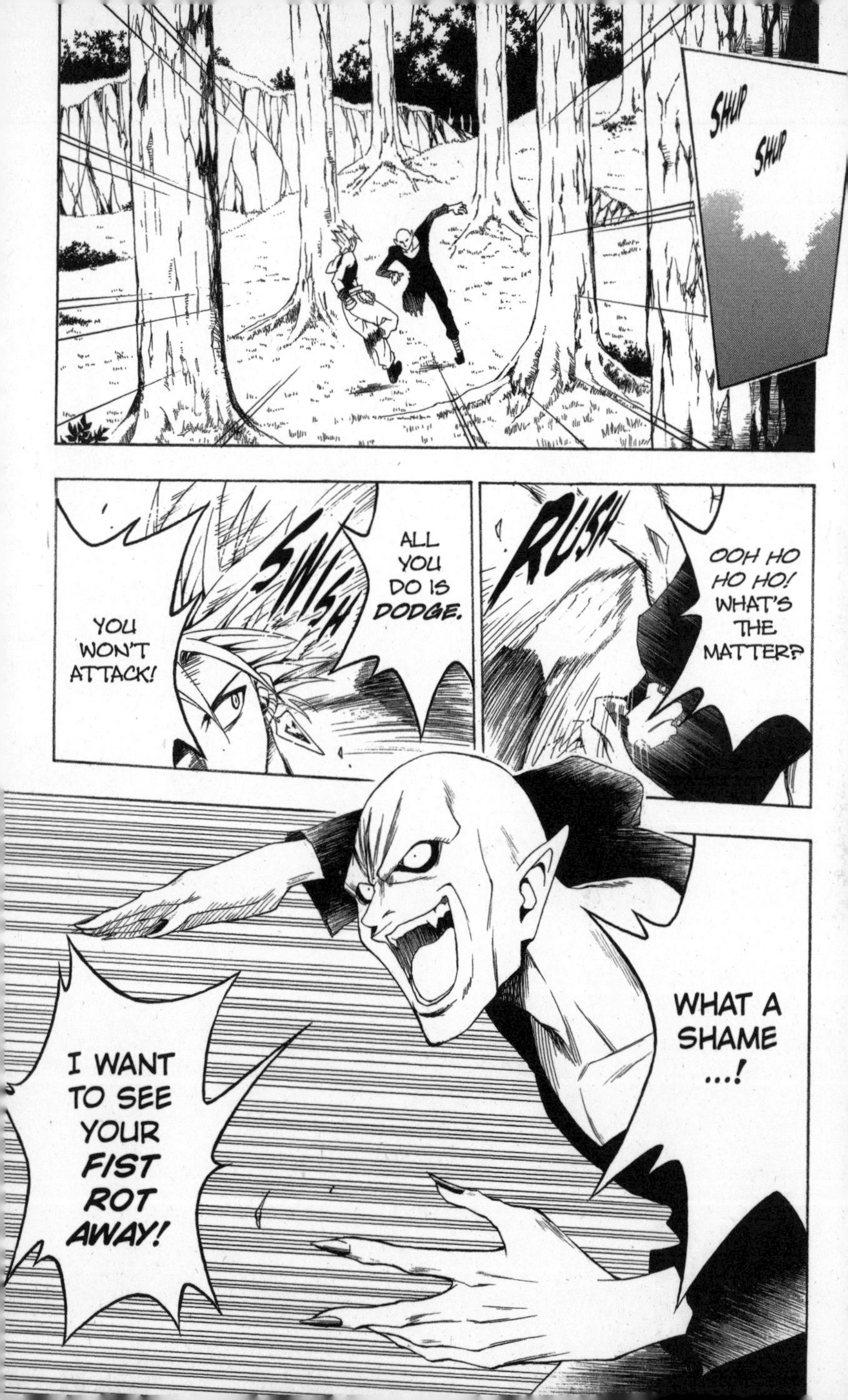
SHUP
SHUP
RUSH
OOH HO HO HO! WHAT'S THE MATTER?
SWISH
ALL YOU DO IS DODGE.
YOU WON'T ATTACK!
WHAT A SHAME ...!
I WANT TO SEE YOUR FIST ROT AWAY!

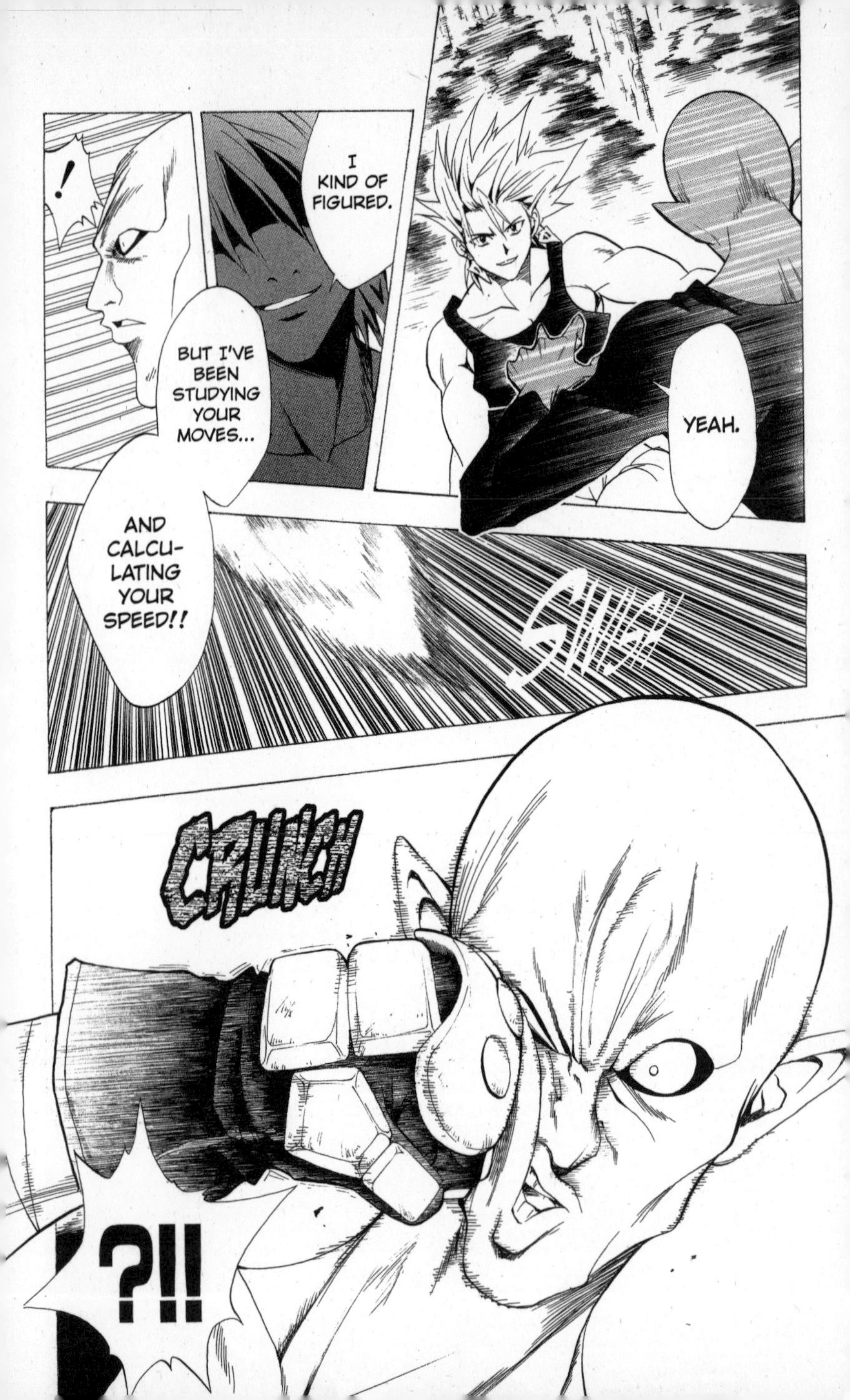
YEAH.
I KIND OF FIGURED.
BUT I'VE BEEN STUDYING YOUR MOVES...
!
AND CALCU-LATING YOUR SPEED!!
CRUNCH
?!!

READ THIS WAY

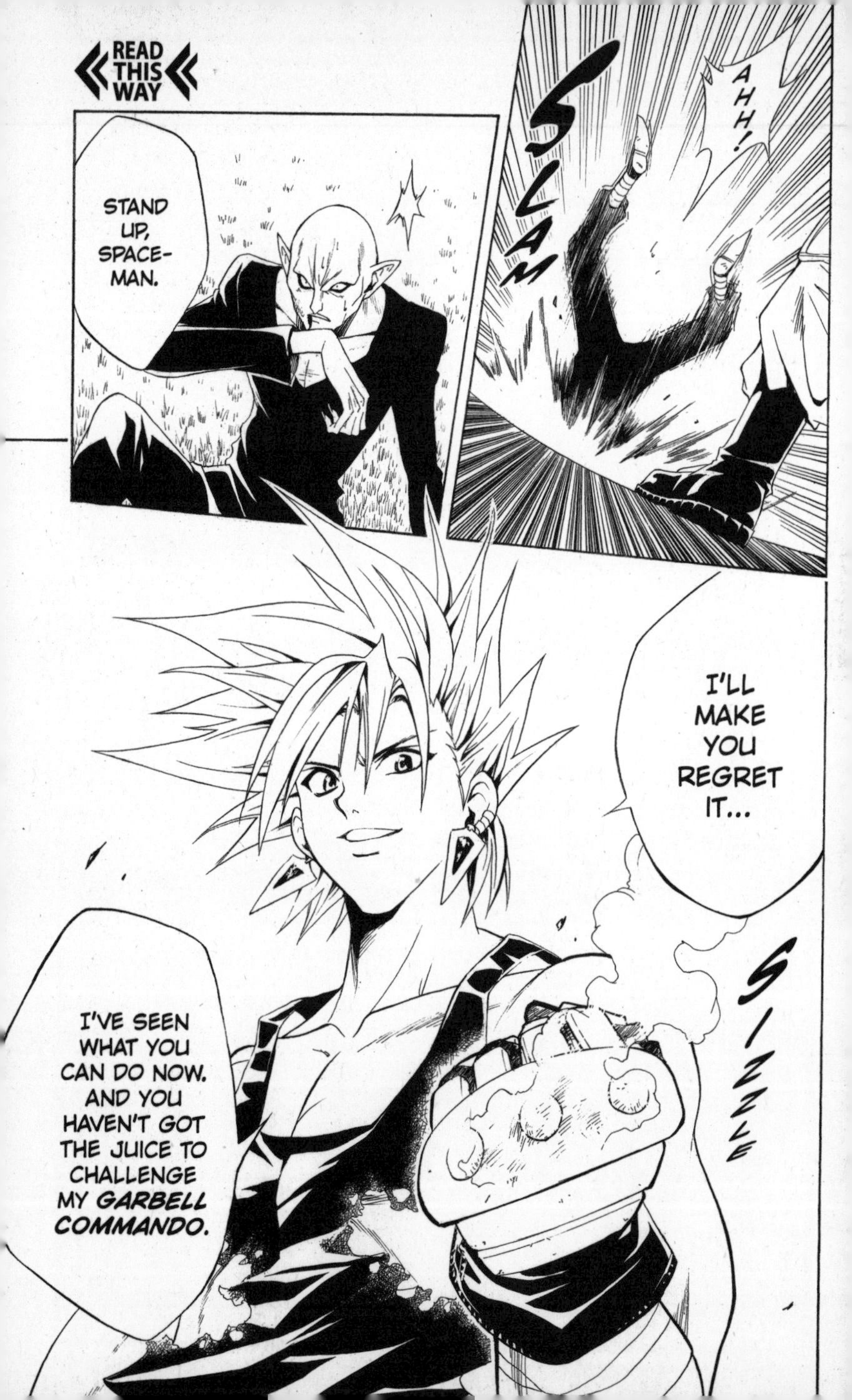
SLAM
AHH!
STAND UP, SPACE-MAN.
I'LL MAKE YOU REGRET IT...
SIZZLE
I'VE SEEN WHAT YOU CAN DO NOW. AND YOU HAVEN'T GOT THE JUICE TO CHALLENGE MY *GARBELL COMMANDO*.

BLACK CAT

profile

PRETA GHOUL

DATA	
BIRTHDATE:	JUNE 6
AGE:	30
BLOOD TYPE:	O
HEIGHT:	181 CM
WEIGHT:	58 KG
POWER:	ERODE
HOBBY:	MAKING VARIOUS THINGS ROT
COMMENTS:	FORMERLY A PRIEST... AND SERIAL KILLER. HE USED TO HAVE HAIR, BUT WHEN HE AWAKENED HIS POWERS, HIS HAIR FELL OUT. (ODDLY, HE NEVER HAD EYEBROWS). DON'T BE DECEIVED BY THE POINTY EARS; HE IS NOT AN ALIEN.

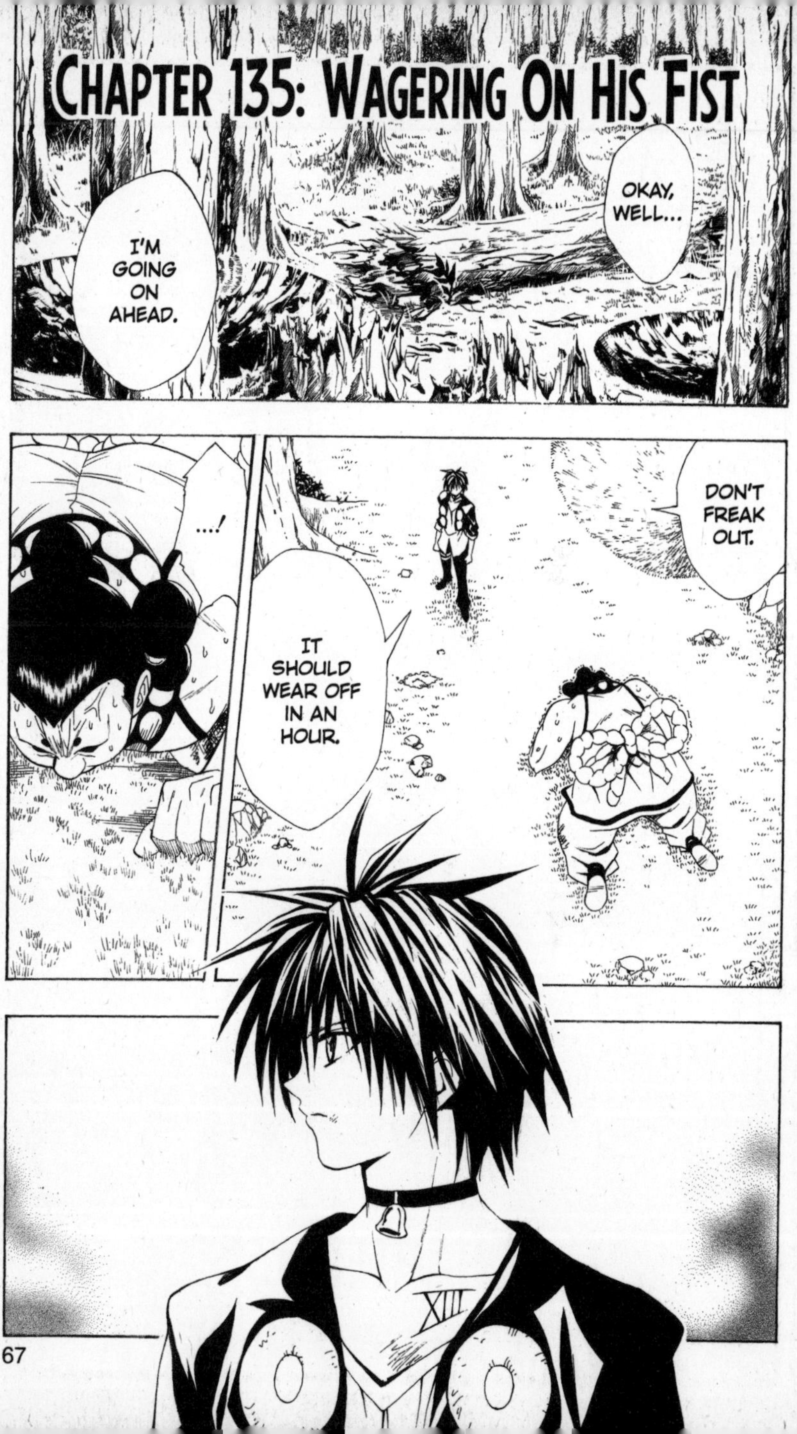
Chapter 135: Wagering On His Fist
OKAY, WELL...
I'M GOING ON AHEAD.
DON'T FREAK OUT.
IT SHOULD WEAR OFF IN AN HOUR.
...!

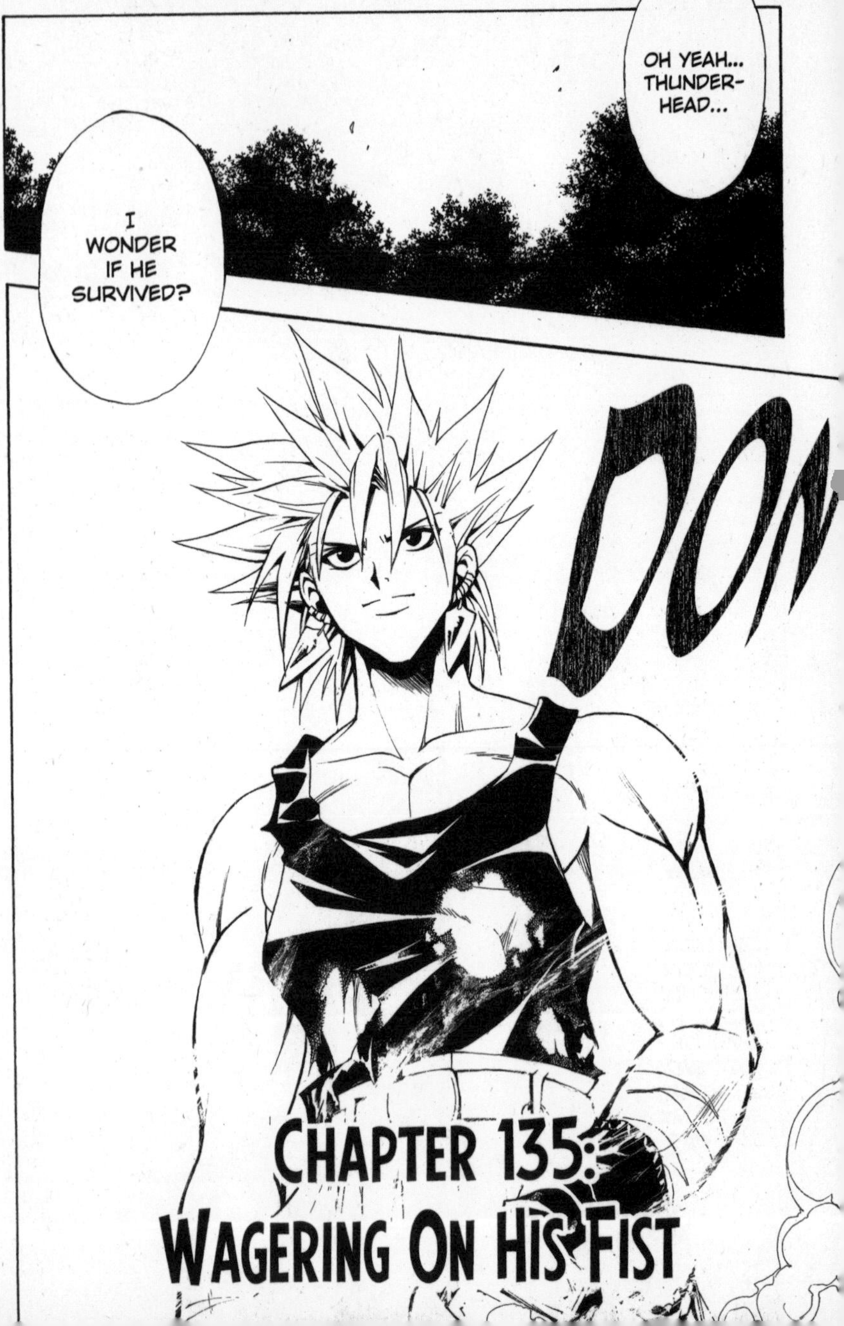
OH YEAH... THUNDER-HEAD...
I WONDER IF HE SURVIVED?
DON
CHAPTER 135:
WAGERING ON HIS FIST

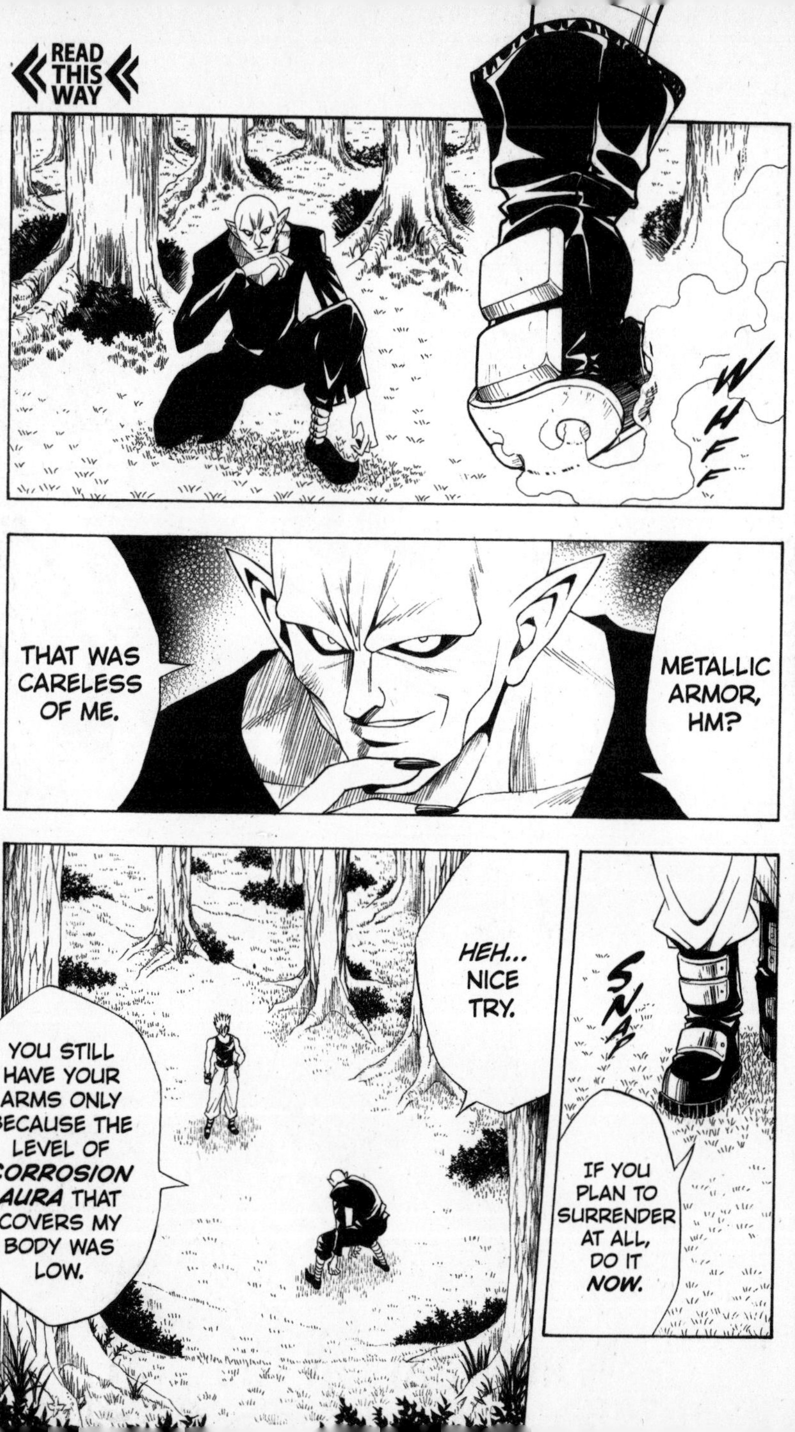
READ THIS WAY
WHFF
METALLIC ARMOR, HM?
THAT WAS CARELESS OF ME.
SNAP
IF YOU PLAN TO SURRENDER AT ALL, DO IT NOW.
HEH... NICE TRY.
YOU STILL HAVE YOUR ARMS ONLY BECAUSE THE LEVEL OF CORROSION AURA THAT COVERS MY BODY WAS LOW.

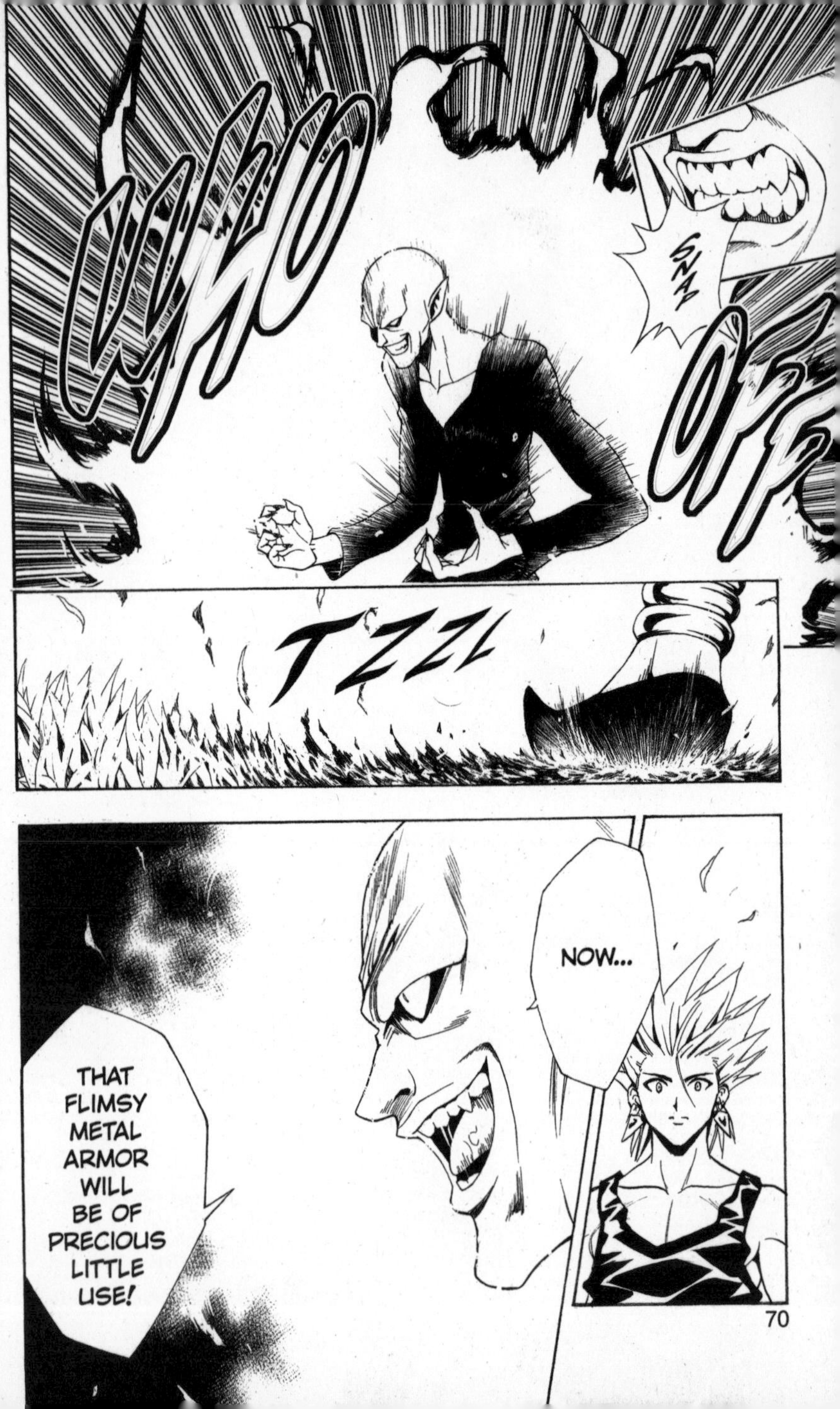
SNAP
TZZZ
NOW...
THAT FLIMSY METAL ARMOR WILL BE OF PRECIOUS LITTLE USE!

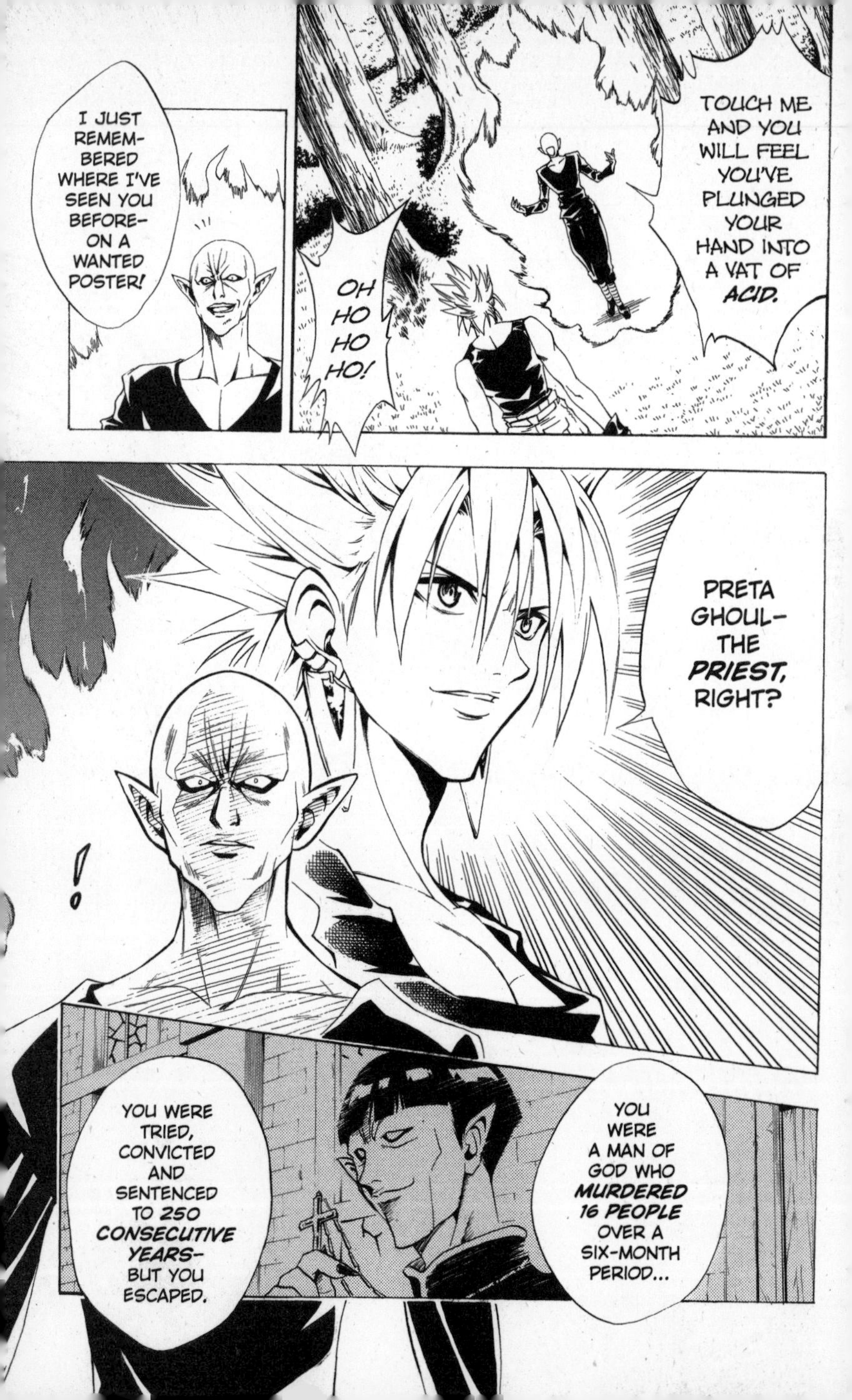
TOUCH ME AND YOU WILL FEEL YOU'VE PLUNGED YOUR HAND INTO A VAT OF ACID.
OH HO HO HO!
I JUST REMEMBERED WHERE I'VE SEEN YOU BEFORE–ON A WANTED POSTER!
PRETA GHOUL–THE PRIEST, RIGHT?
!
YOU WERE A MAN OF GOD WHO MURDERED 16 PEOPLE OVER A SIX-MONTH PERIOD...
YOU WERE TRIED, CONVICTED AND SENTENCED TO 250 CONSECUTIVE YEARS–BUT YOU ESCAPED.

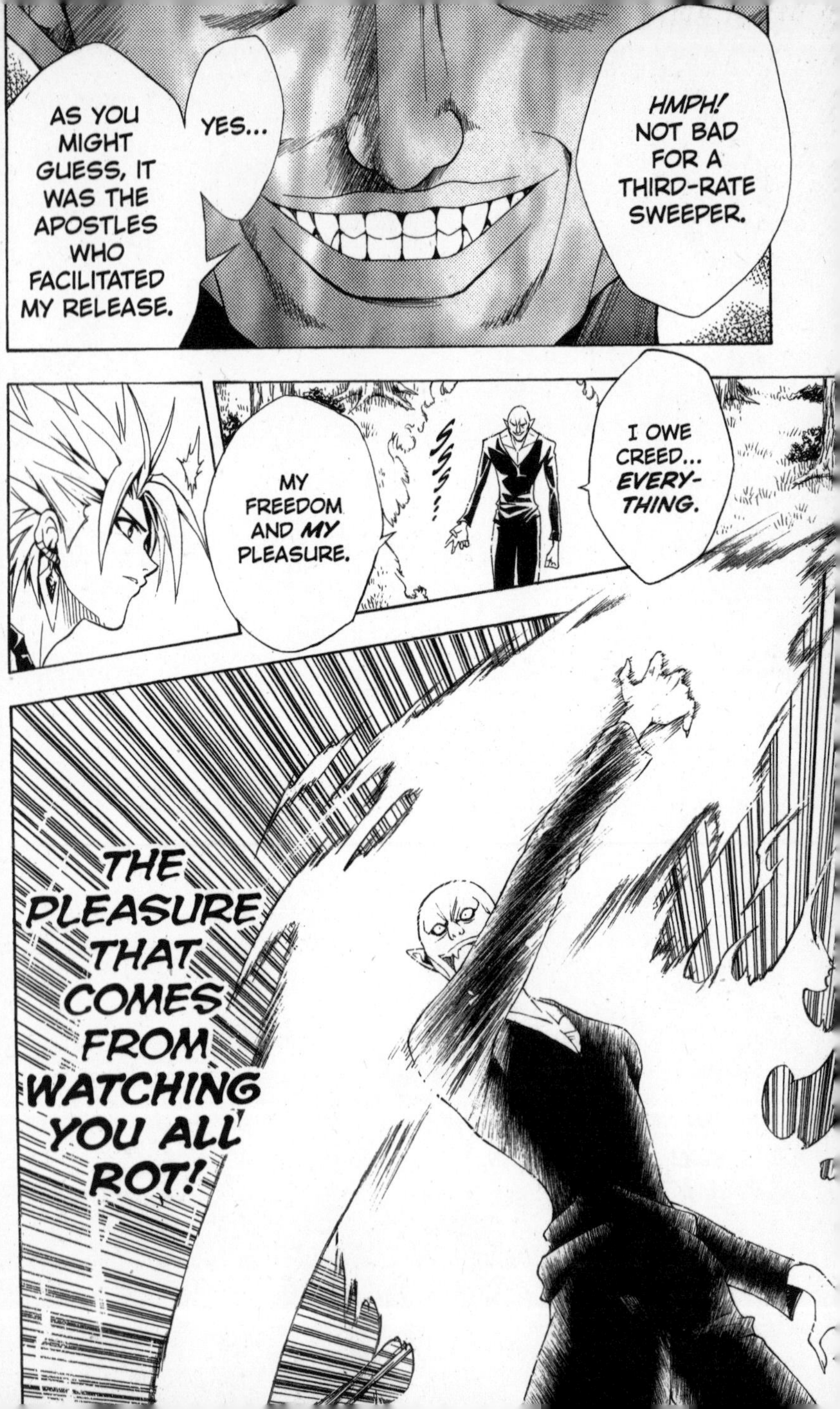
HMPH! NOT BAD FOR A THIRD-RATE SWEEPER.
YES...
AS YOU MIGHT GUESS, IT WAS THE APOSTLES WHO FACILITATED MY RELEASE.
I OWE CREED... EVERYTHING.
MY FREEDOM AND MY PLEASURE.
THE PLEASURE THAT COMES FROM WATCHING YOU ALL ROT!

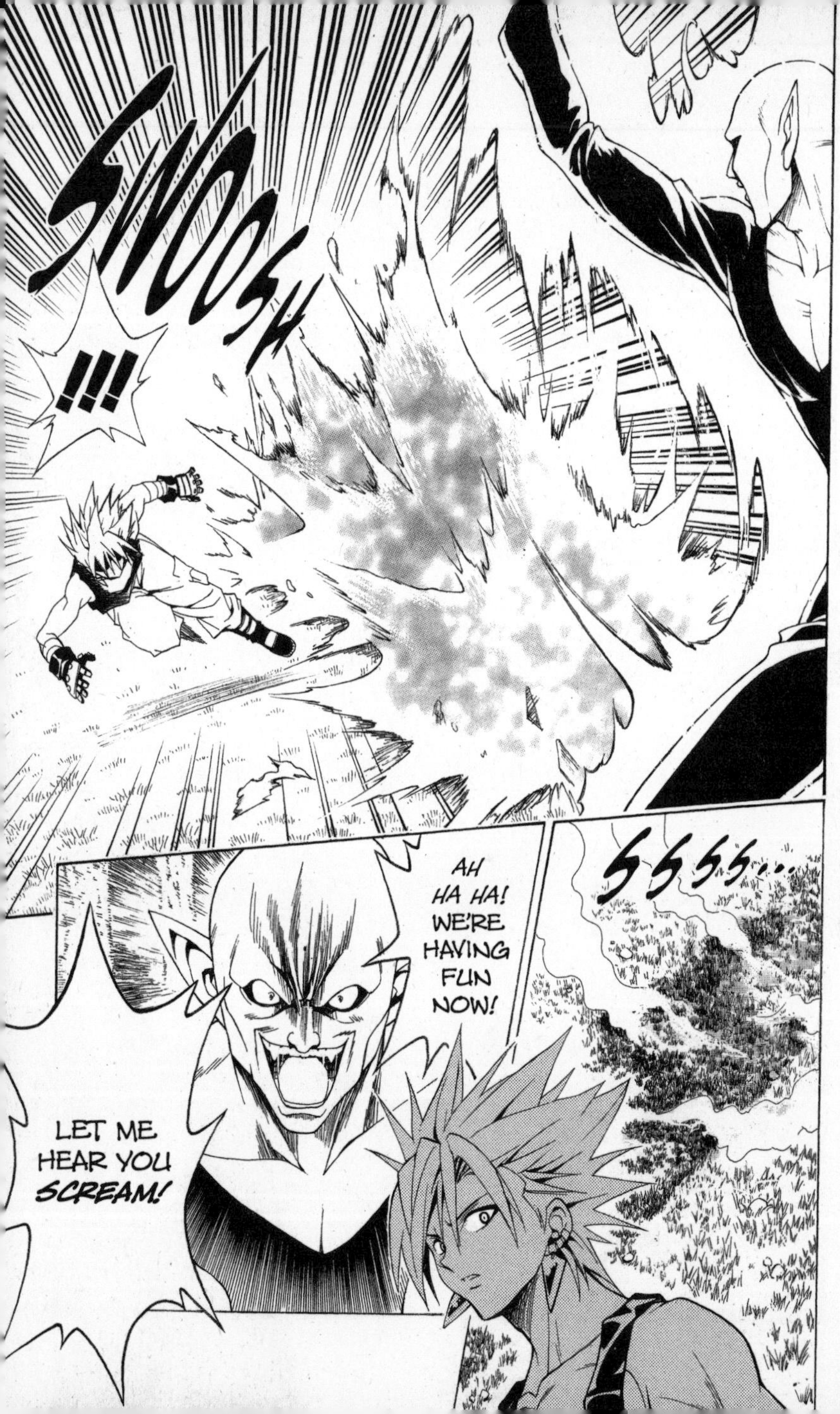
SWOOSH
!!!
SSSS...
AH HA HA! WE'RE HAVING FUN NOW!
LET ME HEAR YOU SCREAM!

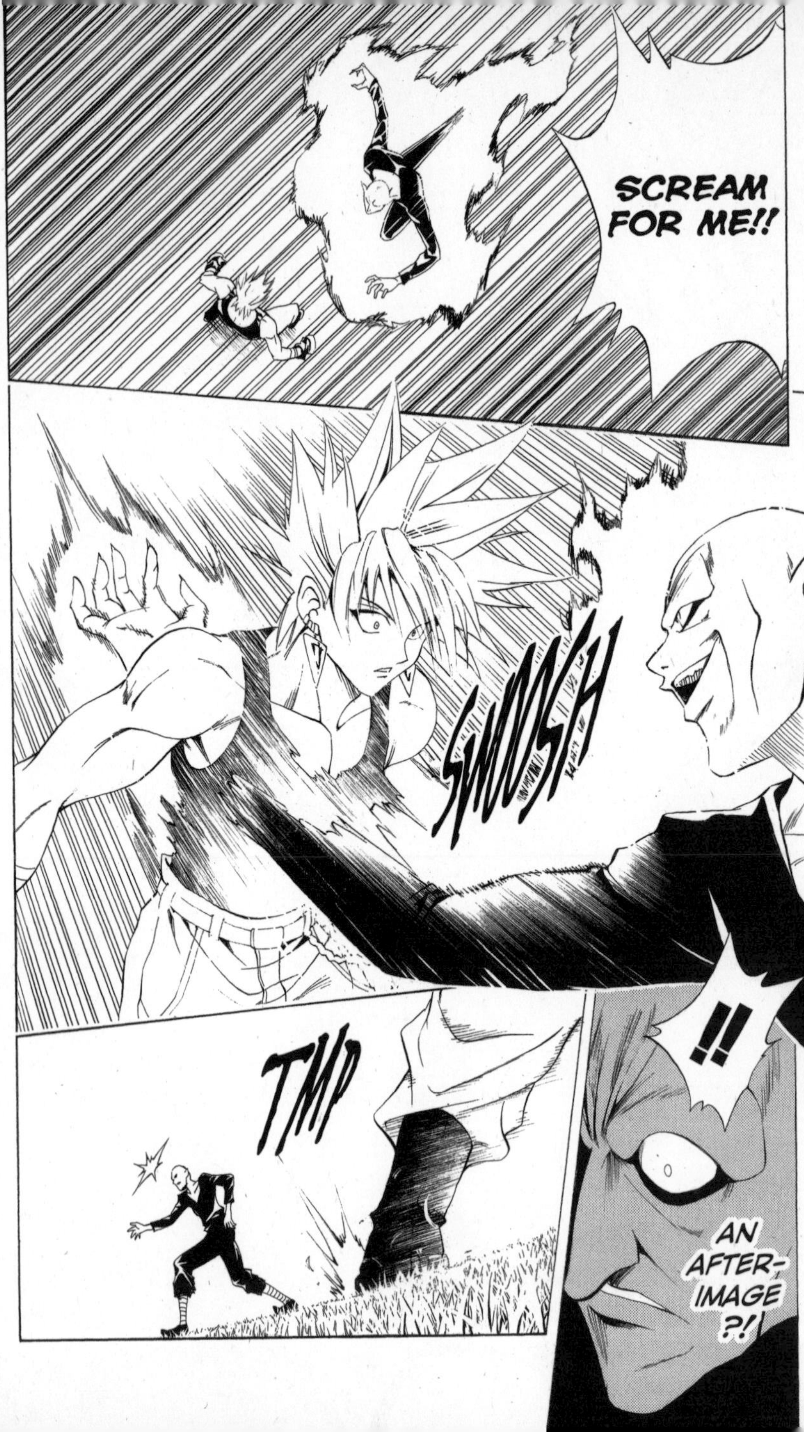
SCREAM FOR ME!!
SWOOSH
!!
AN AFTER-IMAGE ?!
TMP

READ THIS WAY

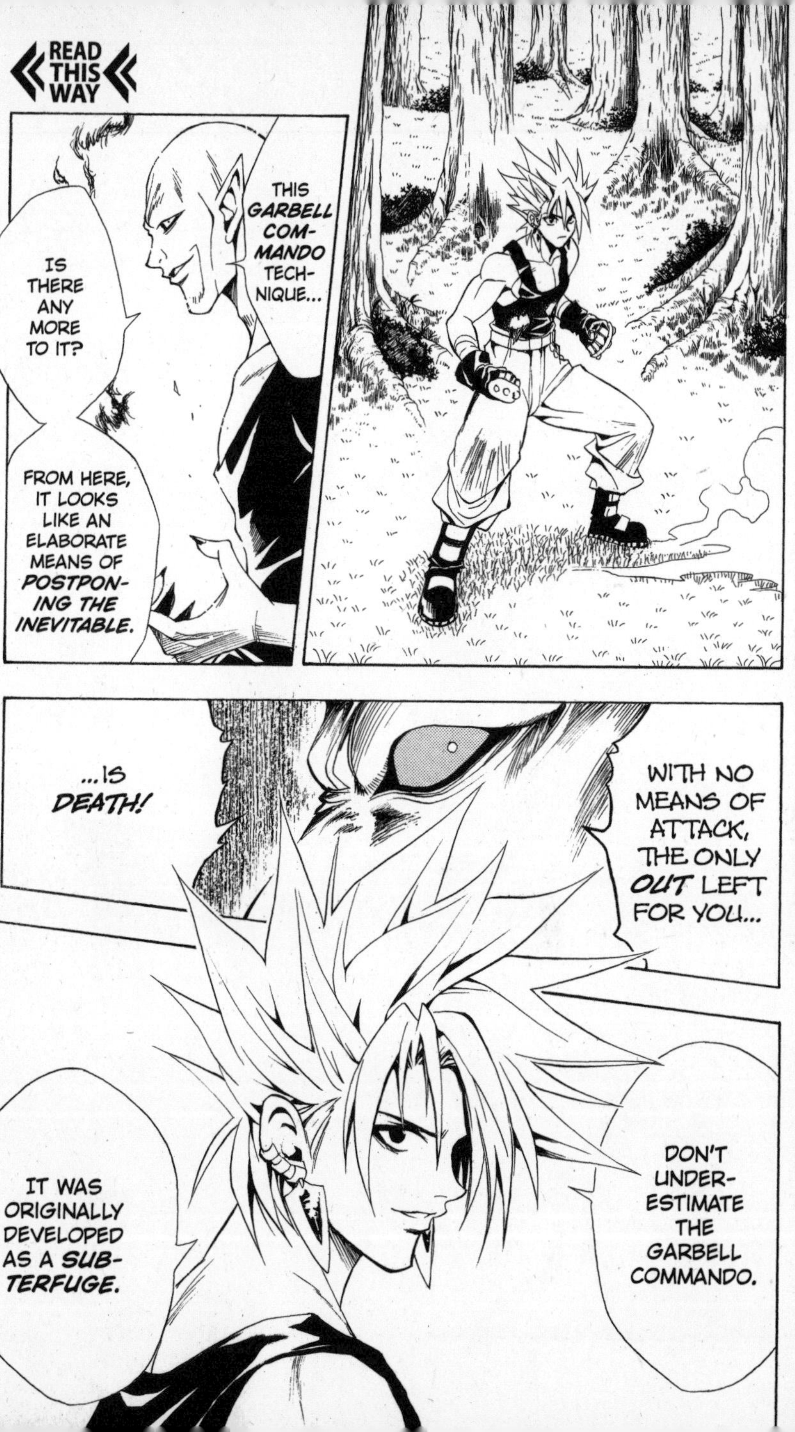
THIS GARBELL COMMANDO TECHNIQUE...
IS THERE ANY MORE TO IT?
FROM HERE, IT LOOKS LIKE AN ELABORATE MEANS OF POSTPONING THE INEVITABLE.
WITH NO MEANS OF ATTACK, THE ONLY OUT LEFT FOR YOU...
...IS DEATH!
DON'T UNDERESTIMATE THE GARBELL COMMANDO.
IT WAS ORIGINALLY DEVELOPED AS A SUBTERFUGE.

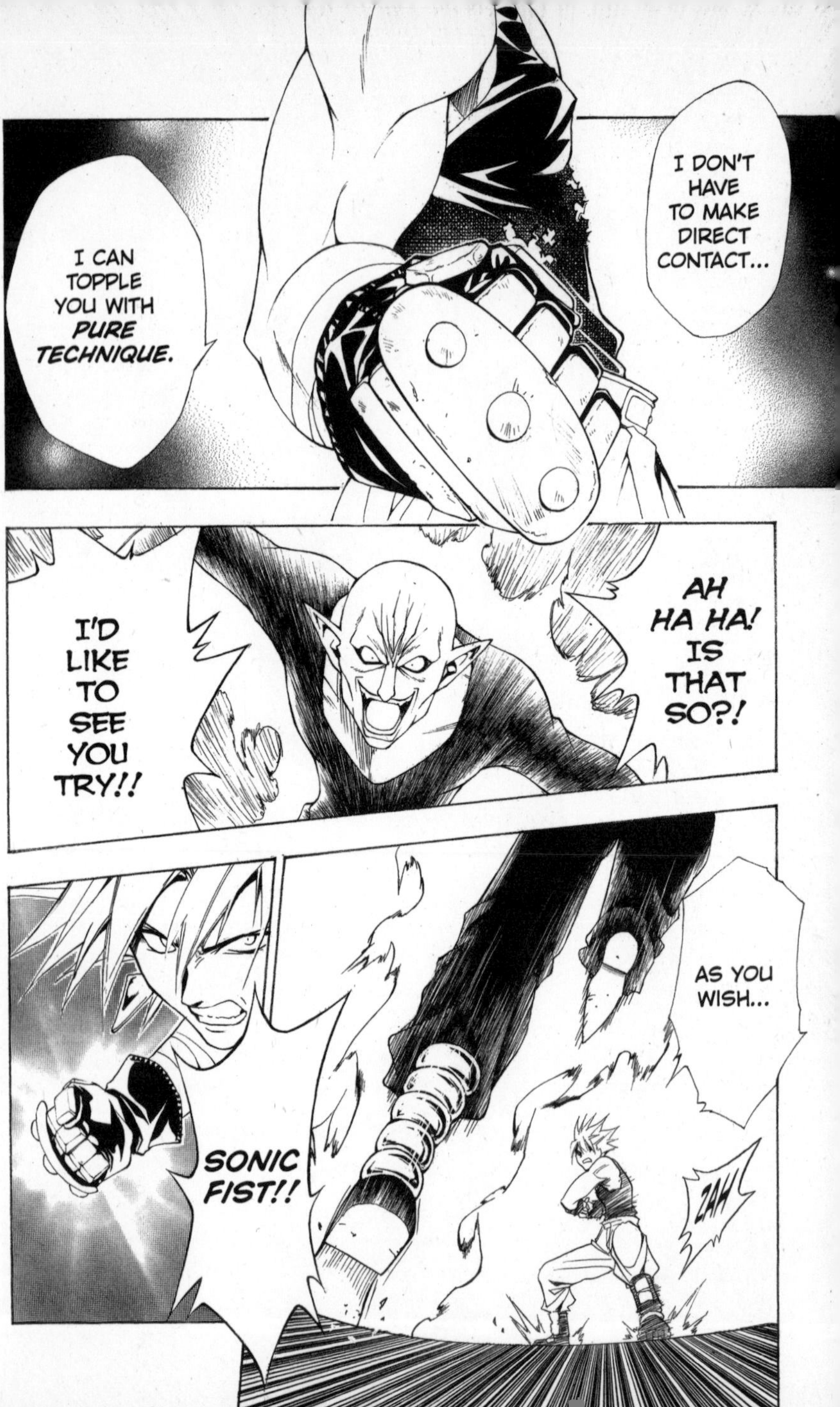
I DON'T HAVE TO MAKE DIRECT CONTACT...
I CAN TOPPLE YOU WITH *PURE TECHNIQUE.*
AH HA HA! IS THAT SO?!
I'D LIKE TO SEE YOU TRY!!
AS YOU WISH...
ZAH
SONIC FIST!!

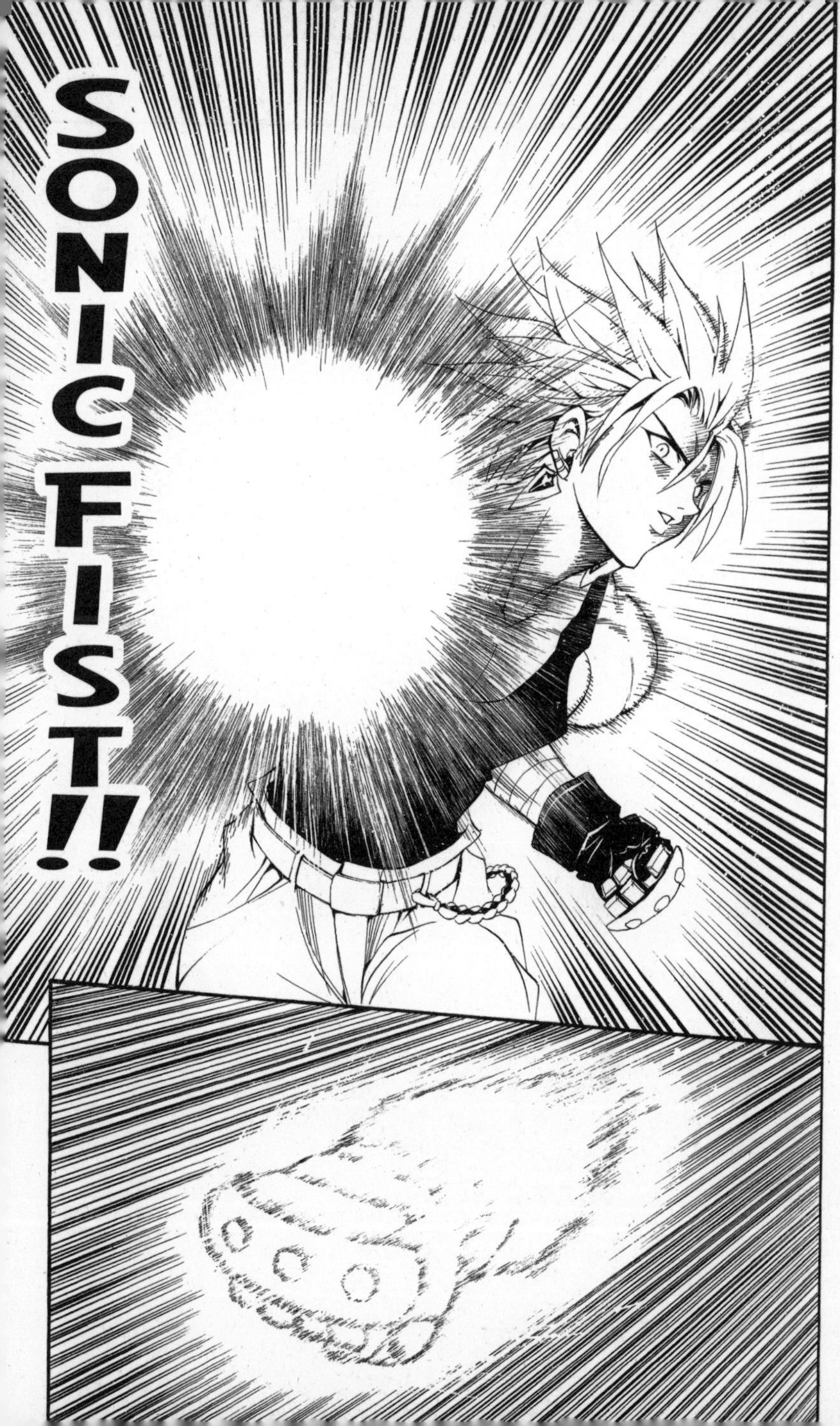
SONIC FIST!!

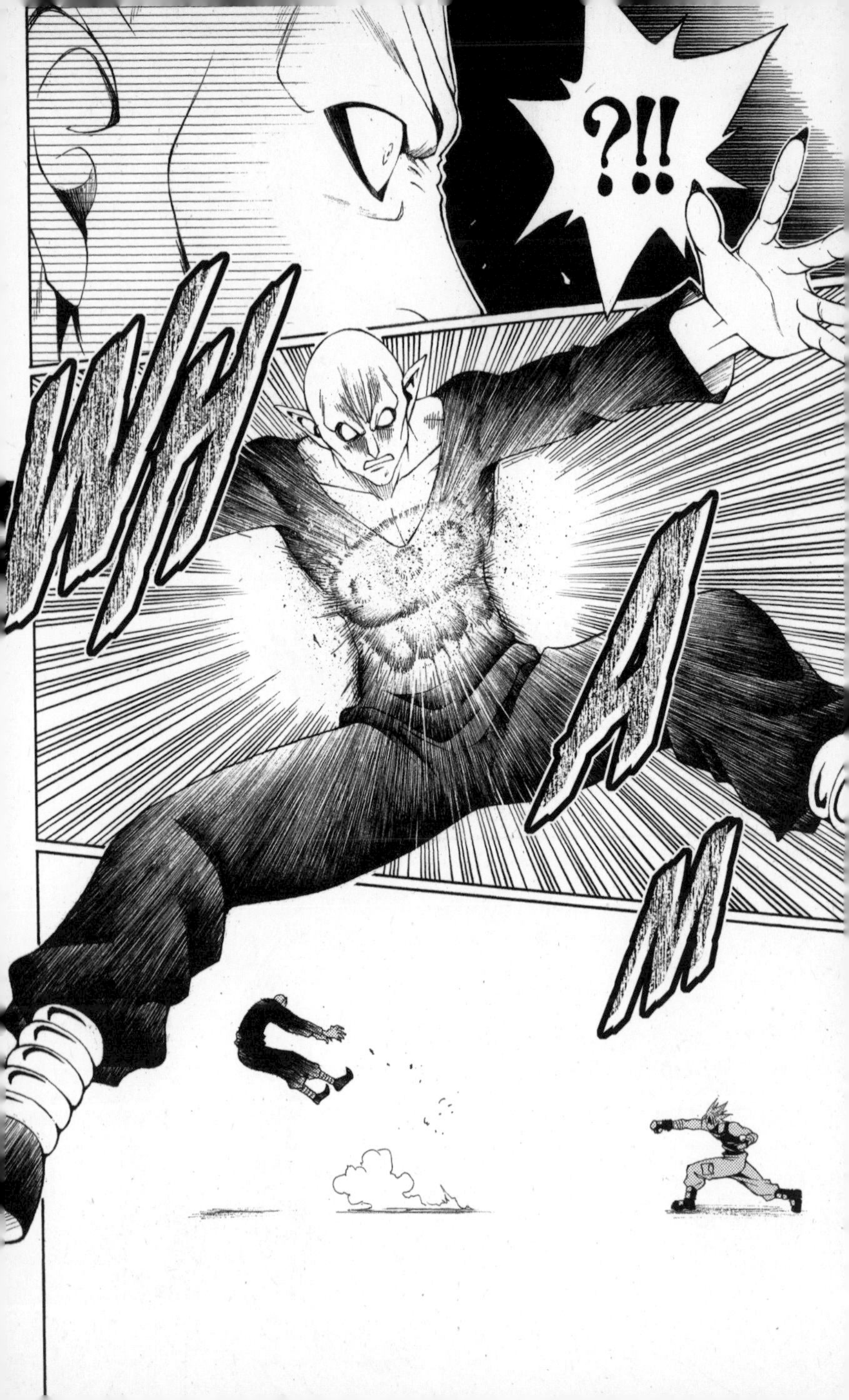
?!!
WHAM

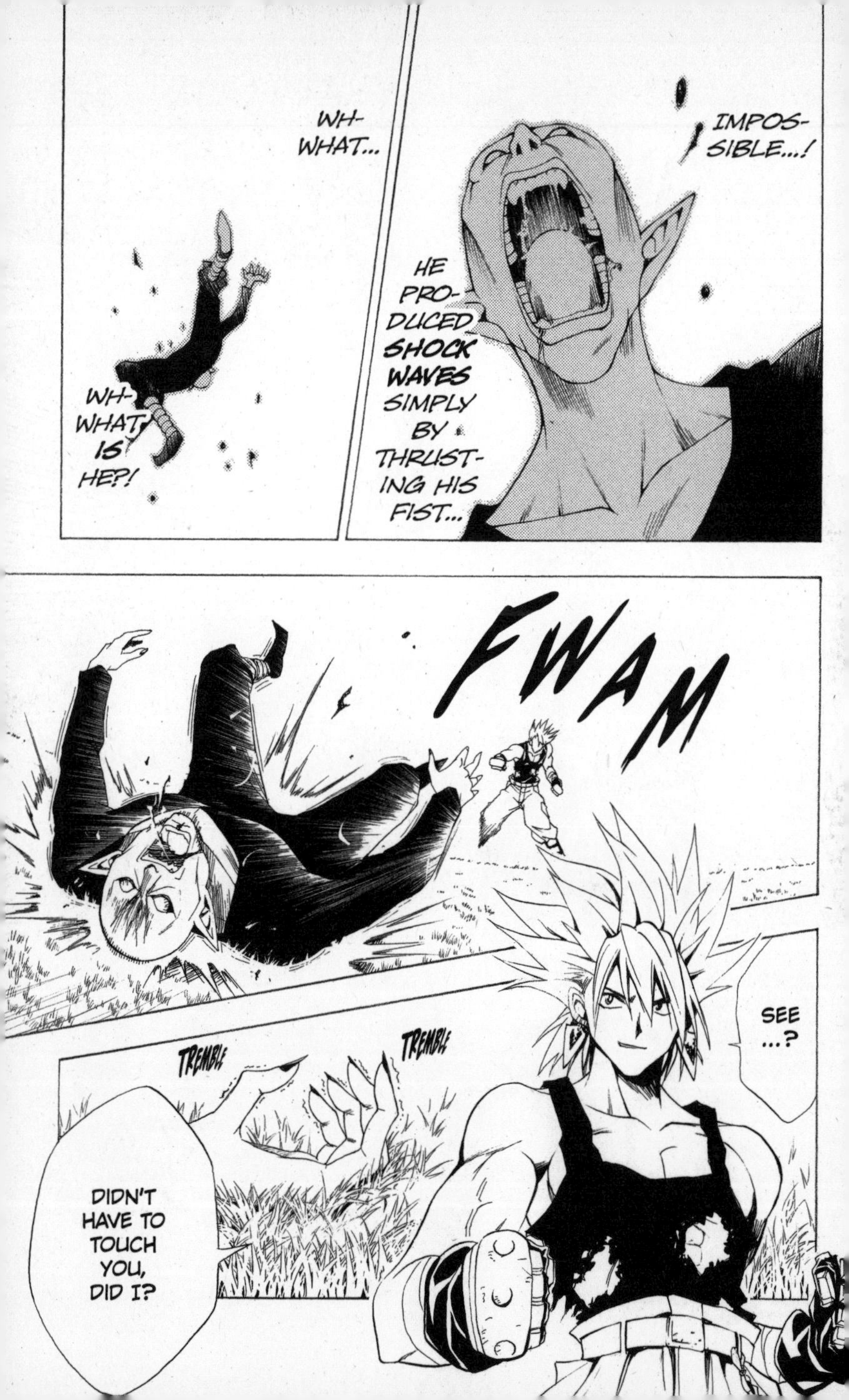
IMPOS-SIBLE...!
HE PRO-DUCED SHOCK WAVES SIMPLY BY THRUST-ING HIS FIST...
WH-WHAT...
WH-WHAT IS HE?!
FWAM
SEE ...?
TREMBLE
TREMBLE
DIDN'T HAVE TO TOUCH YOU, DID I?

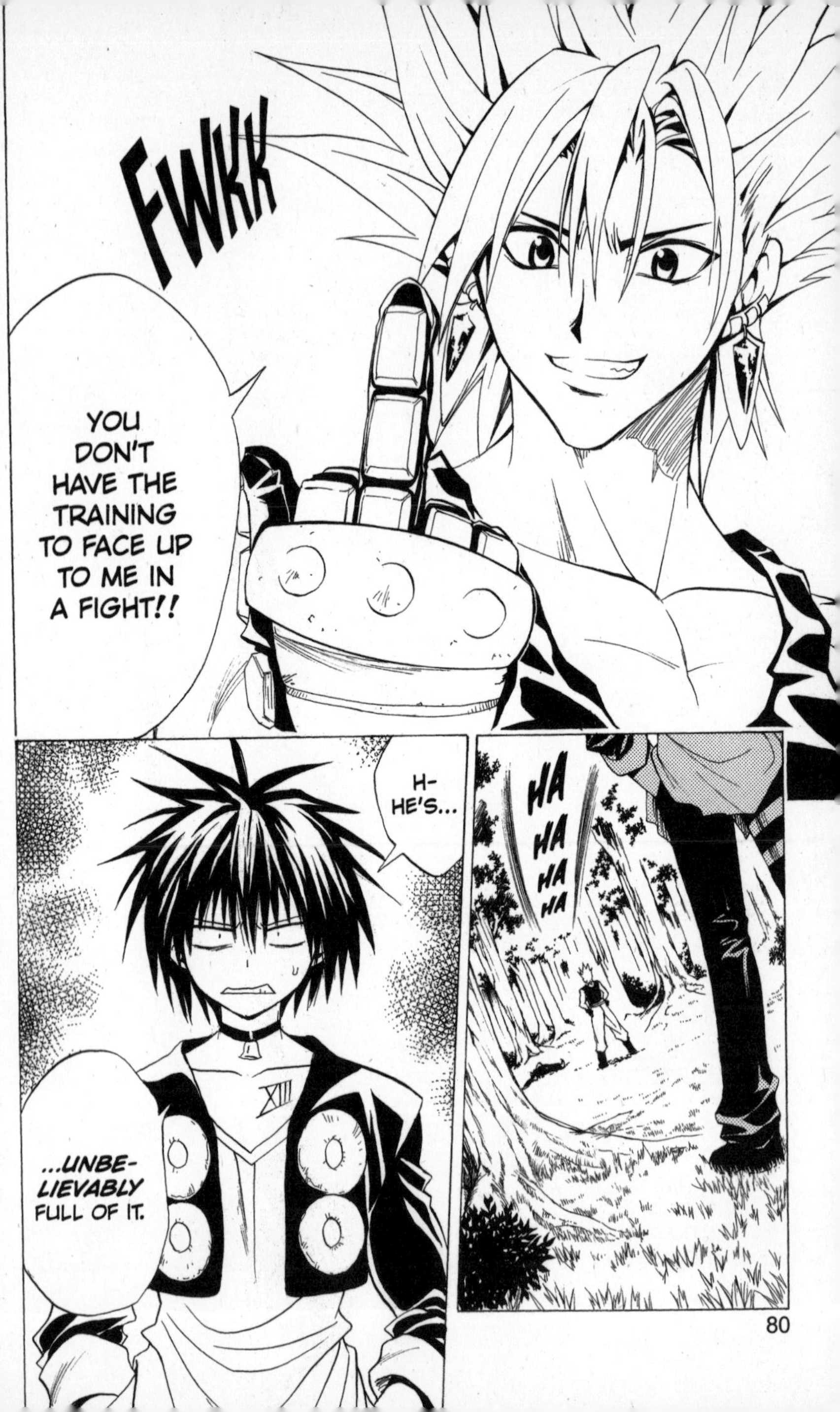

FWKK
YOU DON'T HAVE THE TRAINING TO FACE UP TO ME IN A FIGHT!!
HA HA HA HA HA
H- HE'S...
...UNBE-LIEVABLY FULL OF IT.

READ THIS WAY

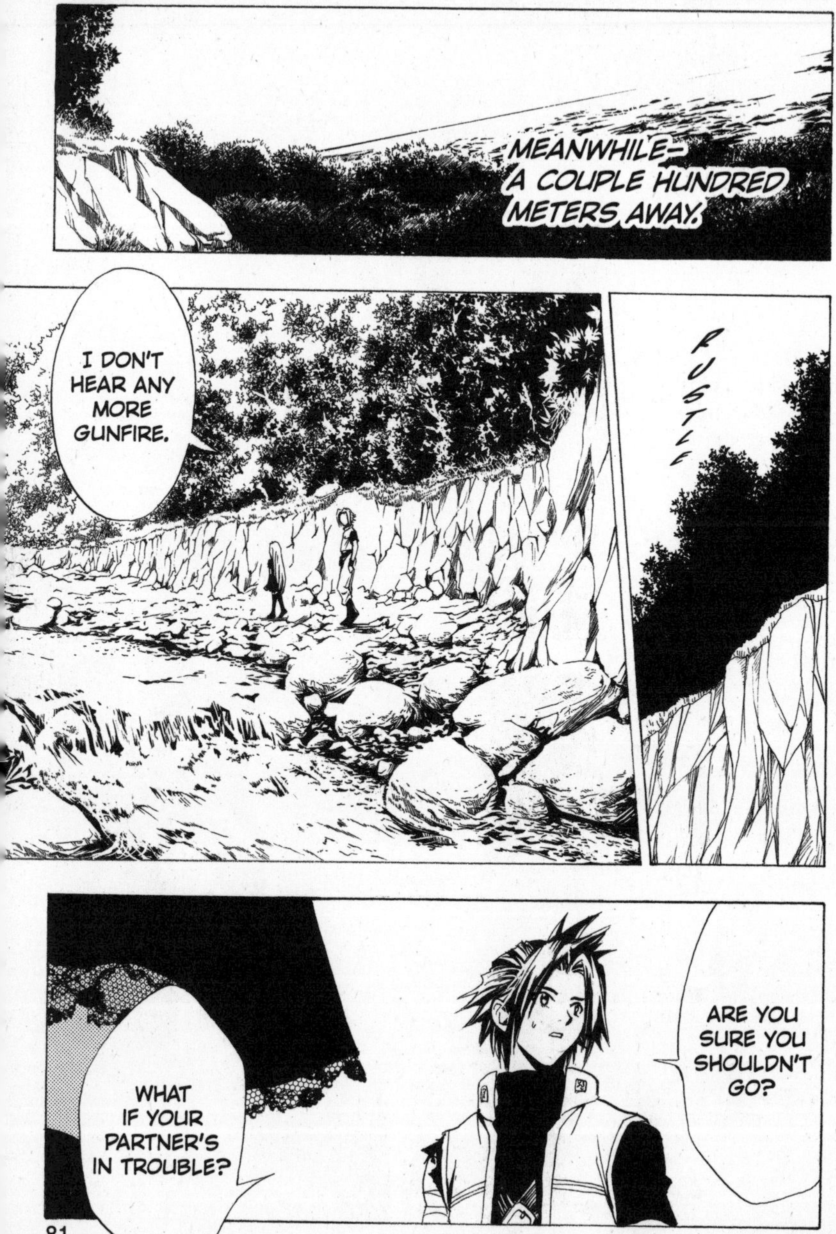
MEANWHILE–
A COUPLE HUNDRED METERS AWAY.
RUSTLE
I DON'T HEAR ANY MORE GUNFIRE.
ARE YOU SURE YOU SHOULDN'T GO?
WHAT IF YOUR PARTNER'S IN TROUBLE?

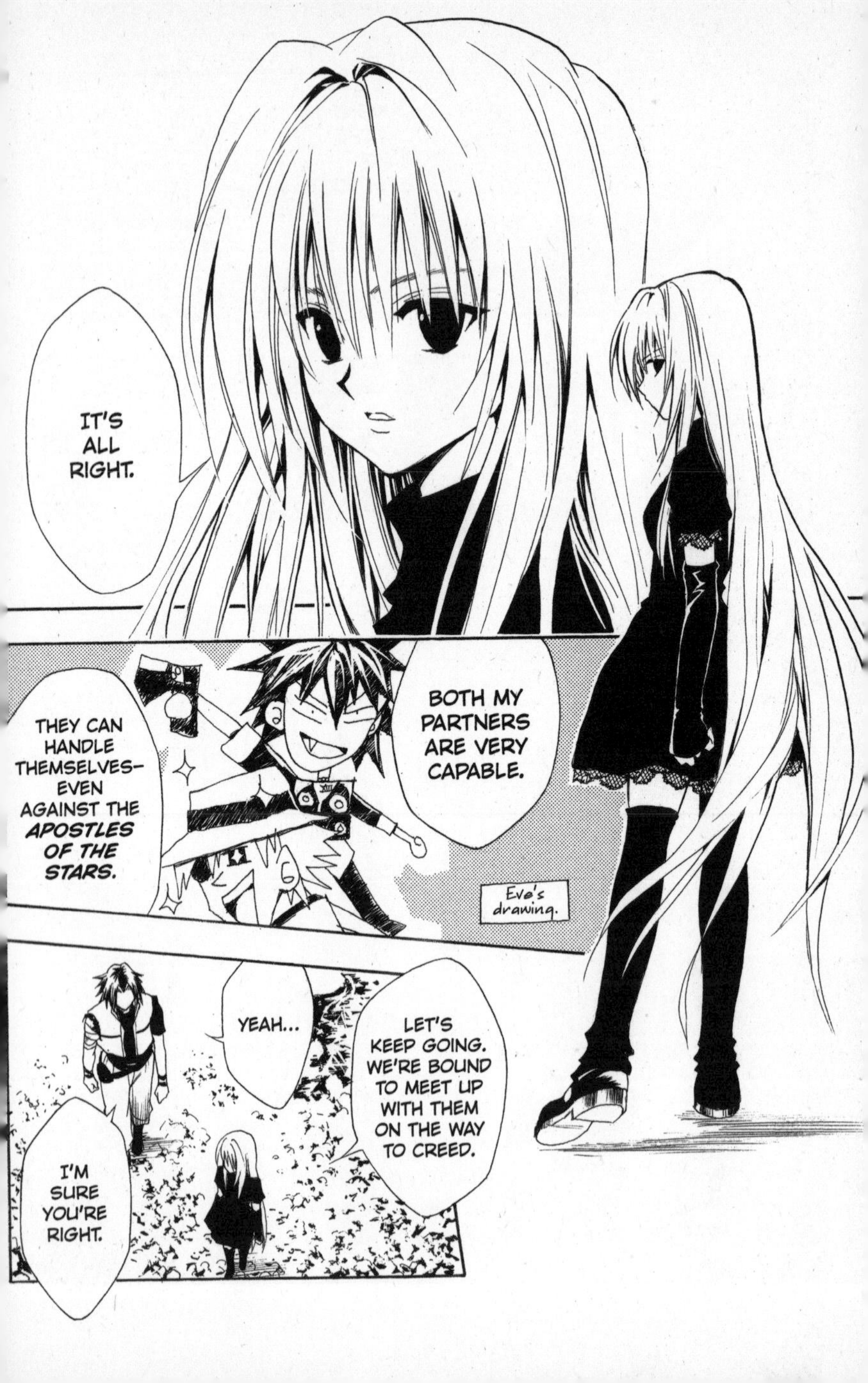

IT'S ALL RIGHT.
BOTH MY PARTNERS ARE VERY CAPABLE.
THEY CAN HANDLE THEMSELVES—EVEN AGAINST THE *APOSTLES OF THE STARS.*
Eve's drawing.
LET'S KEEP GOING. WE'RE BOUND TO MEET UP WITH THEM ON THE WAY TO CREED.
YEAH...
I'M SURE YOU'RE RIGHT.

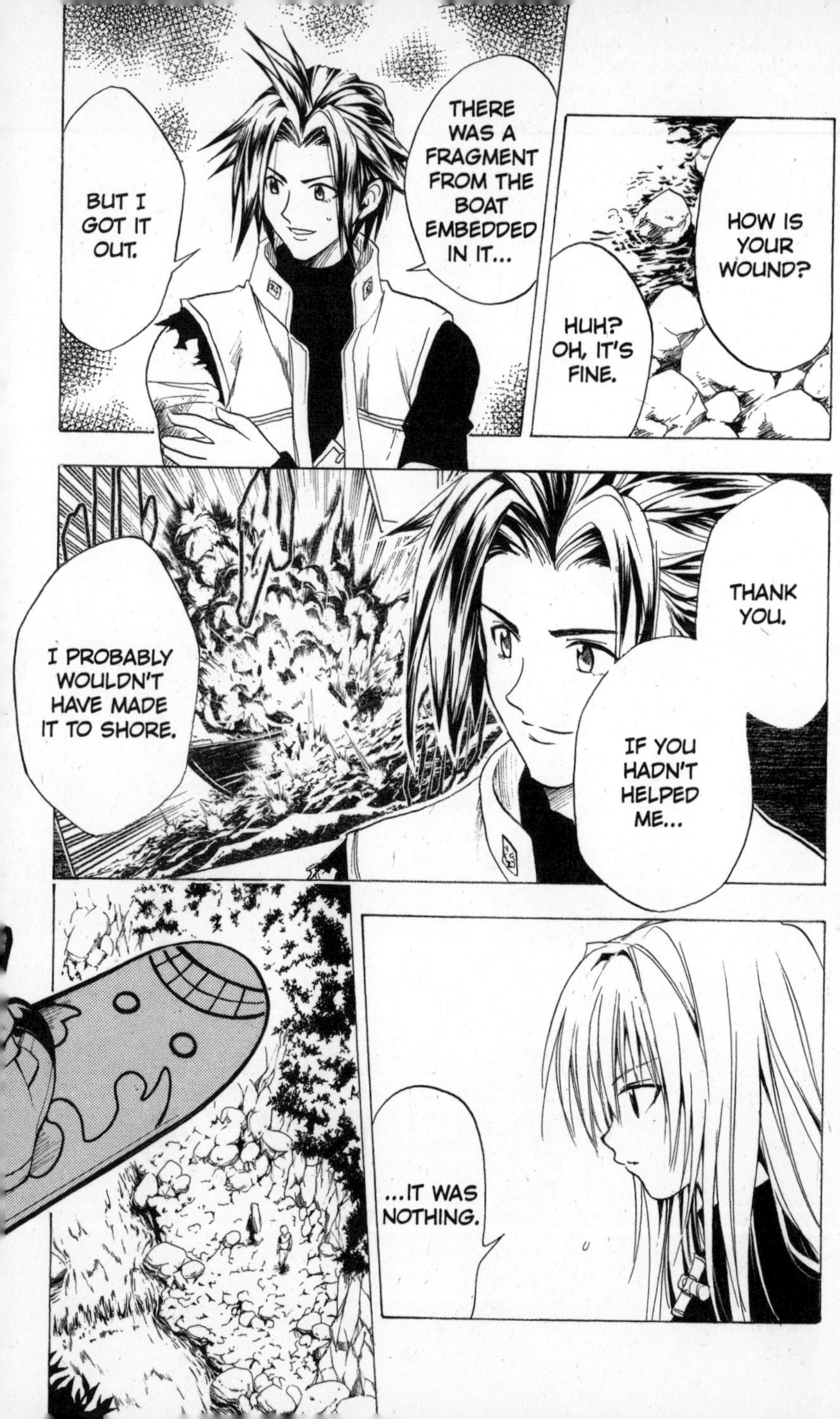
HOW IS YOUR WOUND?
HUH? OH, IT'S FINE.
THERE WAS A FRAGMENT FROM THE BOAT EMBEDDED IN IT...
BUT I GOT IT OUT.
THANK YOU.
IF YOU HADN'T HELPED ME...
I PROBABLY WOULDN'T HAVE MADE IT TO SHORE.
...IT WAS NOTHING.

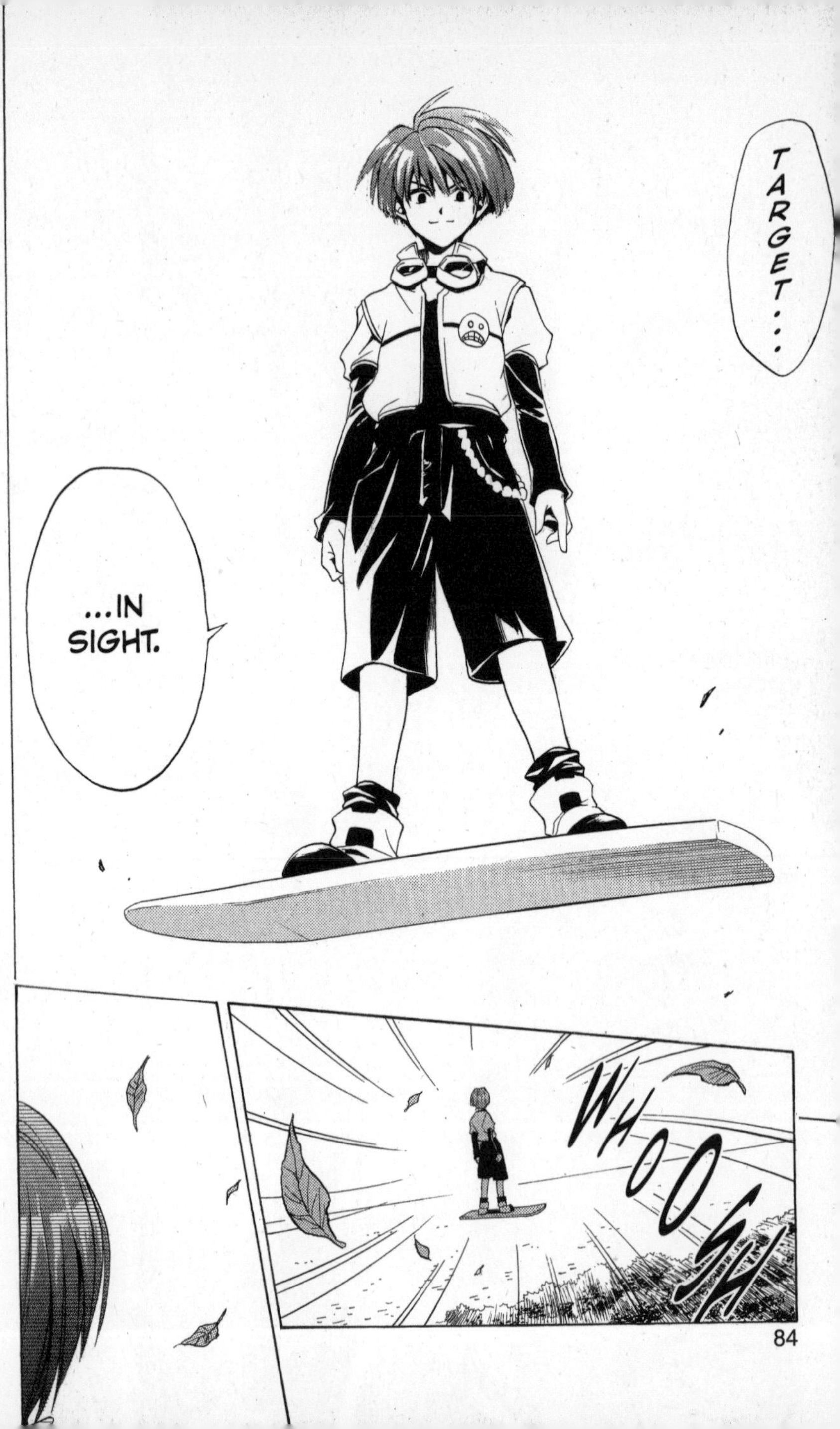
TARGET...
...IN SIGHT.
WHOOSH

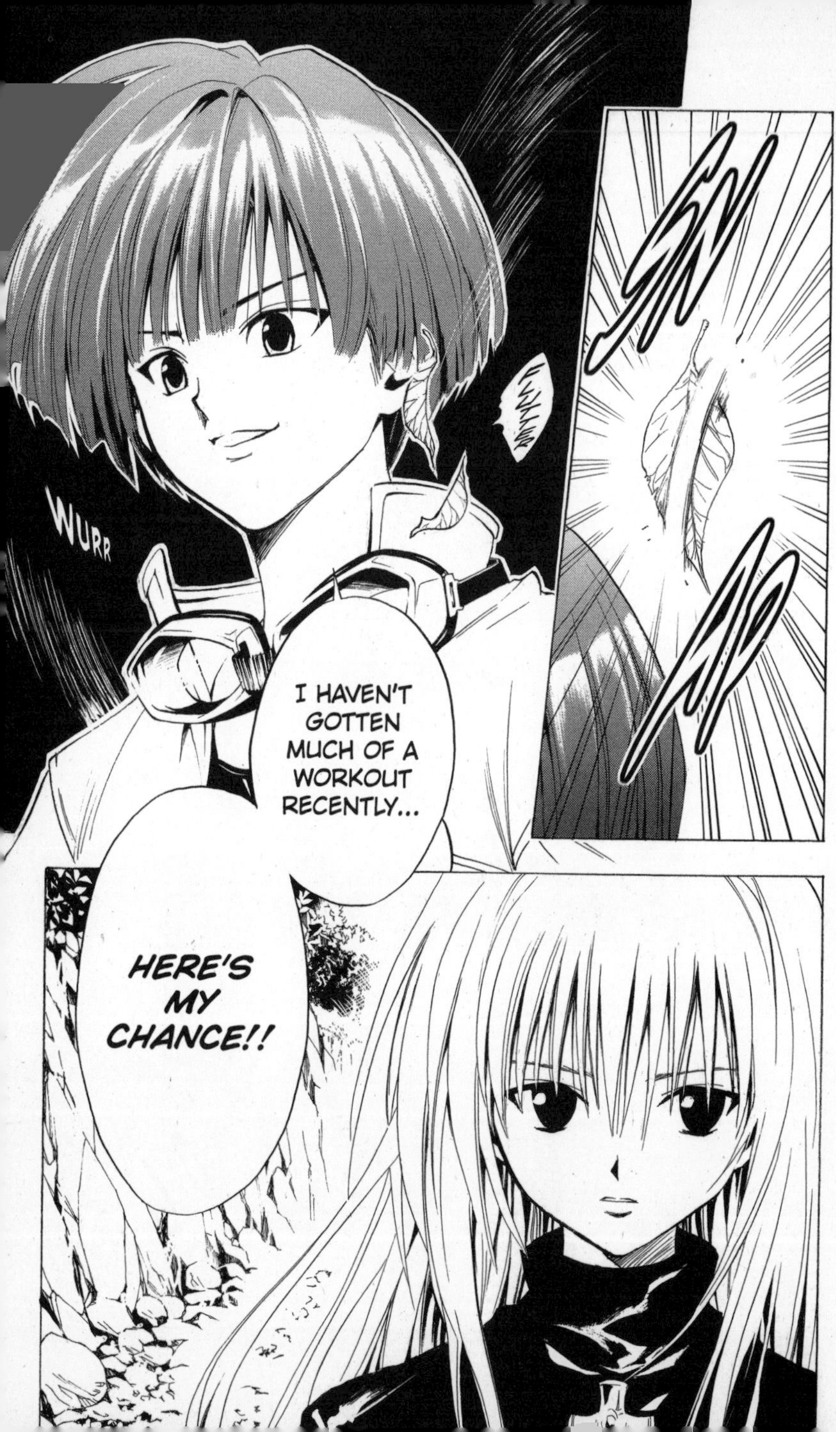
WURR
I HAVEN'T GOTTEN MUCH OF A WORKOUT RECENTLY...
HERE'S MY CHANCE!!

 **FACTOID**

SONIC FIST

A GARBELL COMMANDO TECHNIQUE FOR USE FROM A DISTANCE. A FIST THRUST AT ULTRA HIGH SPEED CREATES A SONIC WAVE POWERFUL ENOUGH TO TOPPLE AN OPPONENT 15 METERS AWAY. NOT AS POWERFUL AS THE CYCLONE GRENADE TECHNIQUE, BUT THE CYCLONE GRENADE MUST BE USED IN CLOSE PROXIMITY.

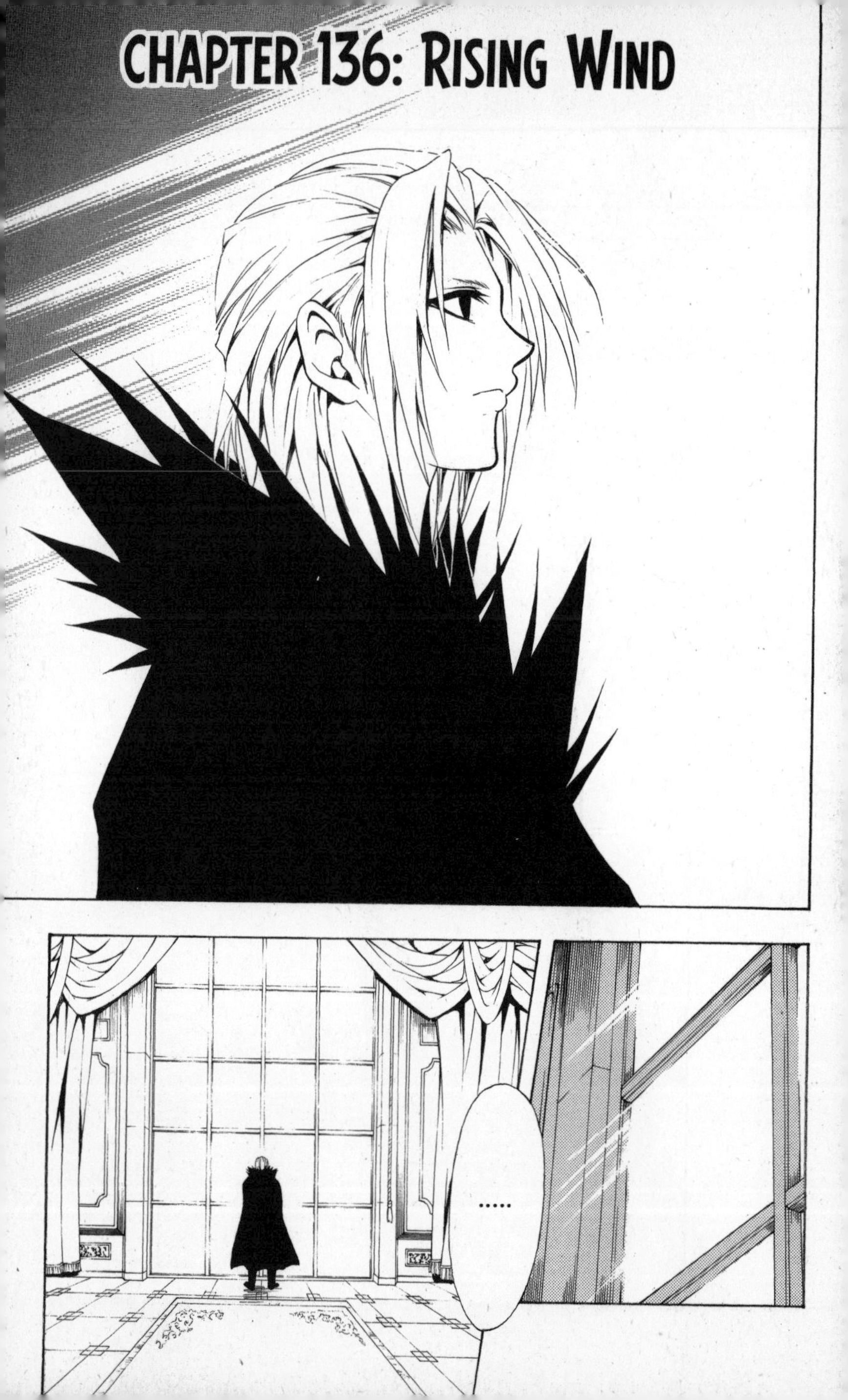
CHAPTER 136: RISING WIND
.....

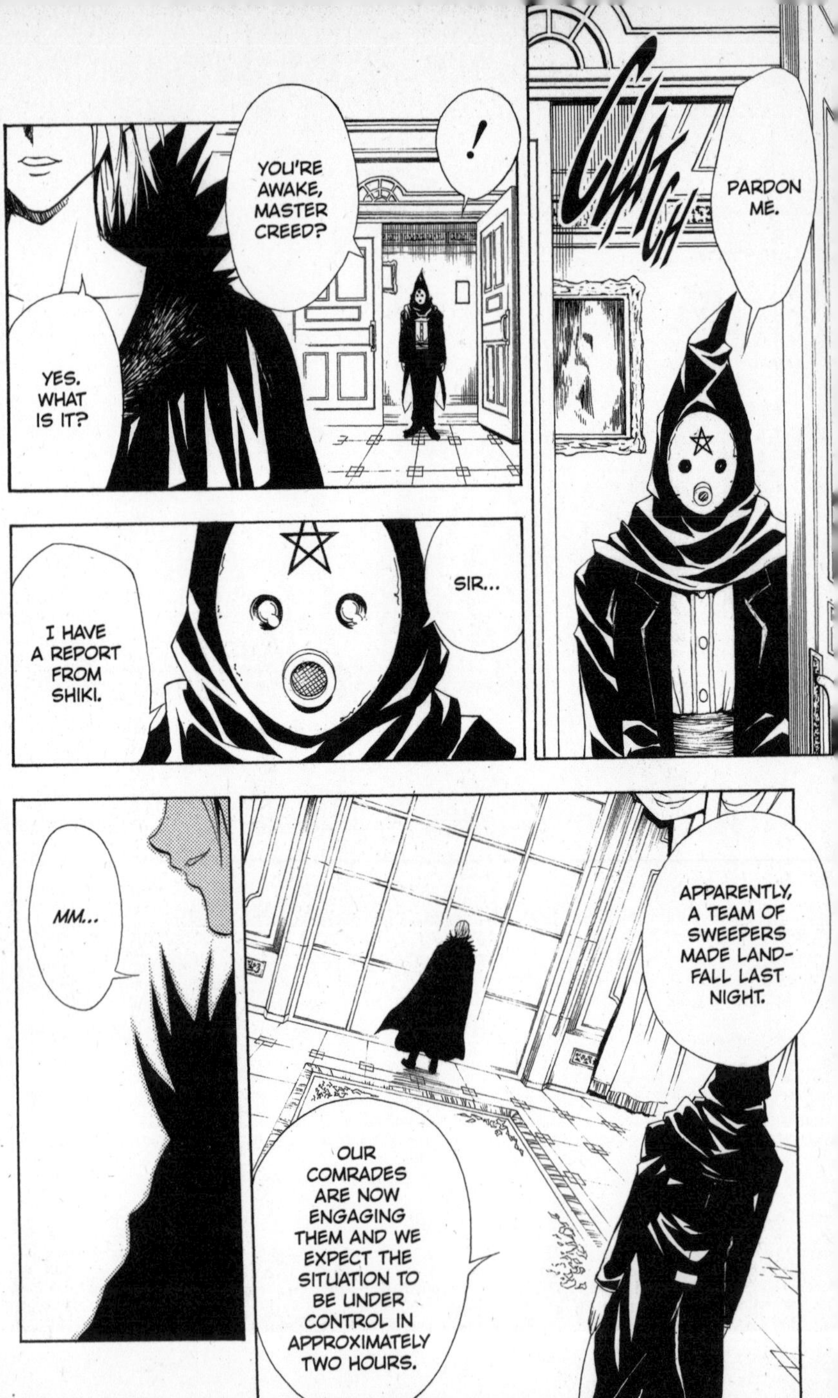
CLATCH
PARDON ME.
!
YOU'RE AWAKE, MASTER CREED?
YES. WHAT IS IT?
SIR...
I HAVE A REPORT FROM SHIKI.
APPARENTLY, A TEAM OF SWEEPERS MADE LAND-FALL LAST NIGHT.
OUR COMRADES ARE NOW ENGAGING THEM AND WE EXPECT THE SITUATION TO BE UNDER CONTROL IN APPROXIMATELY TWO HOURS.
MM...

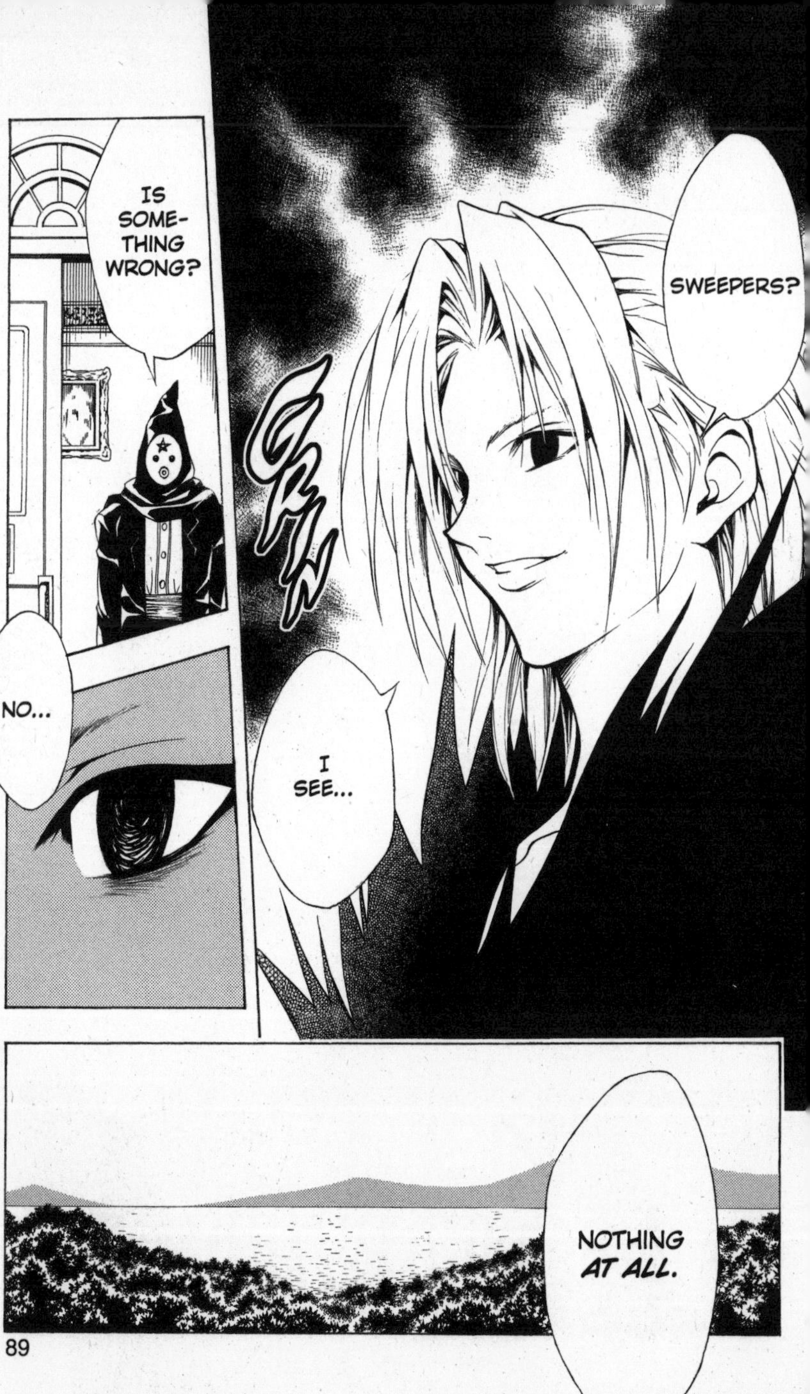
SWEEPERS?
I SEE...
IS SOMETHING WRONG?
NO...
NOTHING AT ALL.

The current locations of the Sweeper Alliance and the Apostles of the Stars

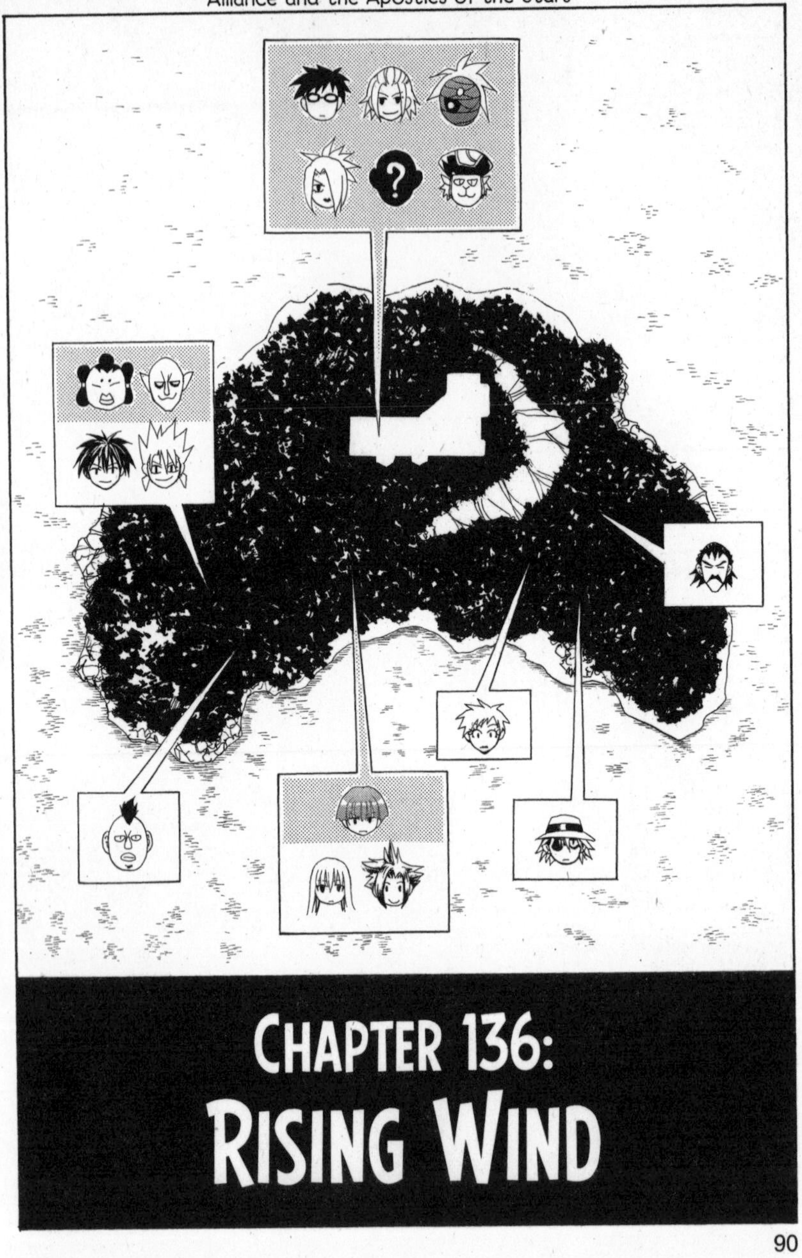

Chapter 136: Rising Wind

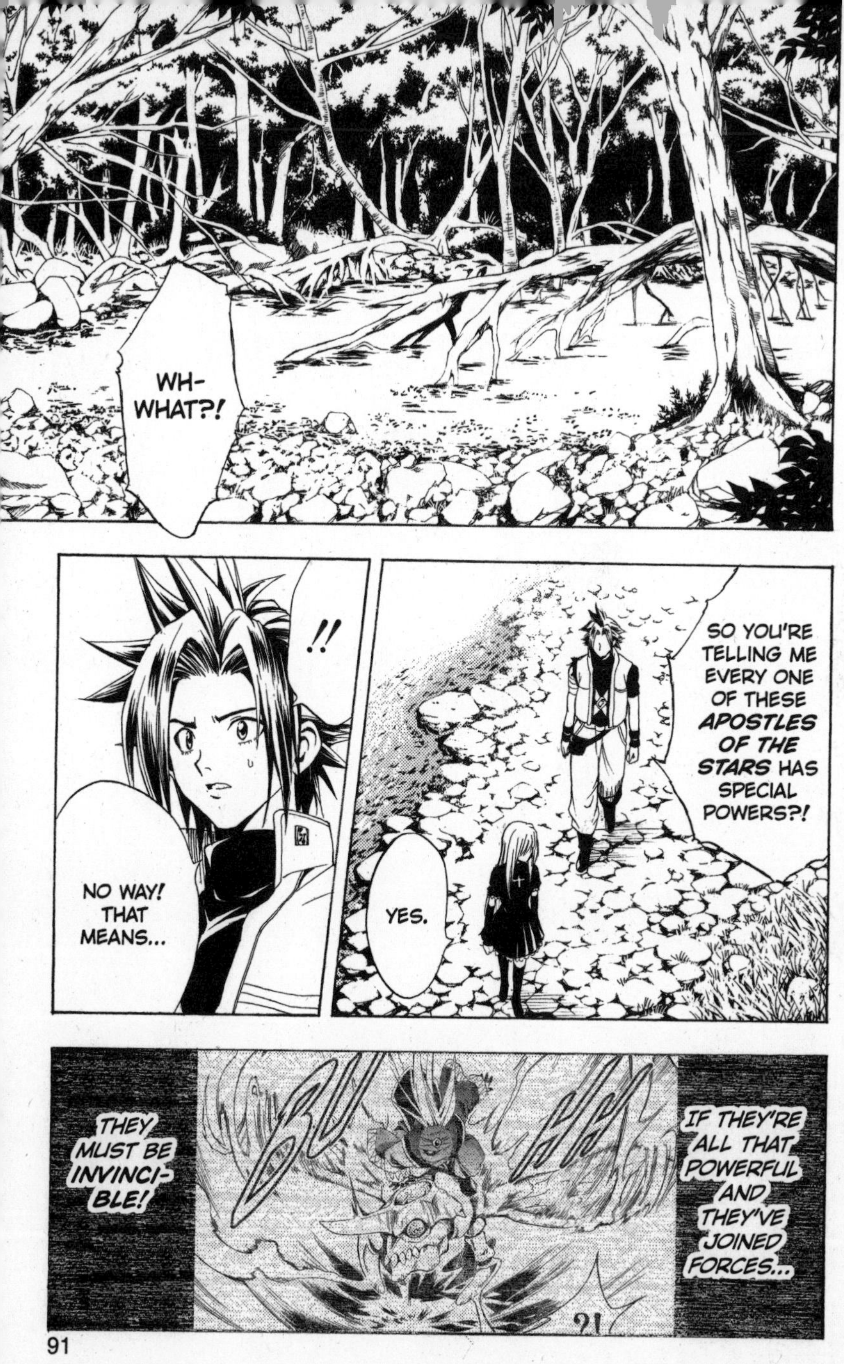
WH- WHAT?!
SO YOU'RE TELLING ME EVERY ONE OF THESE *APOSTLES OF THE STARS* HAS SPECIAL POWERS?!
YES.
!!
NO WAY! THAT MEANS...
IF THEY'RE ALL THAT POWERFUL AND THEY'VE JOINED FORCES...
THEY MUST BE INVINCI- BLE!

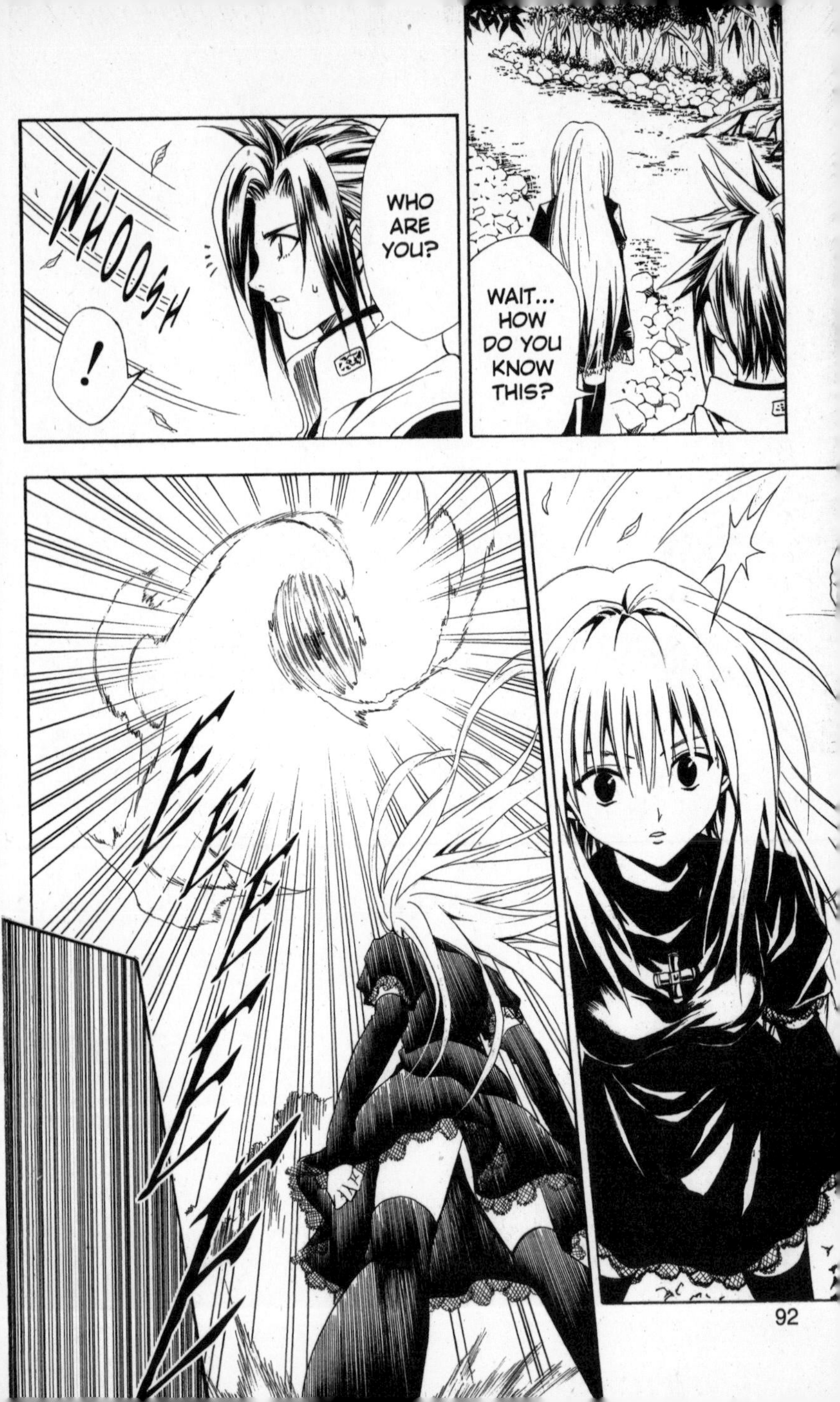
WAIT... HOW DO YOU KNOW THIS?
WHO ARE YOU?
WHOOSH
!

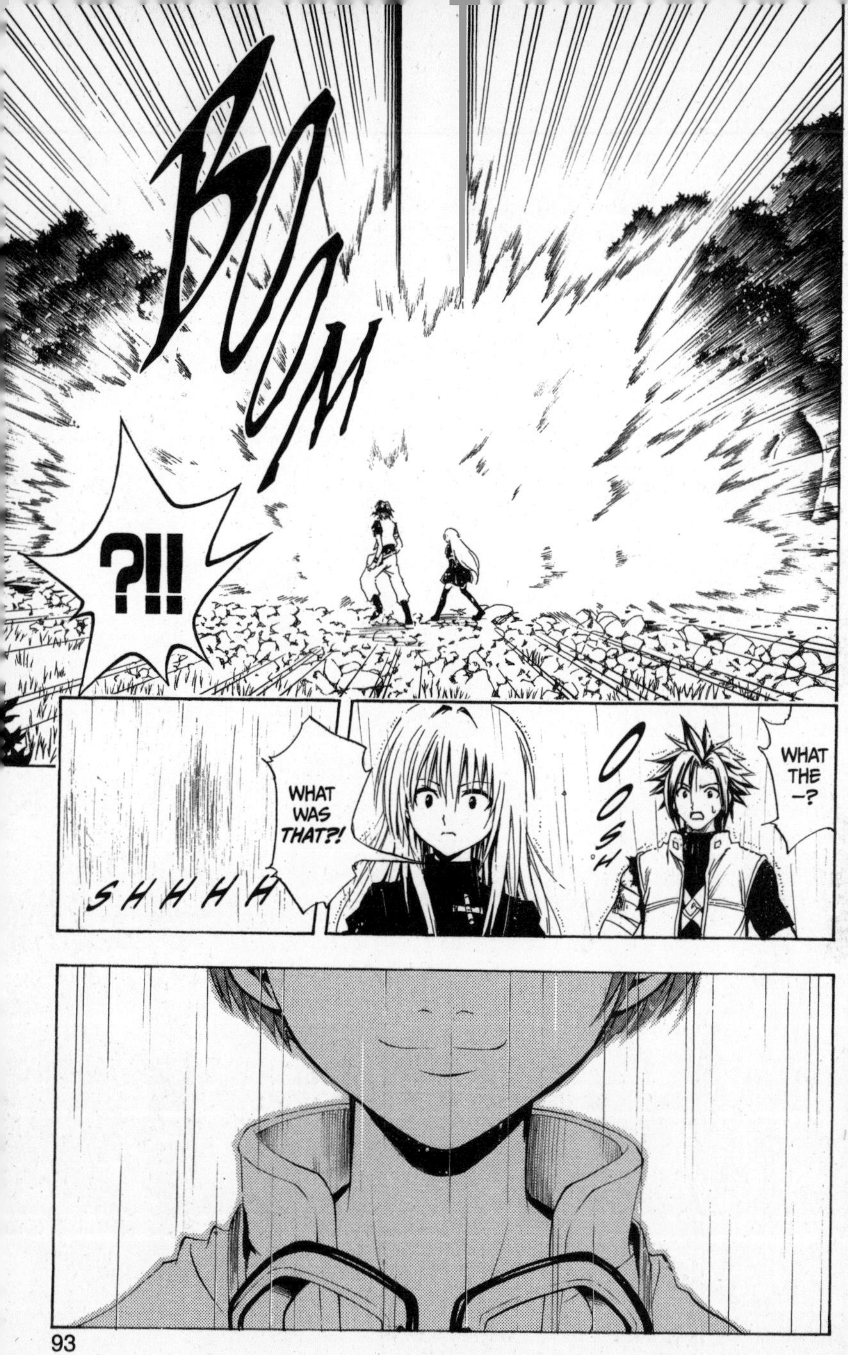
BOOM
?!!
WHAT THE —?
WOOSH
WHAT WAS THAT?!
SHHHH

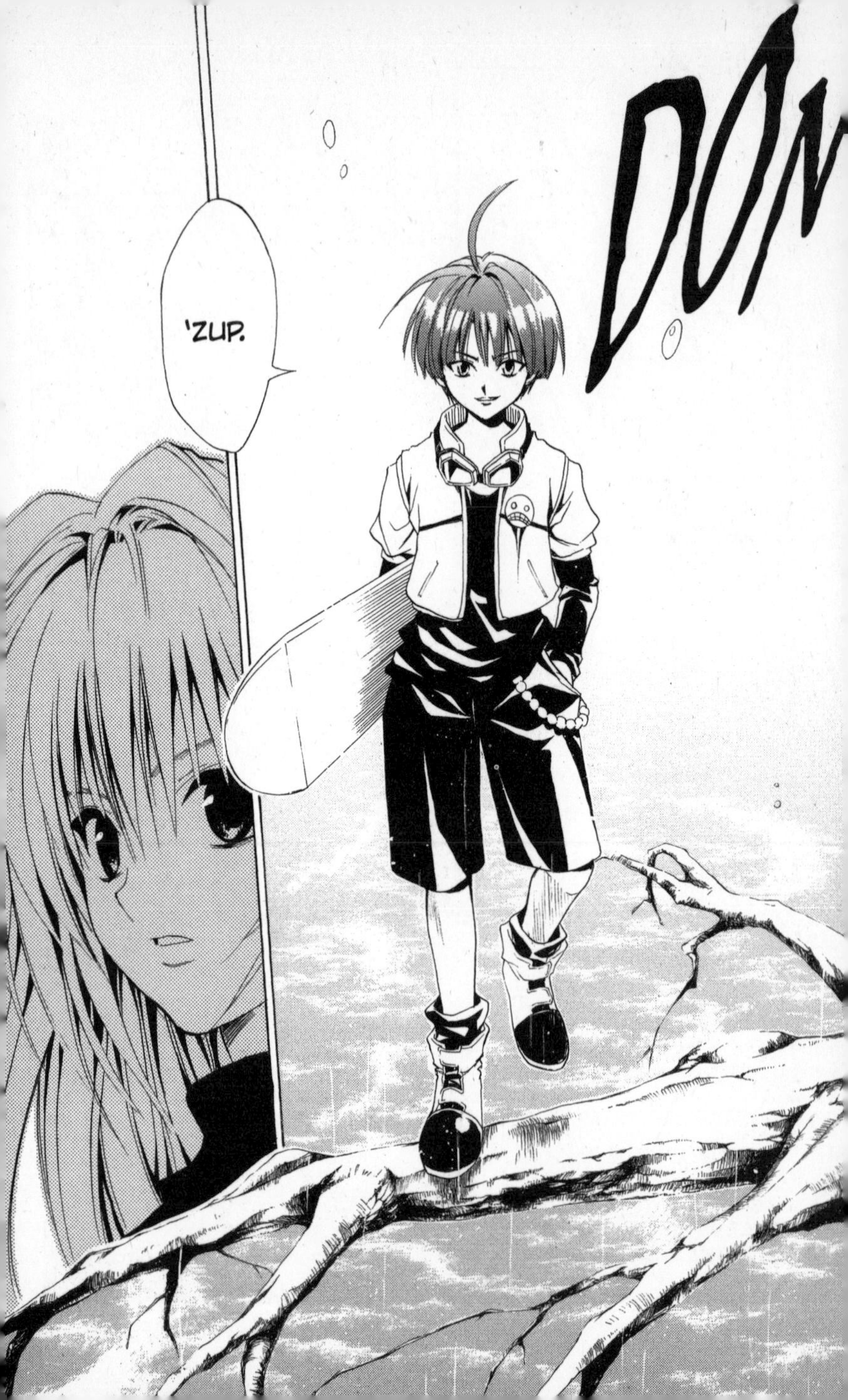
DON
'ZUP.

« READ THIS WAY «

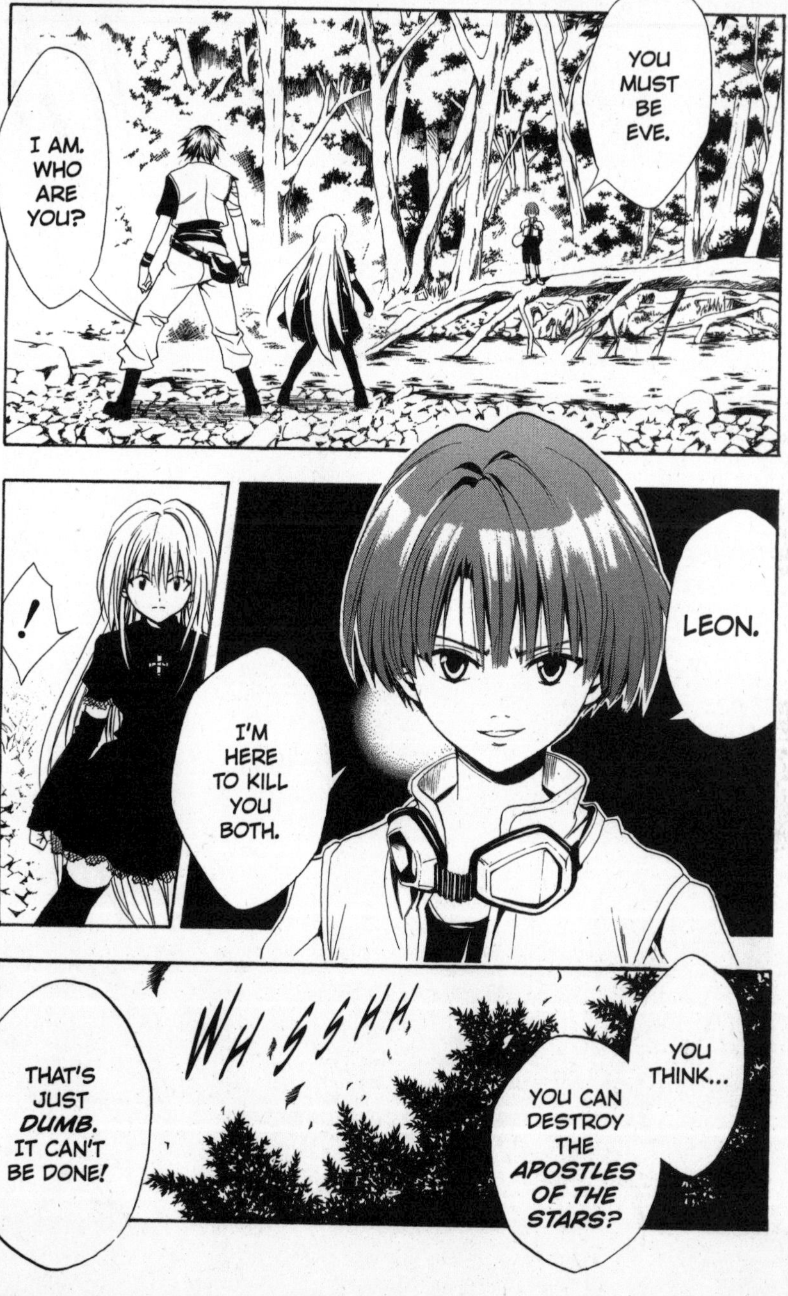
YOU MUST BE EVE.
I AM. WHO ARE YOU?
LEON.
I'M HERE TO KILL YOU BOTH.
!
YOU THINK...
YOU CAN DESTROY THE *APOSTLES OF THE STARS?*
WHSSHH
THAT'S JUST *DUMB.* IT CAN'T BE DONE!

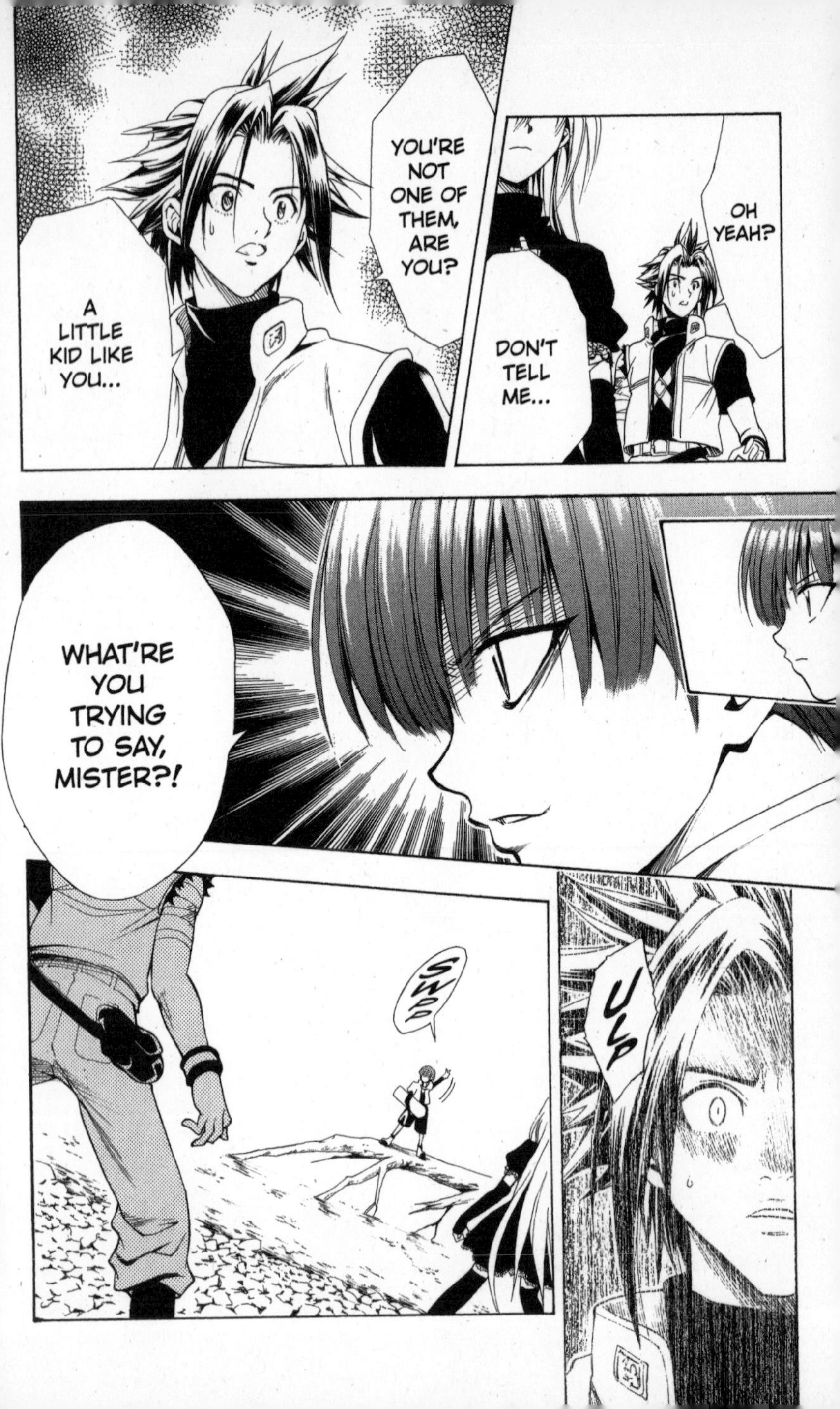
OH YEAH?
DON'T TELL ME...
YOU'RE NOT ONE OF THEM, ARE YOU?
A LITTLE KID LIKE YOU...
WHAT'RE YOU TRYING TO SAY, MISTER?!
ULP
SWPP

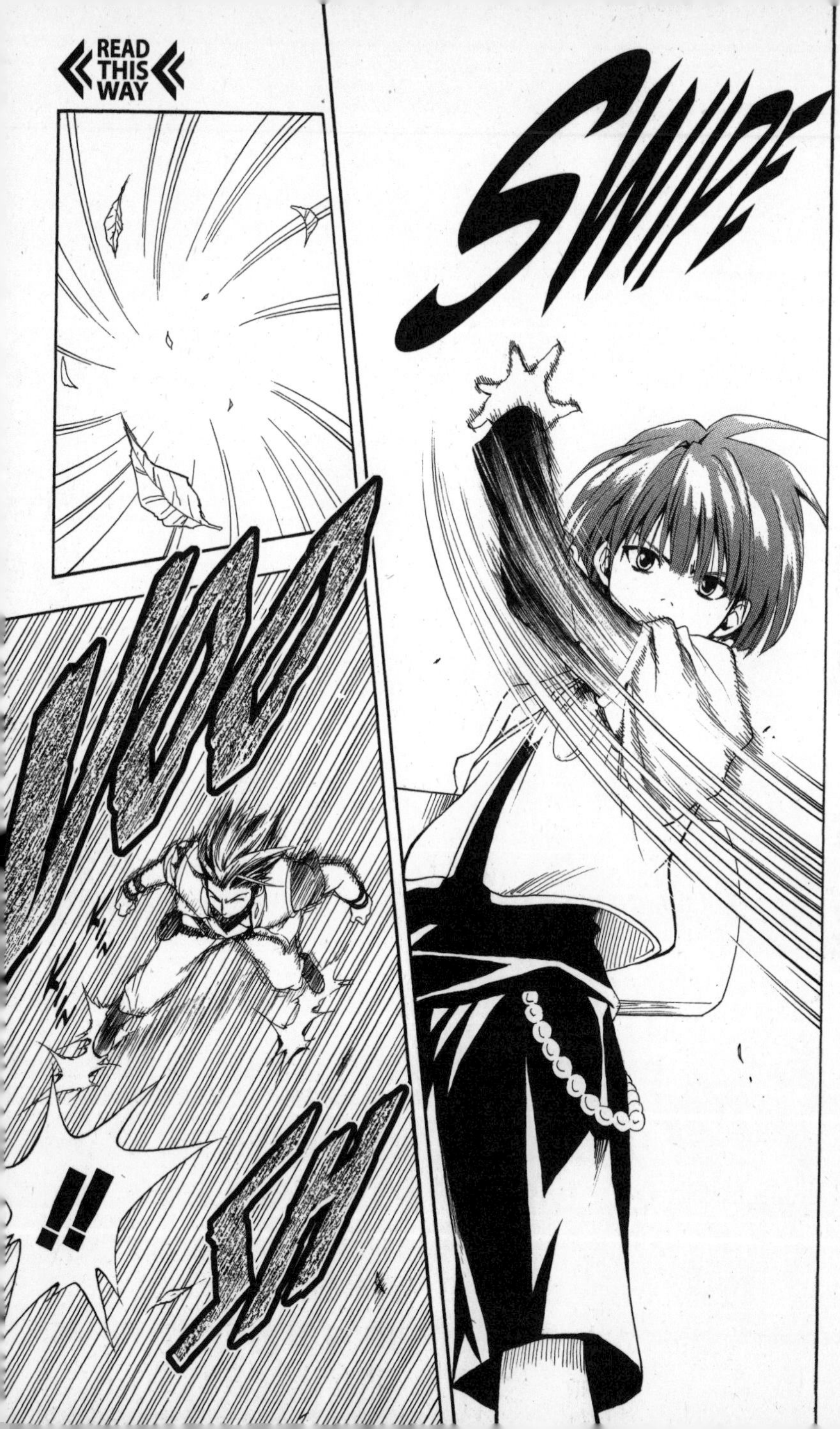
READ THIS WAY
SWIPE
!!

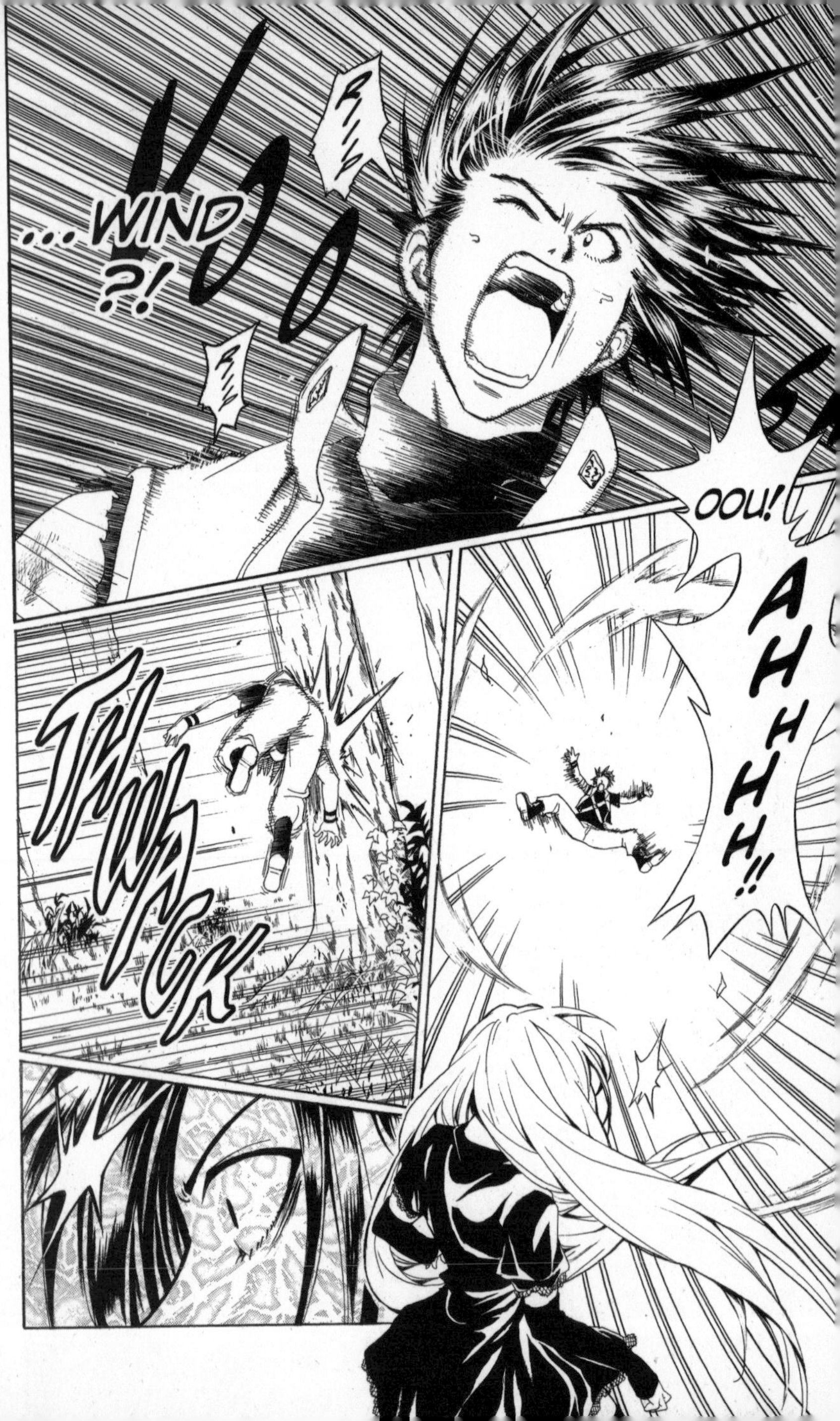
...WIND
?!
OOU!
AHHHHH!!
THWACK

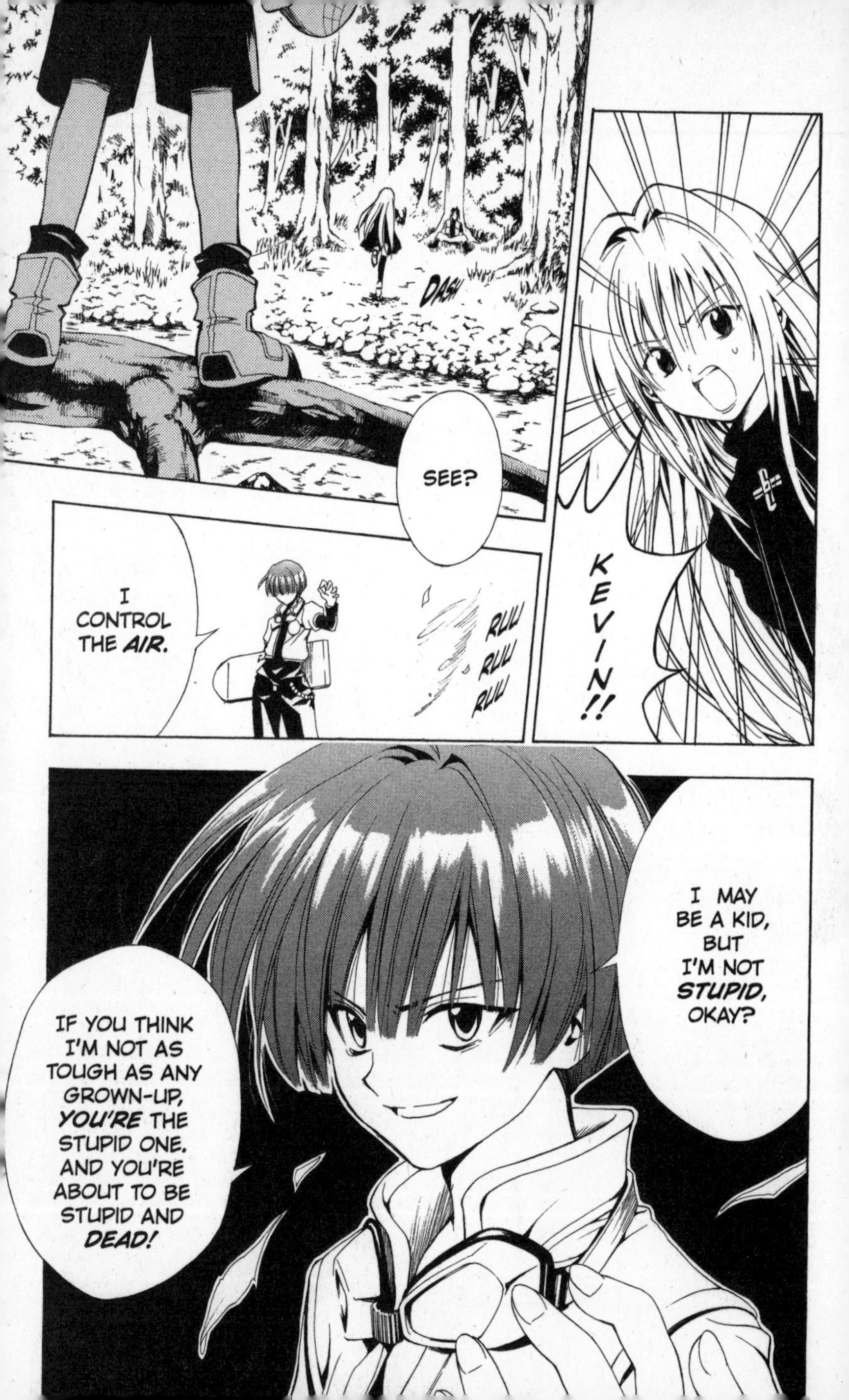

KEVIN!!
DASH
SEE?
I CONTROL THE *AIR*.
RUU RUU RUU
I MAY BE A KID, BUT I'M NOT *STUPID*, OKAY?
IF YOU THINK I'M NOT AS TOUGH AS ANY GROWN-UP, *YOU'RE* THE STUPID ONE. AND YOU'RE ABOUT TO BE STUPID AND *DEAD!*

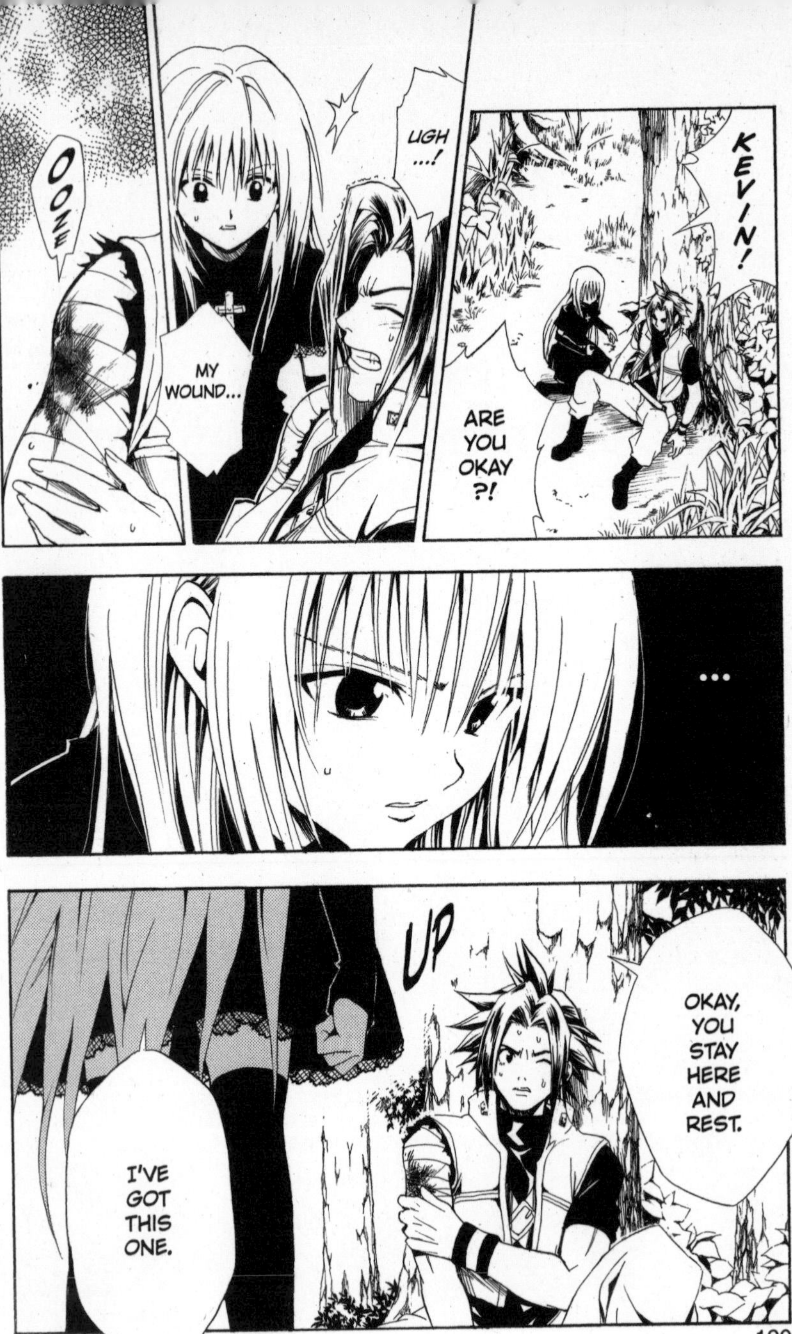
KEVIN!
ARE YOU OKAY?!
UGH...!
MY WOUND...
OOZE
...
OKAY, YOU STAY HERE AND REST.
UP
I'VE GOT THIS ONE.

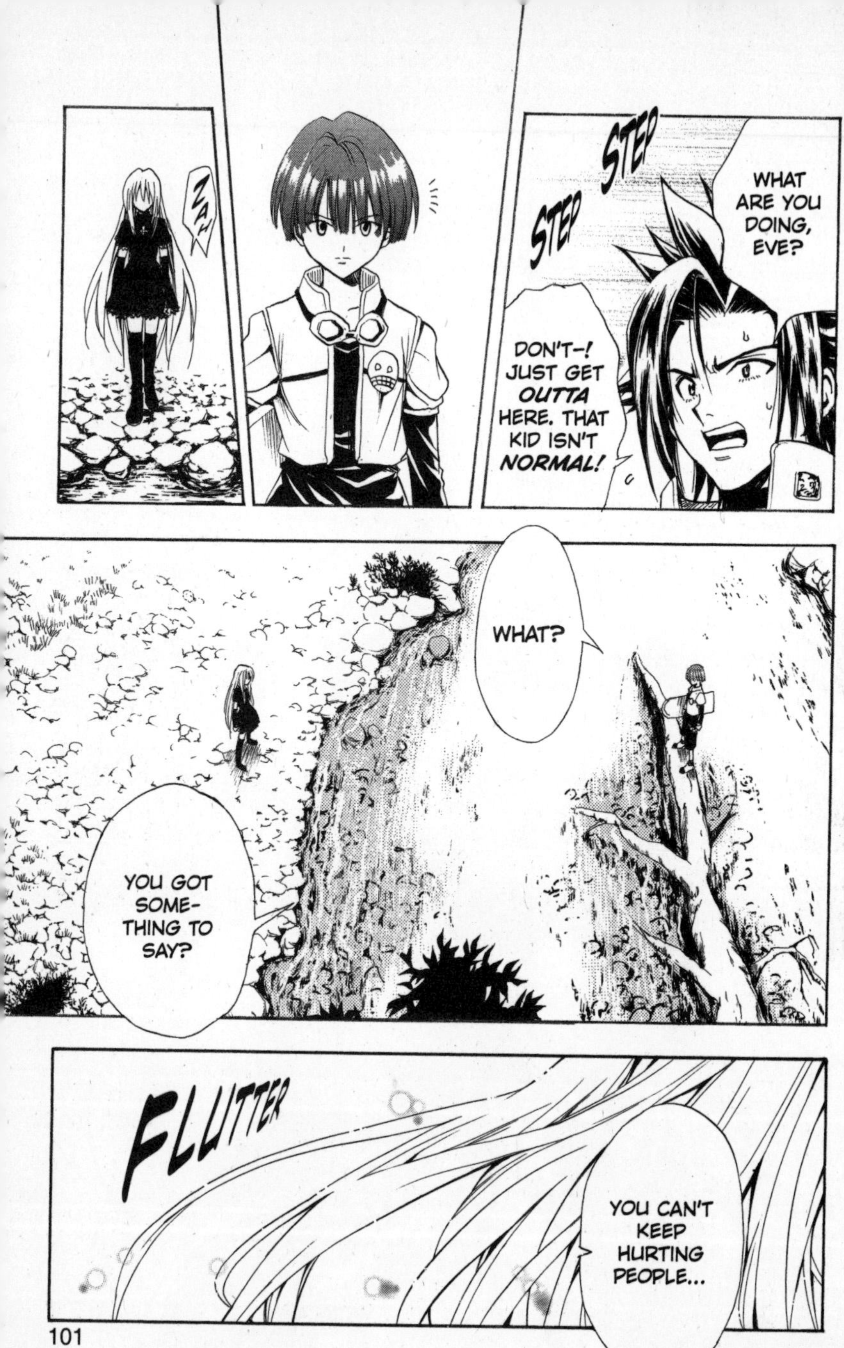
WHAT ARE YOU DOING, EVE?
STEP
STEP
DON'T-! JUST GET OUTTA HERE. THAT KID ISN'T NORMAL!
ZAH
WHAT?
YOU GOT SOME-THING TO SAY?
FLUTTER
YOU CAN'T KEEP HURTING PEOPLE...

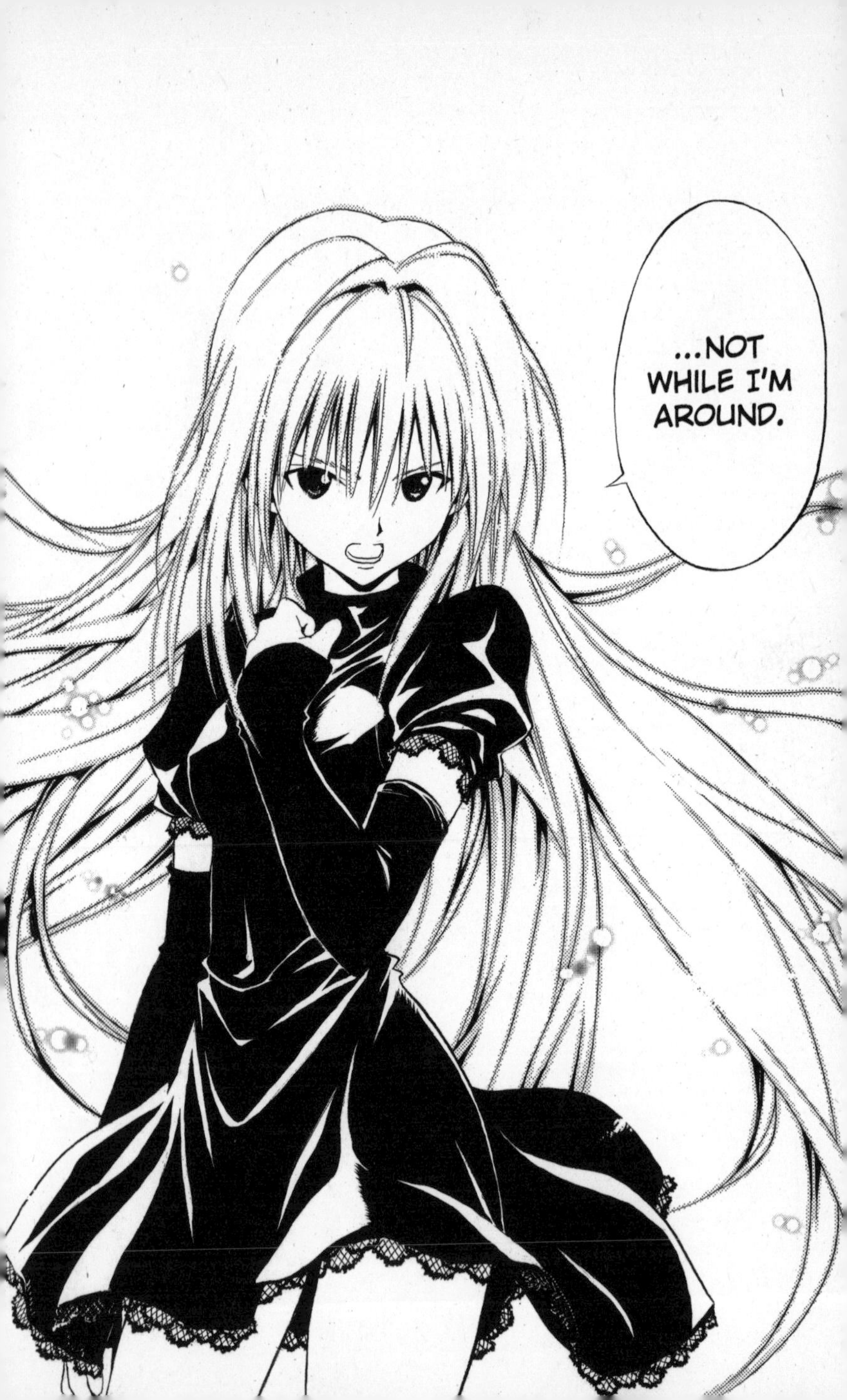
...NOT WHILE I'M AROUND.

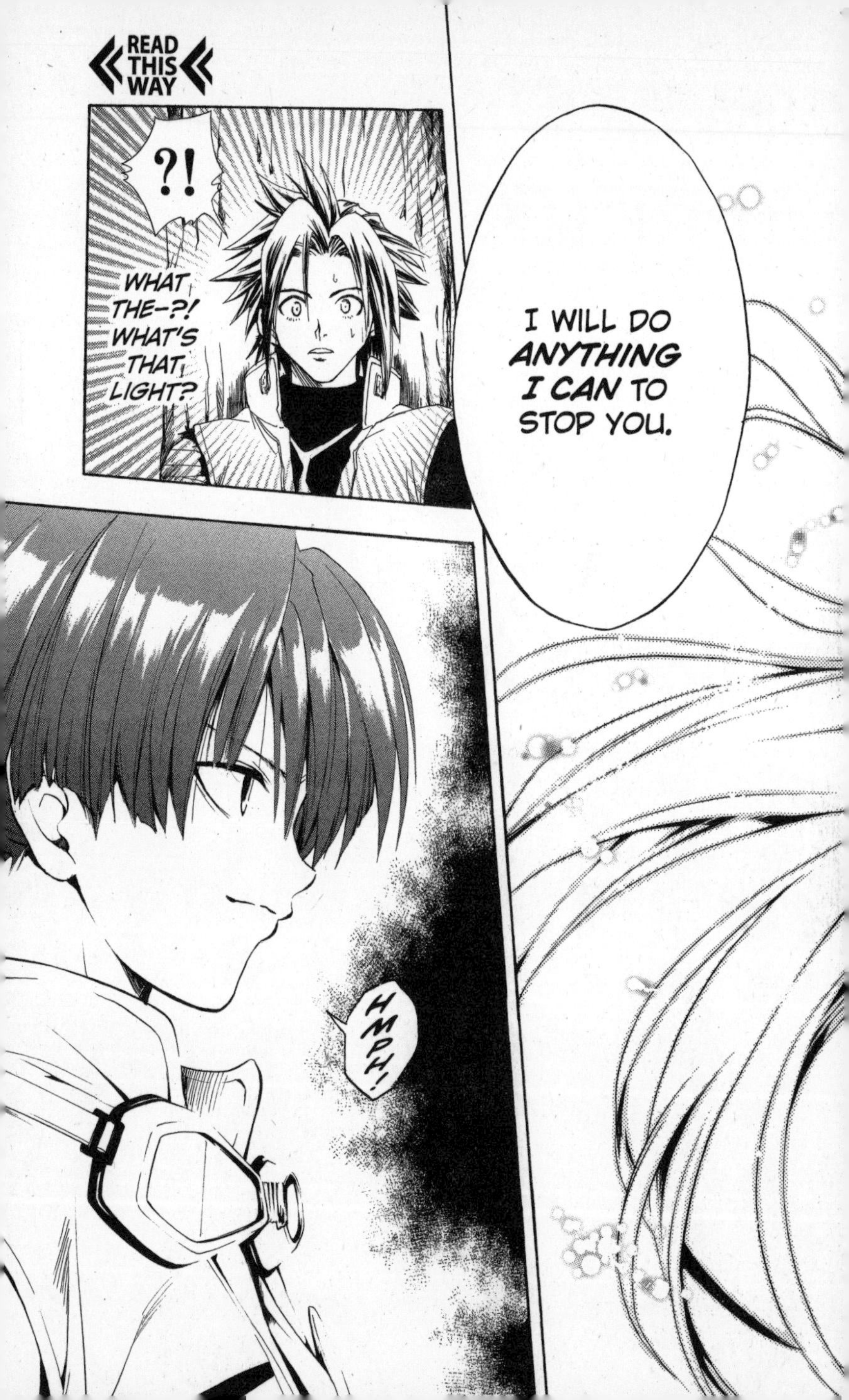
READ THIS WAY
I WILL DO ANYTHING I CAN TO STOP YOU.
?!
WHAT THE-?! WHAT'S THAT LIGHT?
HMPH!

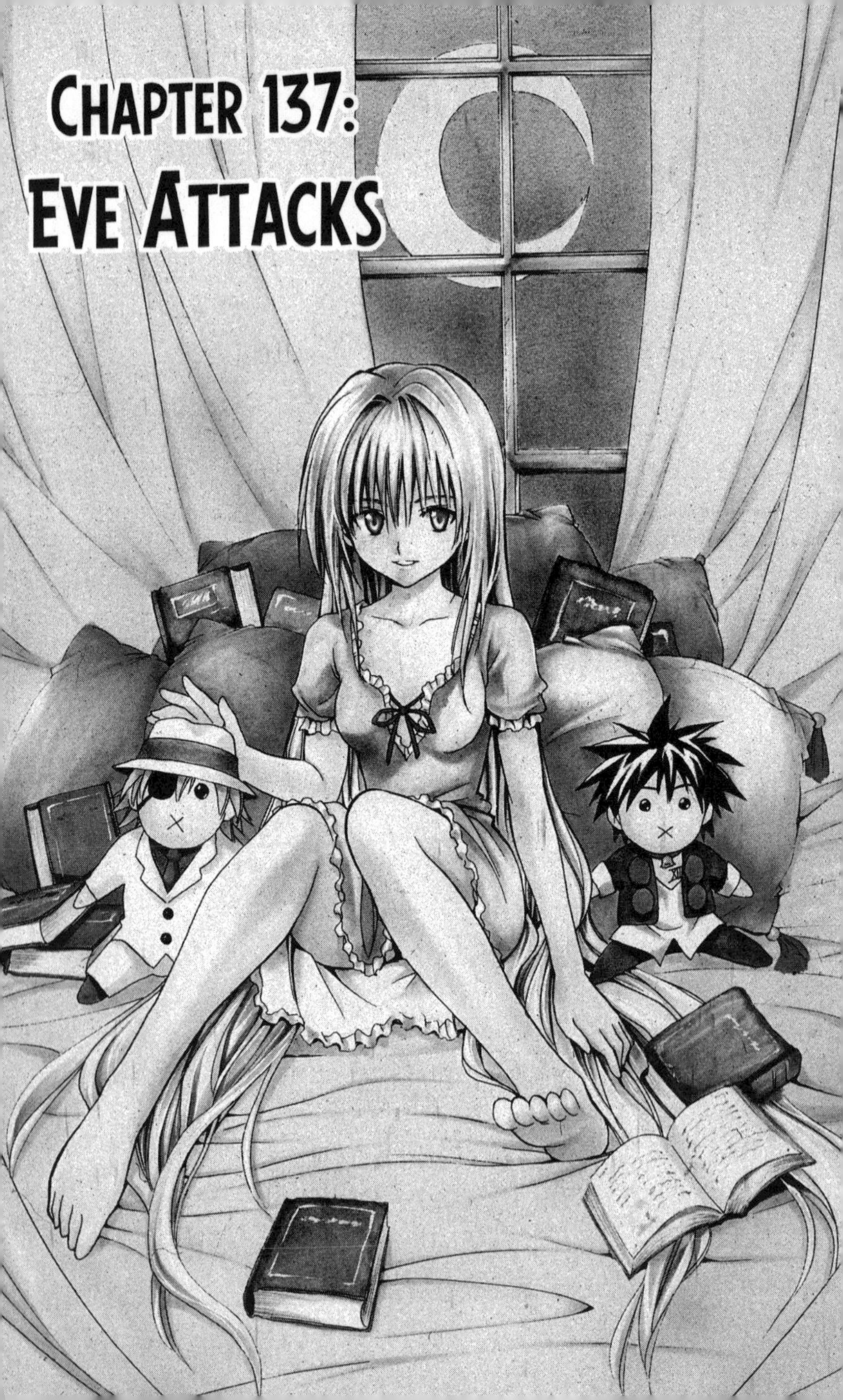
Chapter 137:
Eve Attacks

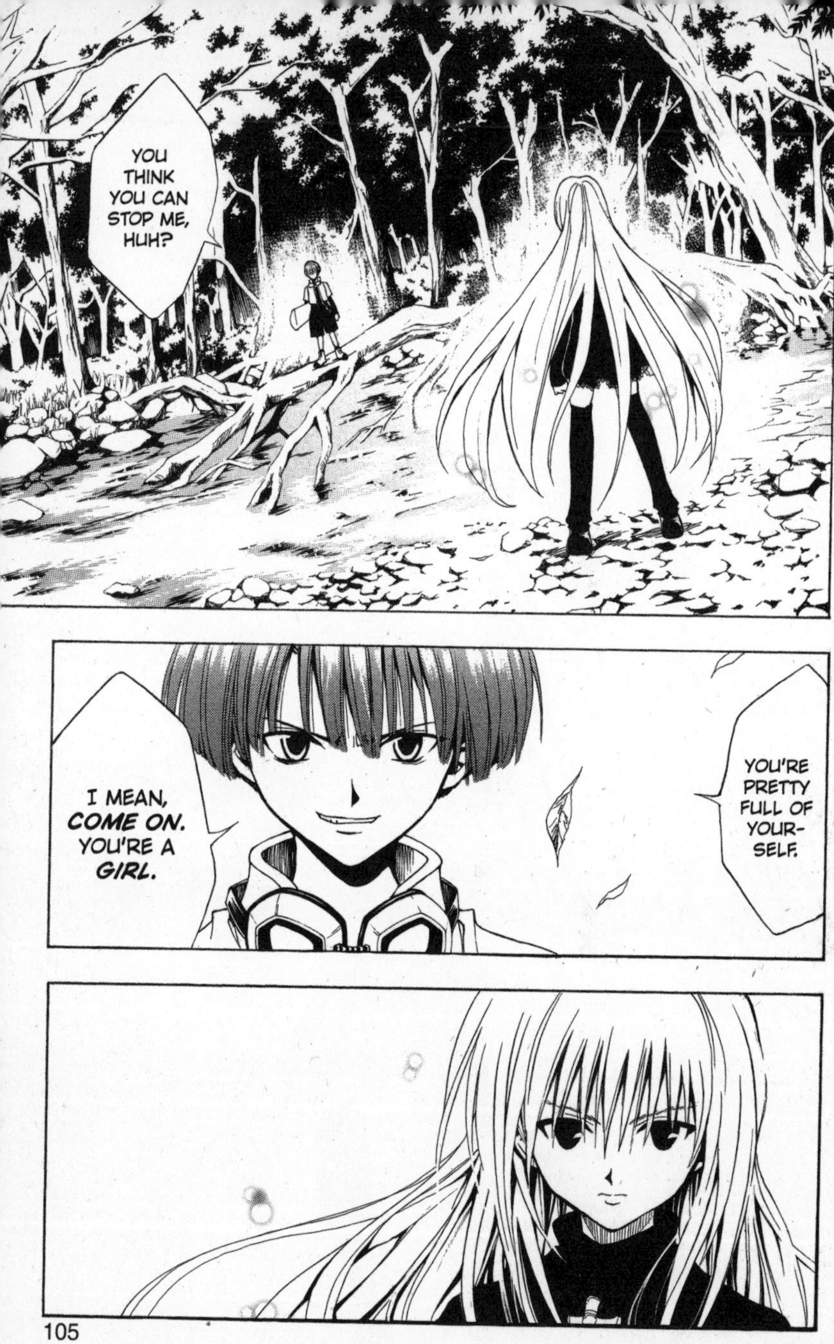
YOU THINK YOU CAN STOP ME, HUH?
YOU'RE PRETTY FULL OF YOUR-SELF.
I MEAN, *COME ON*. YOU'RE A *GIRL*.

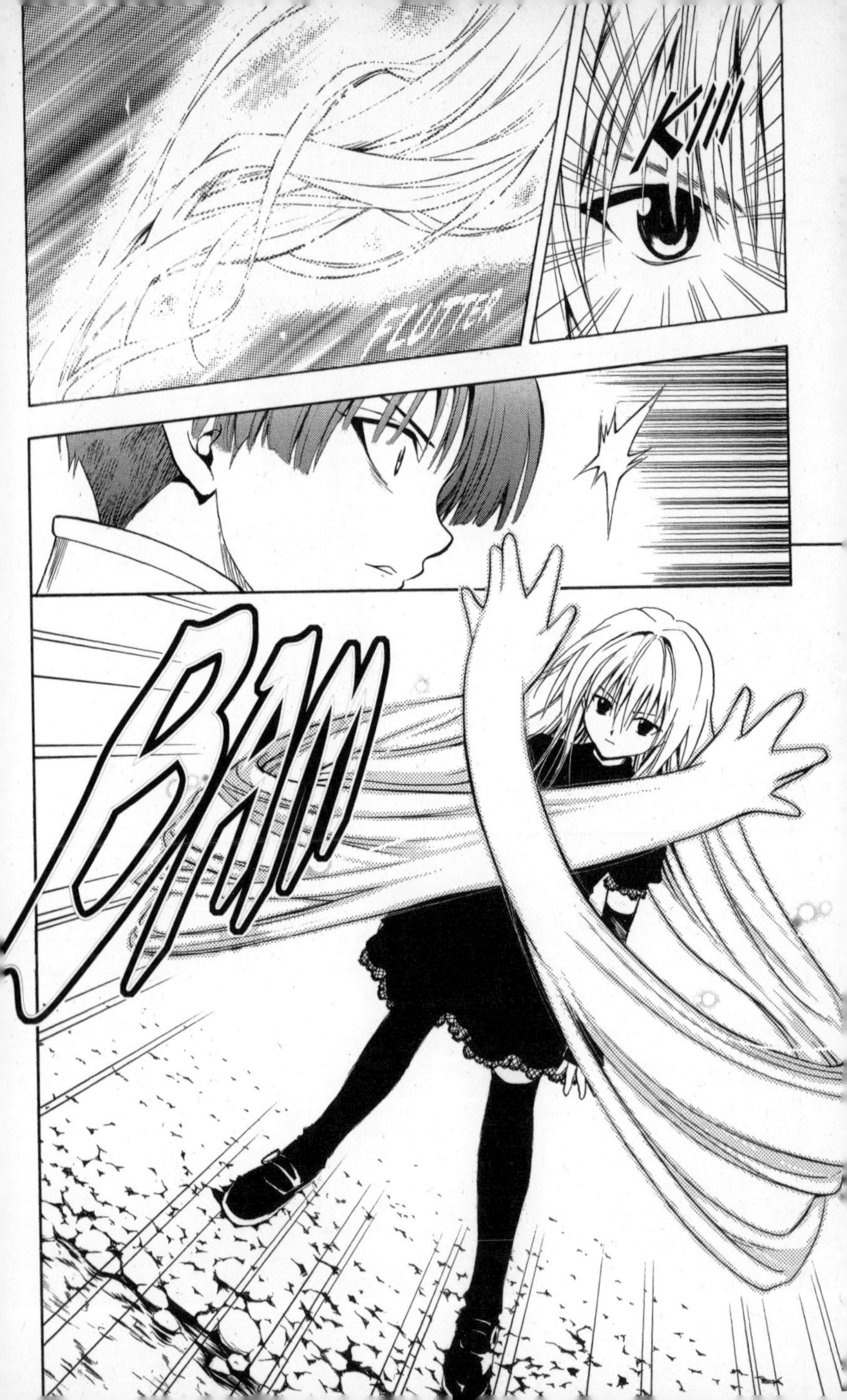
KI!!
FLUTTER
BAM

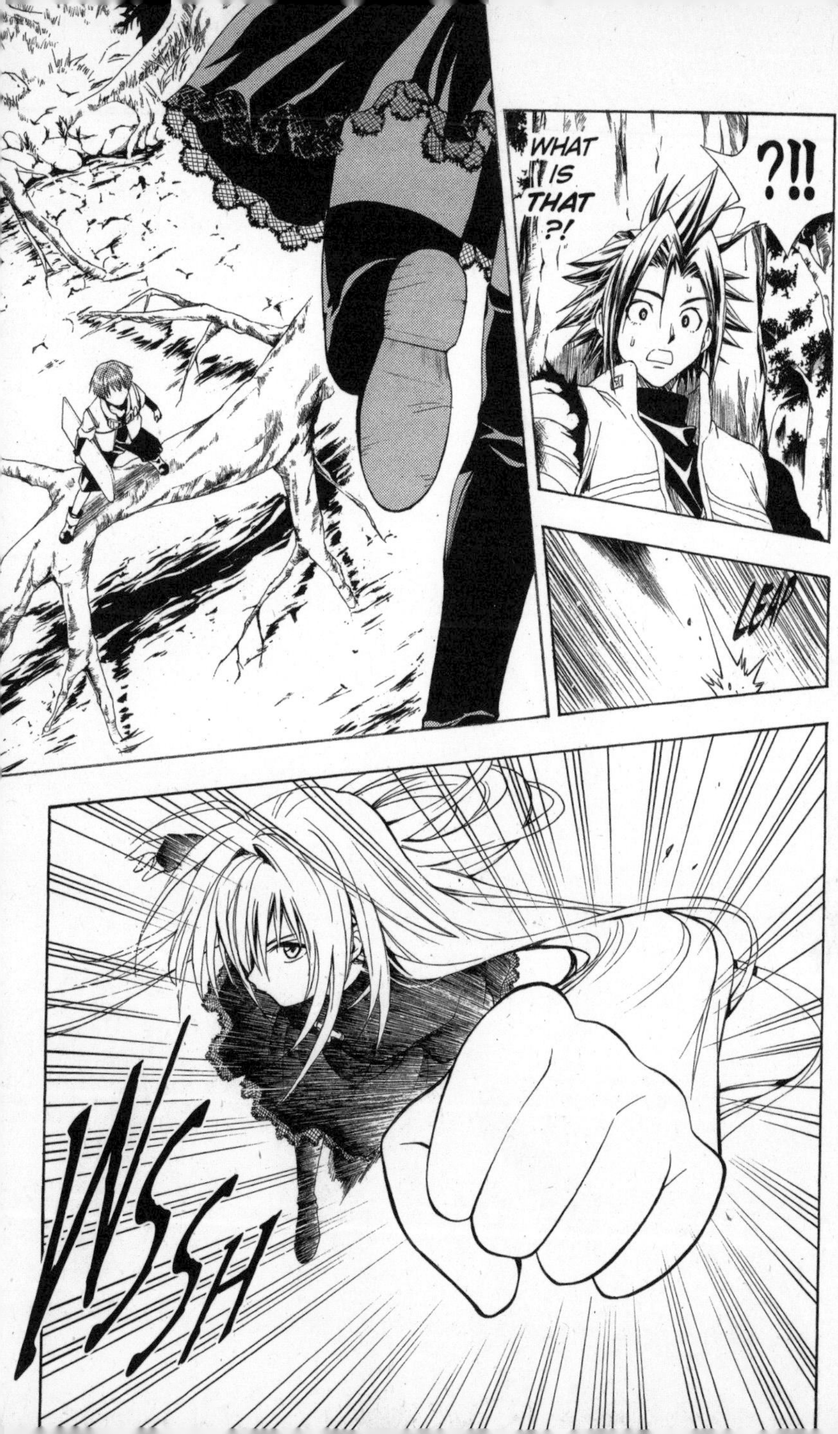
WHAT IS THAT ?!
?!!
LEAP
WSSH

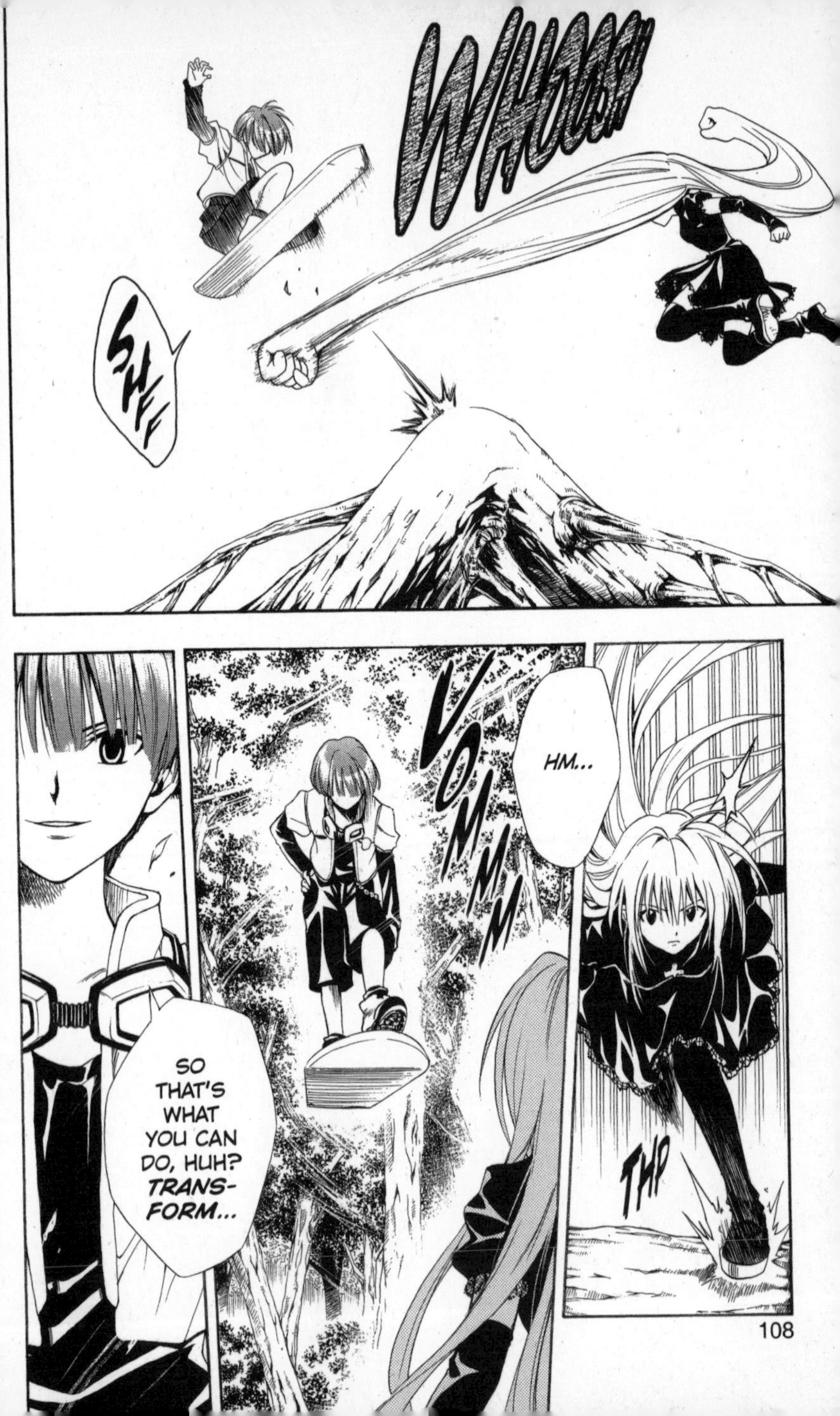
WHOOSH
SHFF
HM...
THP
VOMMMM
SO THAT'S WHAT YOU CAN DO, HUH? *TRANSFORM*...

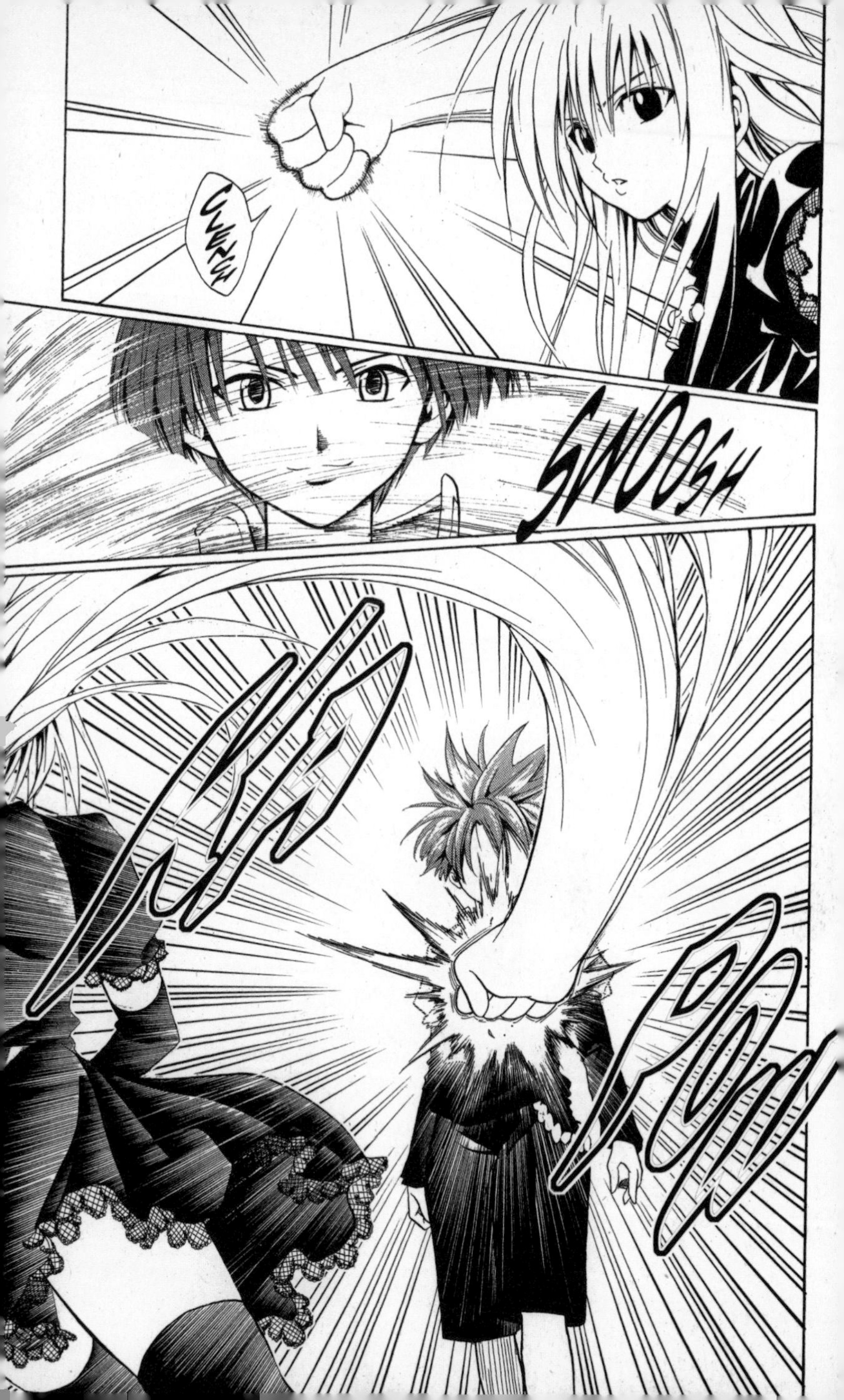
CLENCH
SWOOSH
WHAM
POW

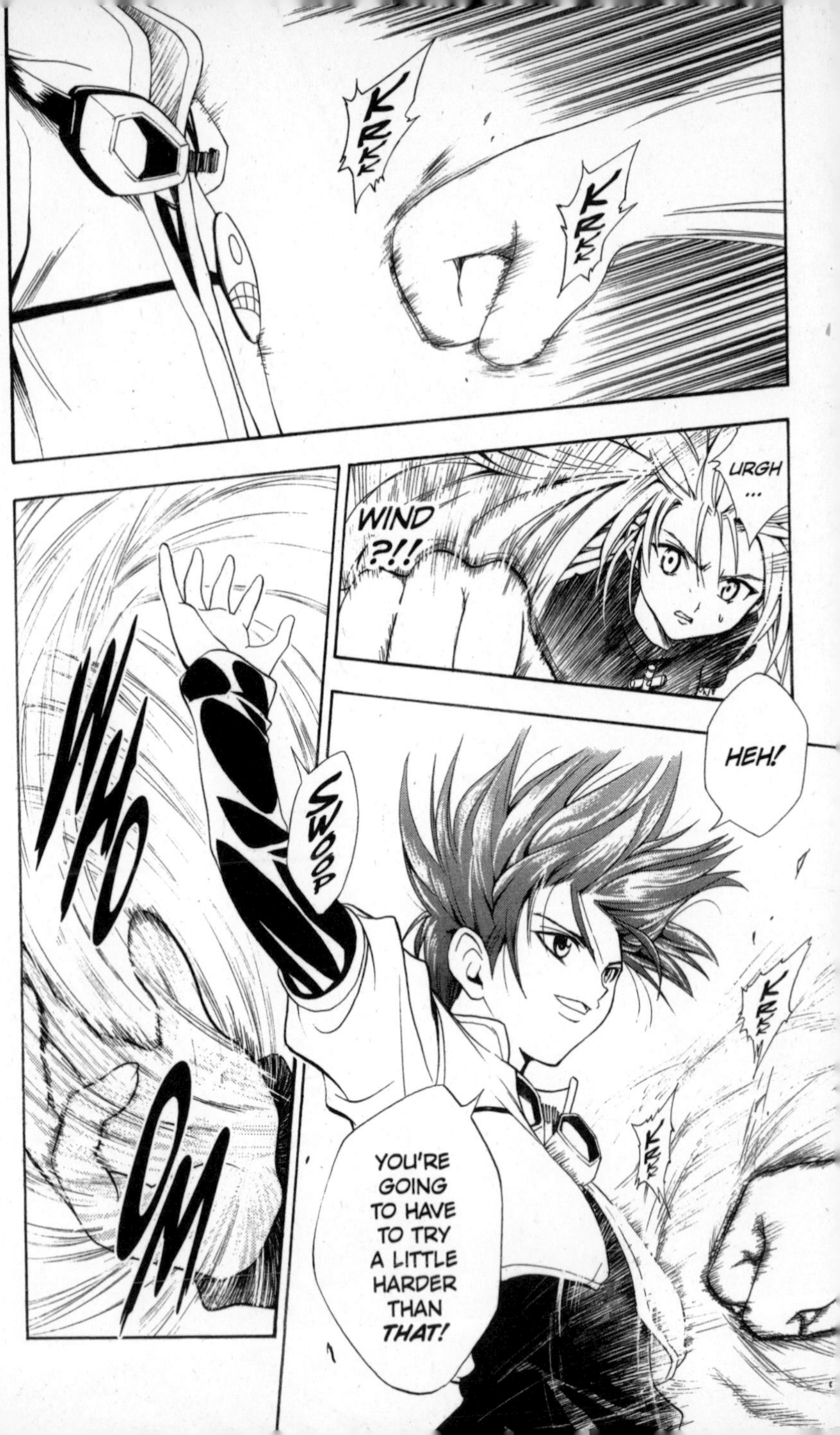

KRKK
KRKK
URGH ...
WIND ?!!
HEH!
KRKK
KRKK
YOU'RE GOING TO HAVE TO TRY A LITTLE HARDER THAN *THAT!*
SWOOP
WHOOSH

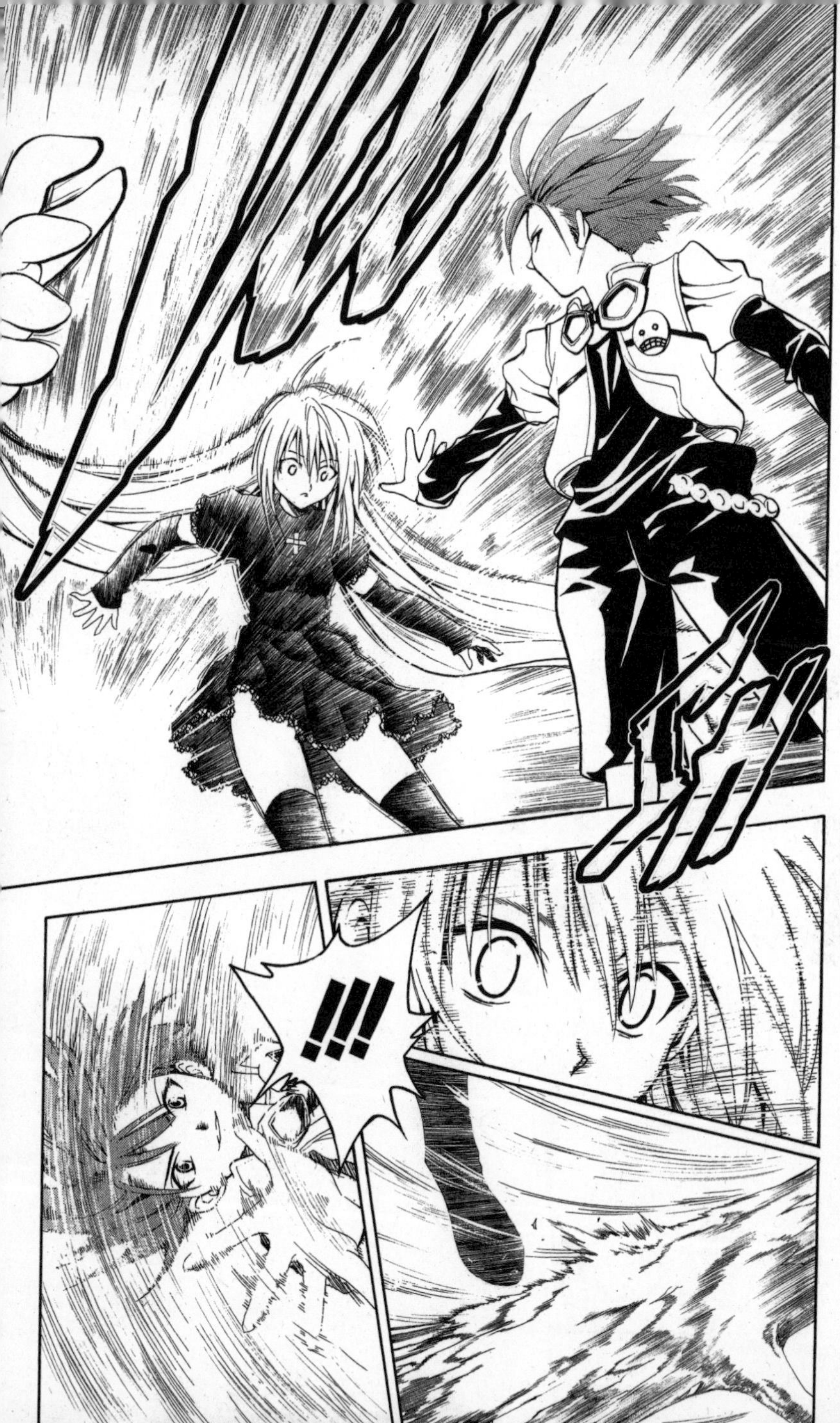
!!!

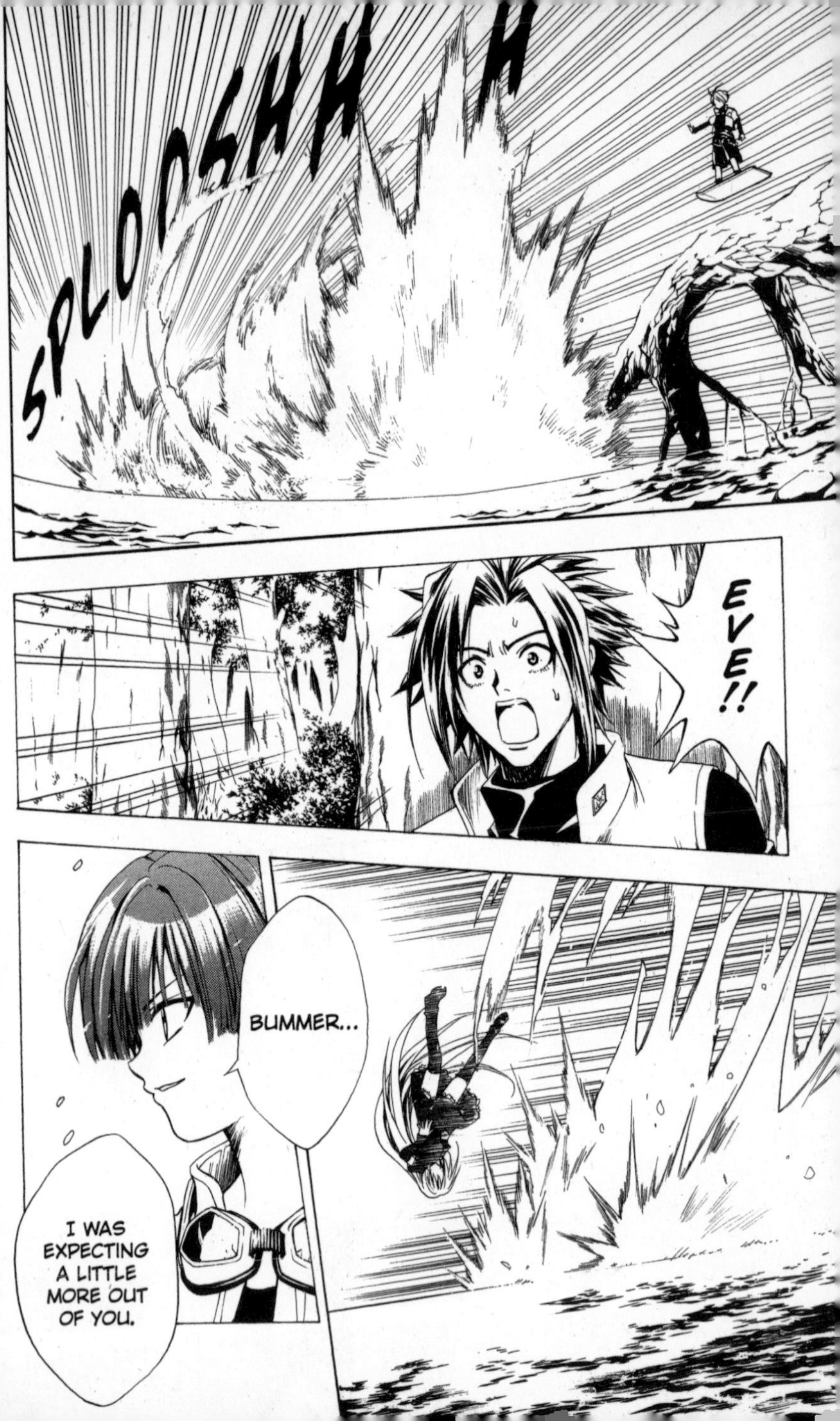
SPLOOSHHH
EVE!!
BUMMER...
I WAS EXPECTING A LITTLE MORE OUT OF YOU.

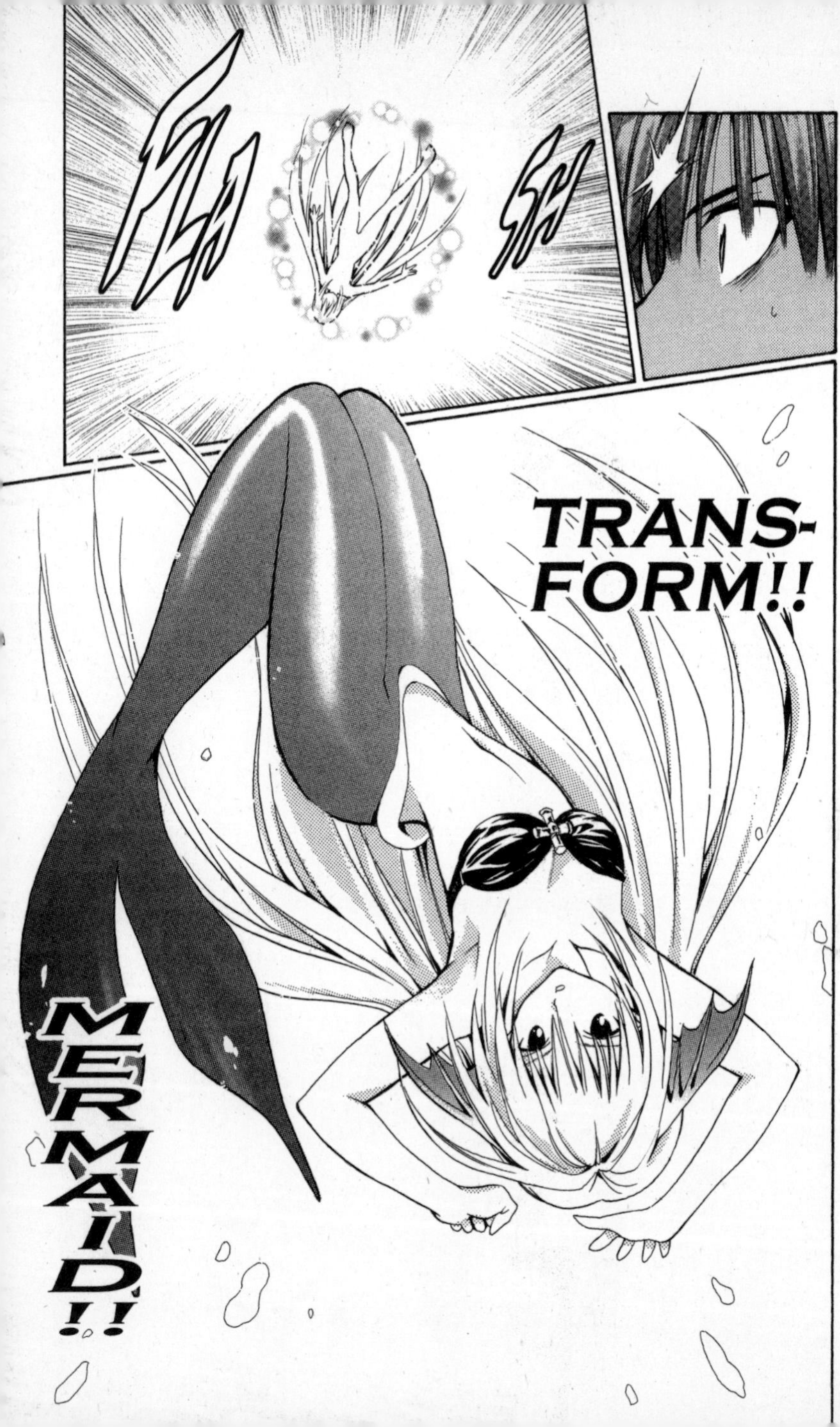
FLASH
TRANS-
FORM!!
MERMAID!!

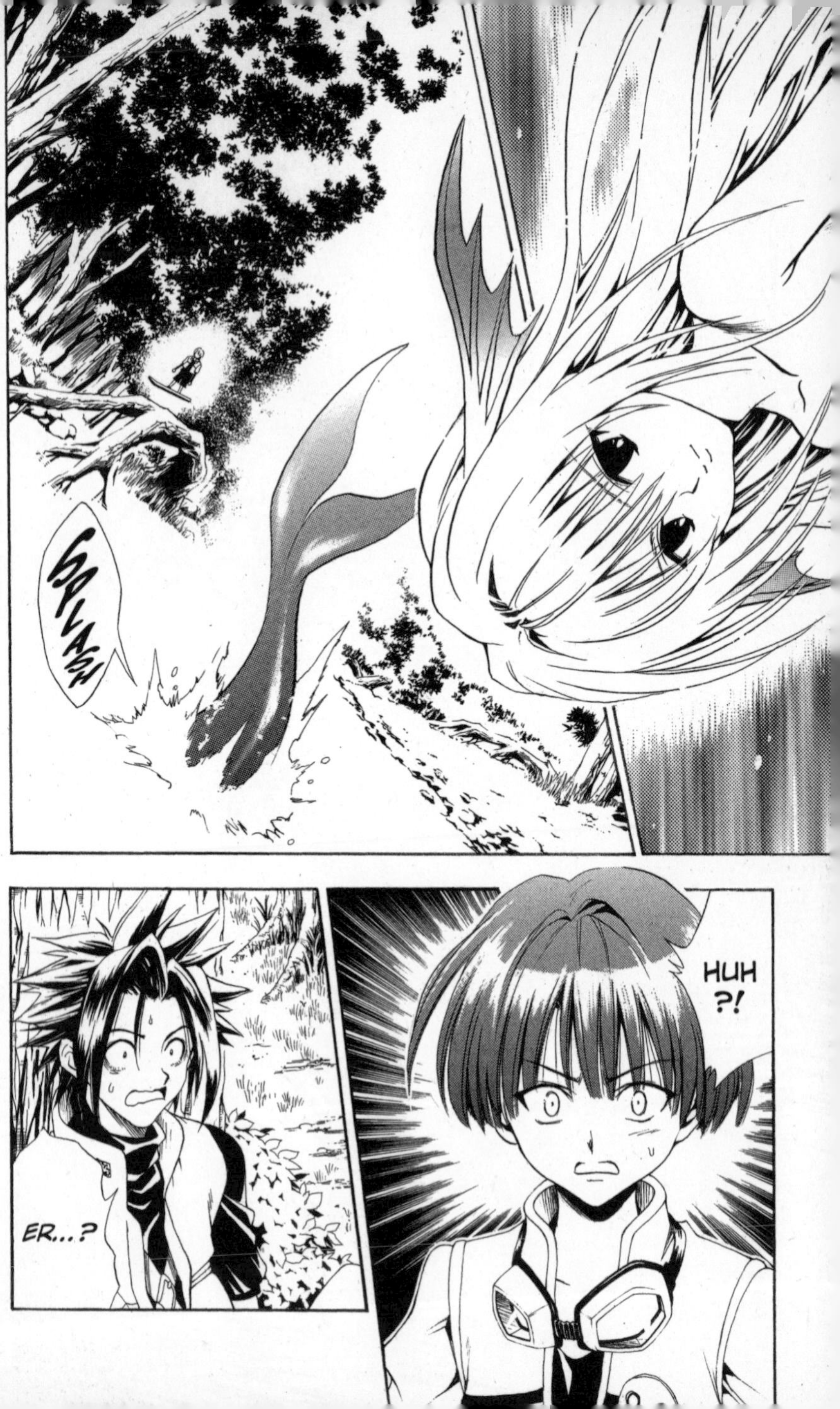
SPLASH
HUH ?!
ER...?

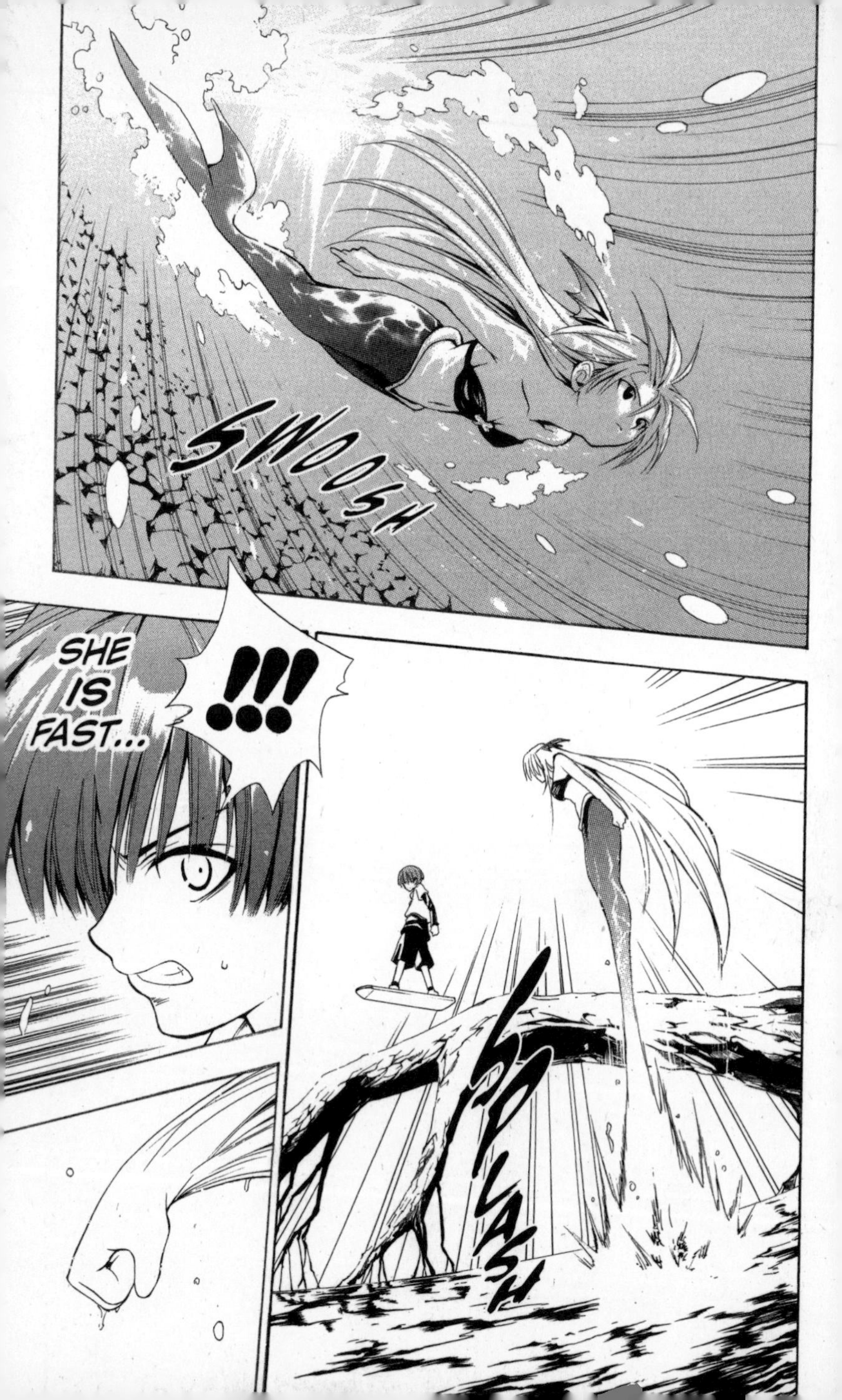
SWOOSH
SPLASH
!!!
SHE IS FAST...

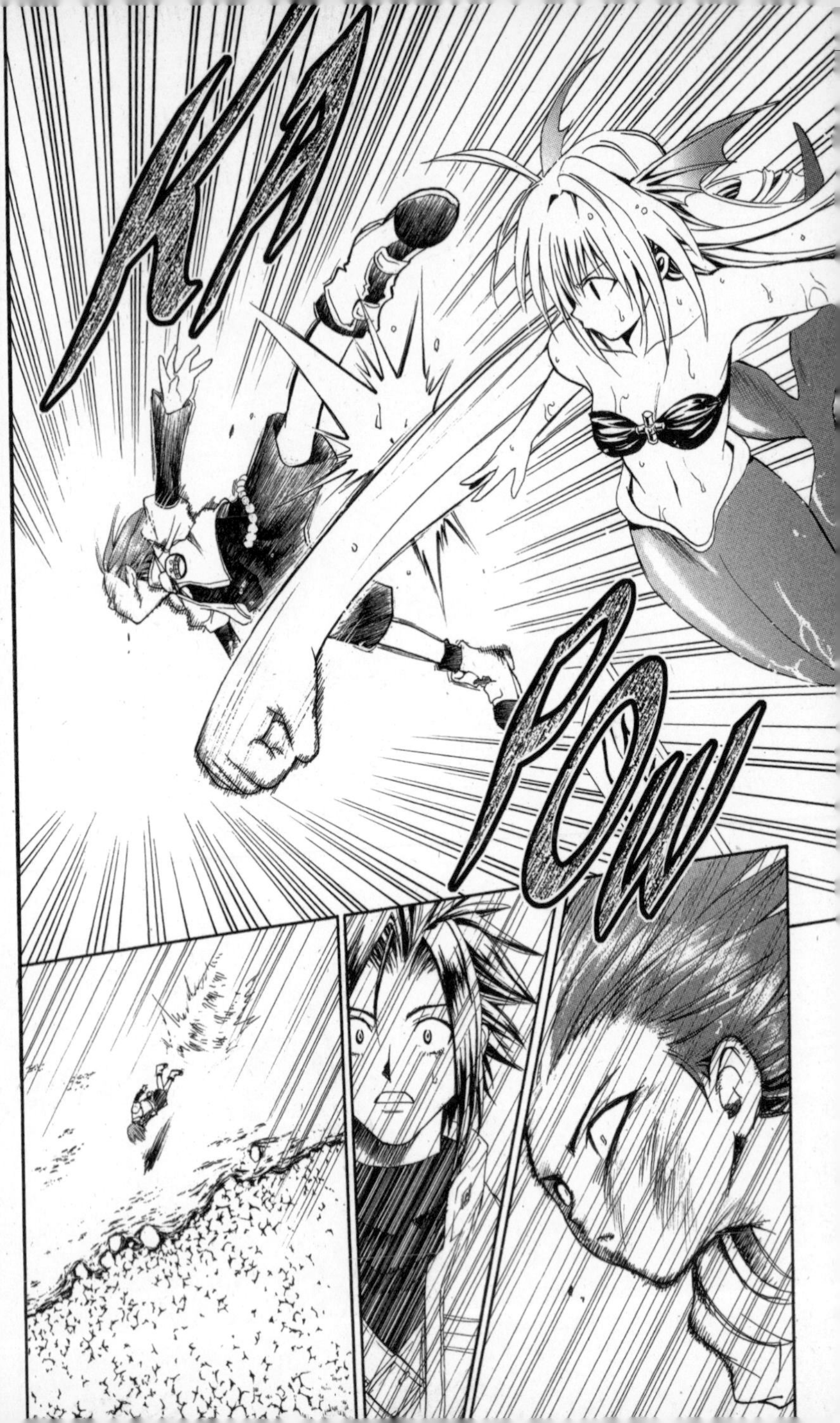
KA
POW

READ THIS WAY

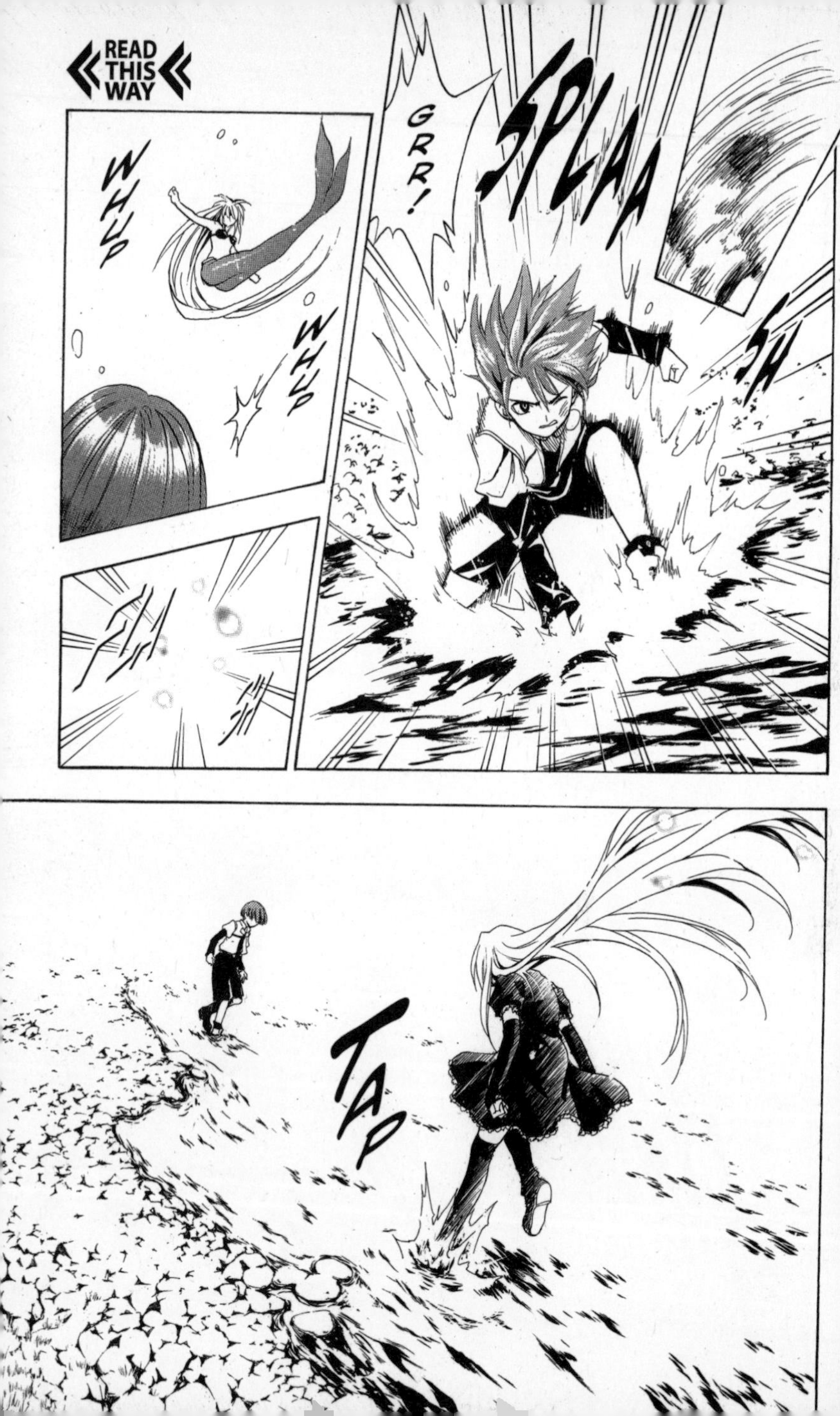
GRR!
SPLAAA
SH
WHUP
WHUP
TAP

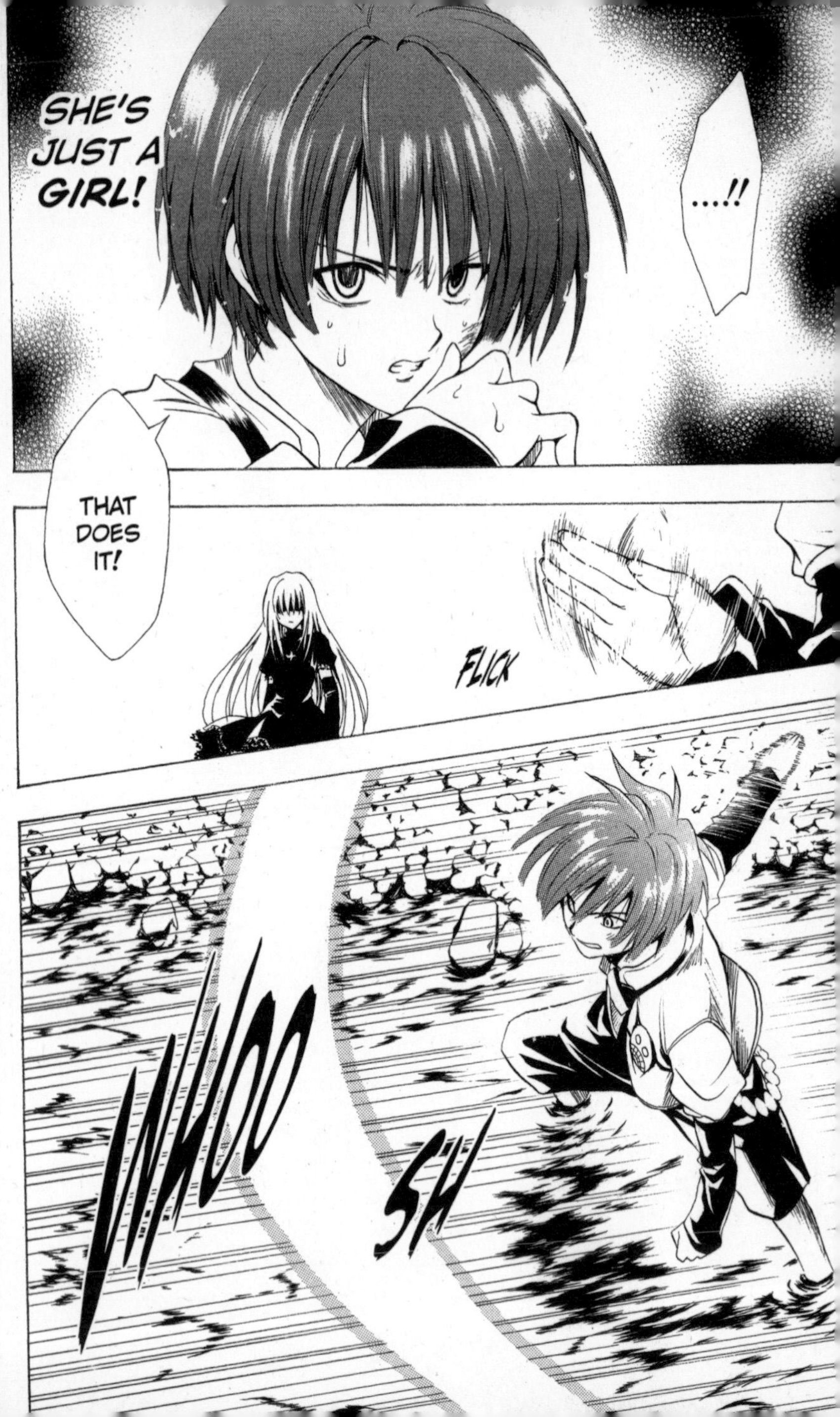
...!!
SHE'S JUST A GIRL!
THAT DOES IT!
FLICK
WHOOSH

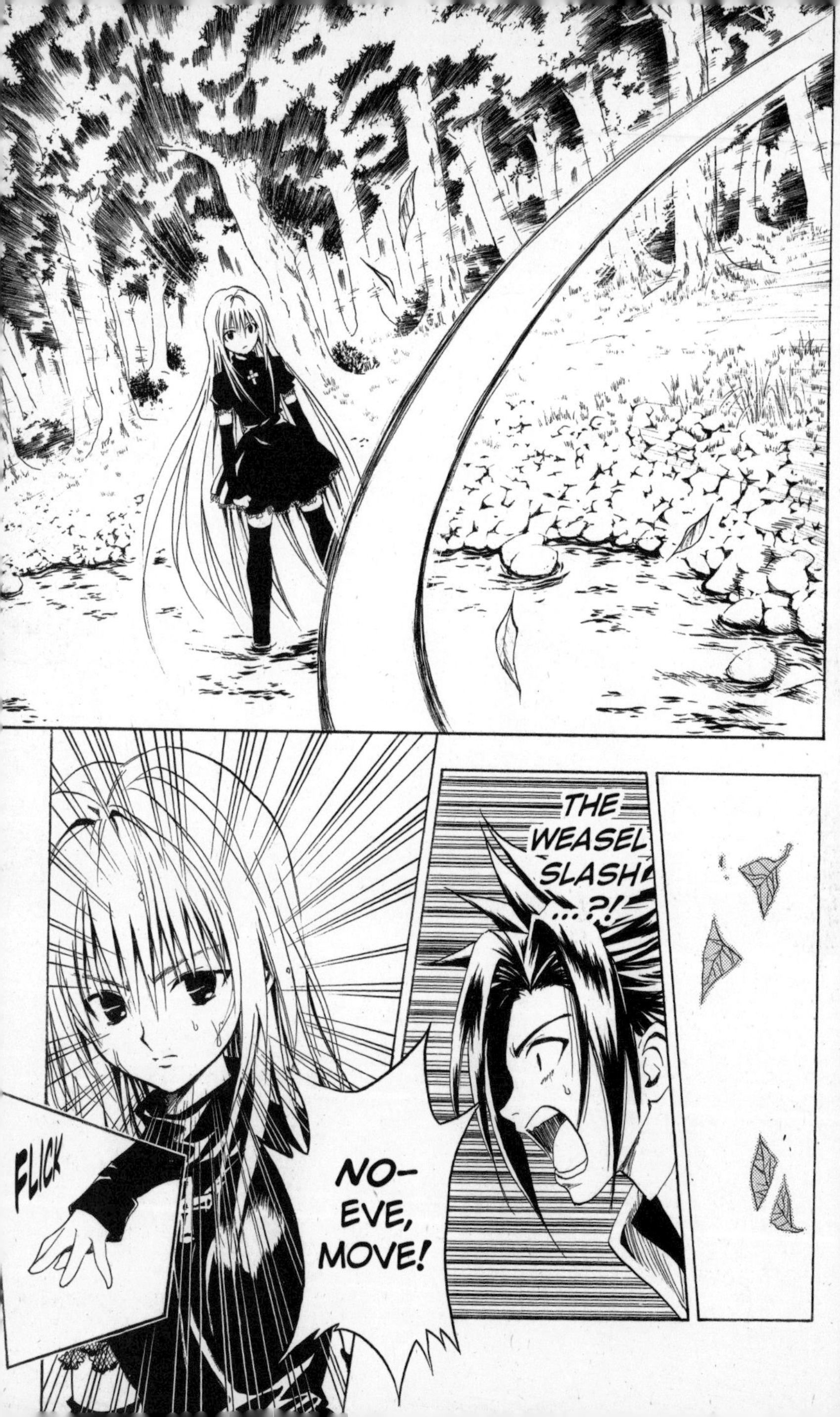
THE WEASEL SLASH ...?!
NO— EVE, MOVE!
FLICK

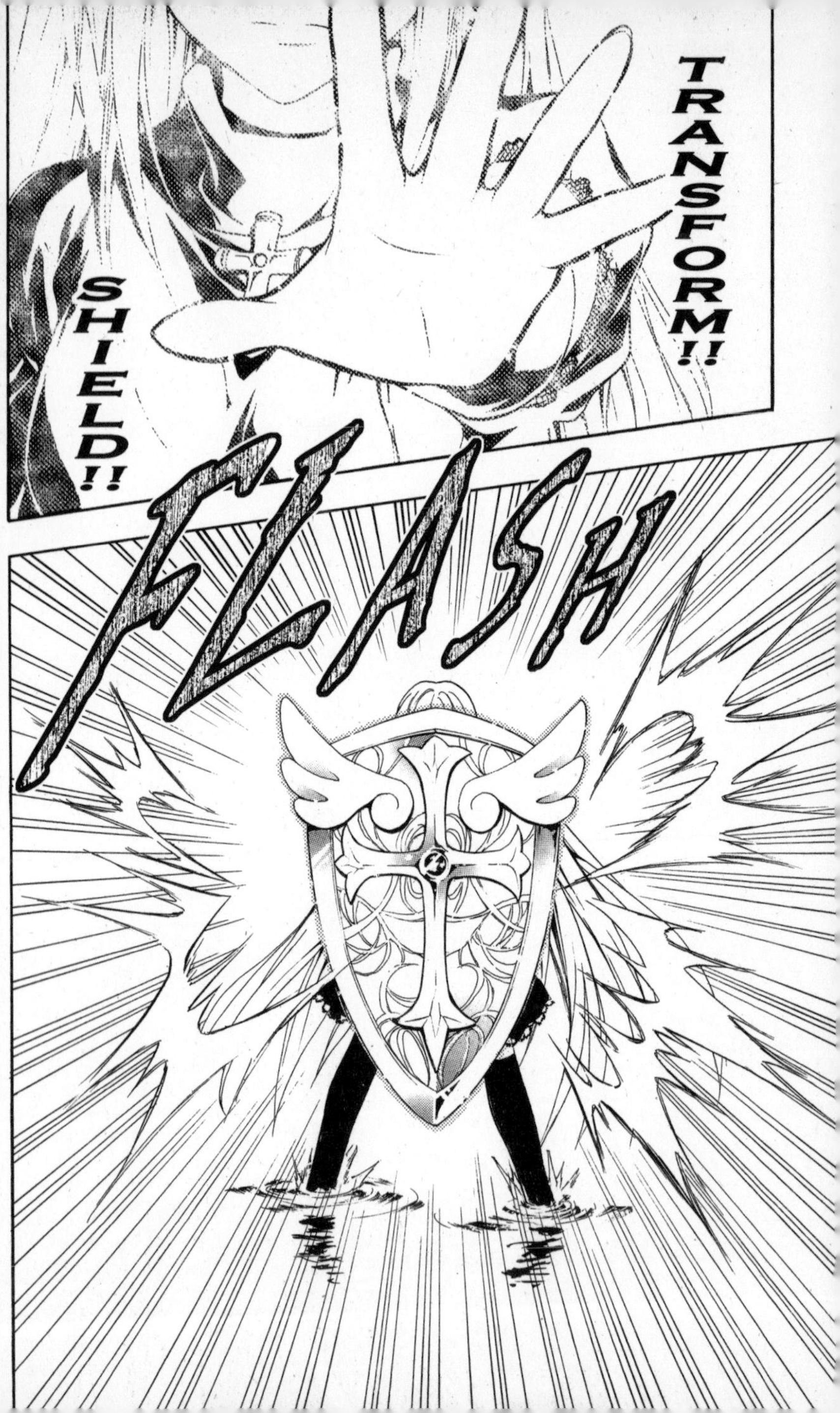
TRANSFORM!!
SHIELD!!
FLASH

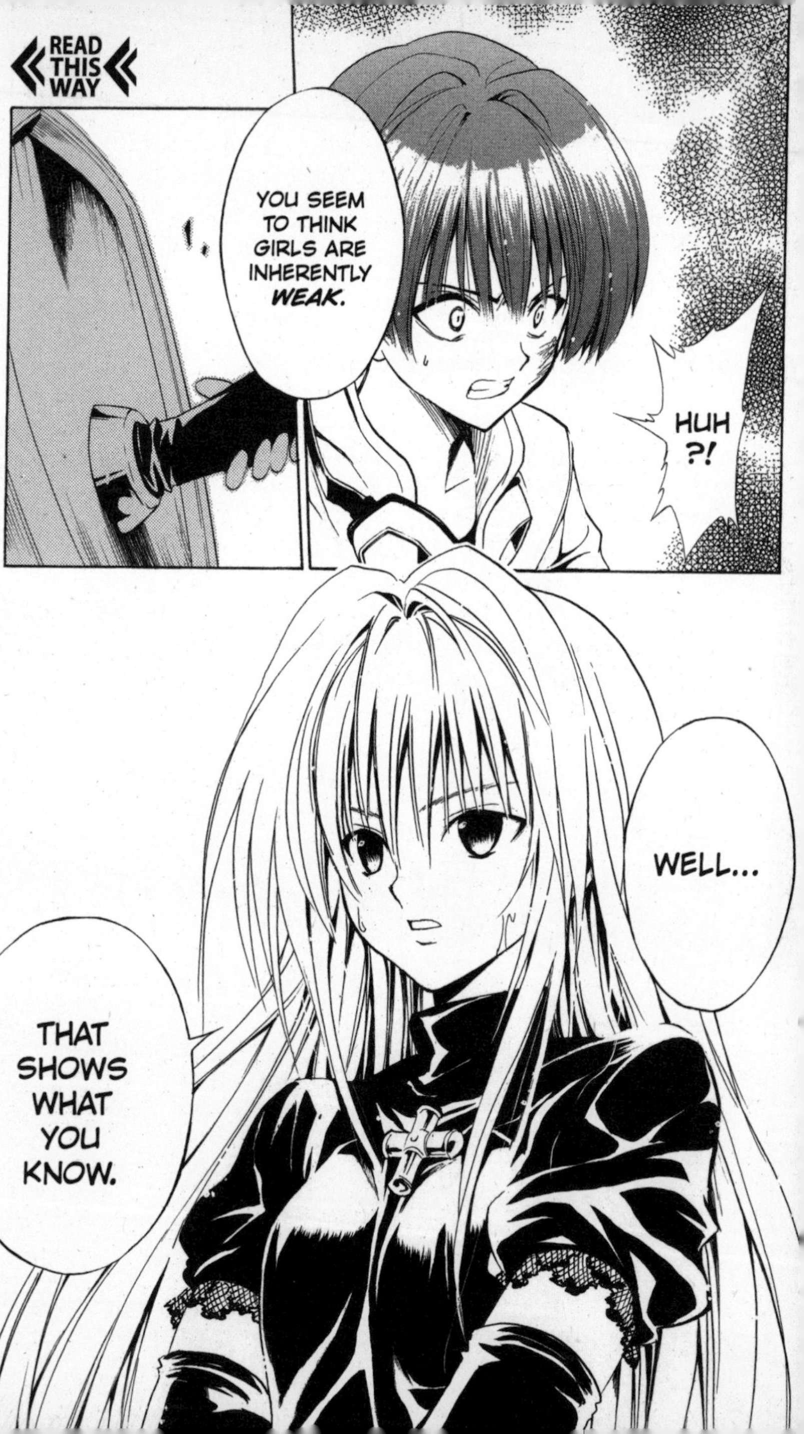
READ THIS WAY
YOU SEEM TO THINK GIRLS ARE INHERENTLY *WEAK.*
HUH ?!
WELL...
THAT SHOWS WHAT YOU KNOW.

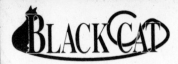

BLACK CAT FACTOID

TRANSFORM: MERMAID

EVE'S FIRST TOTAL TRANSFORMATION. WELL, SHE DID PRACTICE IT SEVERAL TIMES BEFORE SHE TRIED IT OUT IN BATTLE. SO THIS IS HER FIRST TOTAL TRANSFORMATION ***IN BATTLE.*** (CLOTHES ARE BURDENSOME UNDER WATER, SO SHE DISASSEMBLED HER ATOMS AND FORMED A NEW BODY WITH FINS.)

TRANS-FORM!!
MERMAID!!

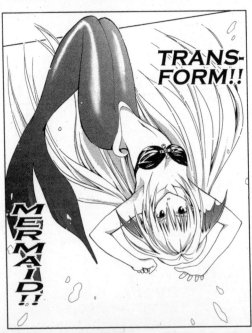

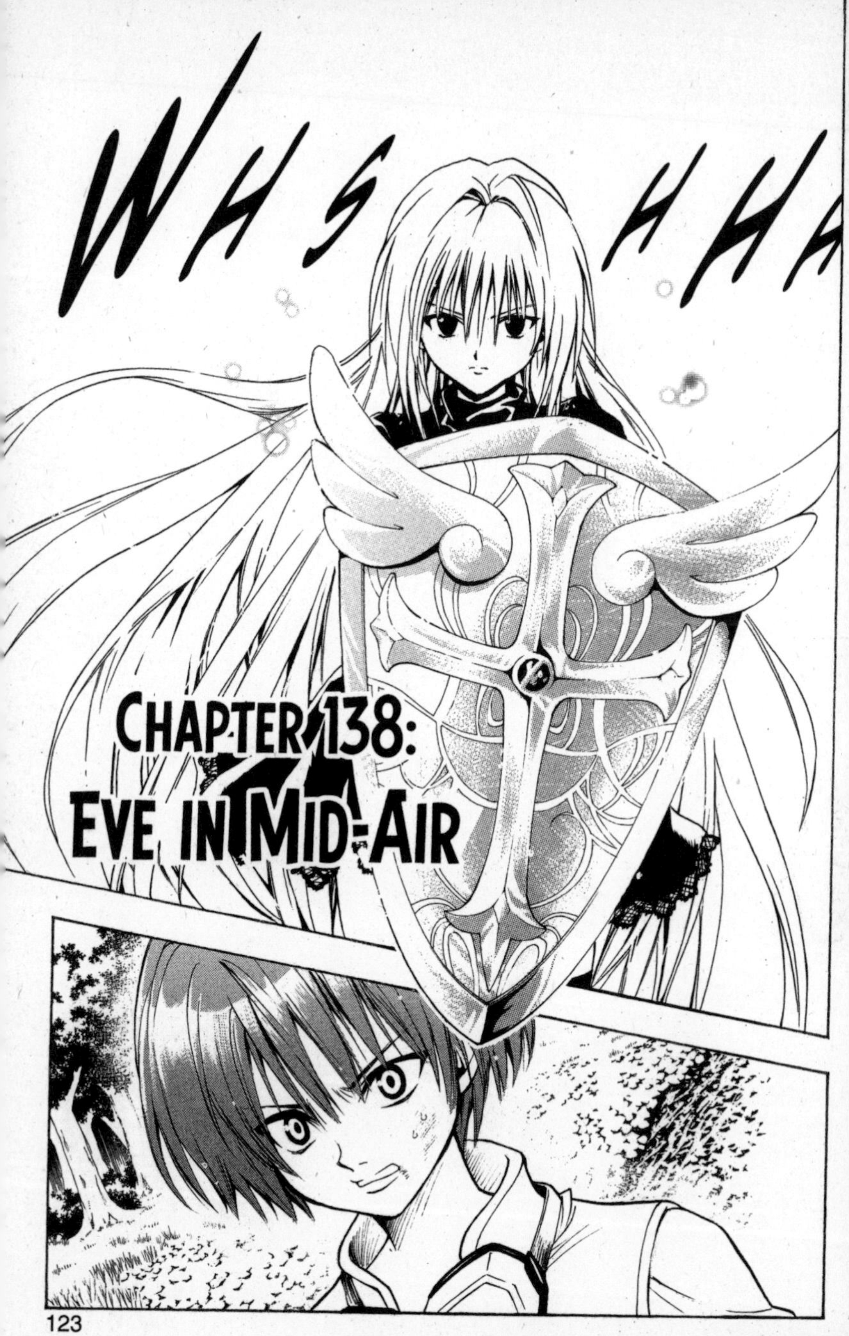
WHSHHH
CHAPTER 138:
EVE IN MID-AIR

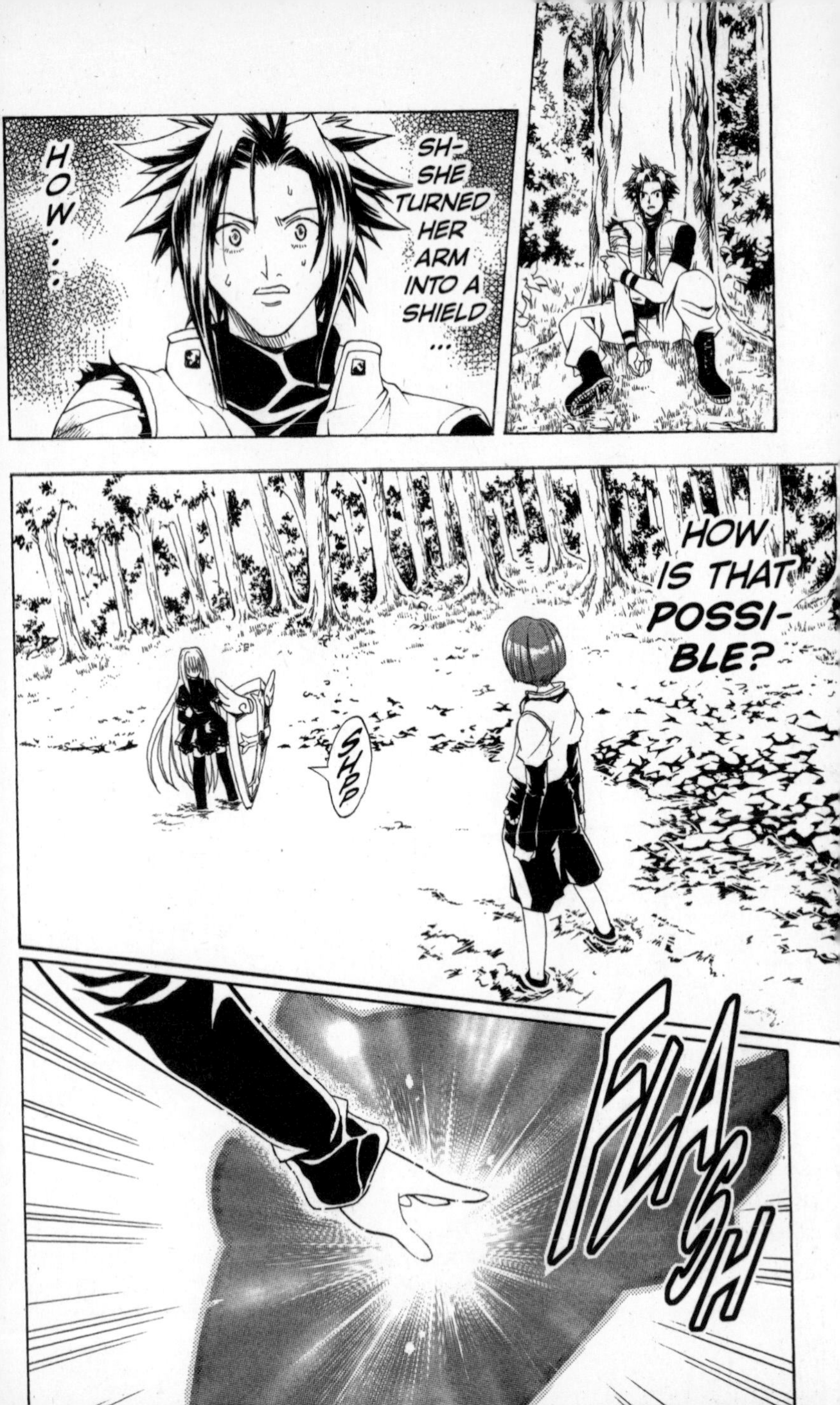
SH-SHE TURNED HER ARM INTO A SHIELD...
HOW...
HOW IS THAT POSSI-BLE?
SHPP
FLASH

READ THIS WAY

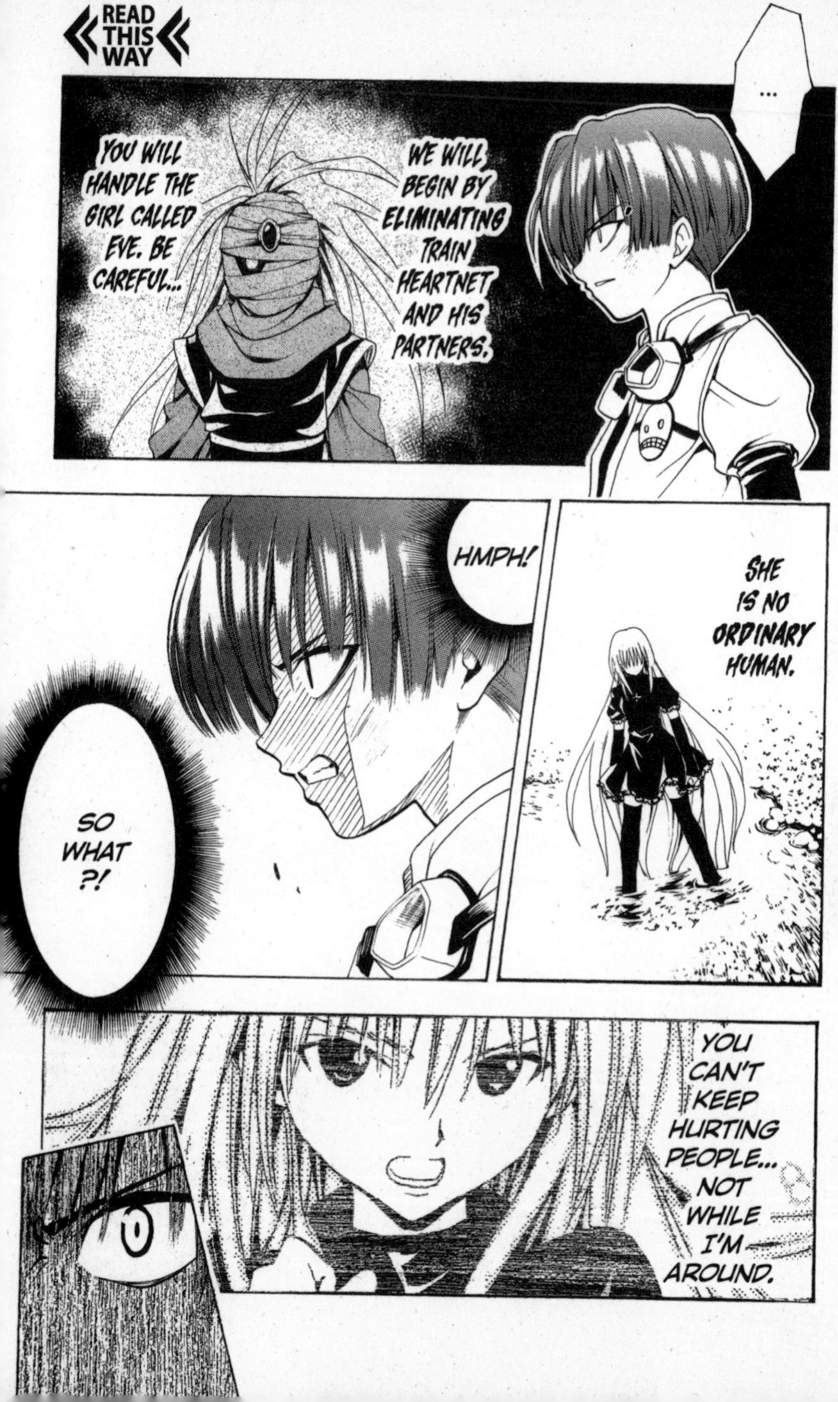
...
WE WILL BEGIN BY ELIMINATING TRAIN HEARTNET AND HIS PARTNERS.
YOU WILL HANDLE THE GIRL CALLED EVE. BE CAREFUL...
SHE IS NO ORDINARY HUMAN.
HMPH!
SO WHAT?!
YOU CAN'T KEEP HURTING PEOPLE... NOT WHILE I'M AROUND.

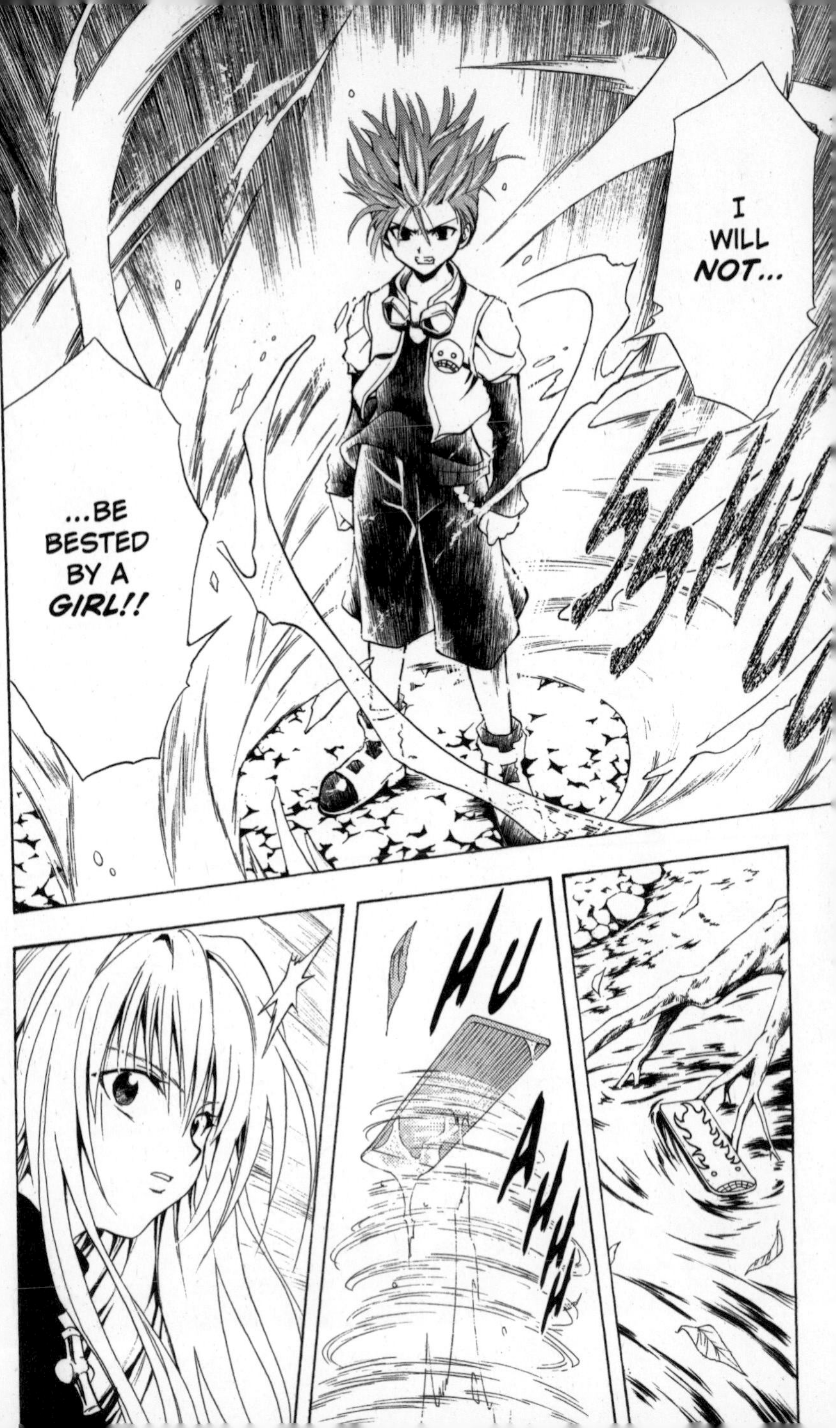
I WILL NOT...
...BE BESTED BY A GIRL!!

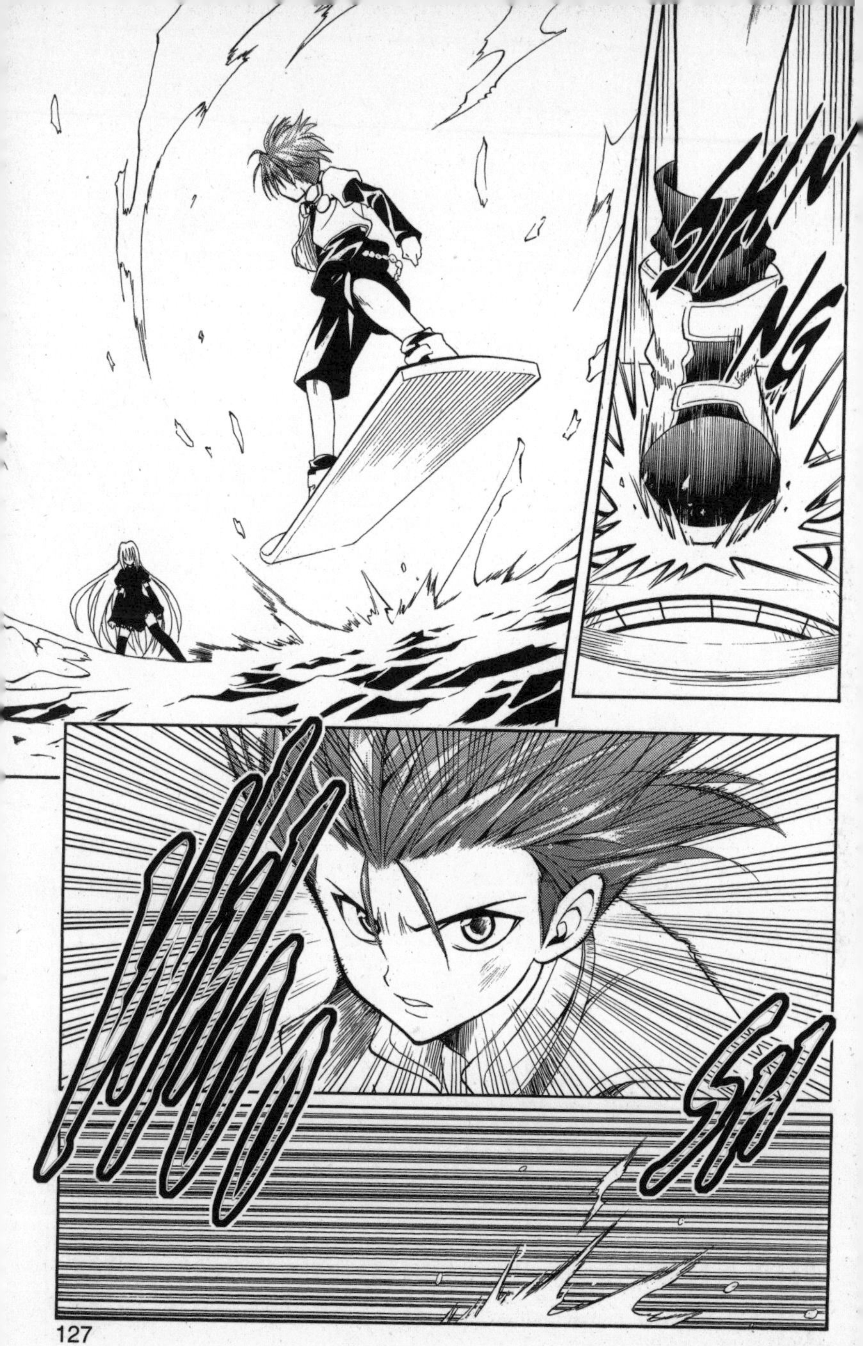

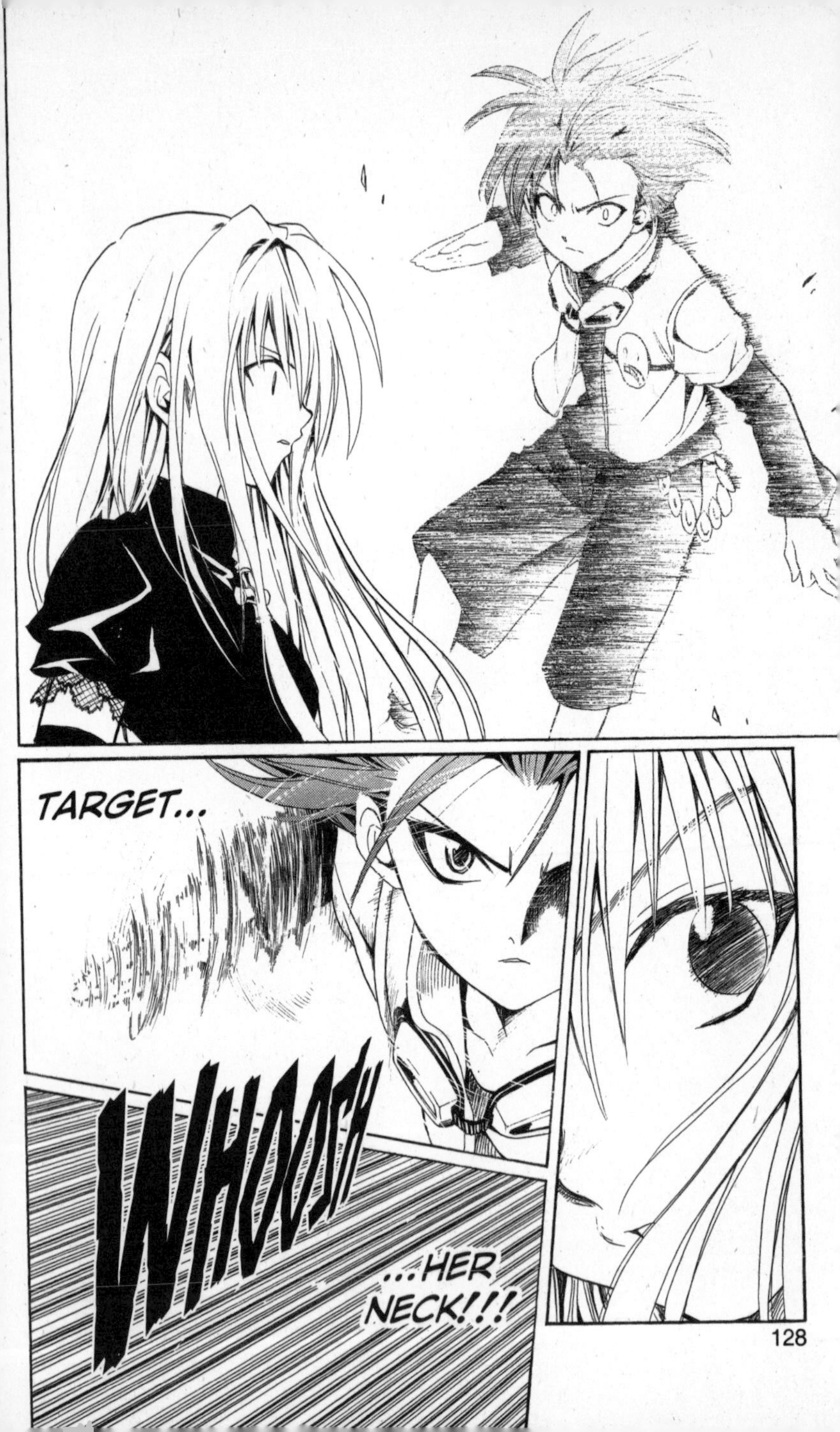
TARGET...
WHOOSH
...HER NECK!!!

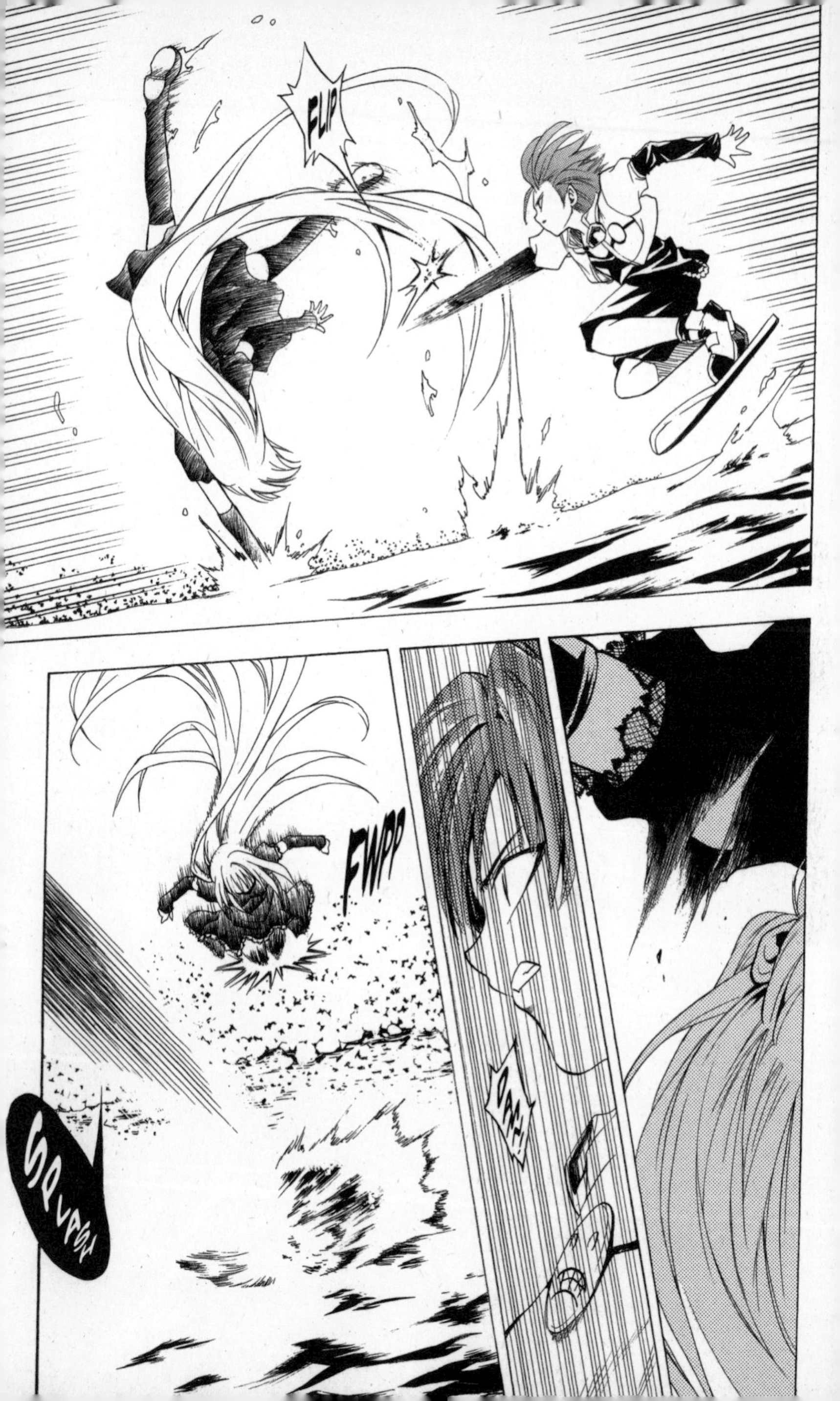
FLIP
FWPP
SPLASH

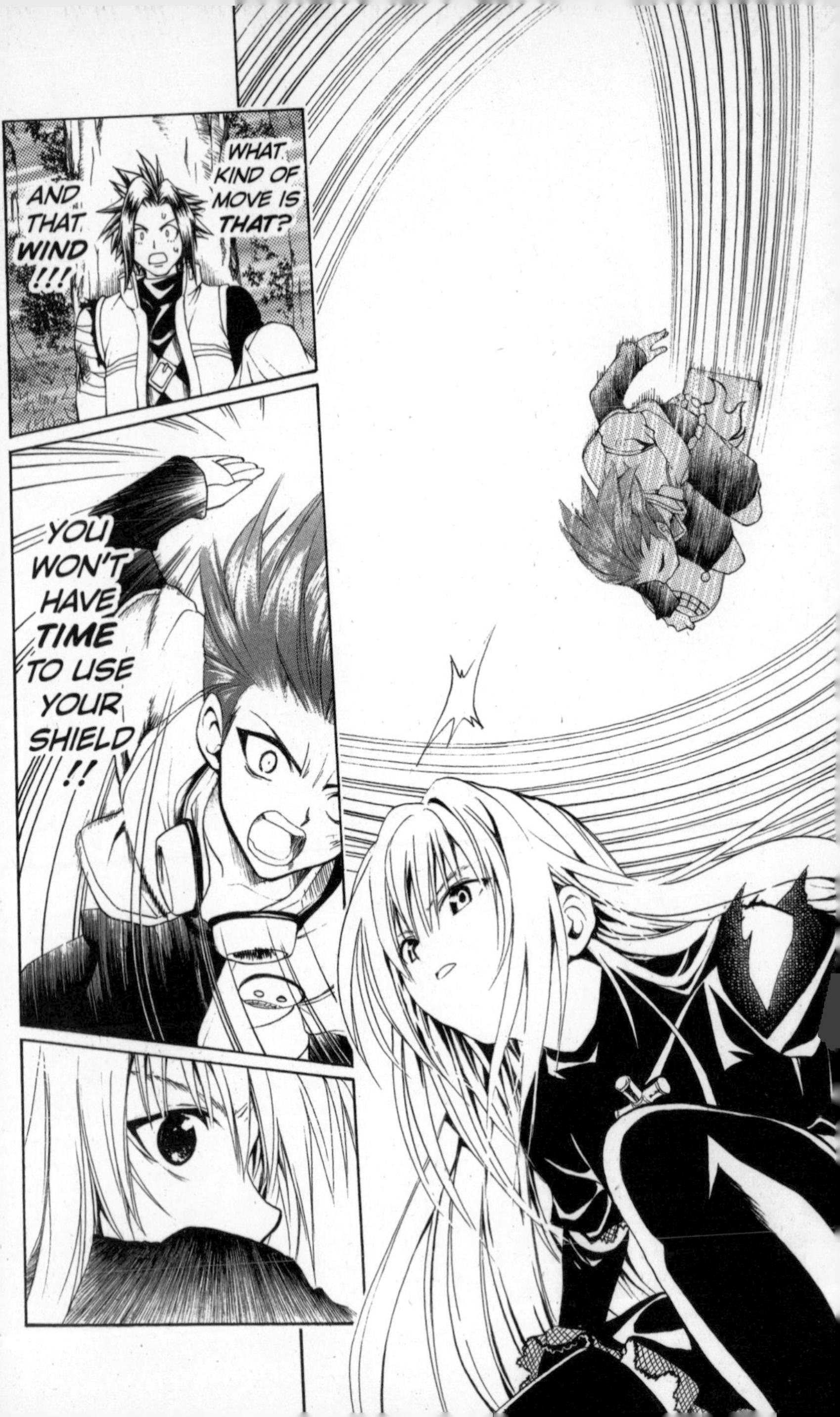
WHAT KIND OF MOVE IS THAT?
AND THAT WIND !!!
YOU WON'T HAVE TIME TO USE YOUR SHIELD !!

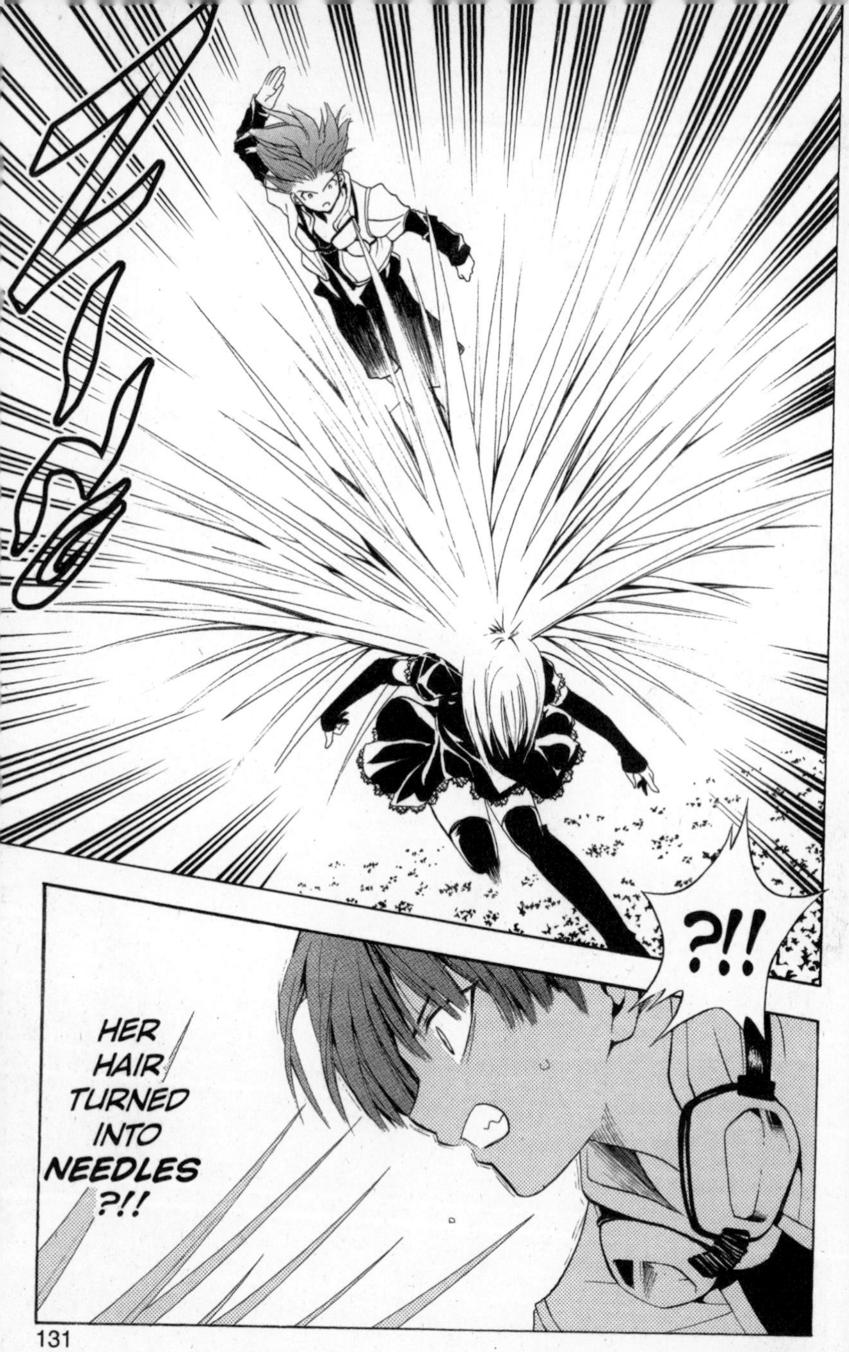
?!!
HER HAIR TURNED INTO NEEDLES ?!!

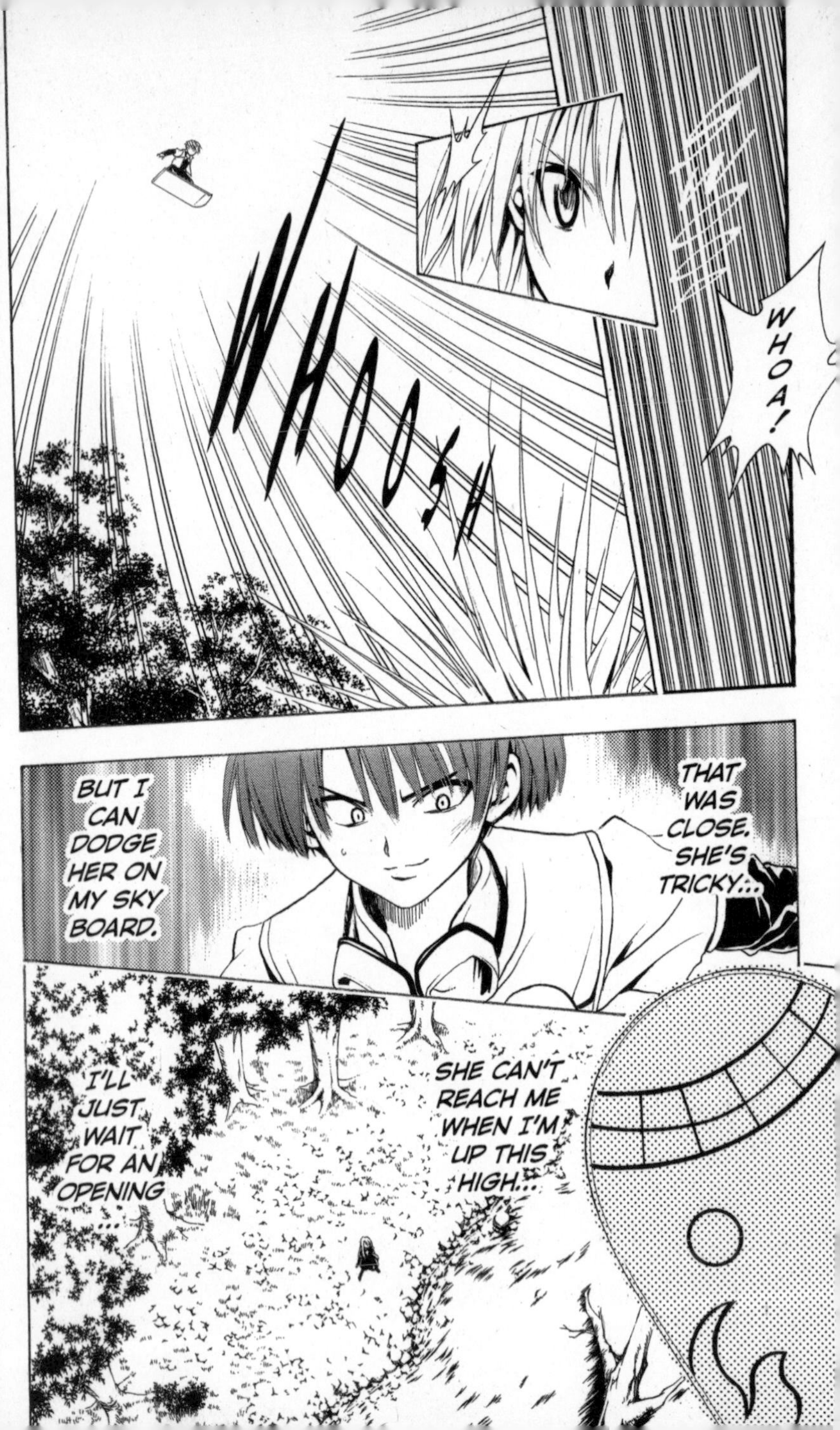
WHOOSH
WHOA!
THAT WAS CLOSE. SHE'S TRICKY...
BUT I CAN DODGE HER ON MY SKY BOARD.
SHE CAN'T REACH ME WHEN I'M UP THIS HIGH...
I'LL JUST WAIT FOR AN OPENING...

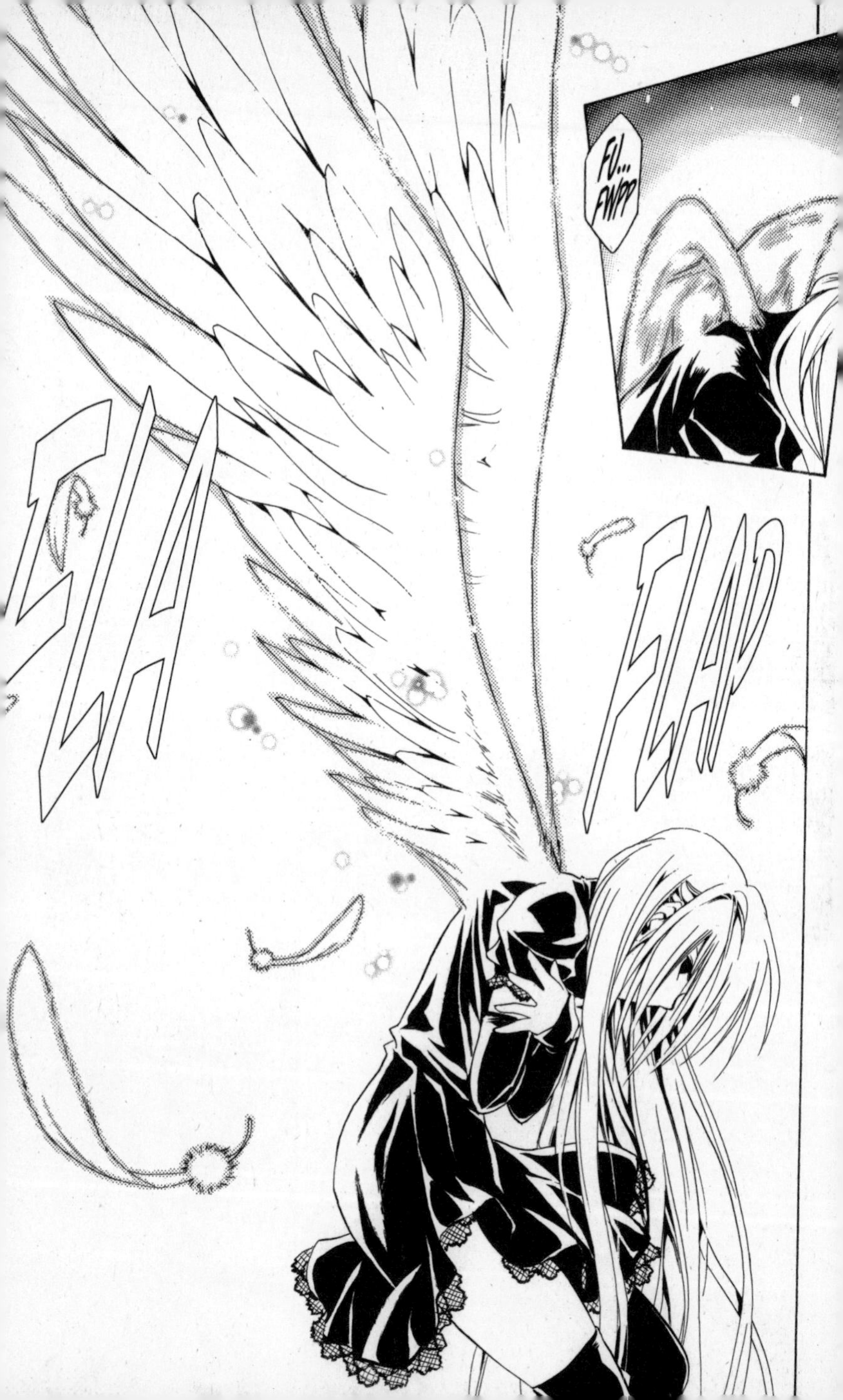
FU... FWPP
FLAP
FLA

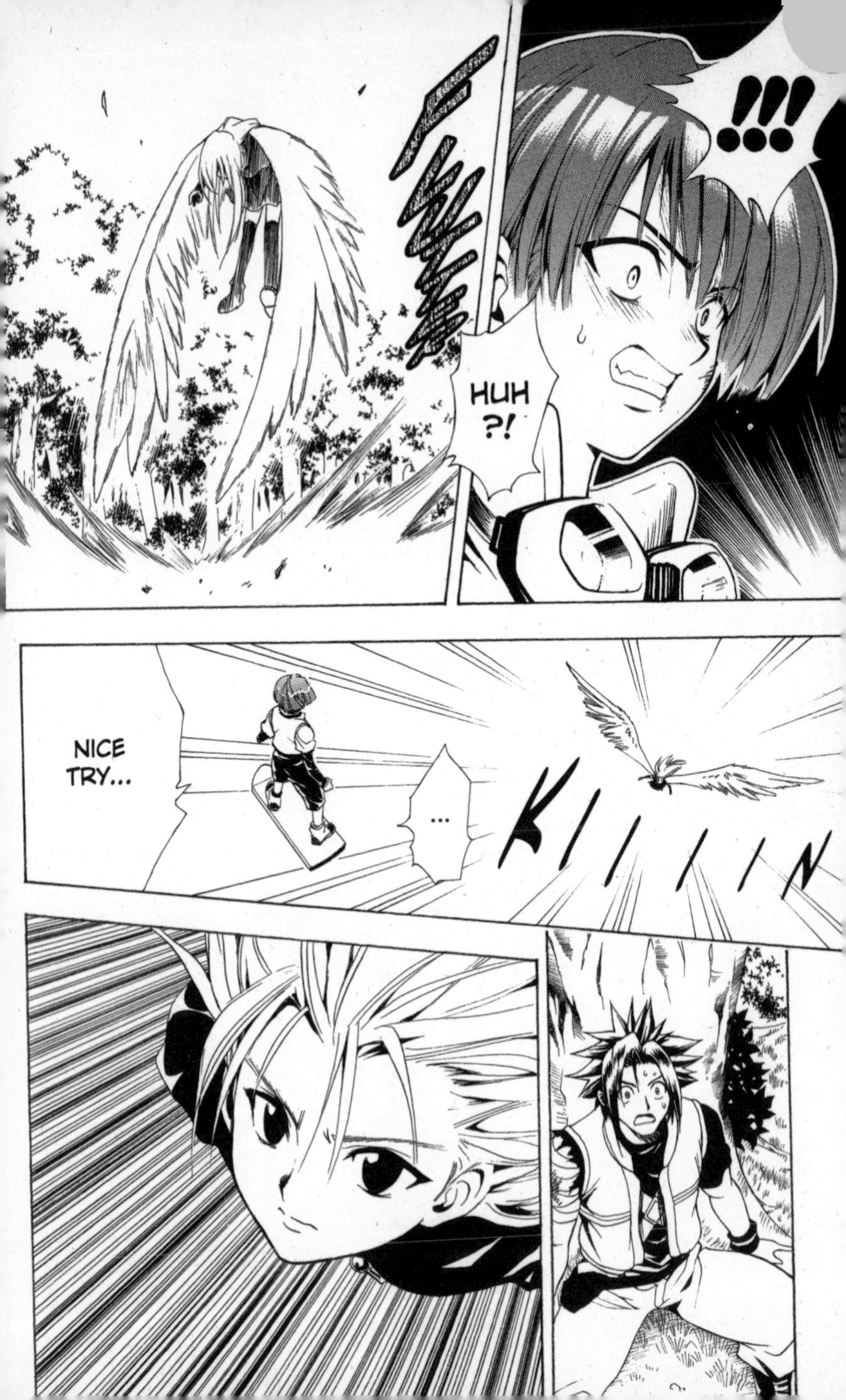
!!!
HUH ?!
...
NICE TRY...
KIIIIN

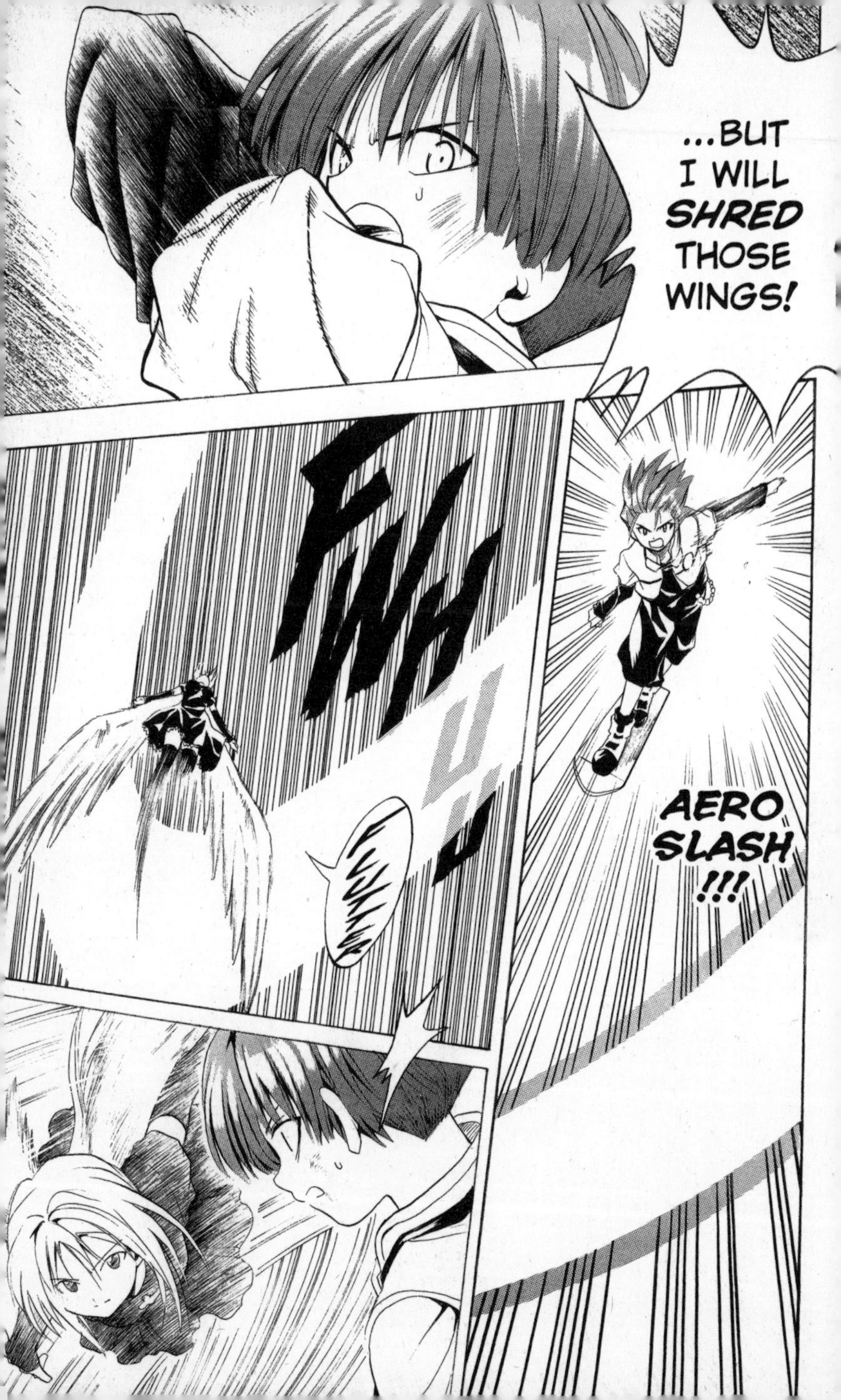
...BUT I WILL SHRED THOSE WINGS!
AERO SLASH!!!

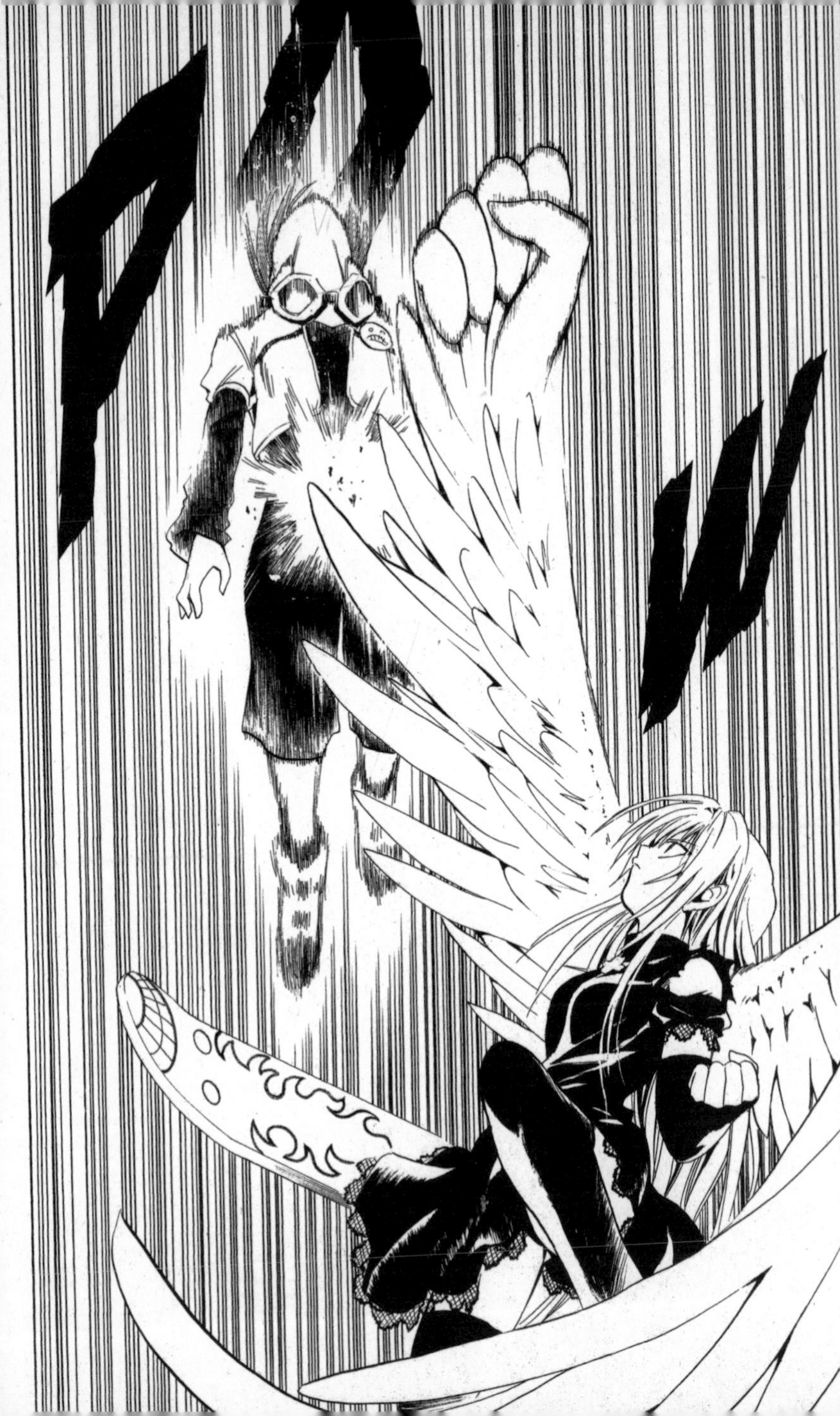

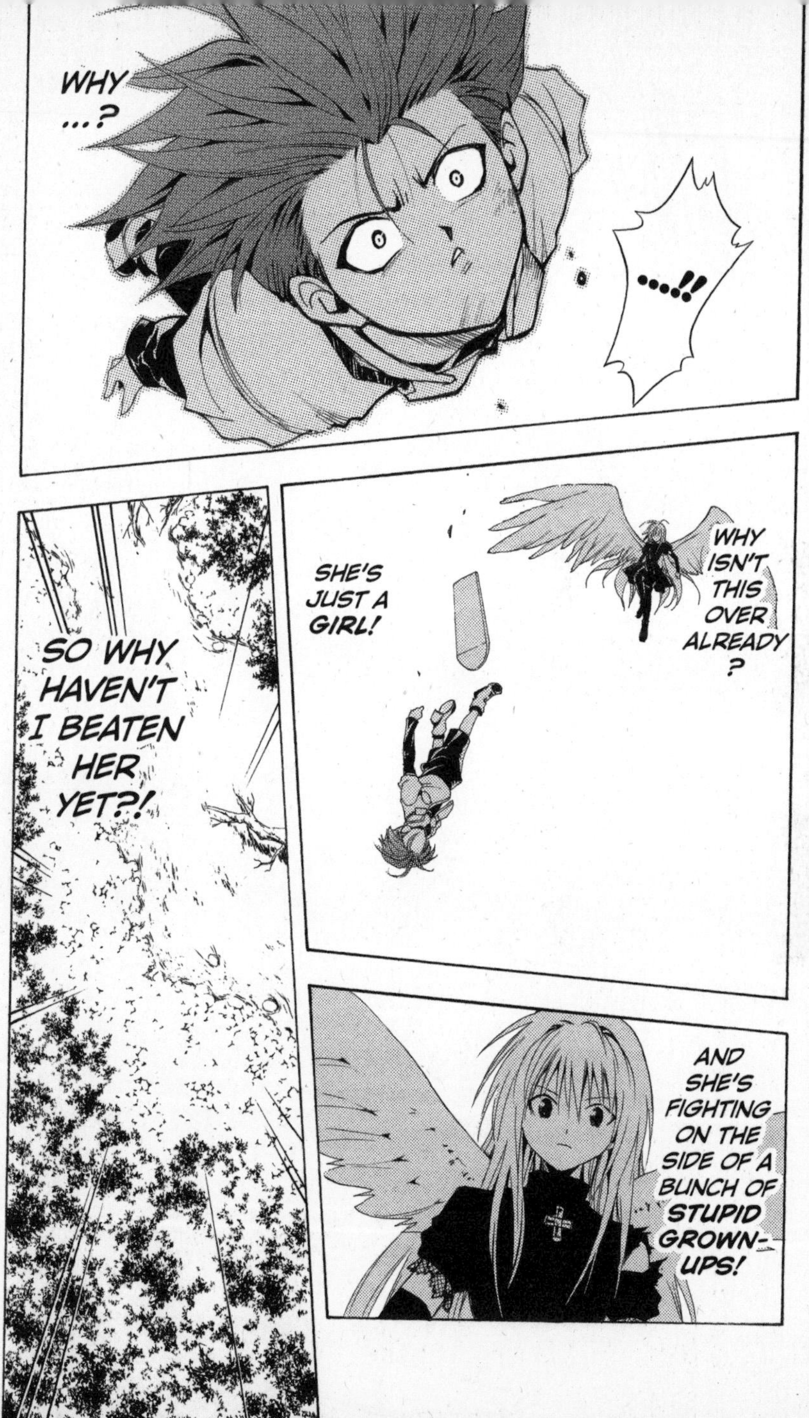

...!!
WHY ...?
WHY ISN'T THIS OVER ALREADY?
SHE'S JUST A GIRL!
AND SHE'S FIGHTING ON THE SIDE OF A BUNCH OF STUPID GROWN-UPS!
SO WHY HAVEN'T I BEATEN HER YET?!

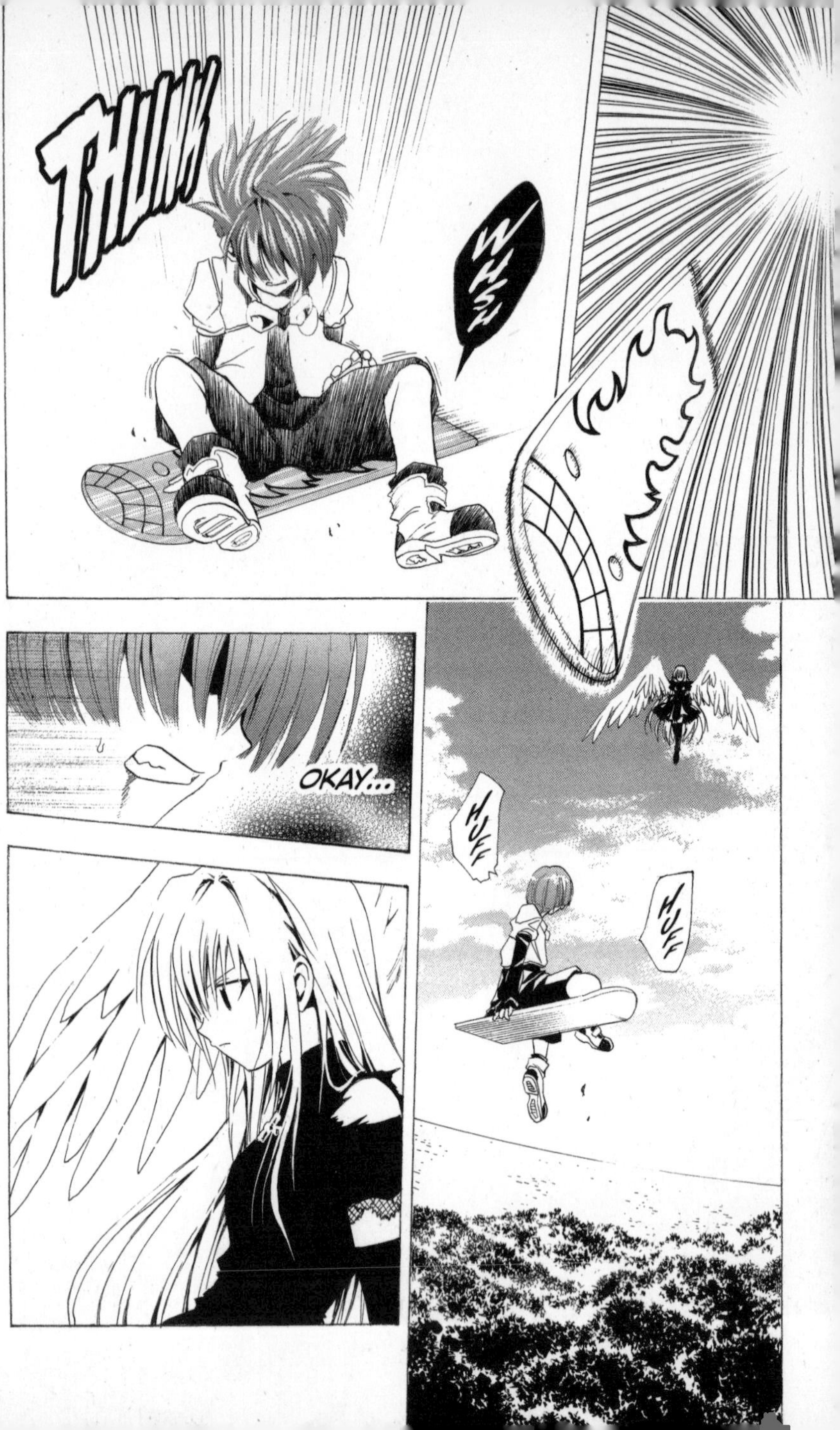
THUNK
WHSH
HUFF
HUFF
OKAY...

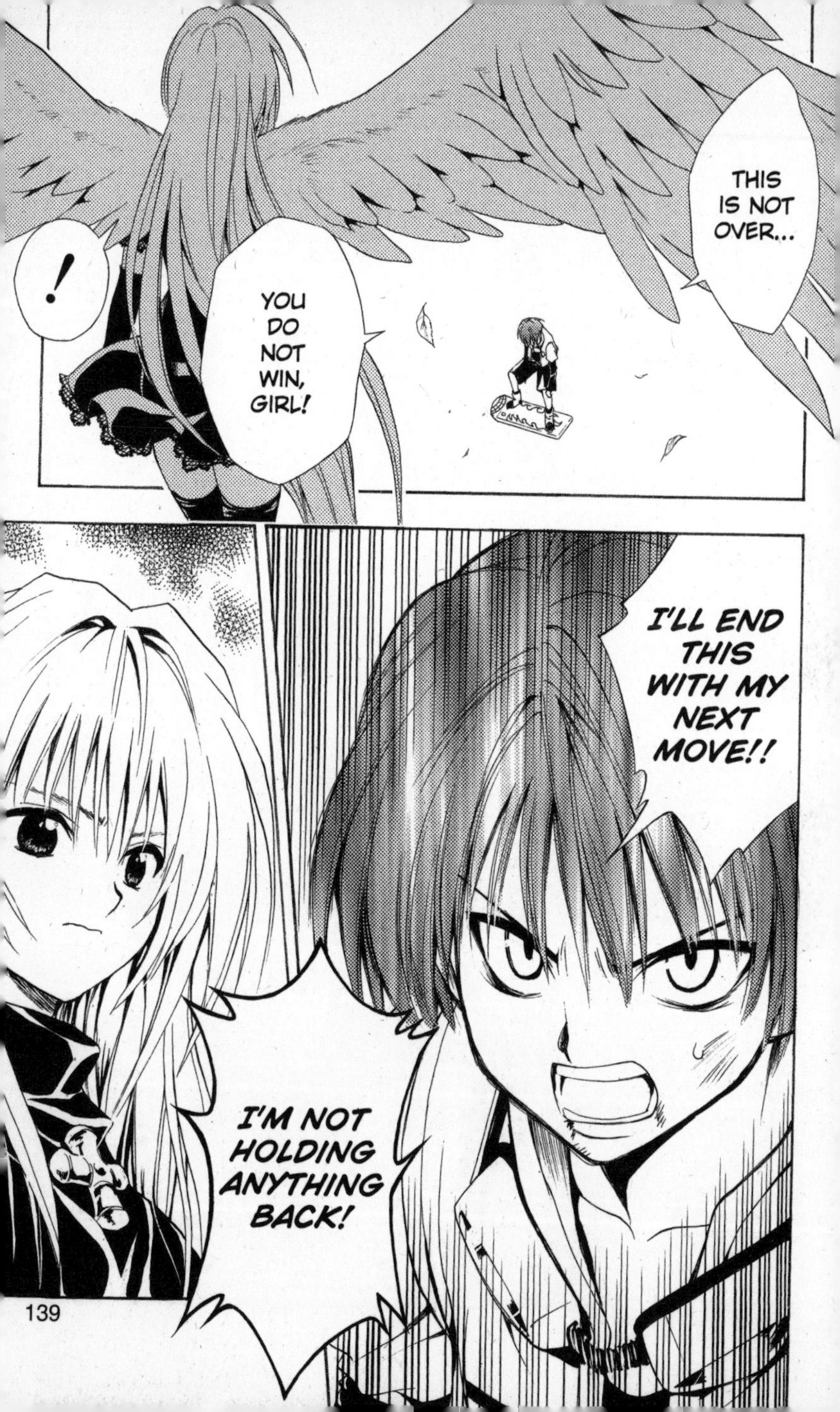
THIS IS NOT OVER...
YOU DO NOT WIN, GIRL!
!
I'LL END THIS WITH MY NEXT MOVE!!
I'M NOT HOLDING ANYTHING BACK!

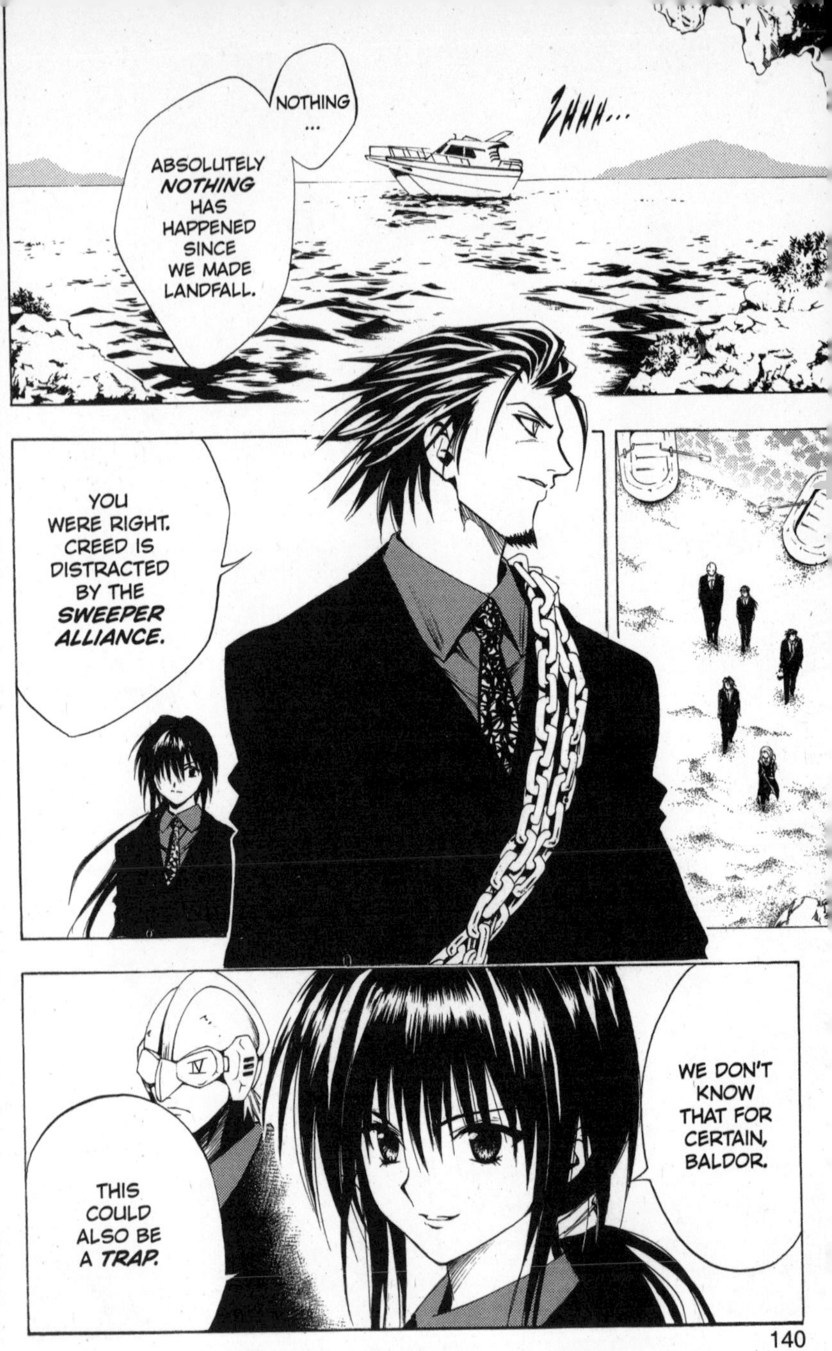

ZHHH...
NOTHING ... ABSOLUTELY ***NOTHING*** HAS HAPPENED SINCE WE MADE LANDFALL.
YOU WERE RIGHT. CREED IS DISTRACTED BY THE ***SWEEPER ALLIANCE.***
WE DON'T KNOW THAT FOR CERTAIN, BALDOR.
THIS COULD ALSO BE A ***TRAP.***

READ THIS WAY

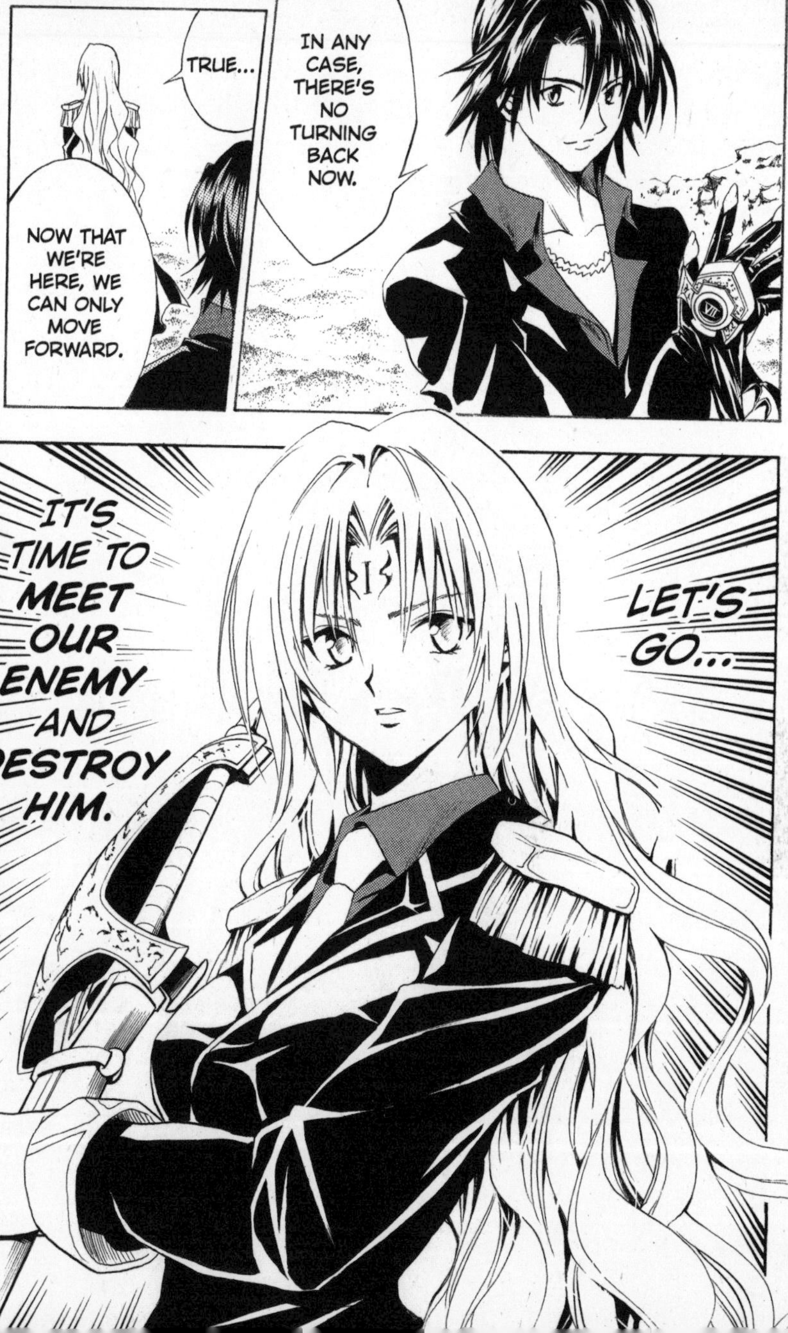
IN ANY CASE, THERE'S NO TURNING BACK NOW.
TRUE...
NOW THAT WE'RE HERE, WE CAN ONLY MOVE FORWARD.
LET'S GO...
IT'S TIME TO MEET OUR ENEMY AND DESTROY HIM.

THIS IS A ROUGH DRAFT OF THE CHAPTER 137 TITLE PAGE. I INTENDED TO SURROUND EVE WITH GUNS AND GRENADES—EVEN THOUGH SHE'S A CHILD, SHE'S STILL A SWEEPER, AFTER ALL—BUT IT LOOKED CREEPIER THAN I THOUGHT IT WOULD, SO I CHANGED IT.

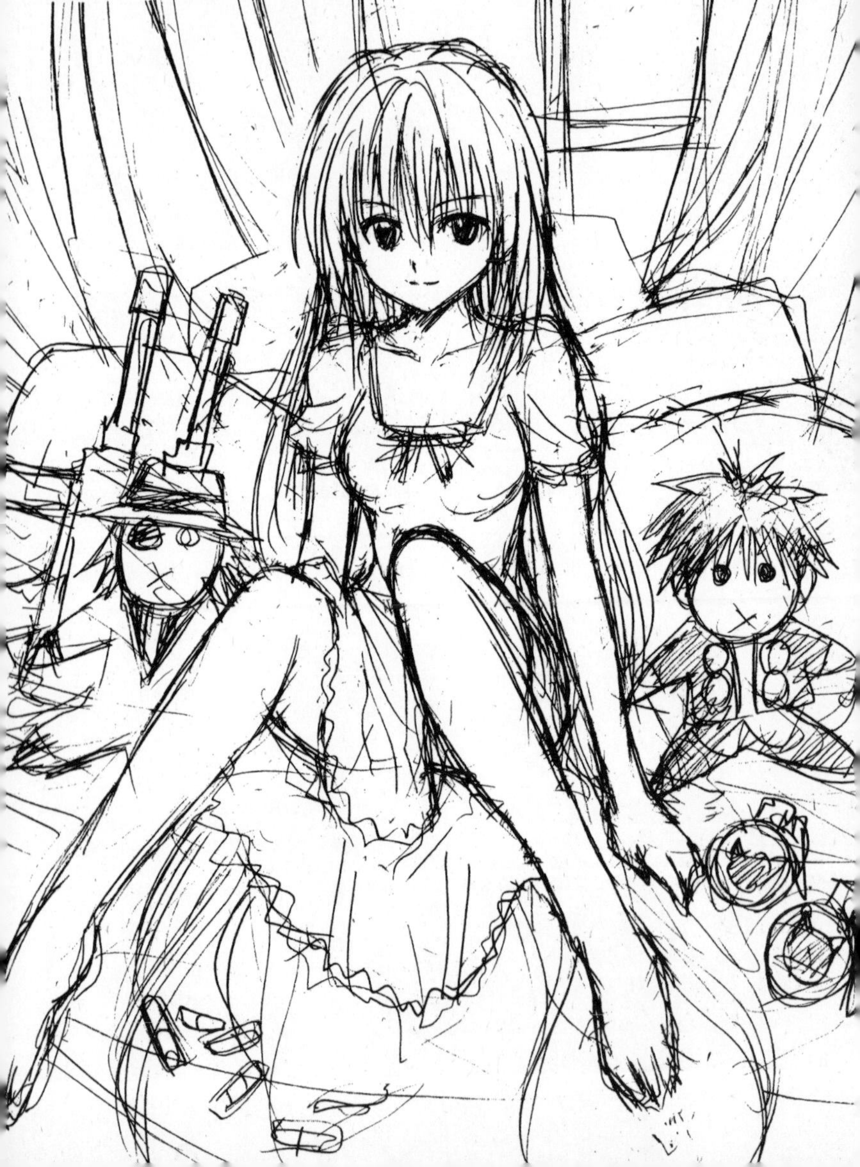

Chapter 139: Deadly Whirlwind

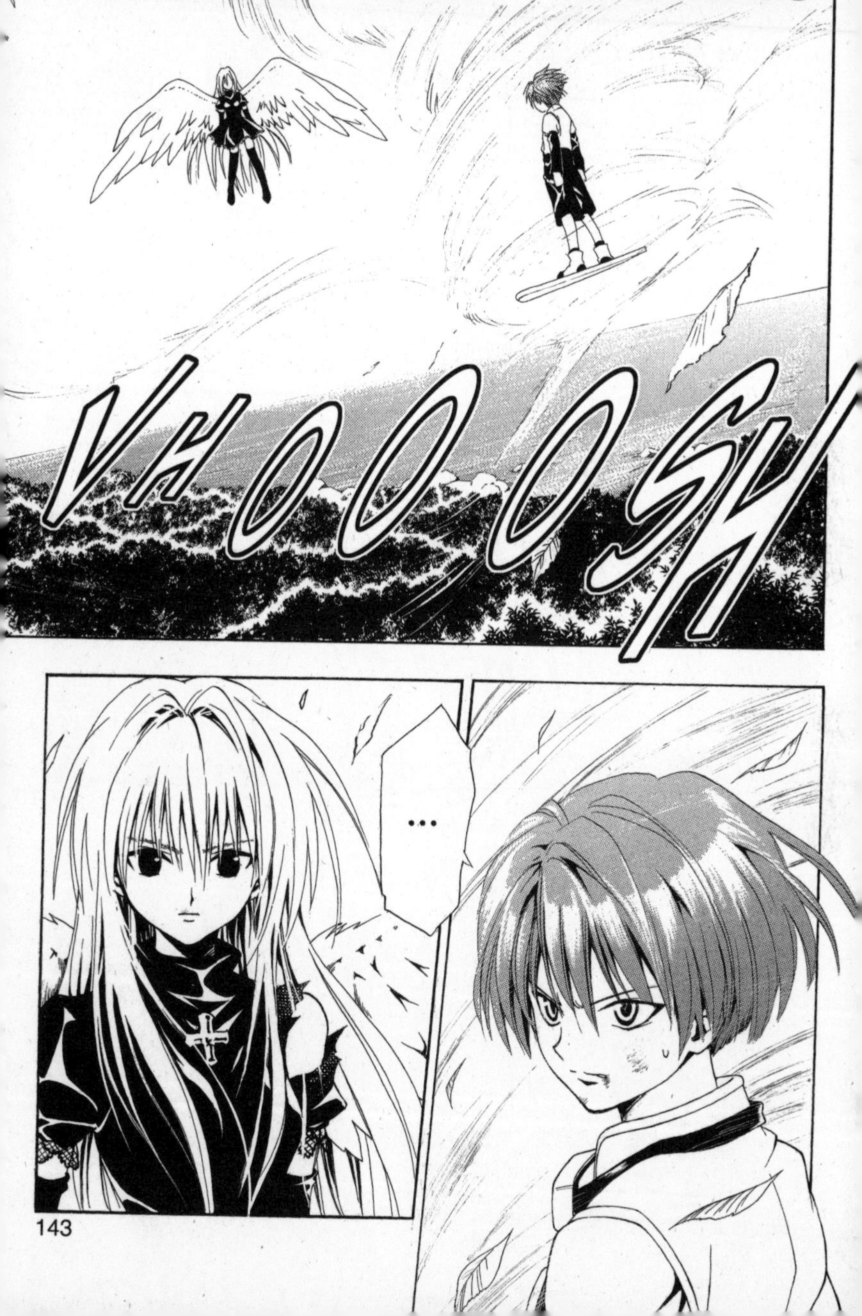
VHOOOSH
...

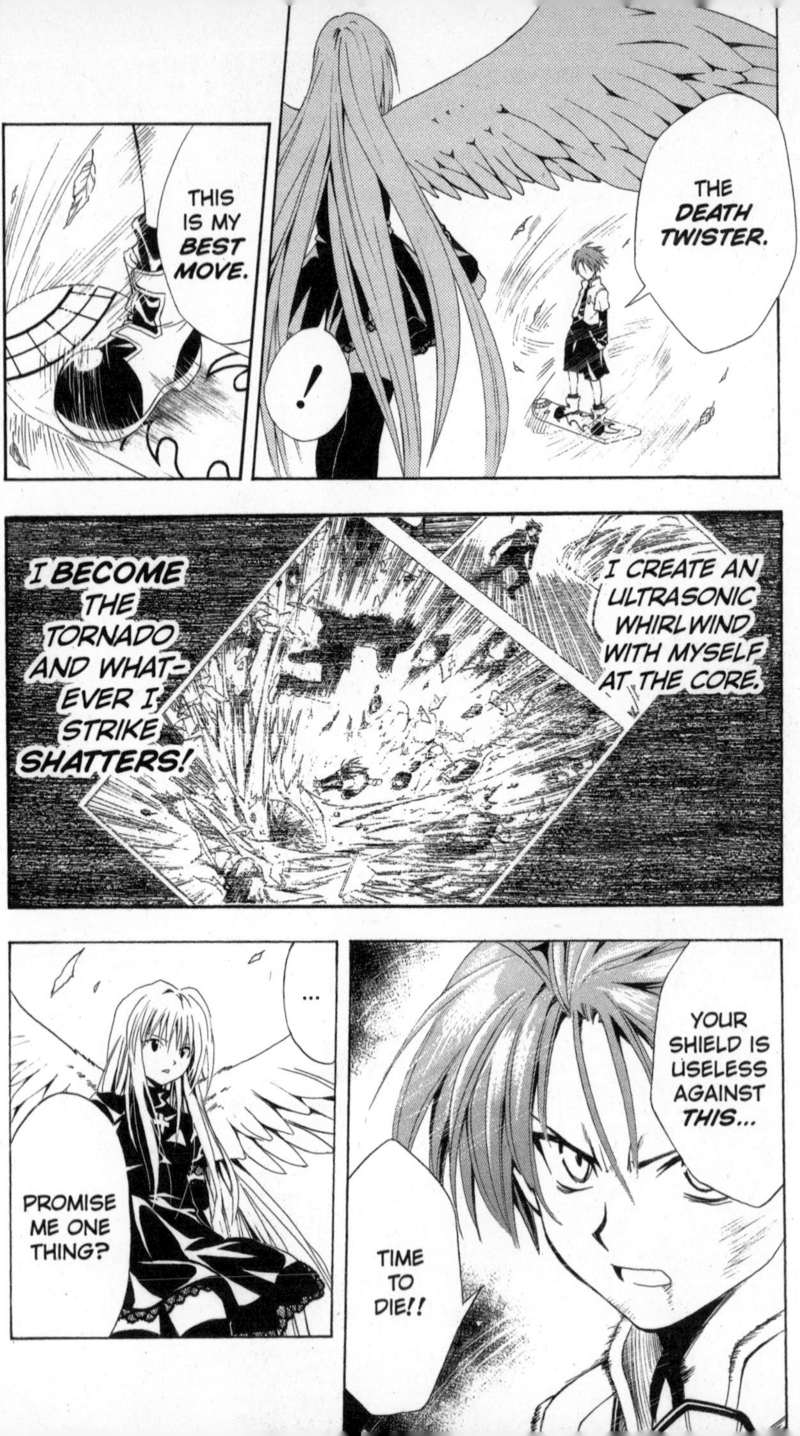
THE DEATH TWISTER.
!
THIS IS MY BEST MOVE.
I CREATE AN ULTRASONIC WHIRLWIND WITH MYSELF AT THE CORE.
I BECOME THE TORNADO AND WHATEVER I STRIKE SHATTERS!
YOUR SHIELD IS USELESS AGAINST THIS...
TIME TO DIE!!
...
PROMISE ME ONE THING?

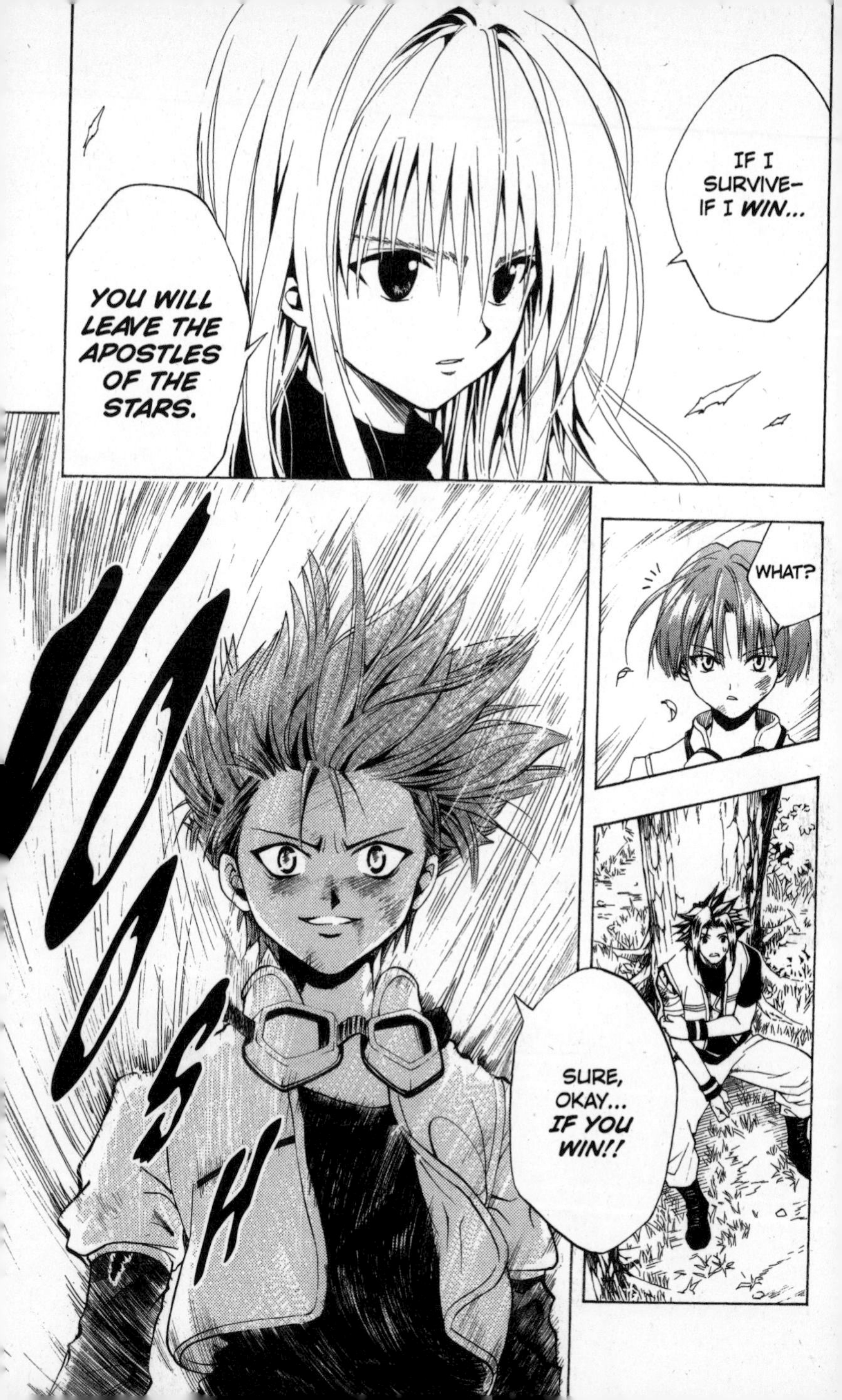
IF I SURVIVE- IF I *WIN*...
YOU WILL LEAVE THE APOSTLES OF THE STARS.
WHAT?
SURE, OKAY... *IF YOU WIN!!*

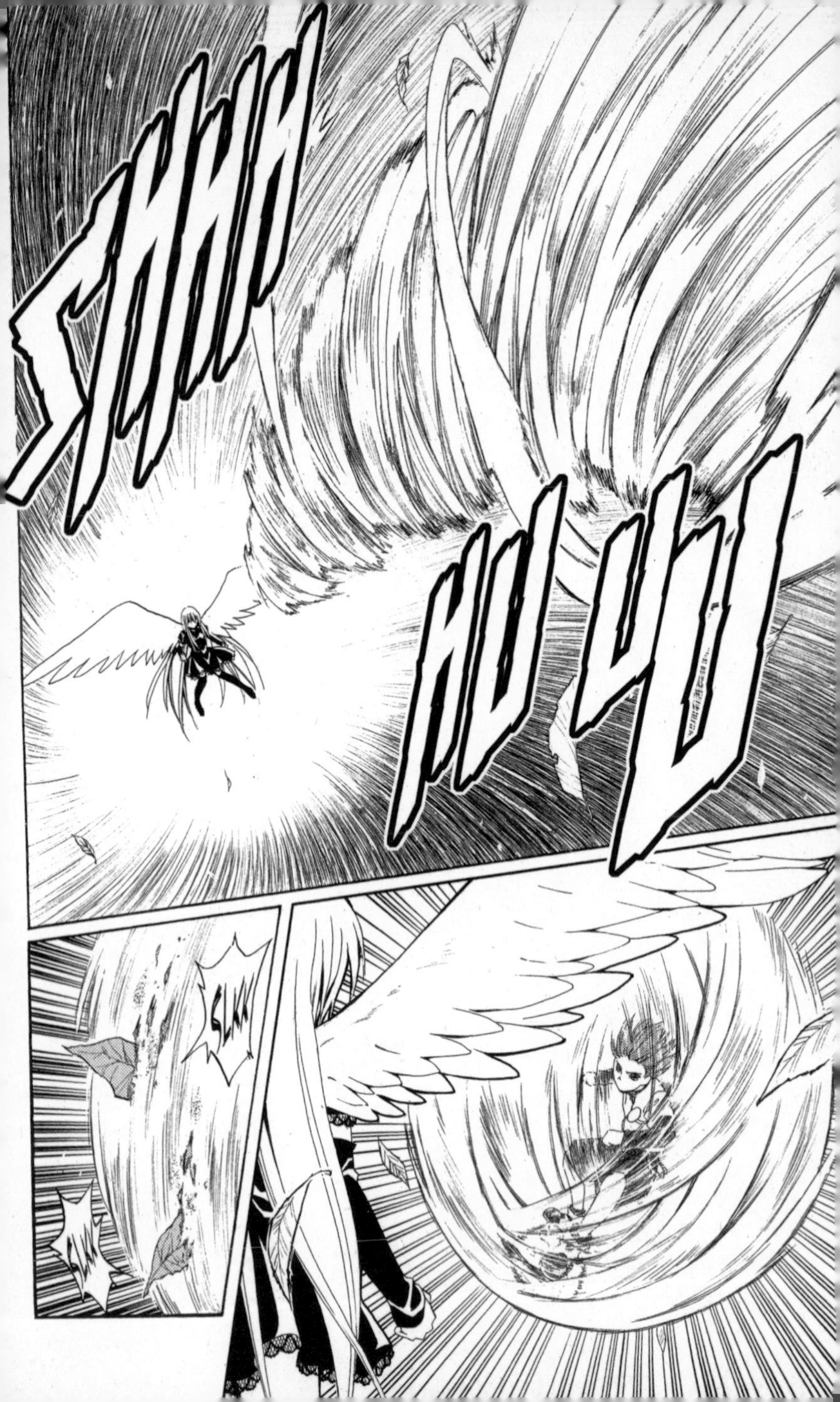
SHHH
SLKK
SLKK

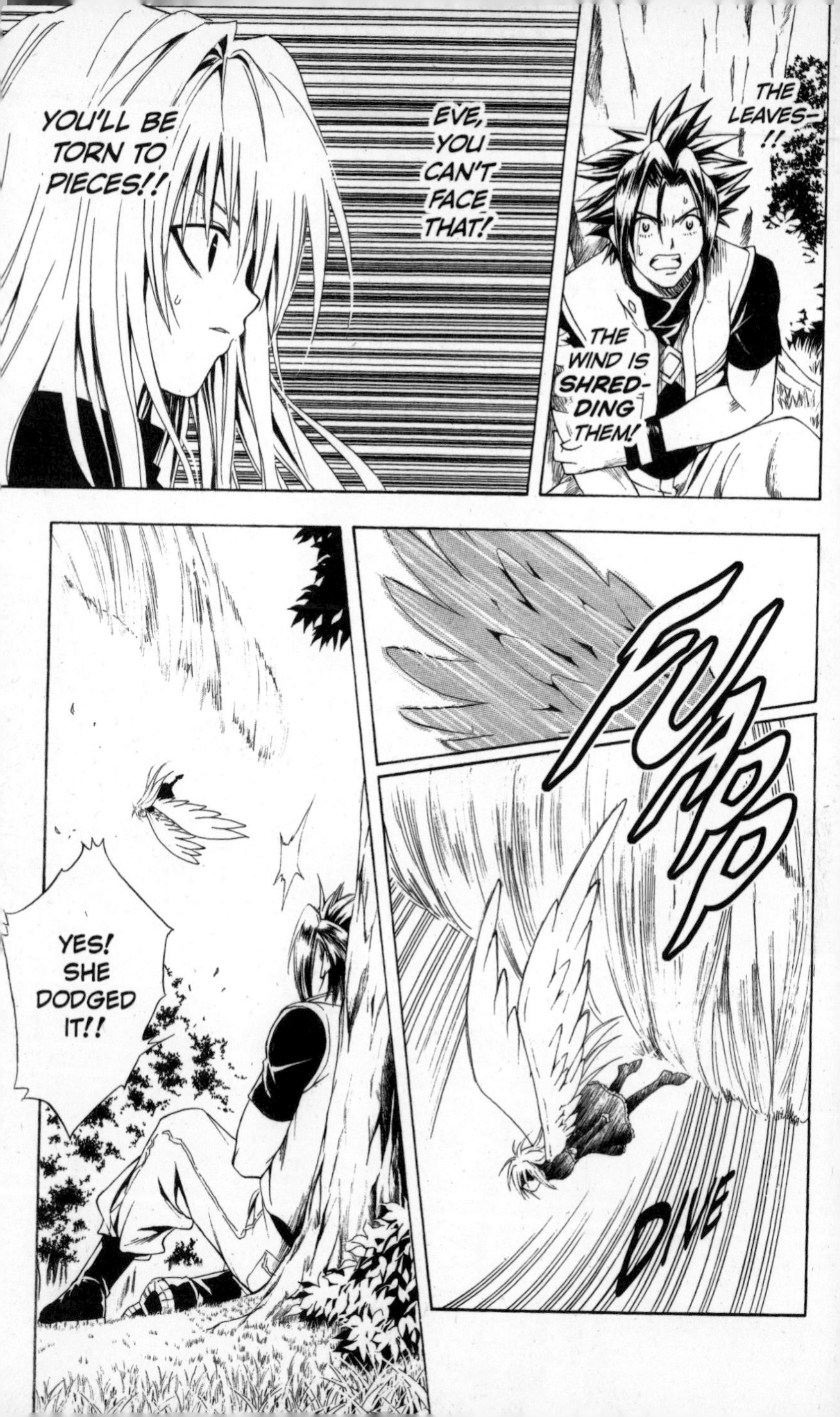
THE LEAVES—!!
THE WIND IS SHREDDING THEM!
EVE, YOU CAN'T FACE THAT!
YOU'LL BE TORN TO PIECES!!
FWOOP
DIVE
YES! SHE DODGED IT!!

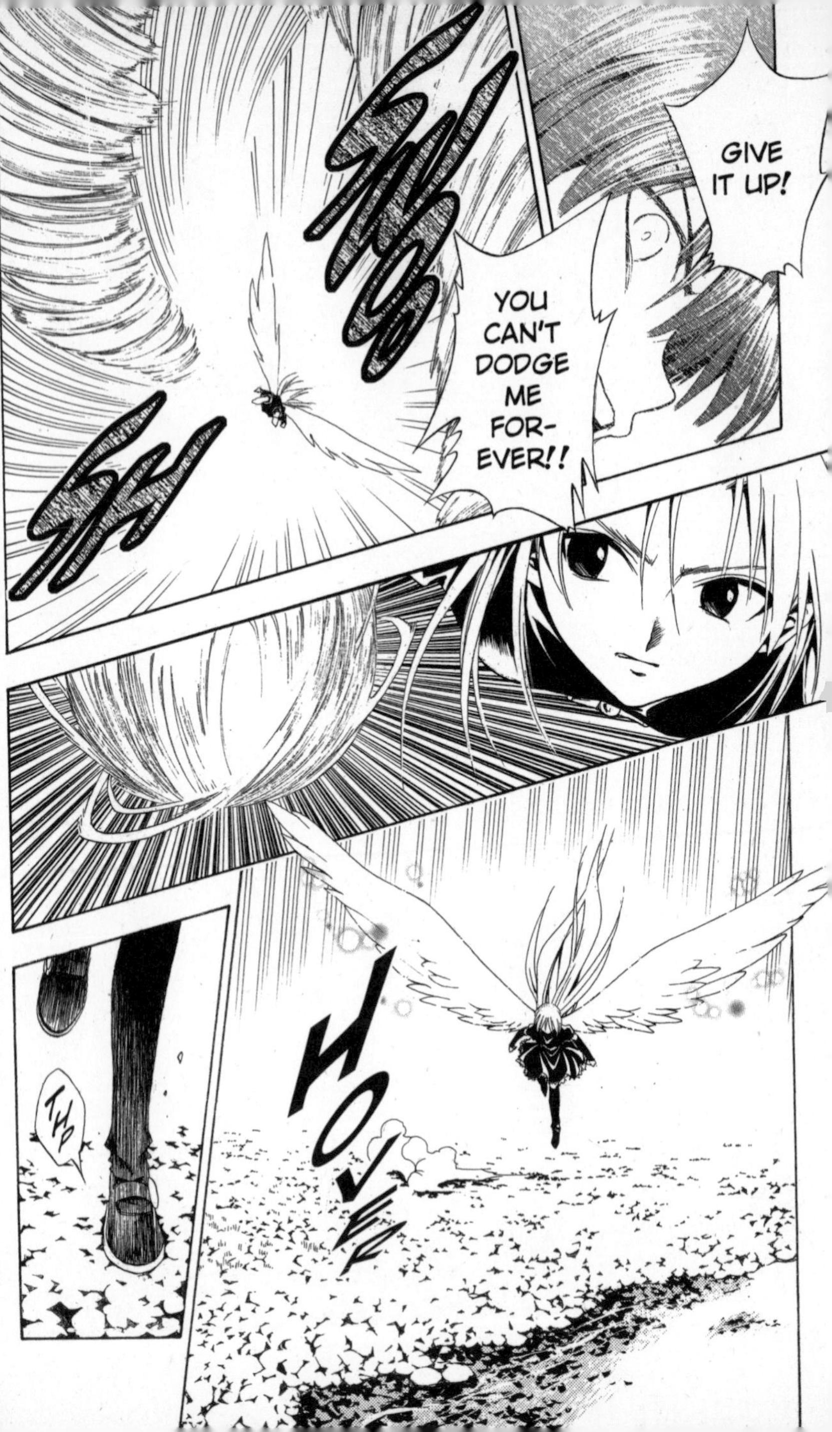
GIVE IT UP!
YOU CAN'T DODGE ME FOR-EVER!!

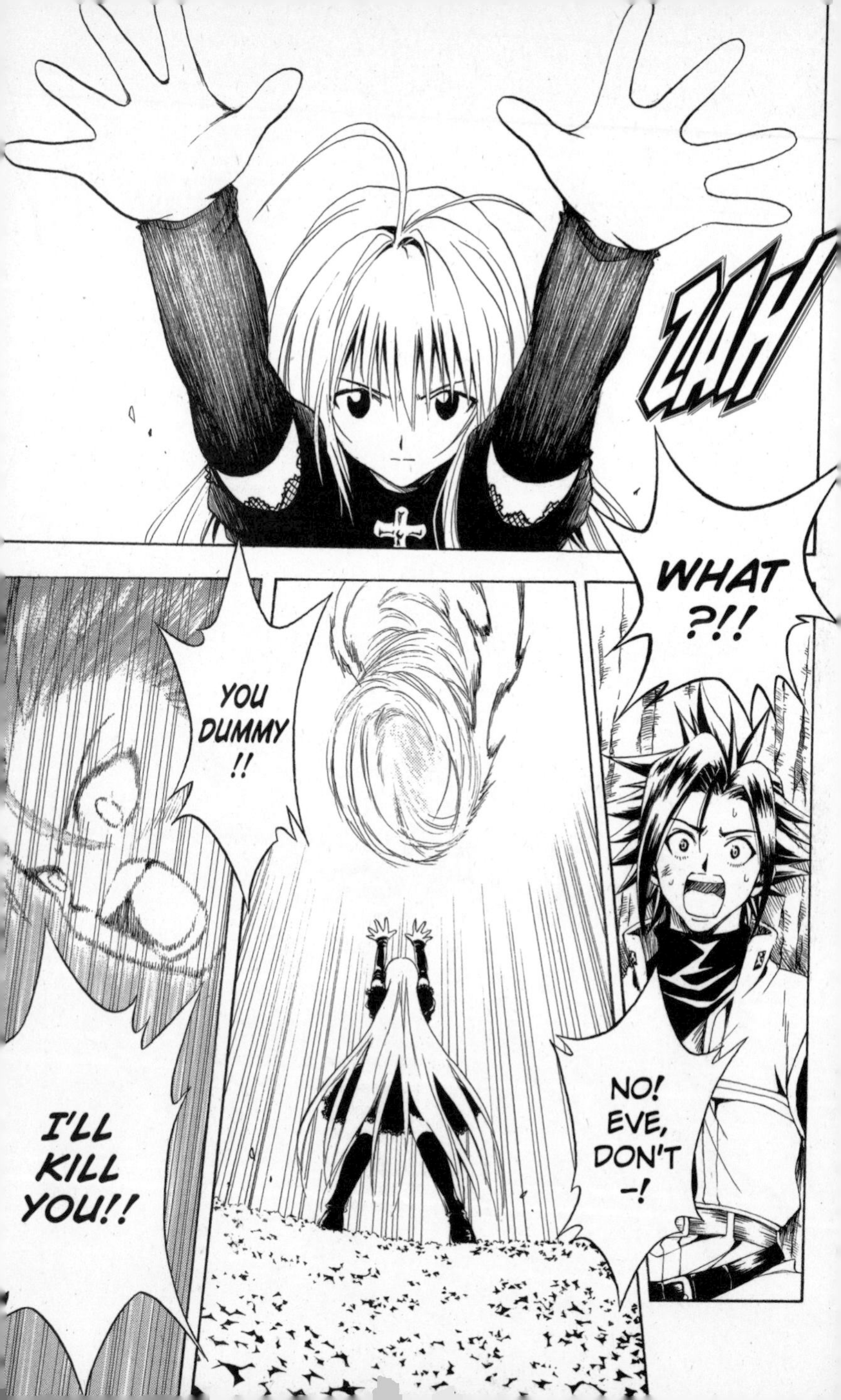
ZAH
WHAT ?!!
NO! EVE, DON'T –!
YOU DUMMY !!
I'LL KILL YOU!!

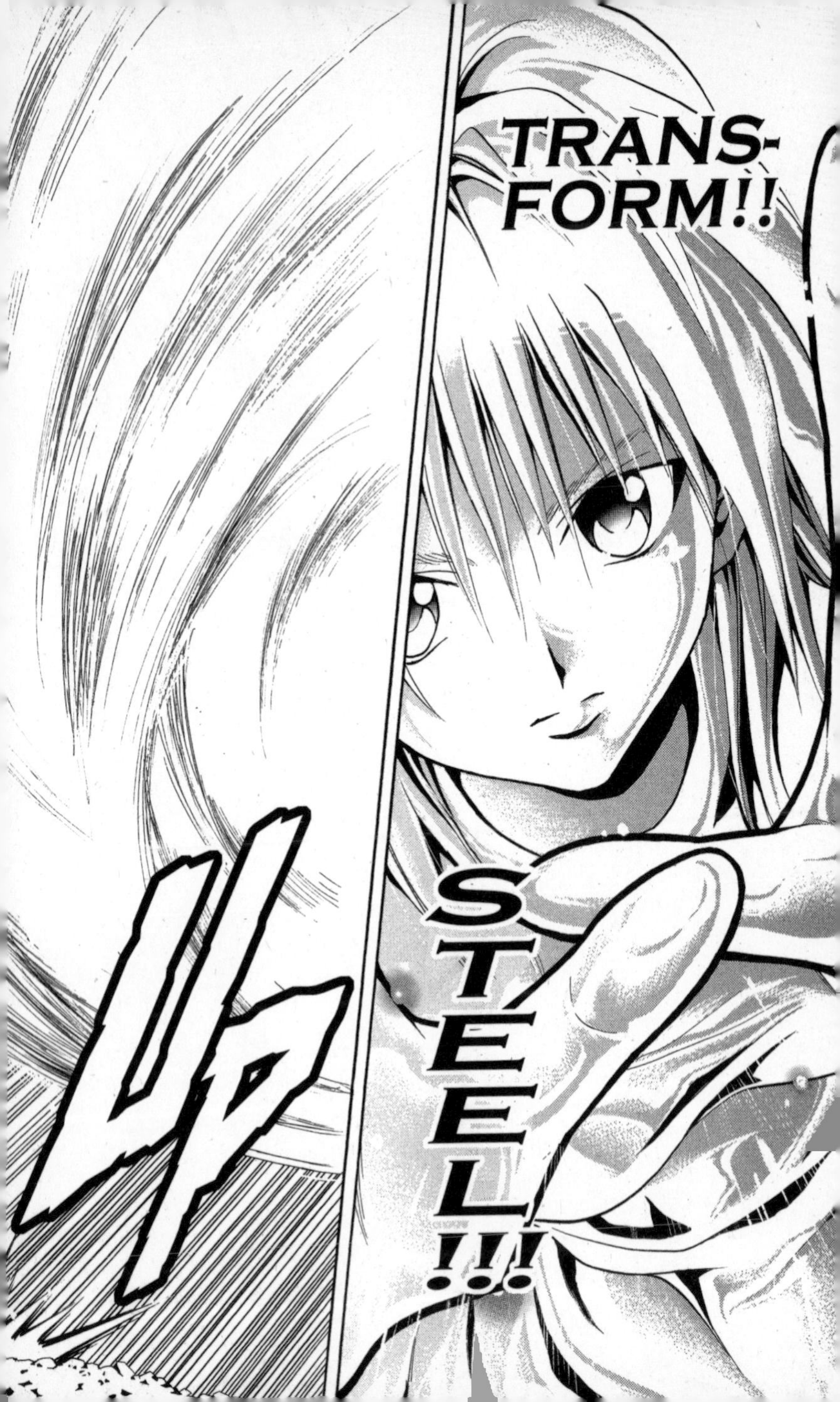
TRANS-
FORM!!
STEEL!!!

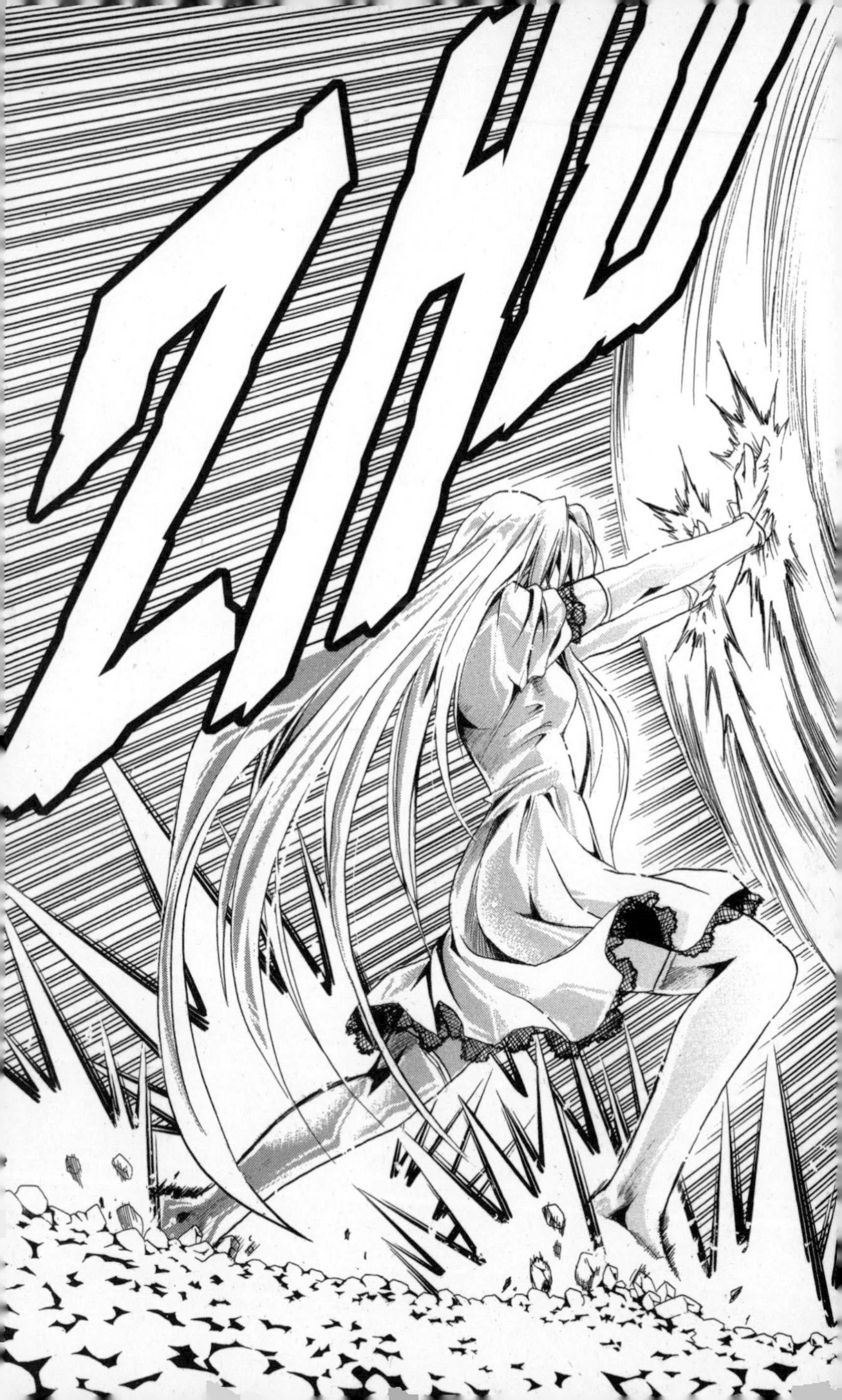

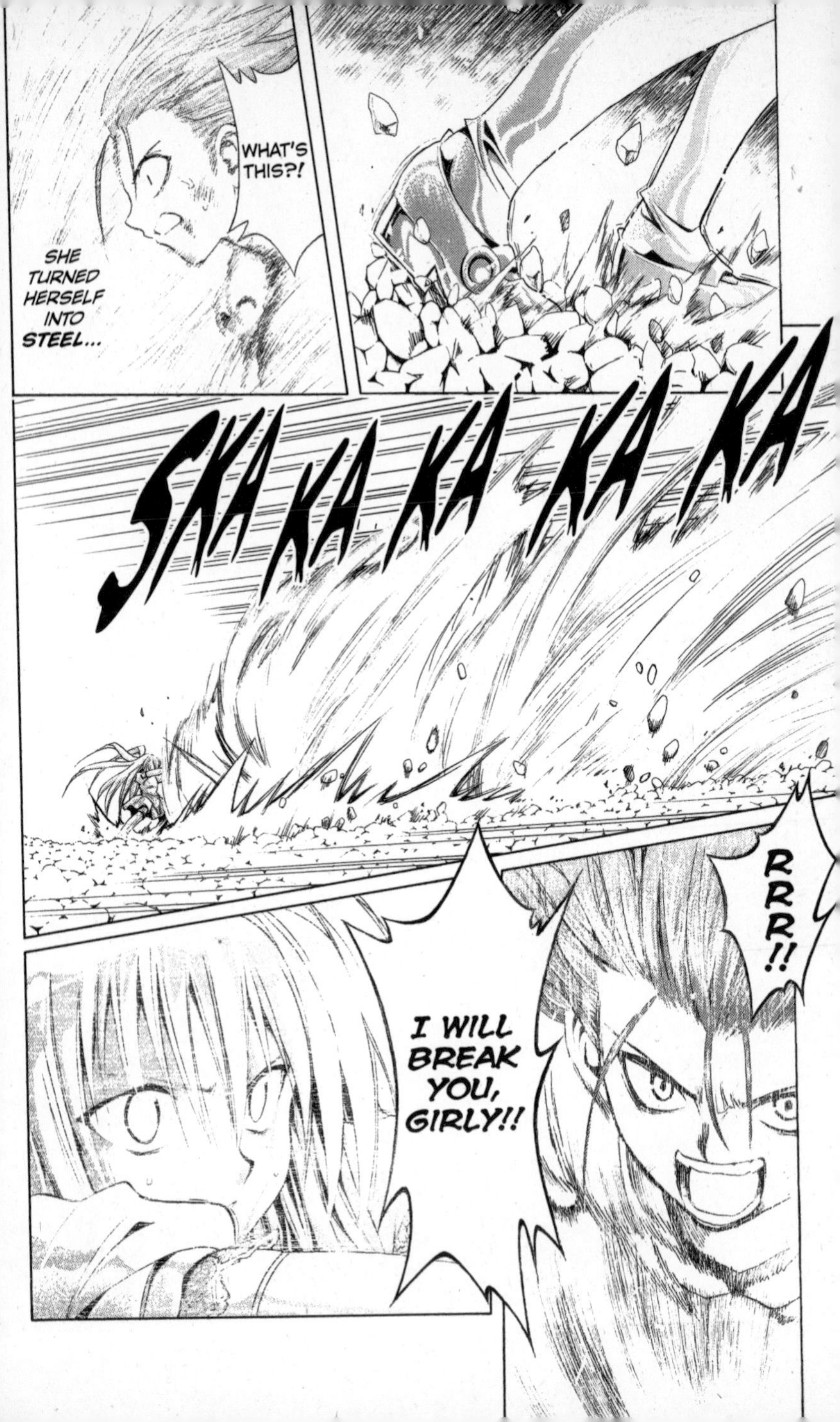
WHAT'S THIS?!
SHE TURNED HERSELF INTO STEEL...
SKA KA KA KA KA
RRR!!
I WILL BREAK YOU, GIRLY!!

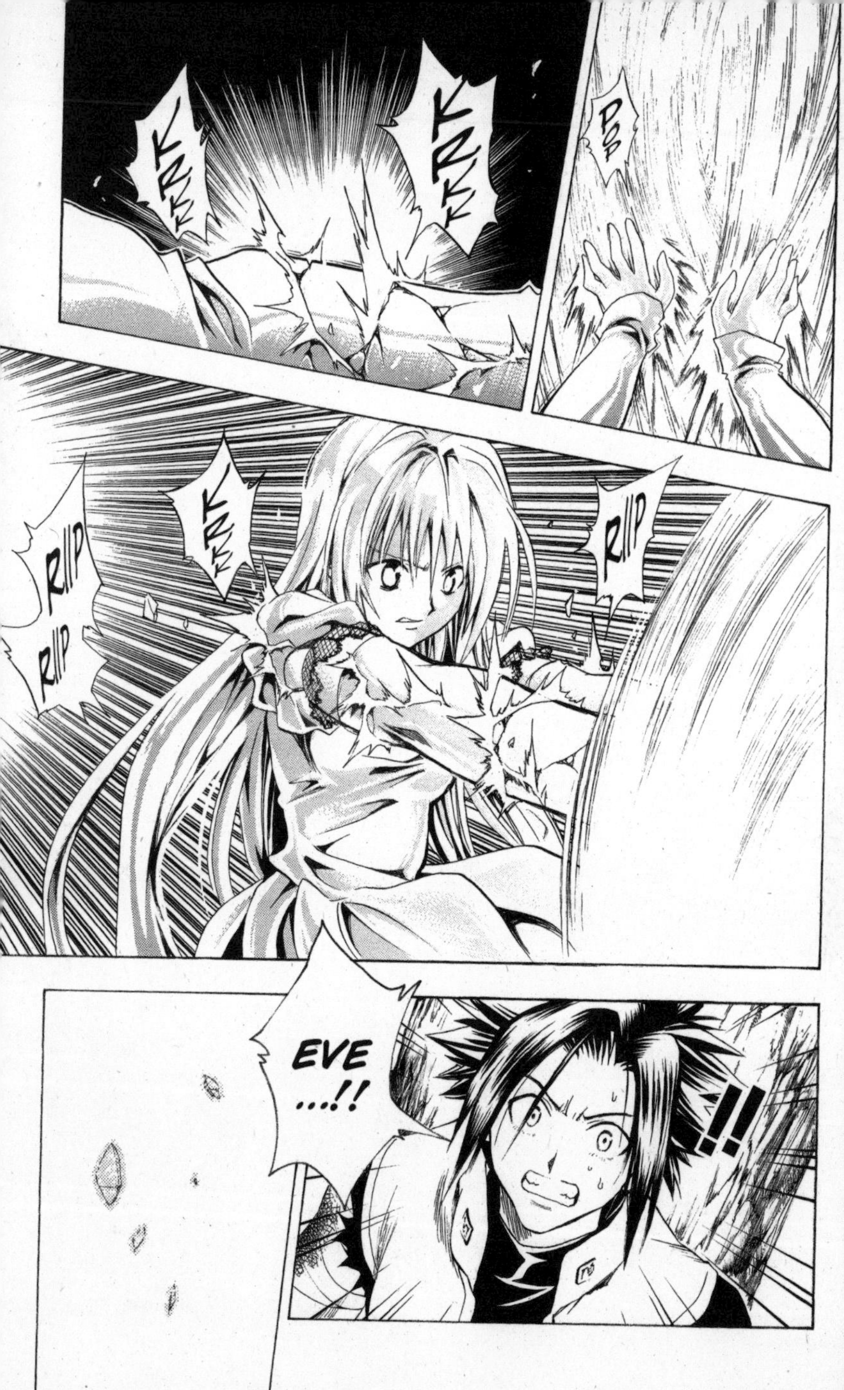
POP
KRKK
KRKK
RIIP
KRKK
RIIP
RIIP
EVE ...!!
!!

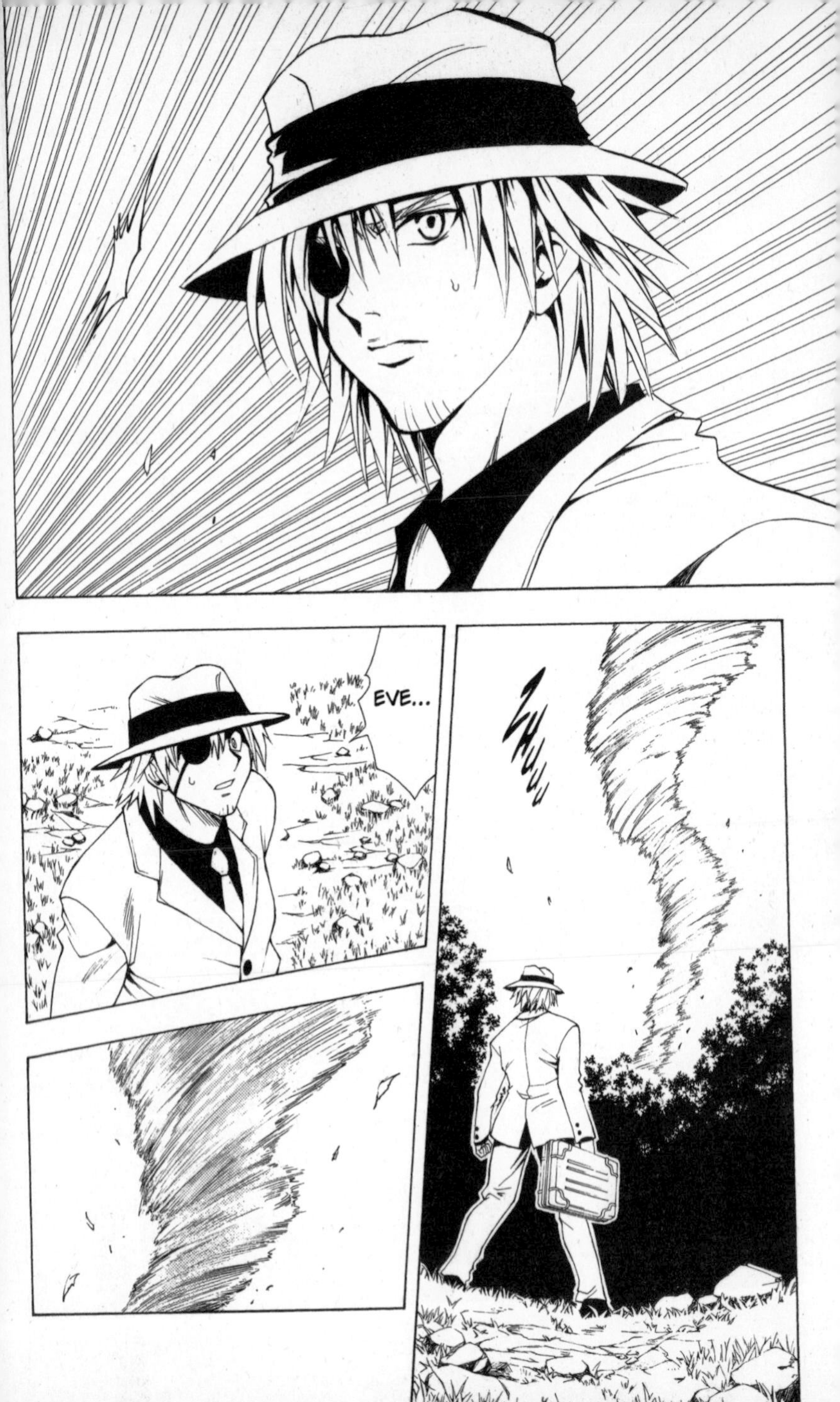
ZHUU
EVE...

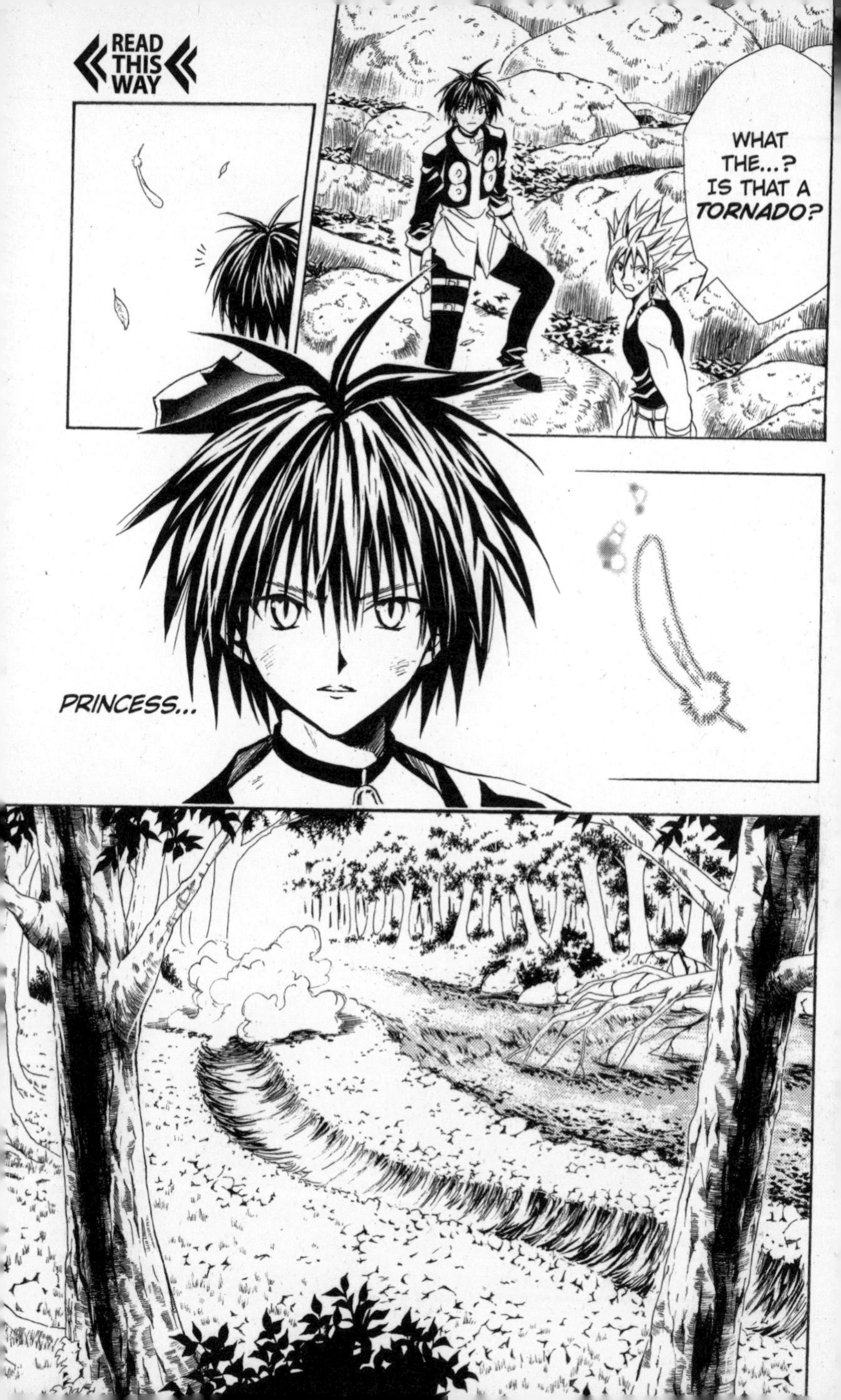
READ THIS WAY
WHAT THE...? IS THAT A *TORNADO?*
PRINCESS...

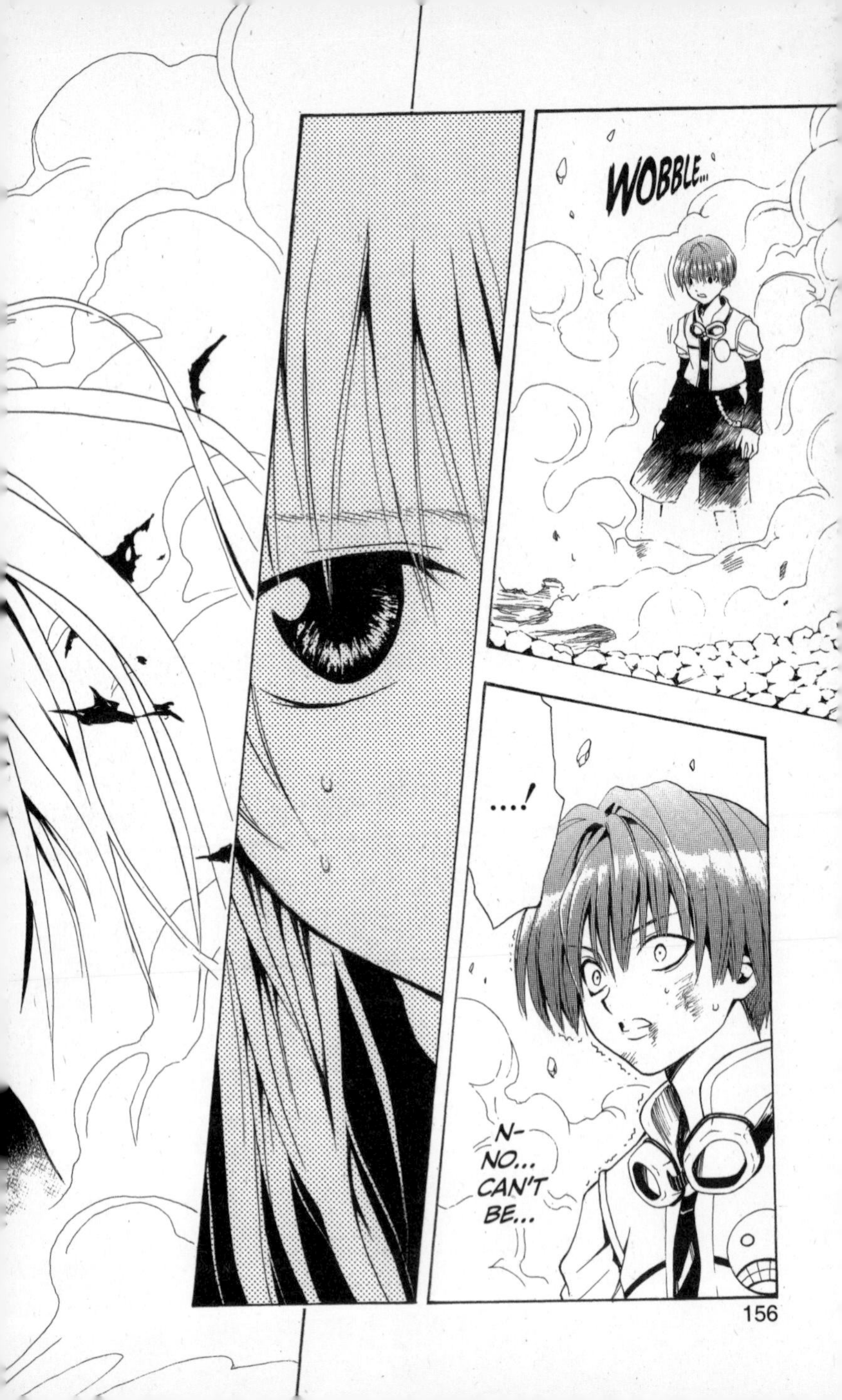
WOBBLE...
...!
N-
NO... CAN'T BE...

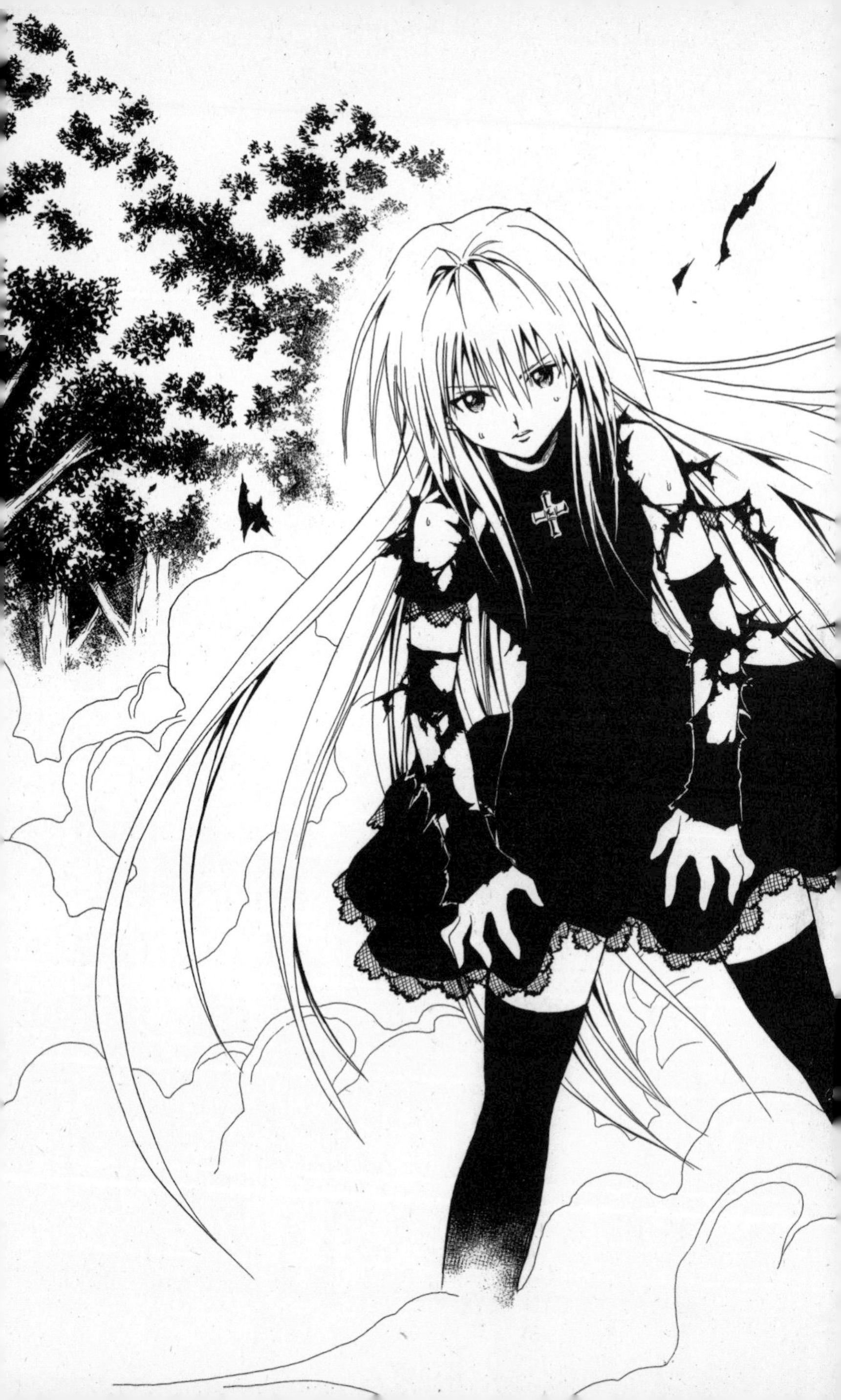

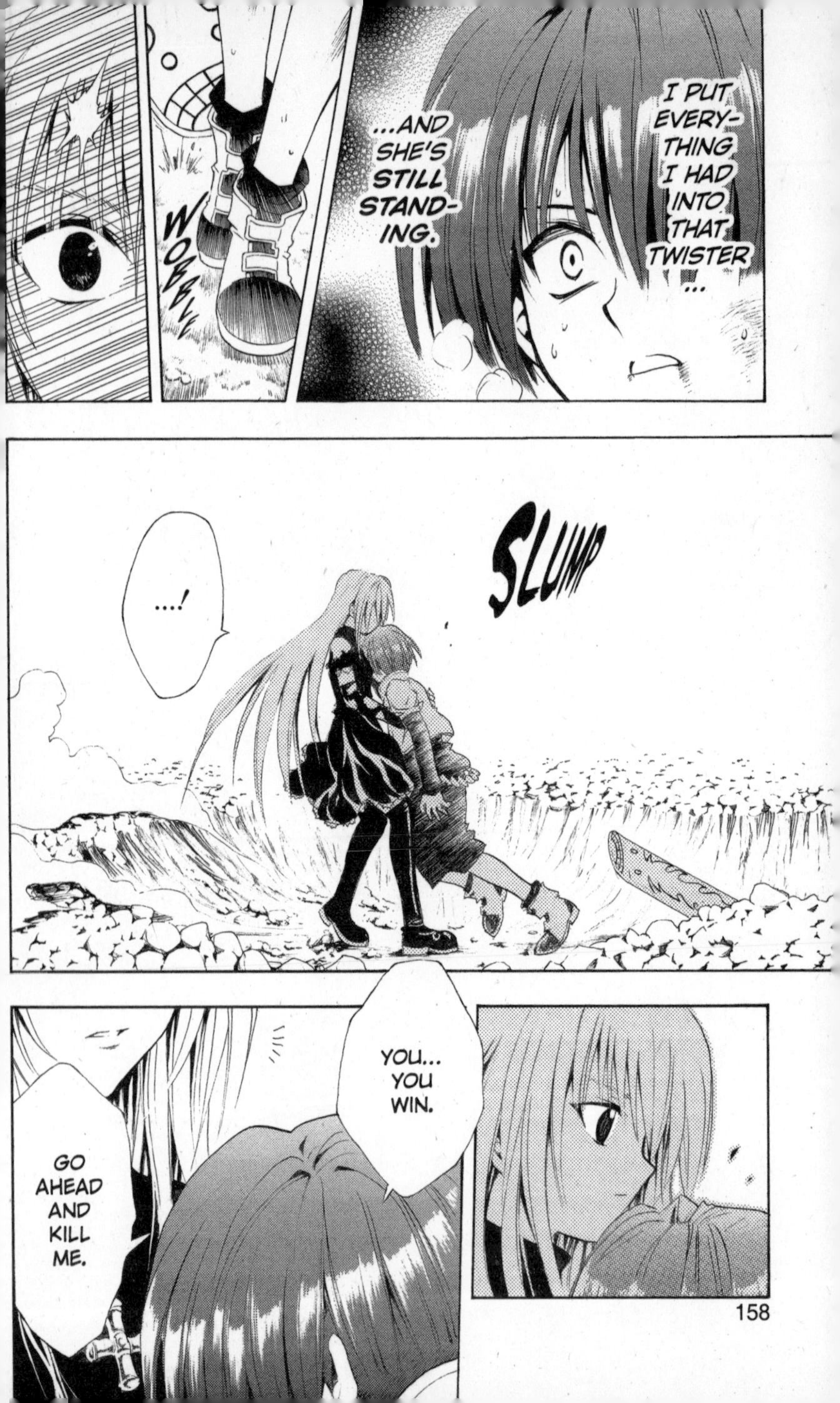
I PUT EVERY-THING I HAD INTO THAT TWISTER ...
...AND SHE'S STILL STAND-ING.
WOBBLY
SLUMP
...!
YOU... YOU WIN.
GO AHEAD AND KILL ME.

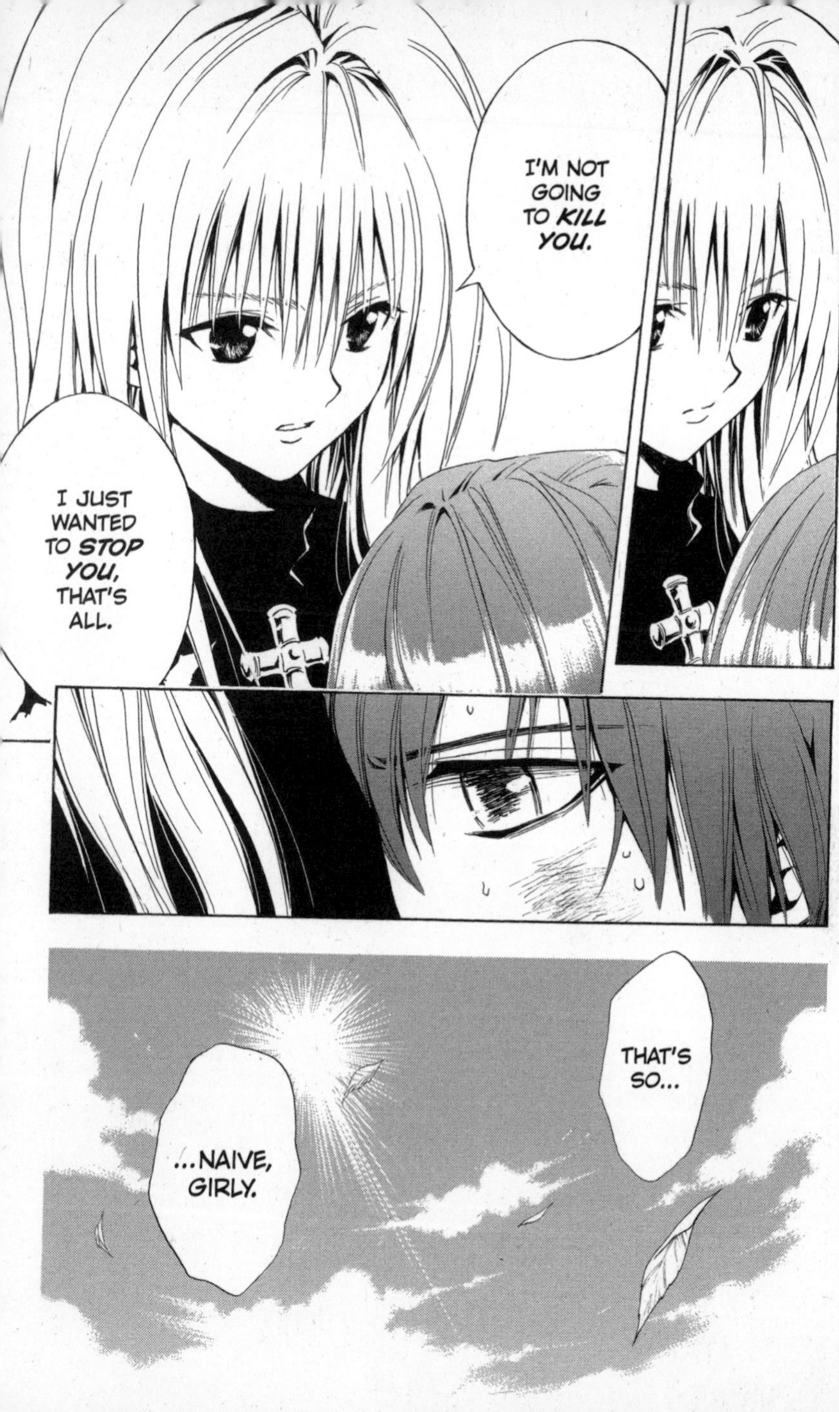
I'M NOT GOING TO *KILL YOU.*
I JUST WANTED TO *STOP YOU,* THAT'S ALL.
THAT'S SO...
...NAIVE, GIRLY.

No pics of
me recently...

Oh.

Chapter 139: The Bullets Are Stopped

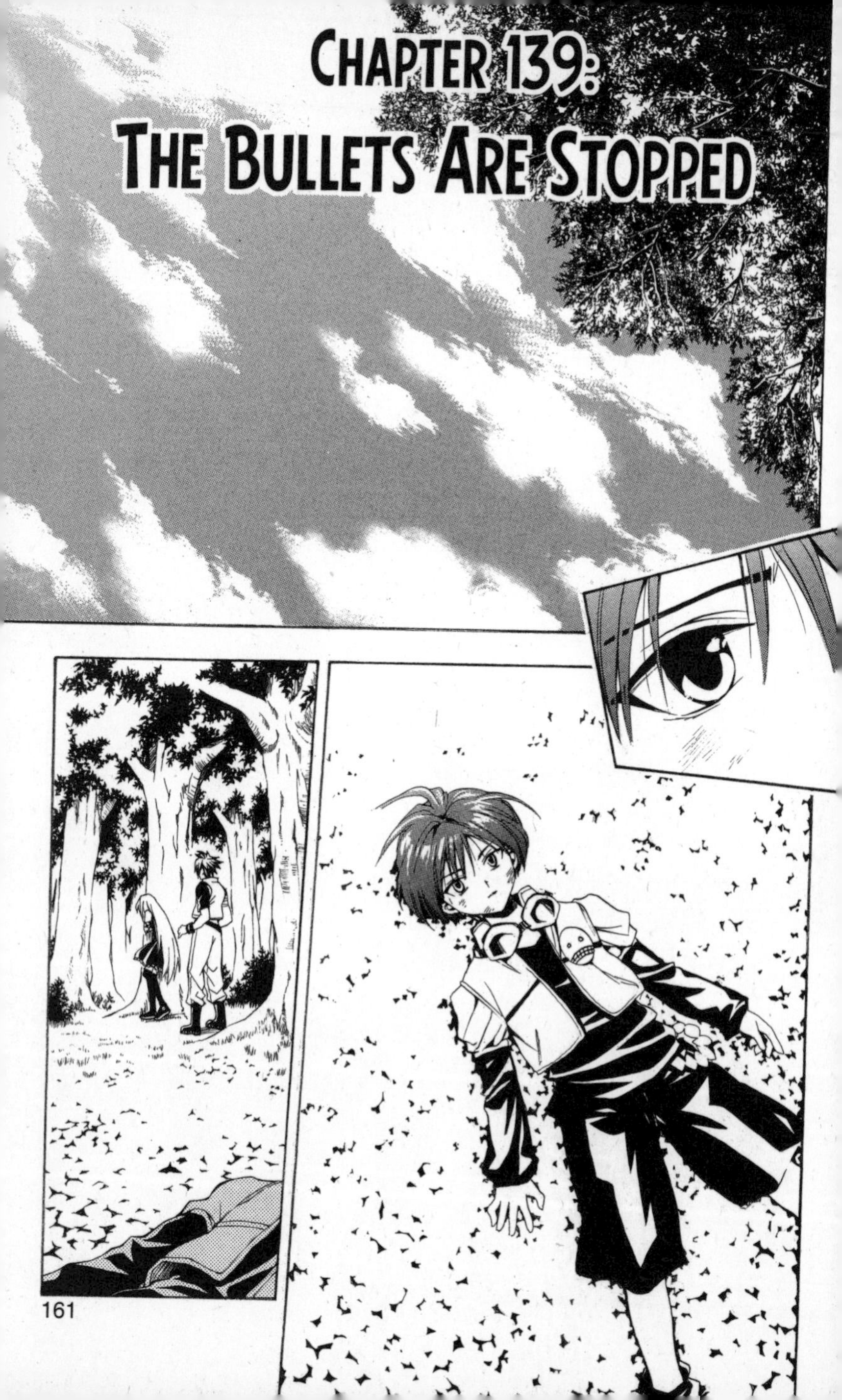

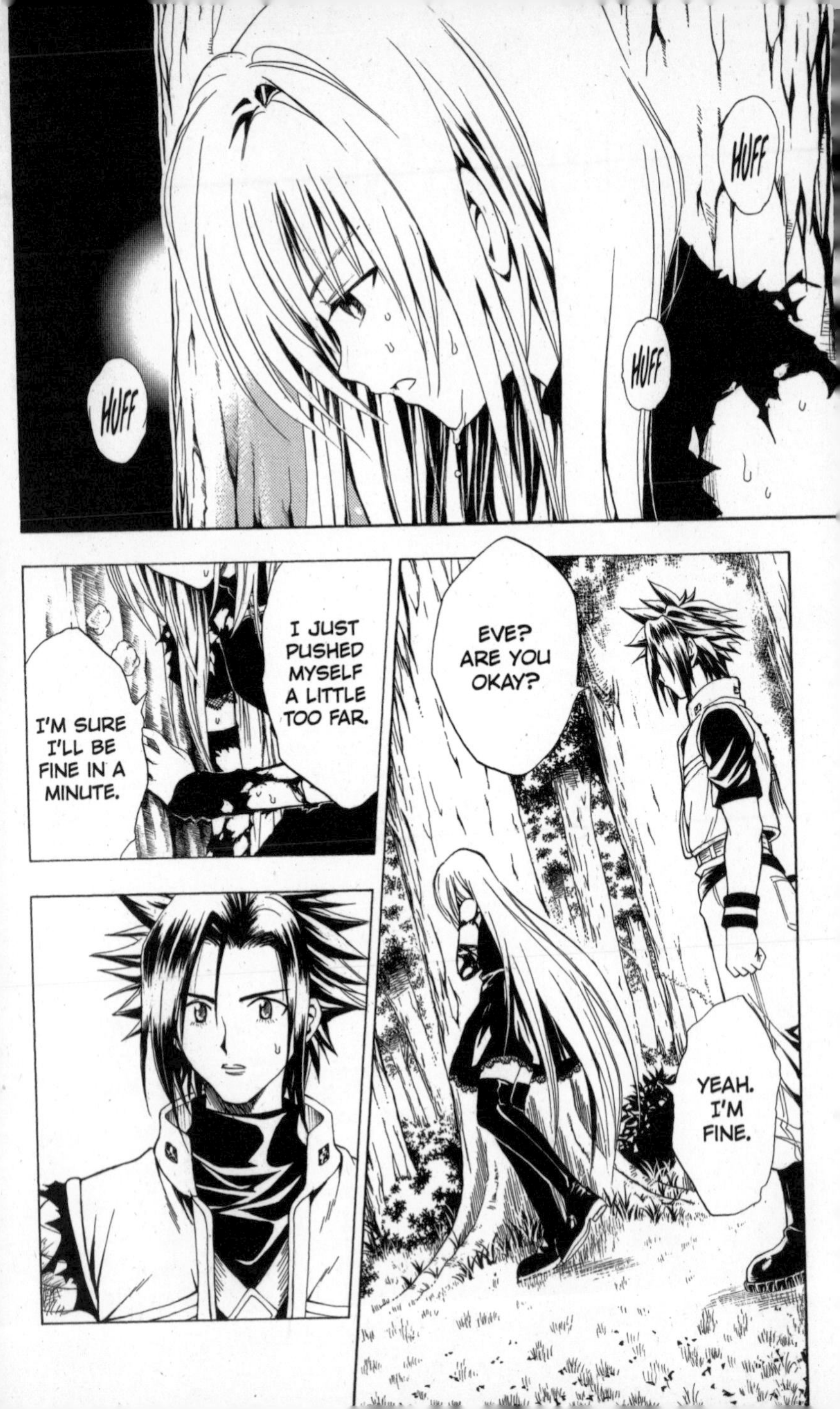
HUFF
HUFF
HUFF
EVE? ARE YOU OKAY?
YEAH. I'M FINE.
I JUST PUSHED MYSELF A LITTLE TOO FAR.
I'M SURE I'LL BE FINE IN A MINUTE.

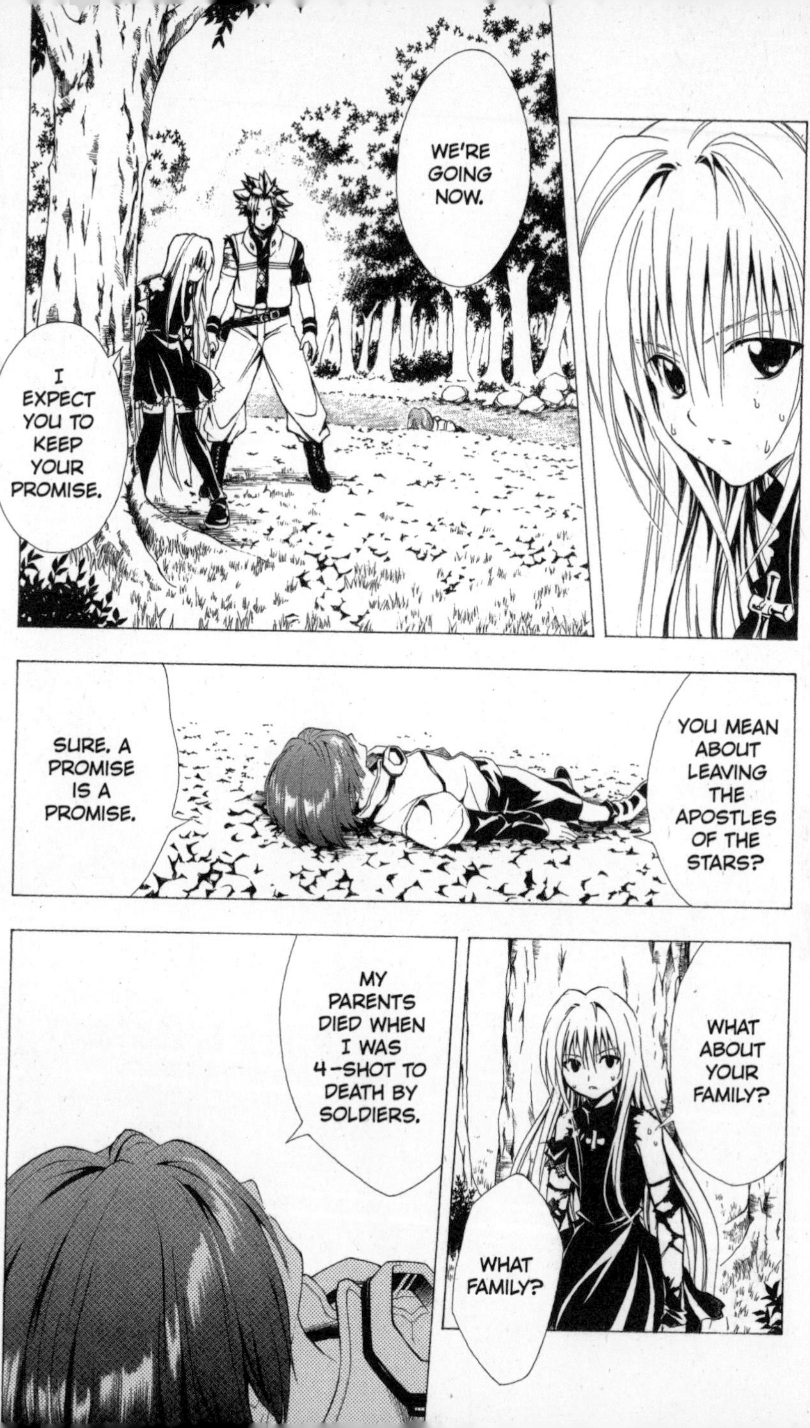
WE'RE GOING NOW.
I EXPECT YOU TO KEEP YOUR PROMISE.
YOU MEAN ABOUT LEAVING THE APOSTLES OF THE STARS?
SURE. A PROMISE IS A PROMISE.
WHAT ABOUT YOUR FAMILY?
WHAT FAMILY?
MY PARENTS DIED WHEN I WAS 4—SHOT TO DEATH BY SOLDIERS.

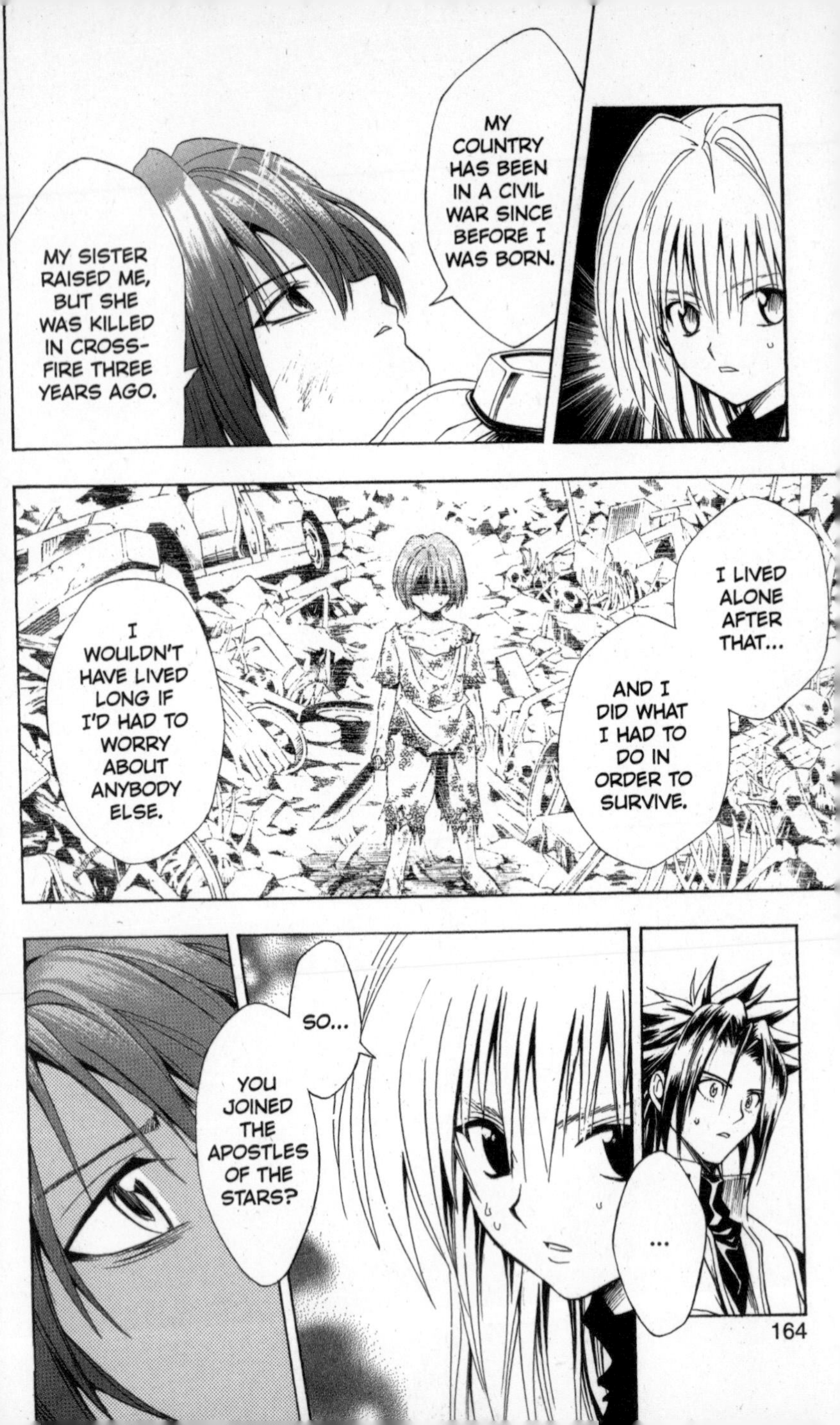
MY COUNTRY HAS BEEN IN A CIVIL WAR SINCE BEFORE I WAS BORN.
MY SISTER RAISED ME, BUT SHE WAS KILLED IN CROSS-FIRE THREE YEARS AGO.
I LIVED ALONE AFTER THAT...
AND I DID WHAT I HAD TO DO IN ORDER TO SURVIVE.
I WOULDN'T HAVE LIVED LONG IF I'D HAD TO WORRY ABOUT ANYBODY ELSE.
...
SO...
YOU JOINED THE APOSTLES OF THE STARS?

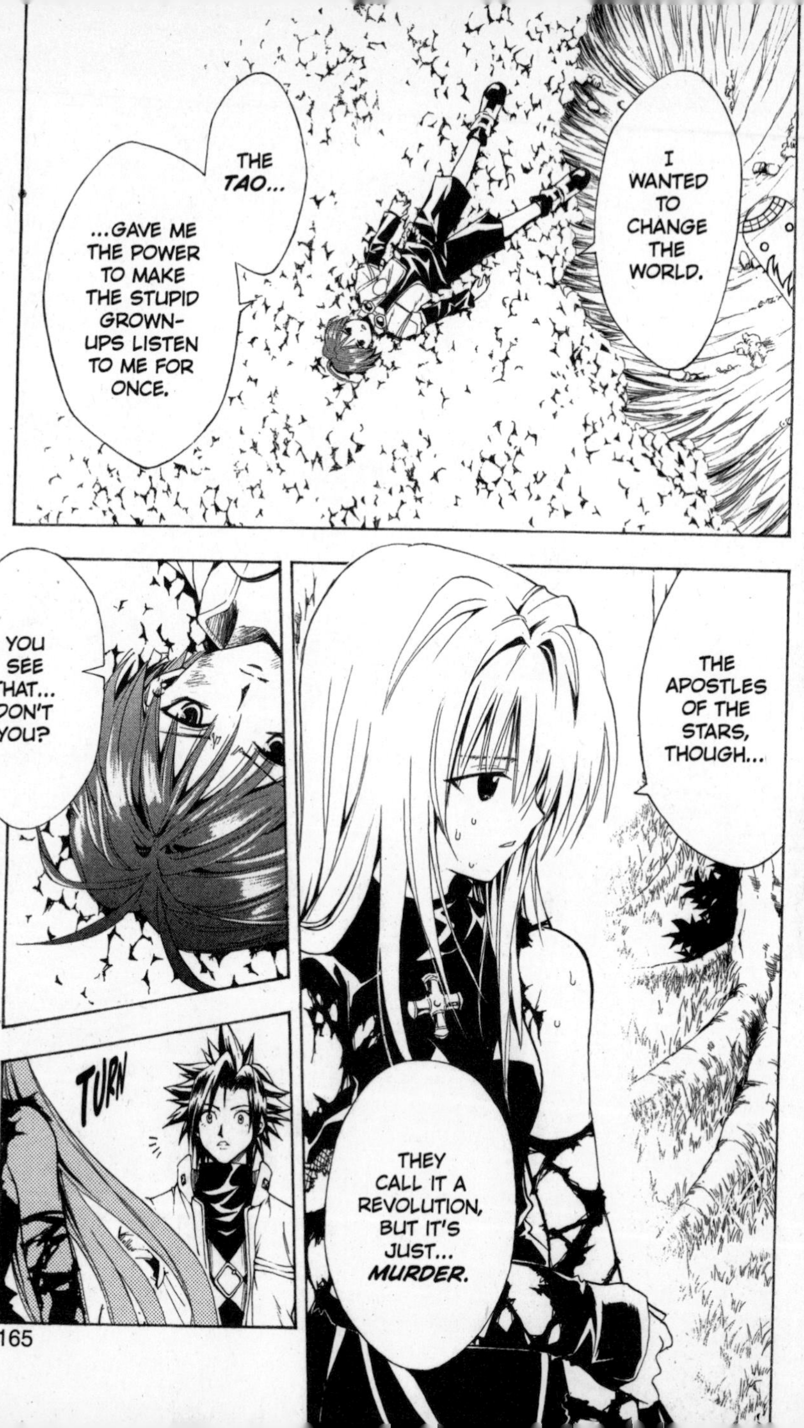

I WANTED TO CHANGE THE WORLD.
THE *TAO*...
...GAVE ME THE POWER TO MAKE THE STUPID GROWN-UPS LISTEN TO ME FOR ONCE.
THE APOSTLES OF THE STARS, THOUGH...
THEY CALL IT A REVOLUTION, BUT IT'S JUST... ***MURDER***.
YOU SEE THAT... DON'T YOU?
TURN

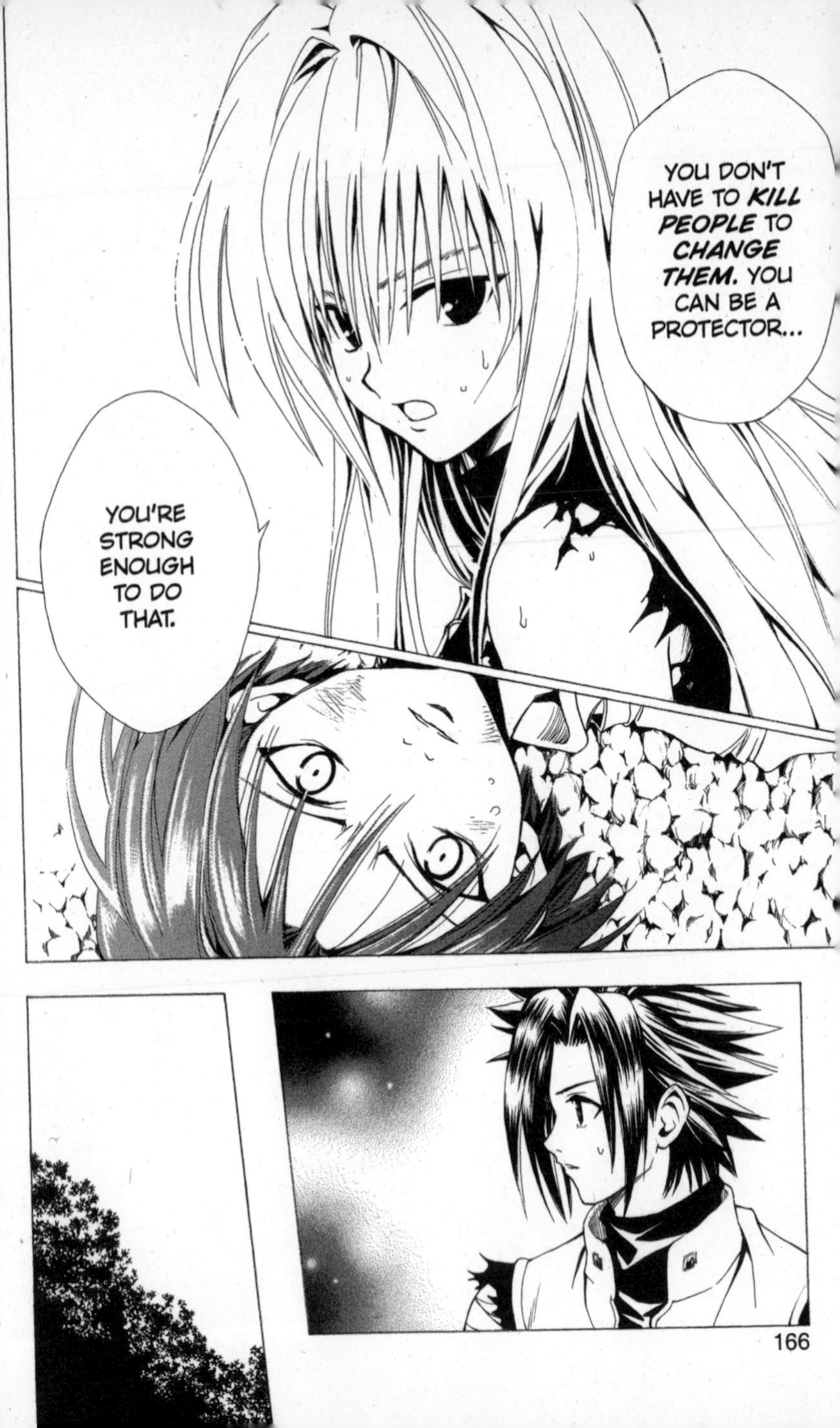
YOU DON'T HAVE TO KILL PEOPLE TO CHANGE THEM. YOU CAN BE A PROTECTOR...
YOU'RE STRONG ENOUGH TO DO THAT.

READ THIS WAY

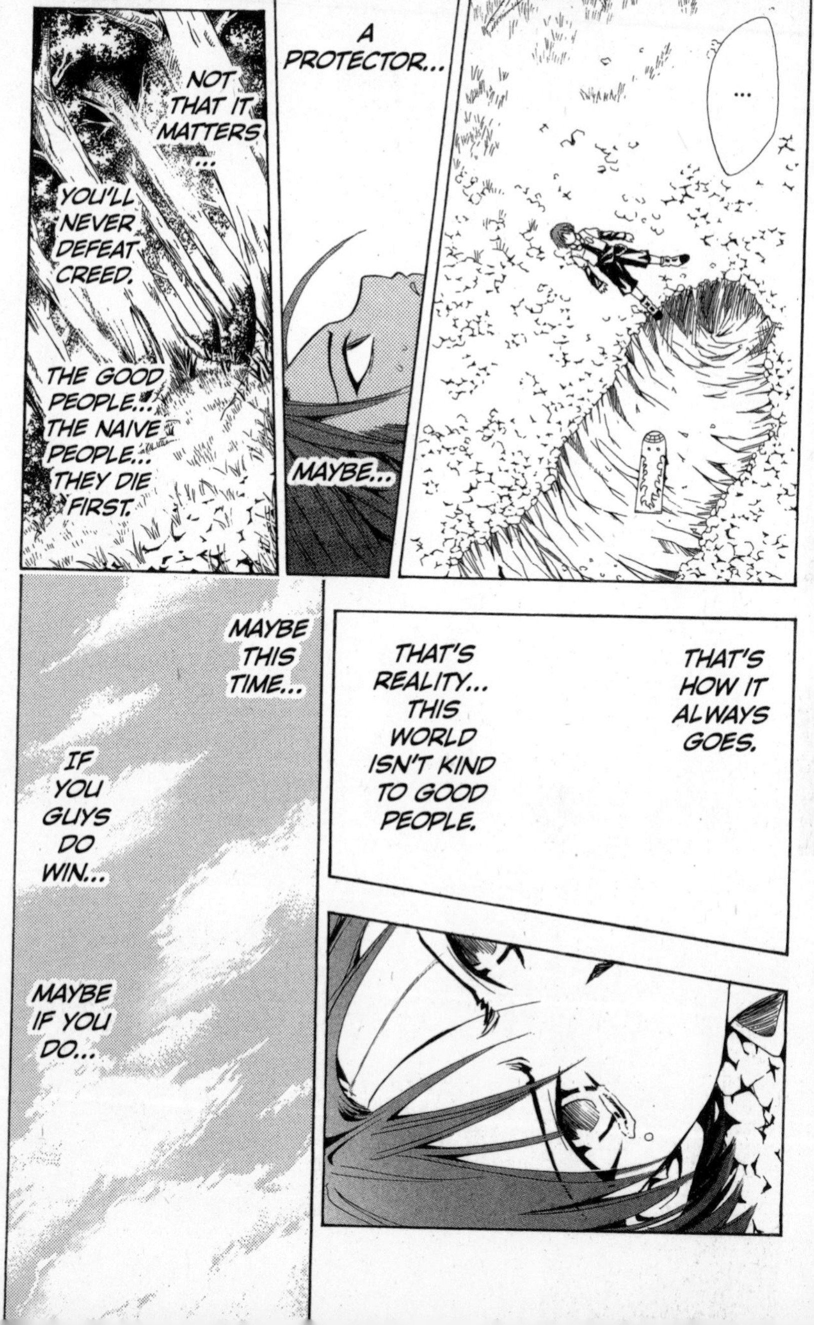
...
A PROTECTOR...
MAYBE...
NOT THAT IT MATTERS...
YOU'LL NEVER DEFEAT CREED.
THE GOOD PEOPLE... THE NAIVE PEOPLE... THEY DIE FIRST.
THAT'S HOW IT ALWAYS GOES.
THAT'S REALITY... THIS WORLD ISN'T KIND TO GOOD PEOPLE.
MAYBE THIS TIME...
IF YOU GUYS DO WIN...
MAYBE IF YOU DO...

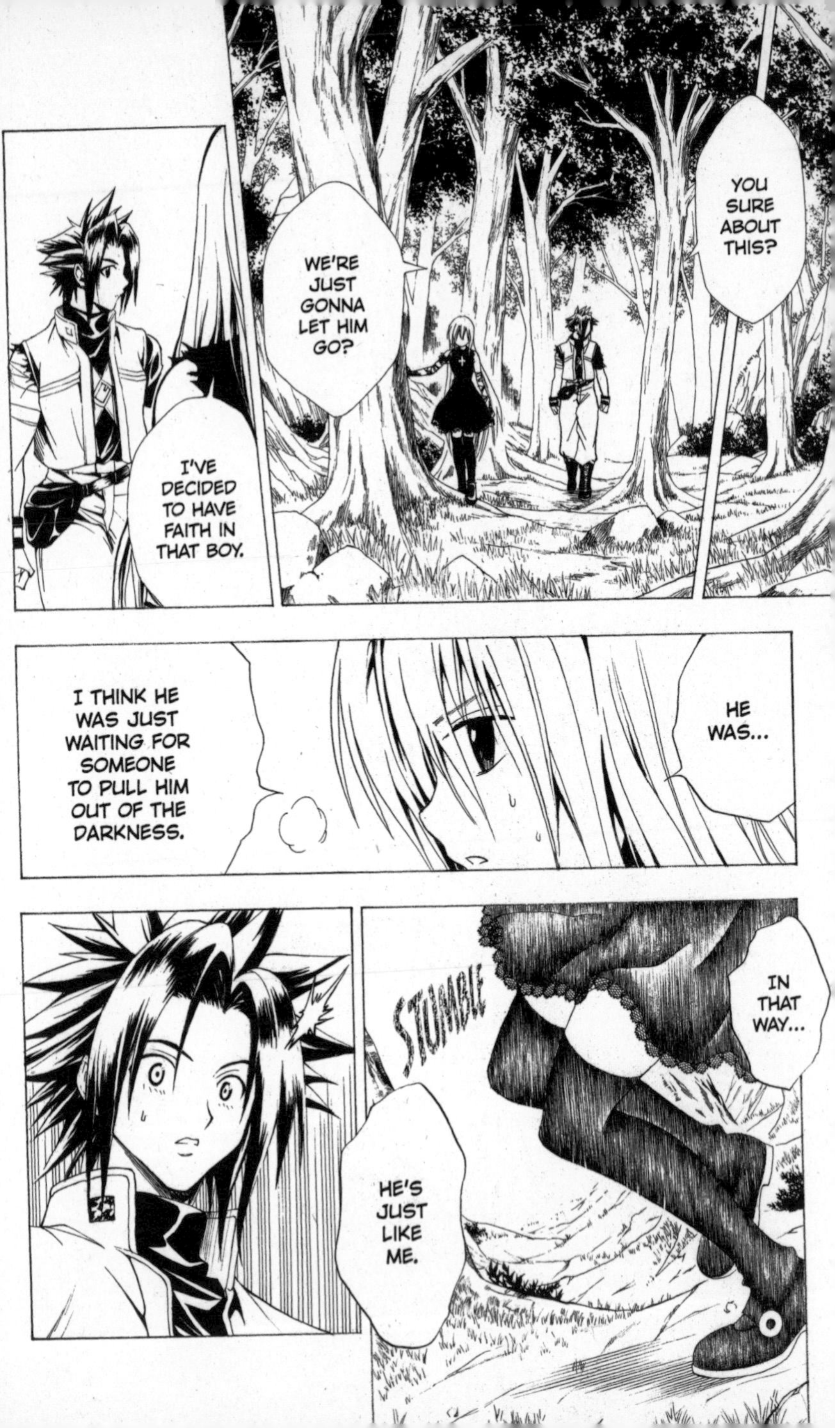
YOU SURE ABOUT THIS?
WE'RE JUST GONNA LET HIM GO?
I'VE DECIDED TO HAVE FAITH IN THAT BOY.
HE WAS...
I THINK HE WAS JUST WAITING FOR SOMEONE TO PULL HIM OUT OF THE DARKNESS.
IN THAT WAY...
STUMBLE
HE'S JUST LIKE ME.

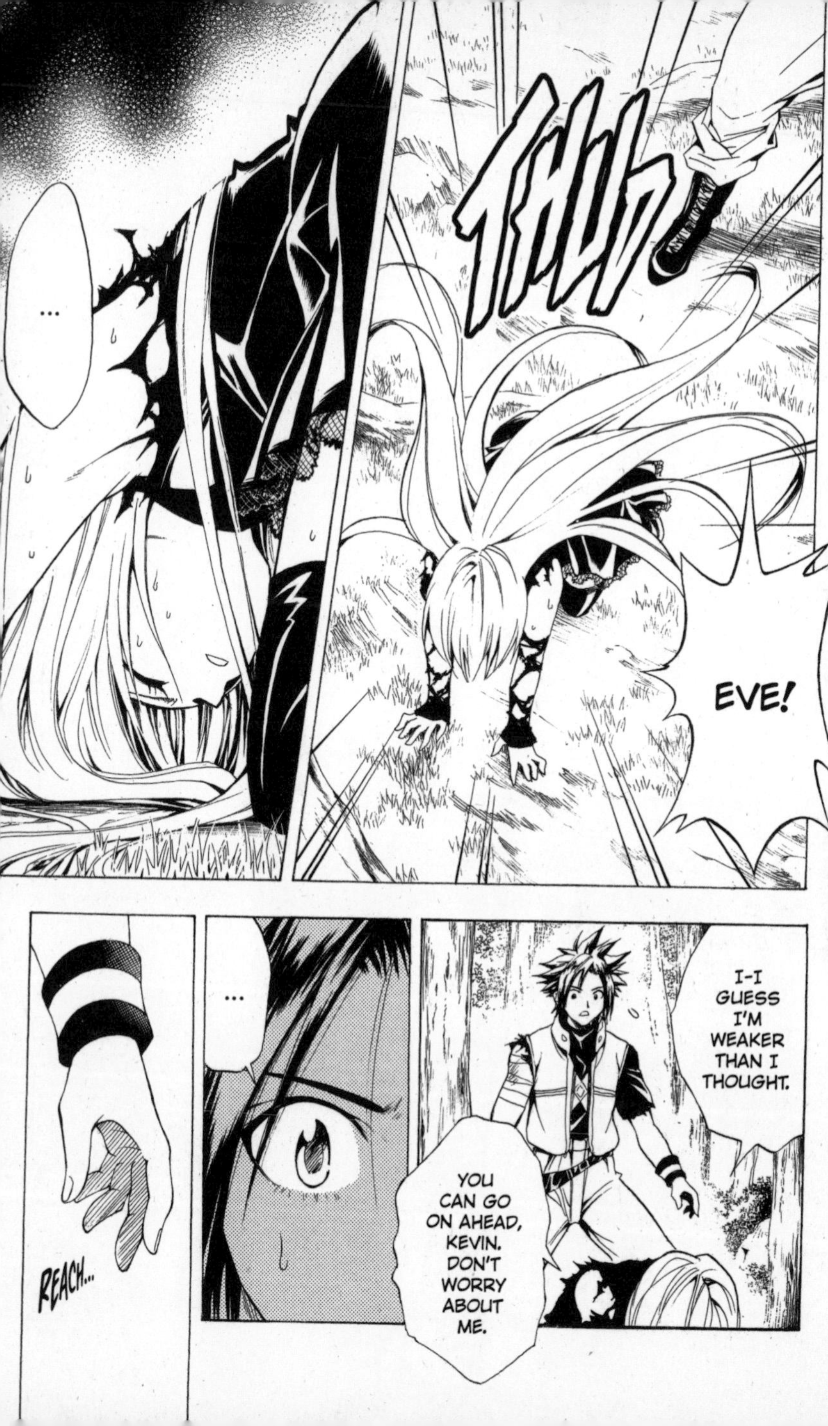
THUD
EVE!
...
I-I GUESS I'M WEAKER THAN I THOUGHT.
YOU CAN GO ON AHEAD, KEVIN. DON'T WORRY ABOUT ME.
...
REACH...

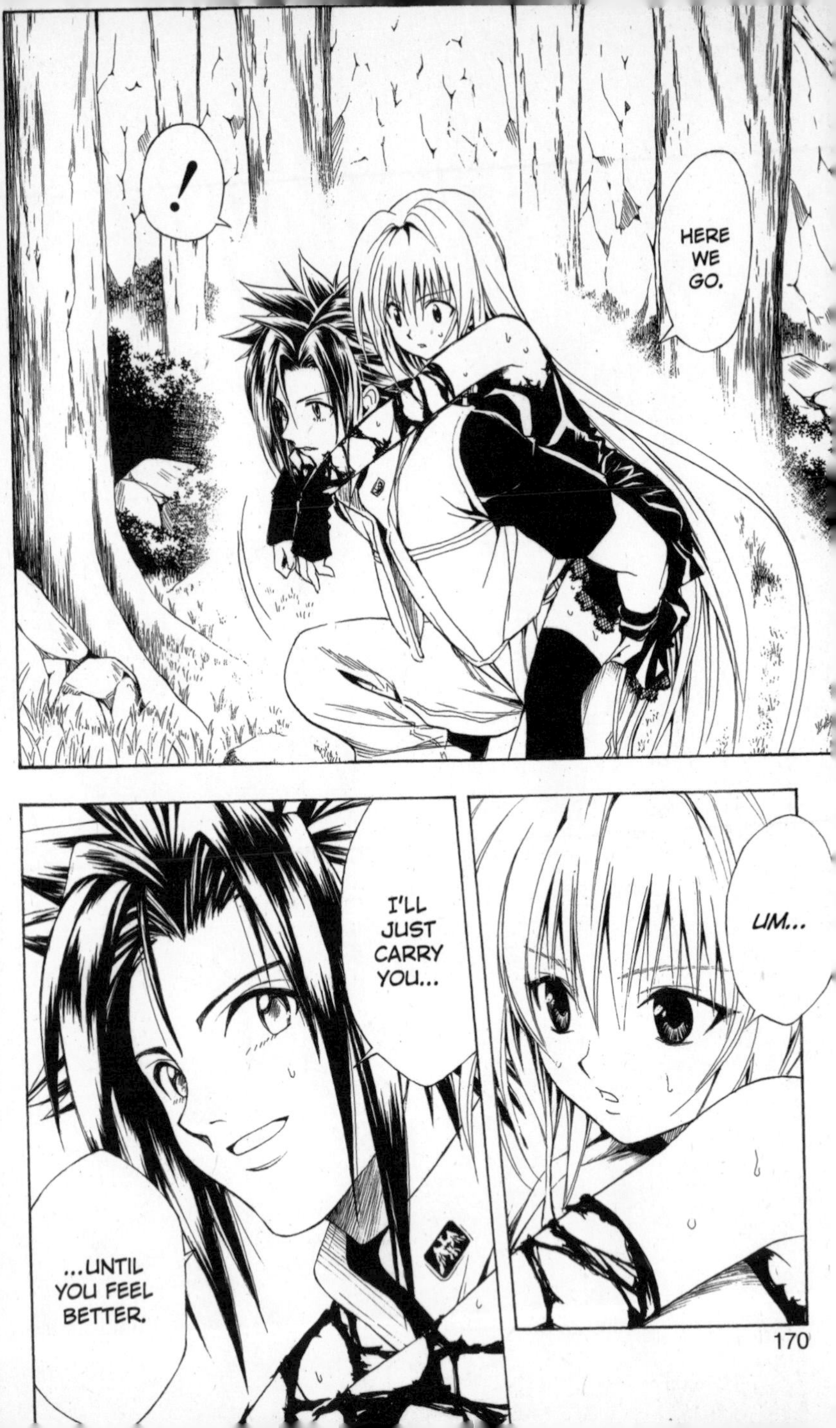
HERE WE GO.
!
UM...
I'LL JUST CARRY YOU...
...UNTIL YOU FEEL BETTER.

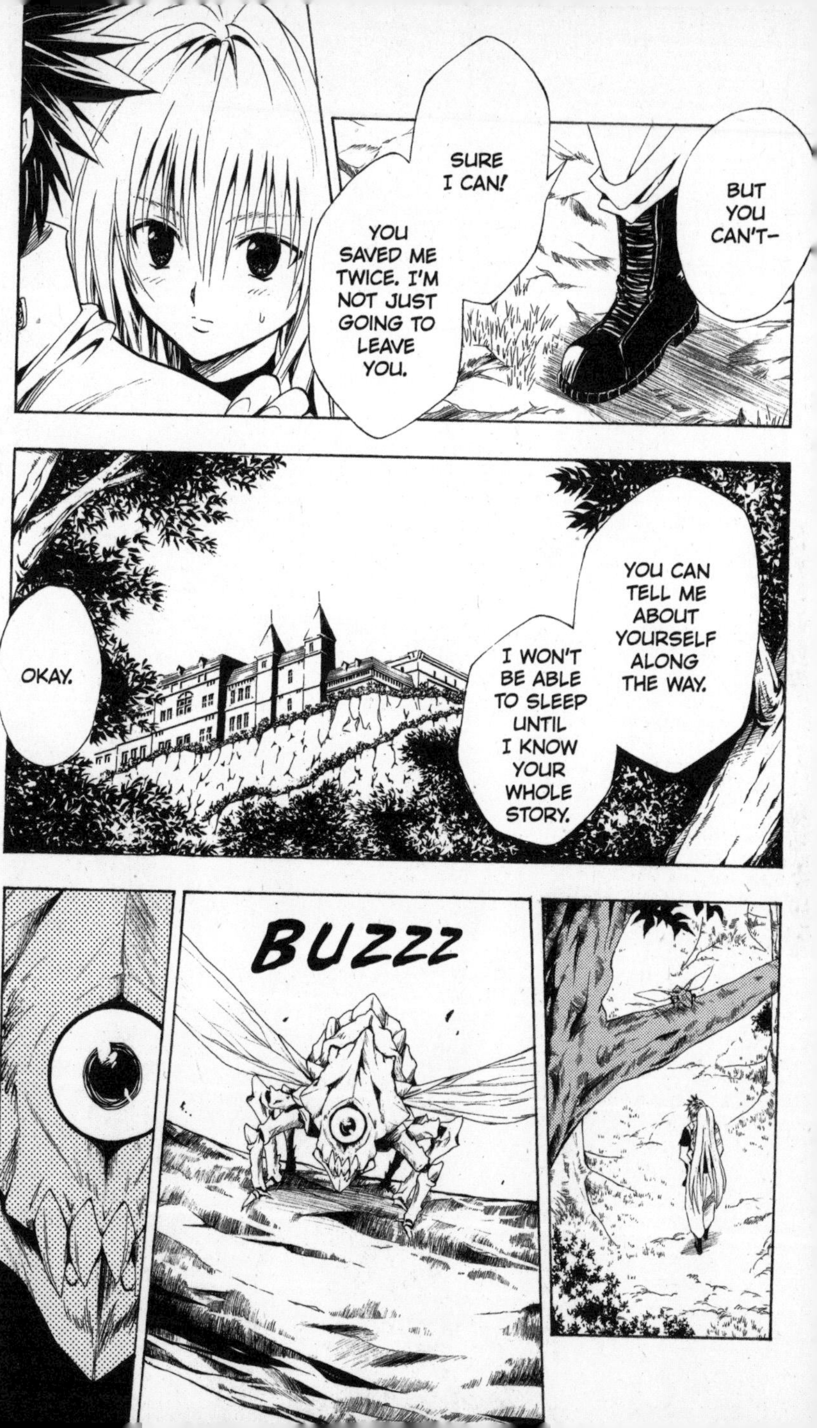
BUT YOU CAN'T-
SURE I CAN!
YOU SAVED ME TWICE. I'M NOT JUST GOING TO LEAVE YOU.
YOU CAN TELL ME ABOUT YOURSELF ALONG THE WAY.
I WON'T BE ABLE TO SLEEP UNTIL I KNOW YOUR WHOLE STORY.
OKAY.
BUZZZ

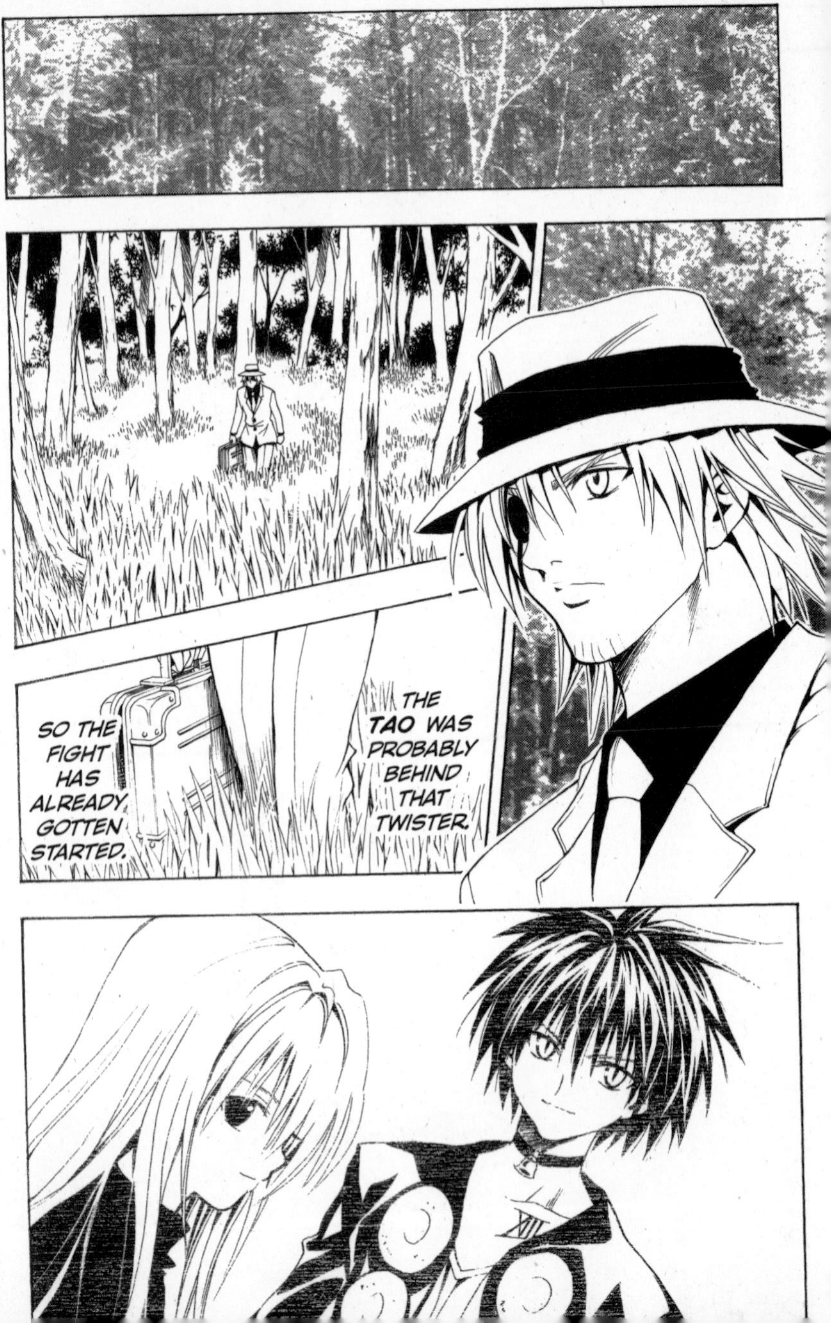
THE TAO WAS PROBABLY BEHIND THAT TWISTER.
SO THE FIGHT HAS ALREADY GOTTEN STARTED.

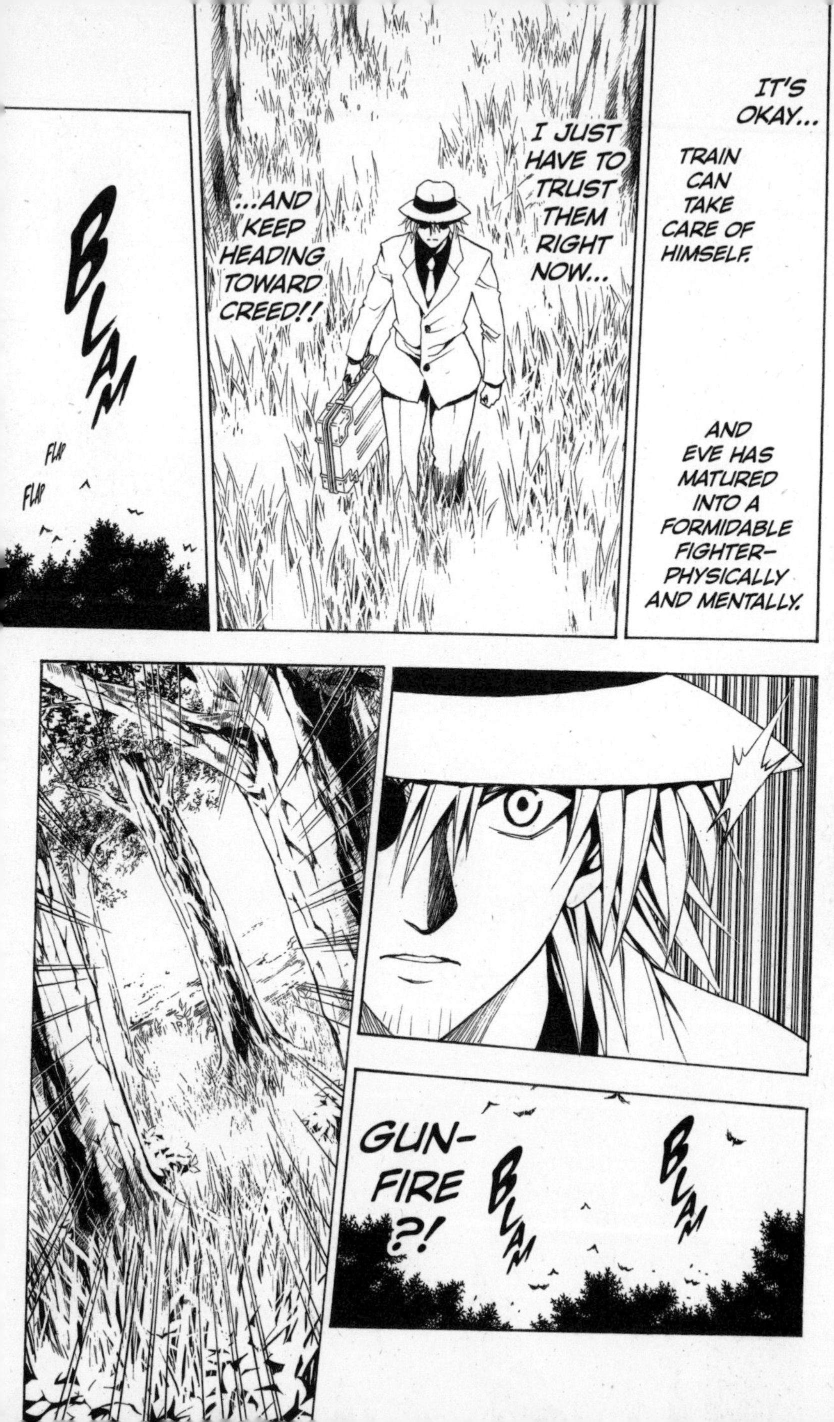
IT'S OKAY...
TRAIN CAN TAKE CARE OF HIMSELF.
AND EVE HAS MATURED INTO A FORMIDABLE FIGHTER—PHYSICALLY AND MENTALLY.
I JUST HAVE TO TRUST THEM RIGHT NOW...
...AND KEEP HEADING TOWARD CREED!!
BLAM
FLAP
FLAP
BLAM
BLAM
GUN-FIRE?!

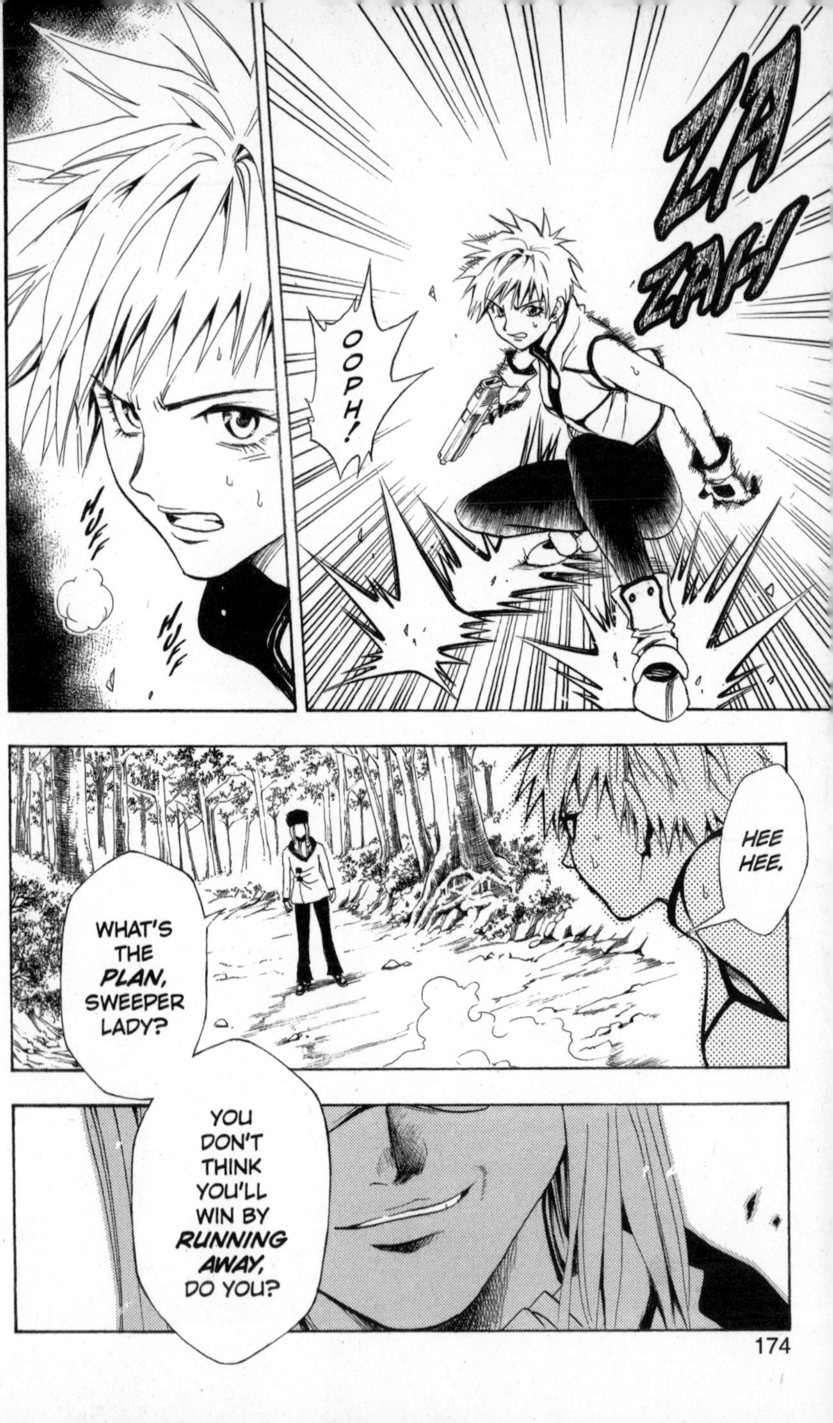

ZA ZAH
OOPH!
HUFF HUFF
HEE HEE.
WHAT'S THE *PLAN,* SWEEPER LADY?
YOU DON'T THINK YOU'LL WIN BY *RUNNING AWAY,* DO YOU?

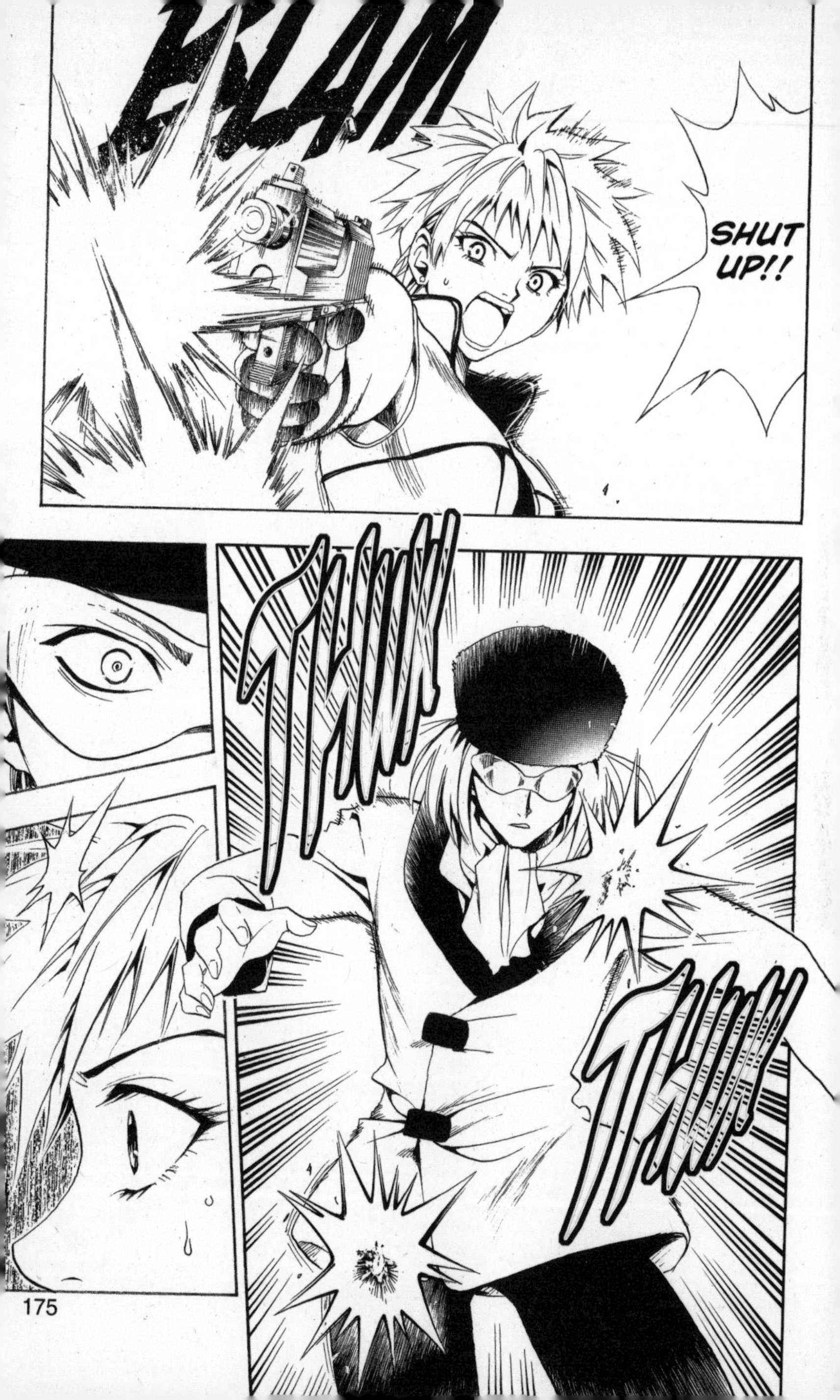
BLAM
SHUT UP!!

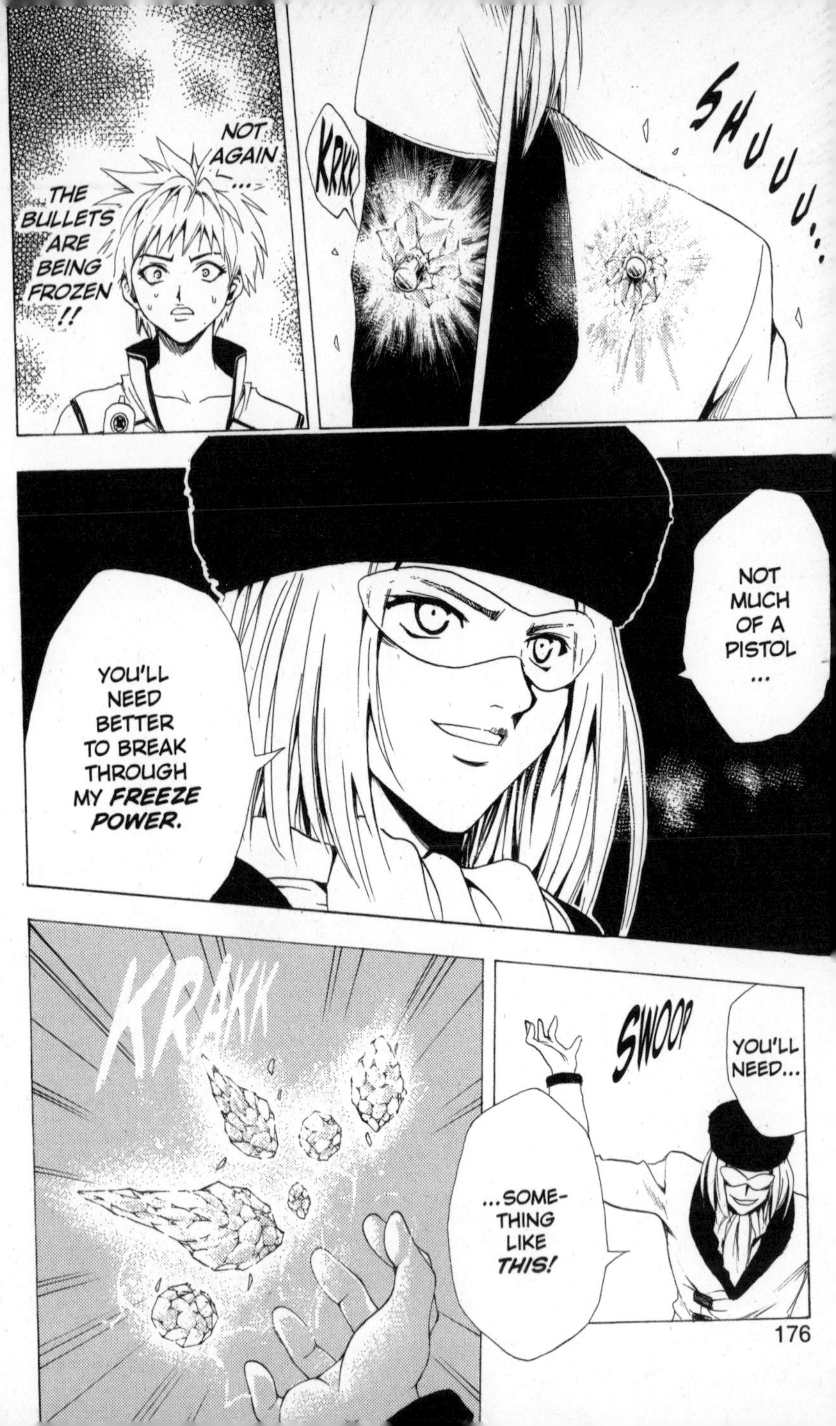
SHUUU...
KRKK
NOT AGAIN...
THE BULLETS ARE BEING FROZEN!!
NOT MUCH OF A PISTOL...
YOU'LL NEED BETTER TO BREAK THROUGH MY *FREEZE POWER*.
SWOOP
YOU'LL NEED...
...SOMETHING LIKE *THIS!*
KRAKK

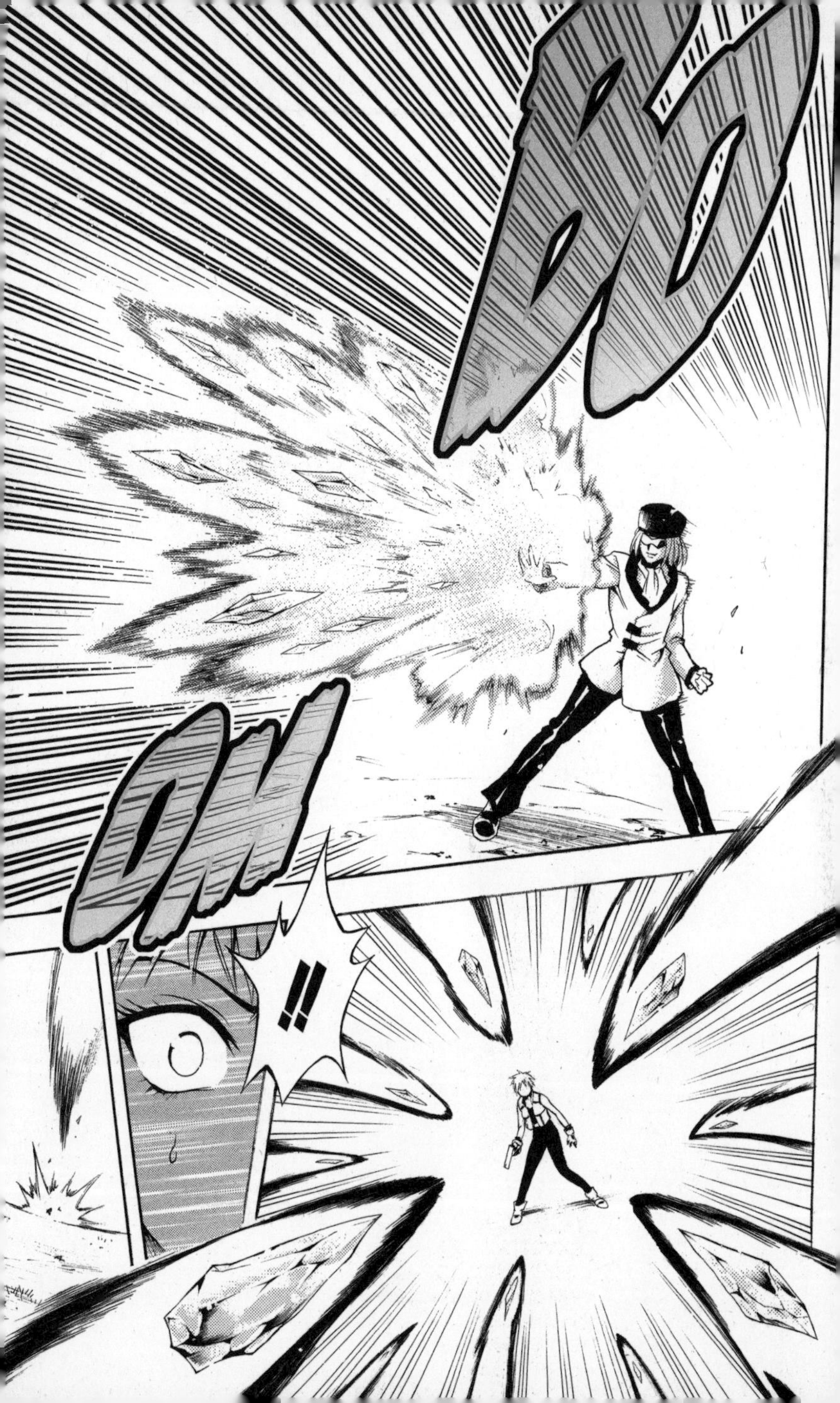
DO
OM
!!

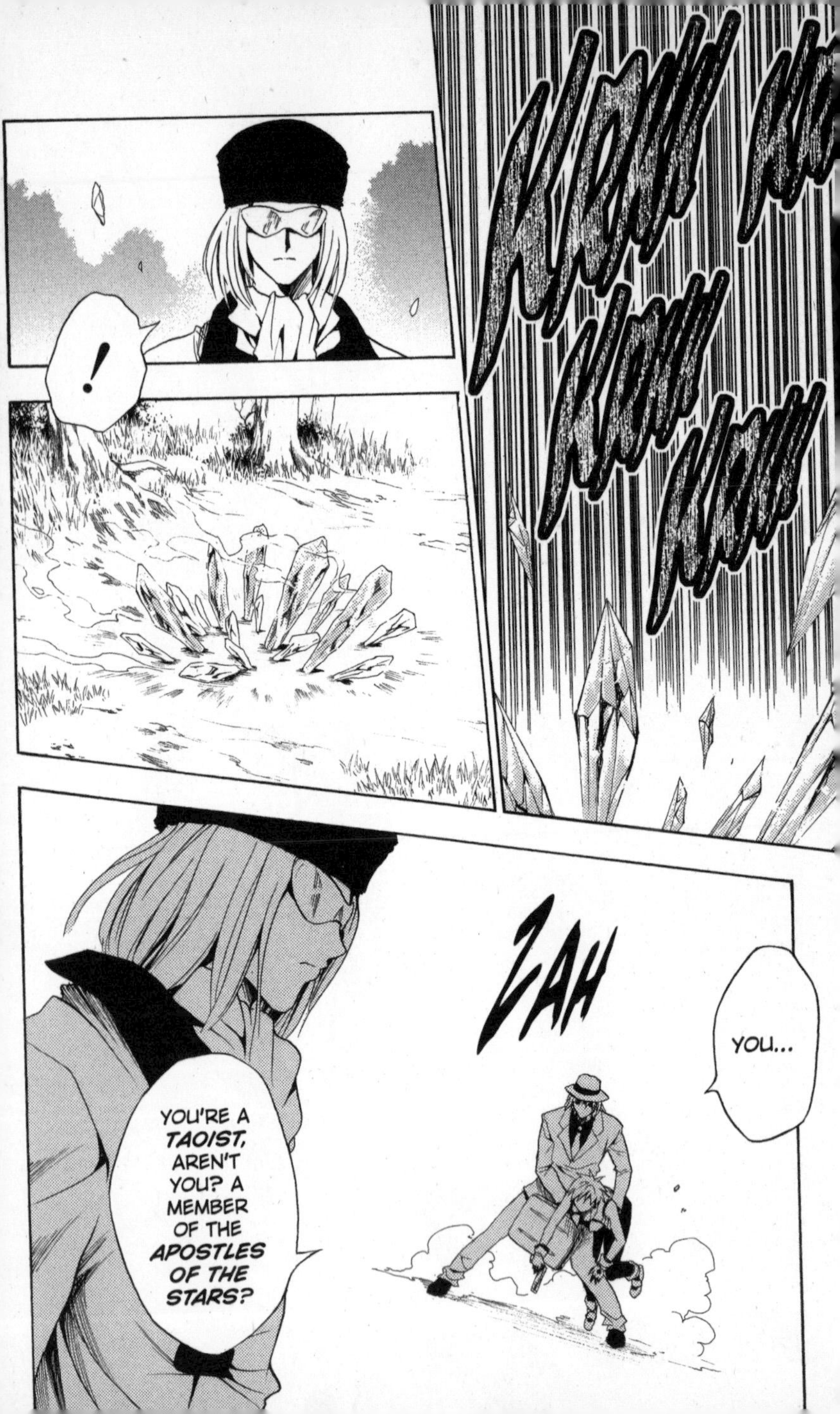
!
ZAH
YOU...
YOU'RE A *TAOIST,* AREN'T YOU? A MEMBER OF THE *APOSTLES OF THE STARS?*

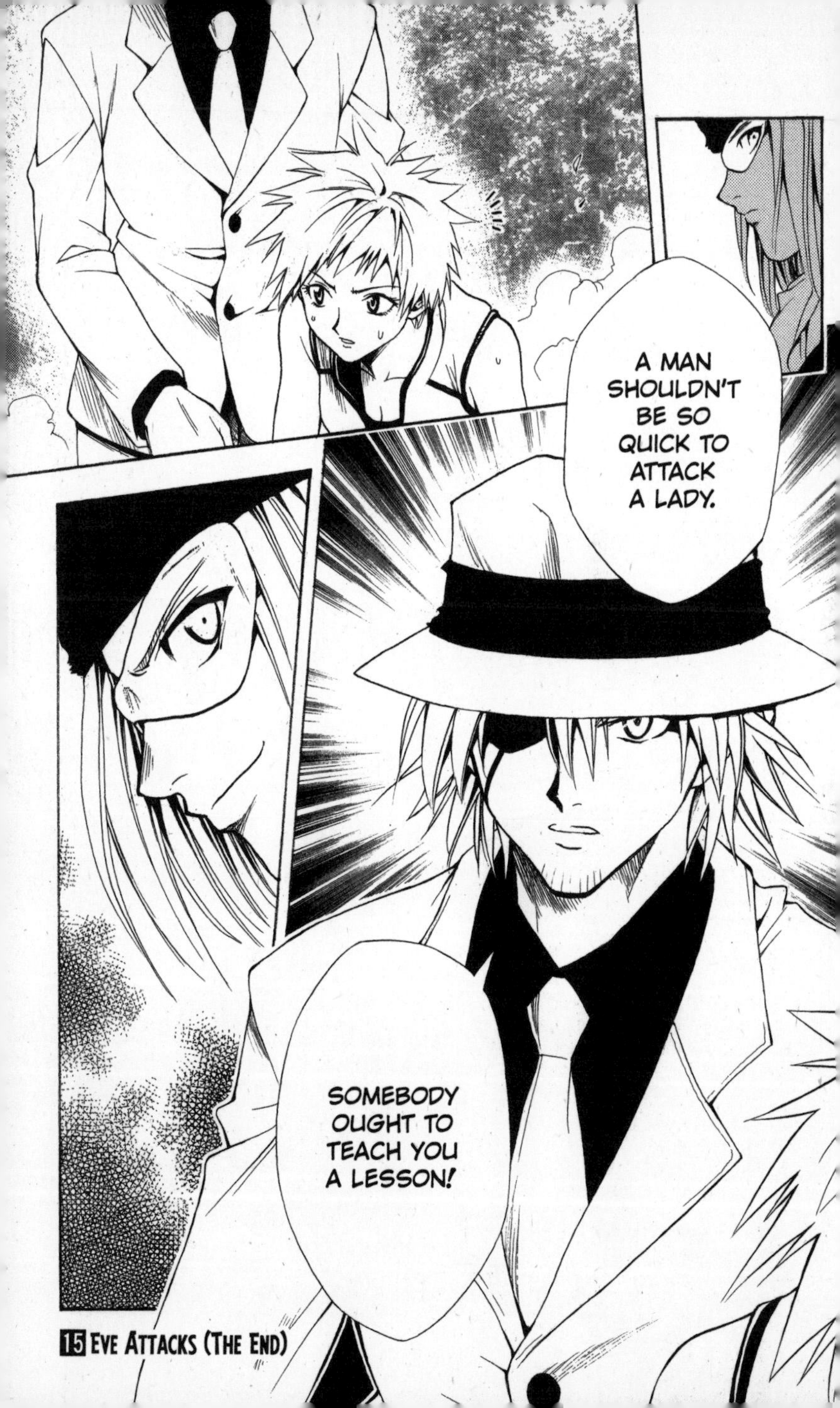
A MAN SHOULDN'T BE SO QUICK TO ATTACK A LADY.
SOMEBODY OUGHT TO TEACH YOU A LESSON!
15 EVE ATTACKS (THE END)

YABUKI SENSEI AND I START A GHOST-LOVER'S CLUB BY AKIRA MIYAZAKI

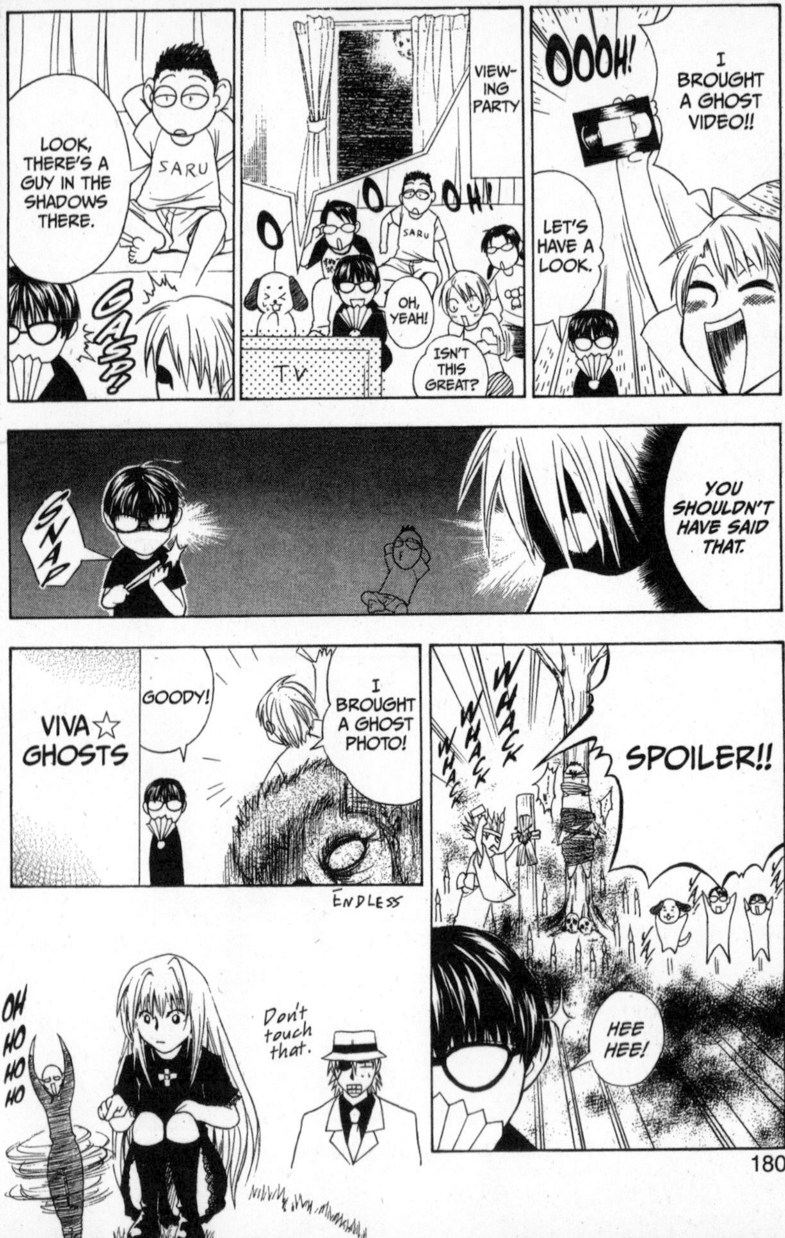
OOOH!
I BROUGHT A GHOST VIDEO!!
LET'S HAVE A LOOK.
VIEWING PARTY
OOOH!
OH, YEAH!
ISN'T THIS GREAT?
LOOK, THERE'S A GUY IN THE SHADOWS THERE.
GASP!
SARU
YOU SHOULDN'T HAVE SAID THAT.
SNAP
SPOILER!!
WHACK
WHACK
WHACK
HEE HEE!
I BROUGHT A GHOST PHOTO!
GOODY!
VIVA☆ GHOSTS
ENDLESS
OH HO HO HO HO
Don't touch that.

EDITOR'S NOTE: [THEY'VE TIED UP SARU FOR SPOILING THE SHOW; SOMEONE IS CURSING HIM BY STAKING HIS VOODOO DOLL]

CREED'S FLOWER BED

DAS BLUMENBEETE SÜR CREED

KOZATO TAI

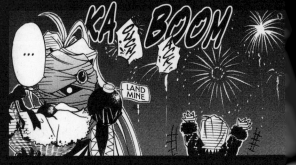

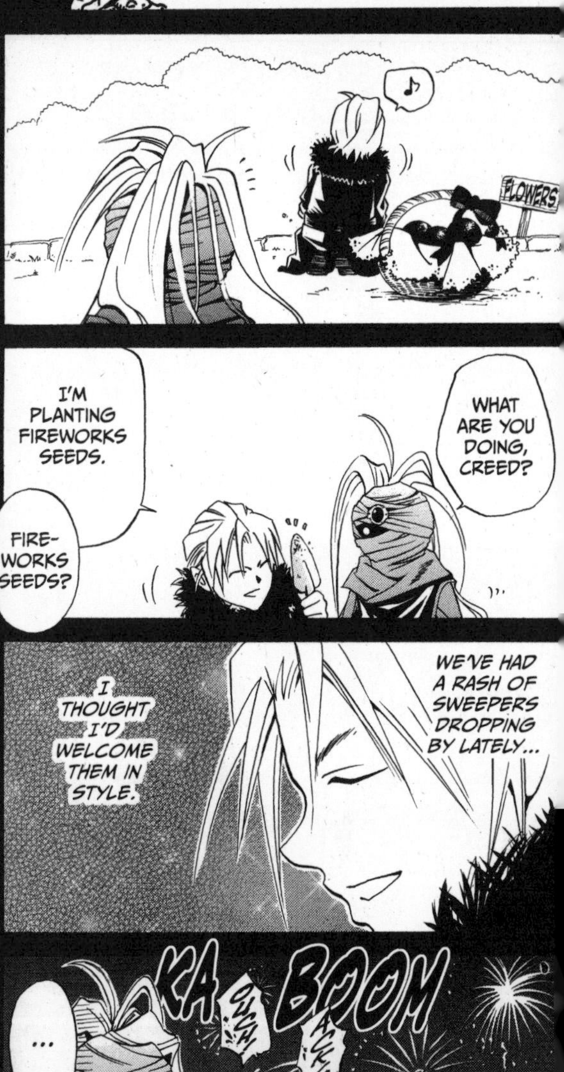

♪
FLOWERS
WHAT ARE YOU DOING, CREED?
I'M PLANTING FIREWORKS SEEDS.
FIRE-WORKS SEEDS?
WE'VE HAD A RASH OF SWEEPERS DROPPING BY LATELY...
I THOUGHT I'D WELCOME THEM IN STYLE.
KA BOOM
OUCH!
ACK!
LAND MINE
...
2003.10

BRAGGING ABOUT DAD

by Katsunori Hida

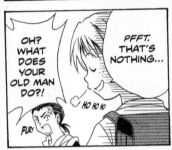

MY DAD PLAYS PROFES-SIONAL BASEBALL. COOL, HUH?
YEAH? MY DAD'S A PILOT.
PFFT. THAT'S NOTHING...
HO HO HO
OH? WHAT DOES YOUR OLD MAN DO?!
FURY
HE'S A WARRIOR...
BEAM
HE MAKES THE WORLD A SAFER PLACE!
WHAC
KRKK
KRKK
THUNDER-HEAD!
ALWAYS AIM FOR THE FACE!!
M-MY SON...
HANG IN THERE, DAD.

THIS IS NOT REALLY PART OF OUR STORY...

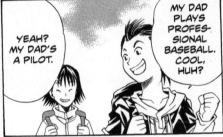

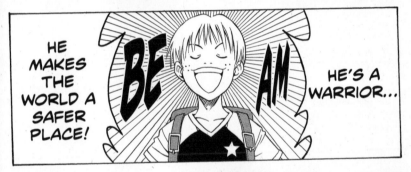

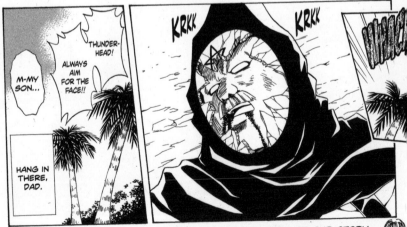

A POINTLESS, PUNLESS, MEANINGLESS AD

(BY KENTARO HONNA)

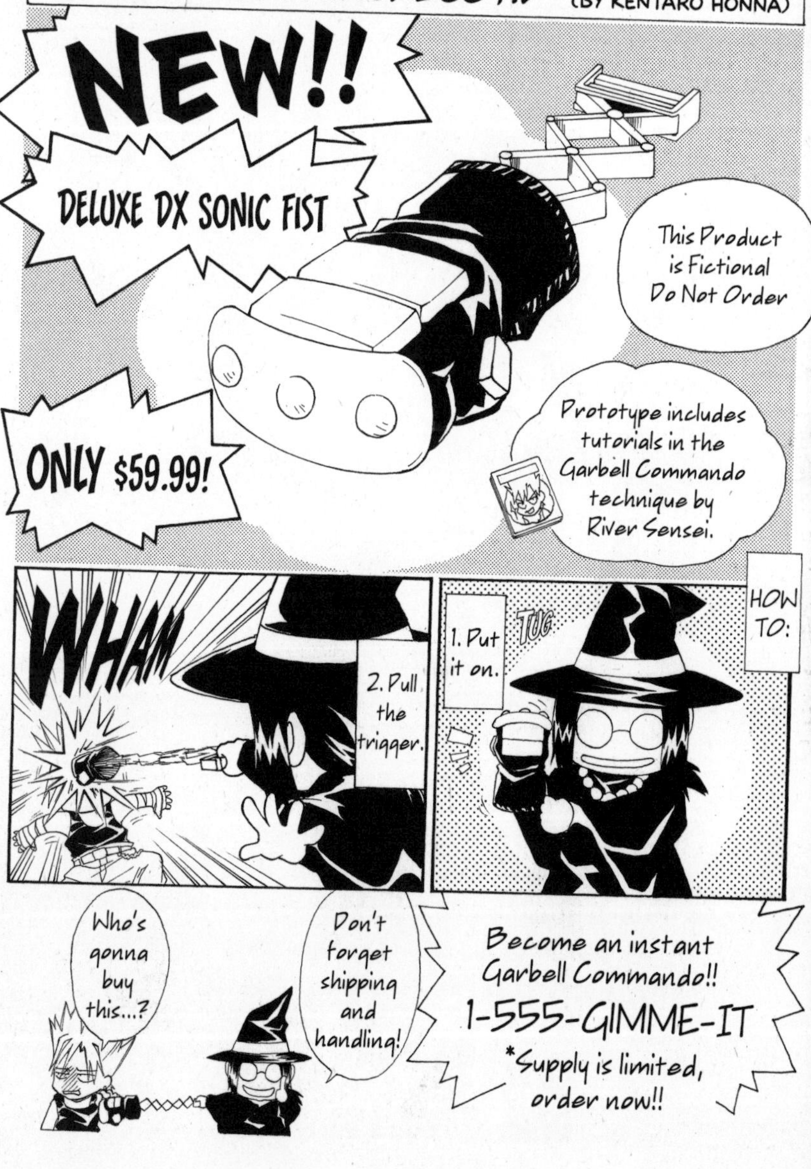

NEW!!
DELUXE DX SONIC FIST
This Product is Fictional Do Not Order
ONLY $59.99!
Prototype includes tutorials in the Garbell Commando technique by River Sensei.
HOW TO:
1. Put it on.
TUG
2. Pull the trigger.
WHAM
Become an instant Garbell Commando!!
1-555-GIMME-IT
*Supply is limited, order now!!
Don't forget shipping and handling!
Who's gonna buy this...?

IN THE NEXT VOLUME...

As the Apostles of the Stars attack, the members of the Sweeper Alliance must put their differences aside and battle together in order to survive. Facing Train and River, Shiki demonstrates the full range of his Taoist power. Will the combined strength of the Sweepers be enough to prevail?

AVAILABLE SEPTEMBER 2008!

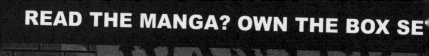

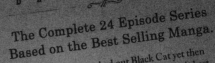

The Complete 24 Episode Series
Based on the Best Selling Manga.

"If you haven't checked out Black Cat yet then you're missing out on one of FUNimation's best and newest series." - DVD Talk.com

"Score: 10 out of 10" - IGN.com

The Complete Series Includes:
24 Episodes on 6 DVDs
24-Page Booklet

OWN THE SERIES TODAY!

"I've come to deliver some bad luck."

WWW.BLACKCAT-TV.COM | WWW.FUNIMATION.COM

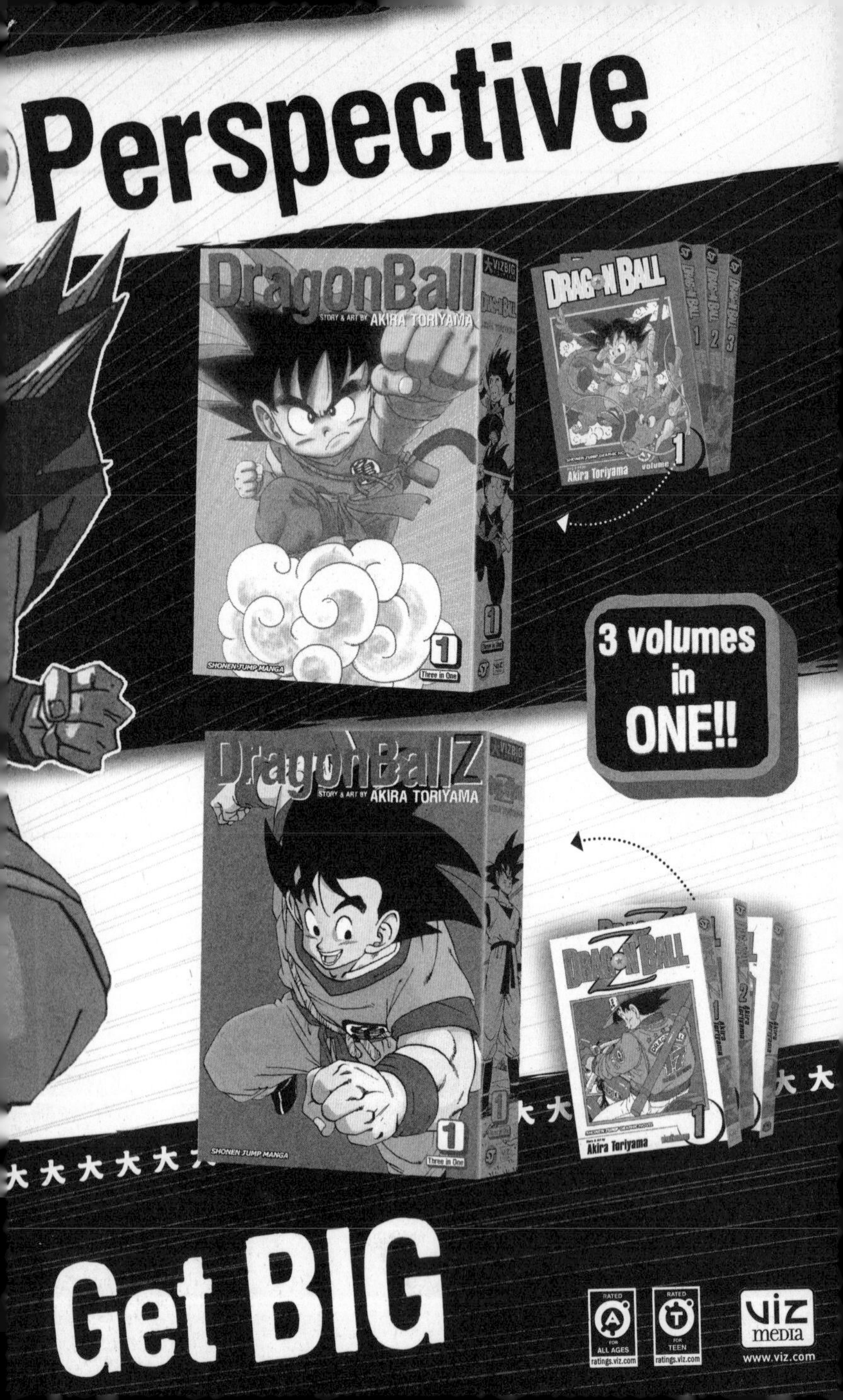
Perspective
DragonBall
STORY & ART BY AKIRA TORIYAMA
SHONEN JUMP MANGA
Three in One
3 volumes in ONE!!
DragonBall Z
STORY & ART BY AKIRA TORIYAMA
SHONEN JUMP MANGA
Three in One
Akira Toriyama
Get BIG
RATED A FOR ALL AGES ratings.viz.com
RATED T FOR TEEN ratings.viz.com
VIZ media
www.viz.com

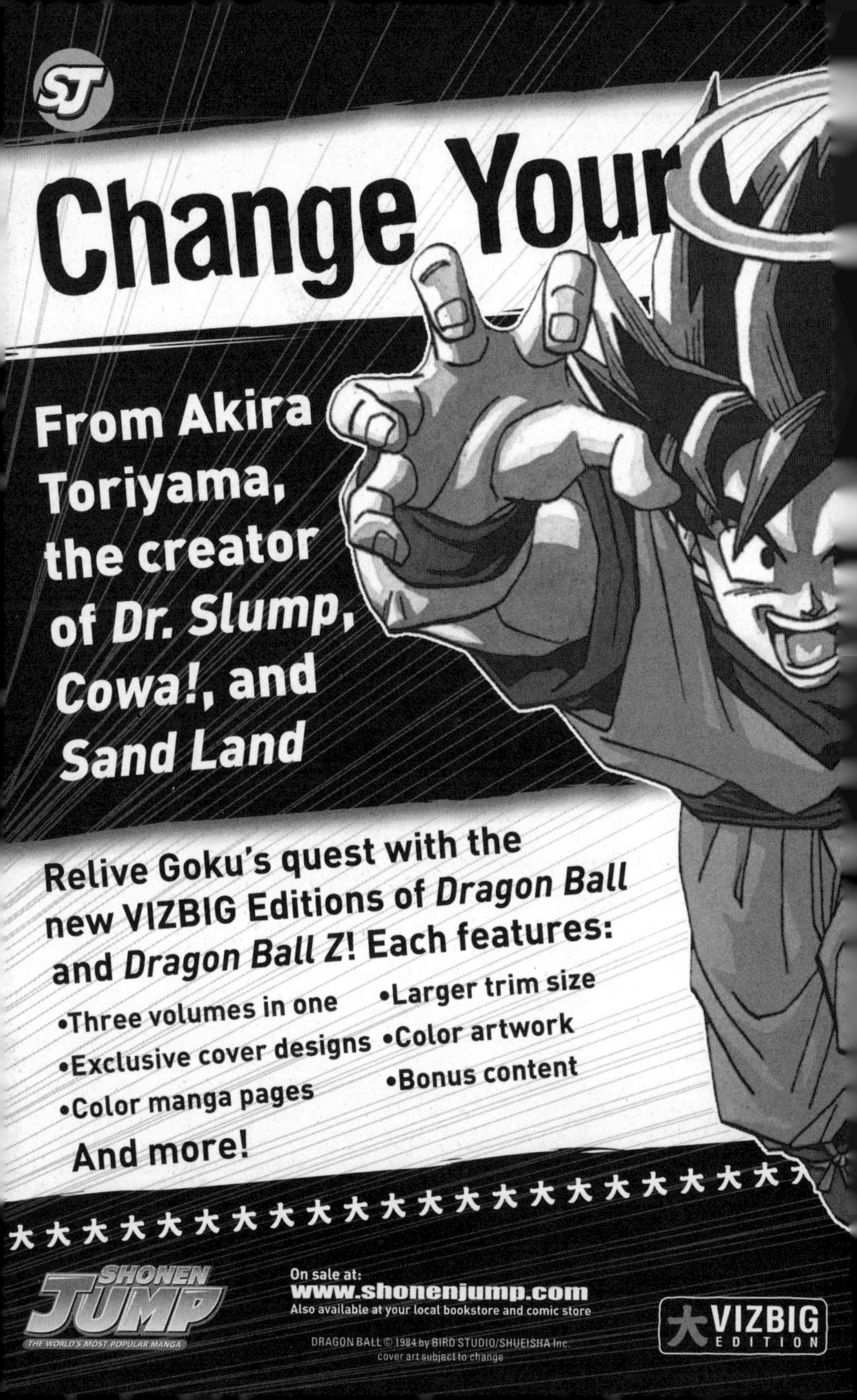
SJ
Change Your
From Akira Toriyama, the creator of *Dr. Slump*, *Cowa!*, and *Sand Land*
Relive Goku's quest with the new VIZBIG Editions of *Dragon Ball* and *Dragon Ball Z*! Each features:
•Three volumes in one
•Exclusive cover designs
•Color manga pages
•Larger trim size
•Color artwork
•Bonus content
And more!
SHONEN JUMP
THE WORLD'S MOST POPULAR MANGA
On sale at:
www.shonenjump.com
Also available at your local bookstore and comic store
DRAGON BALL © 1984 by BIRD STUDIO/SHUEISHA Inc.
cover art subject to change
大 VIZBIG EDITION

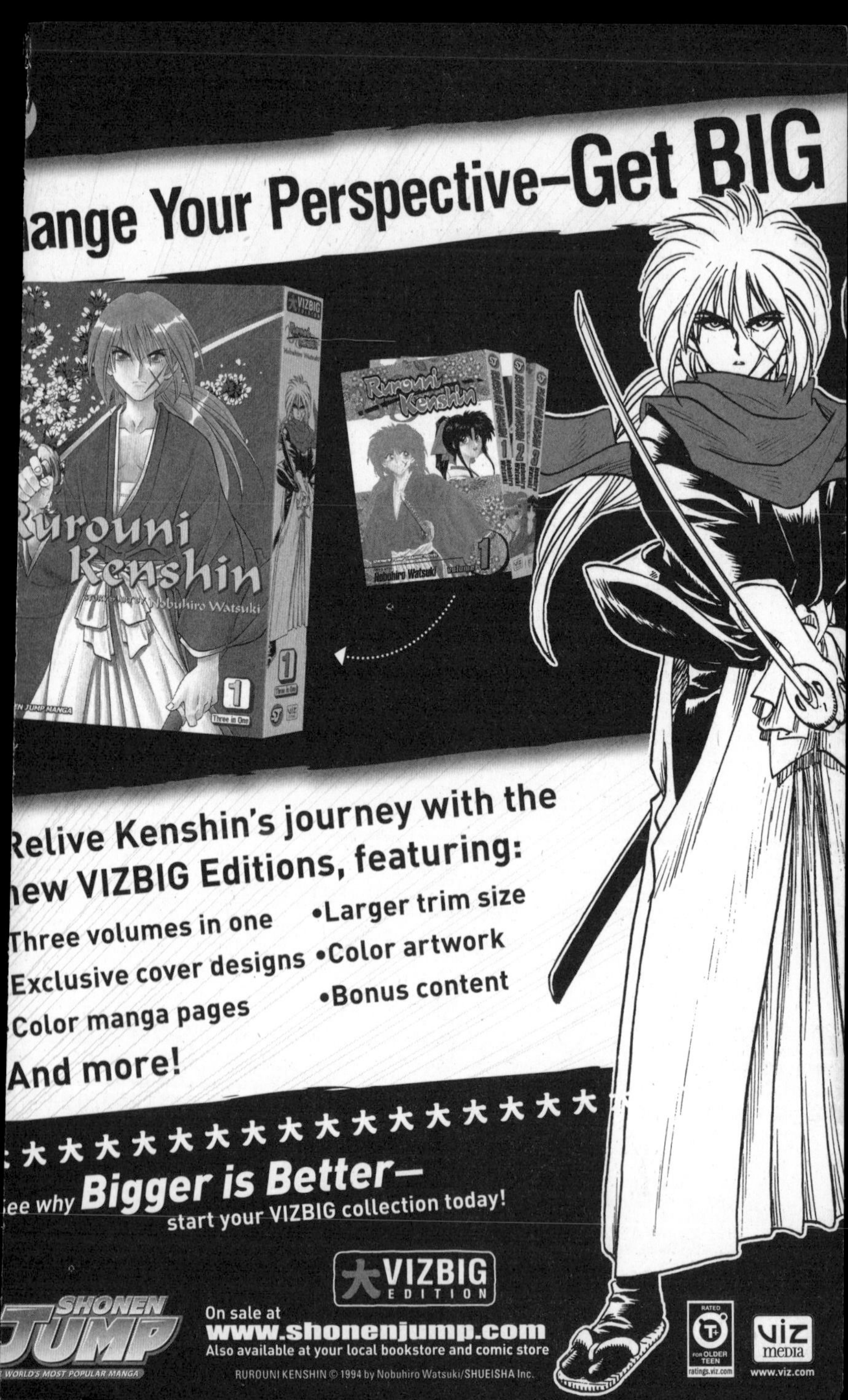
ange Your Perspective–Get BIG
Rurouni Kenshin
Nobuhiro Watsuki
1
Three in One
Relive Kenshin's journey with the
new VIZBIG Editions, featuring:
Three volumes in one
Exclusive cover designs
Color manga pages
•Larger trim size
•Color artwork
•Bonus content
And more!
ee why Bigger is Better—
start your VIZBIG collection today!
VIZBIG EDITION
SHONEN JUMP
WORLD'S MOST POPULAR MANGA
On sale at
www.shonenjump.com
Also available at your local bookstore and comic store
RUROUNI KENSHIN © 1994 by Nobuhiro Watsuki/SHUEISHA Inc.
RATED T+ FOR OLDER TEEN
ratings.viz.com
VIZ media
www.viz.com

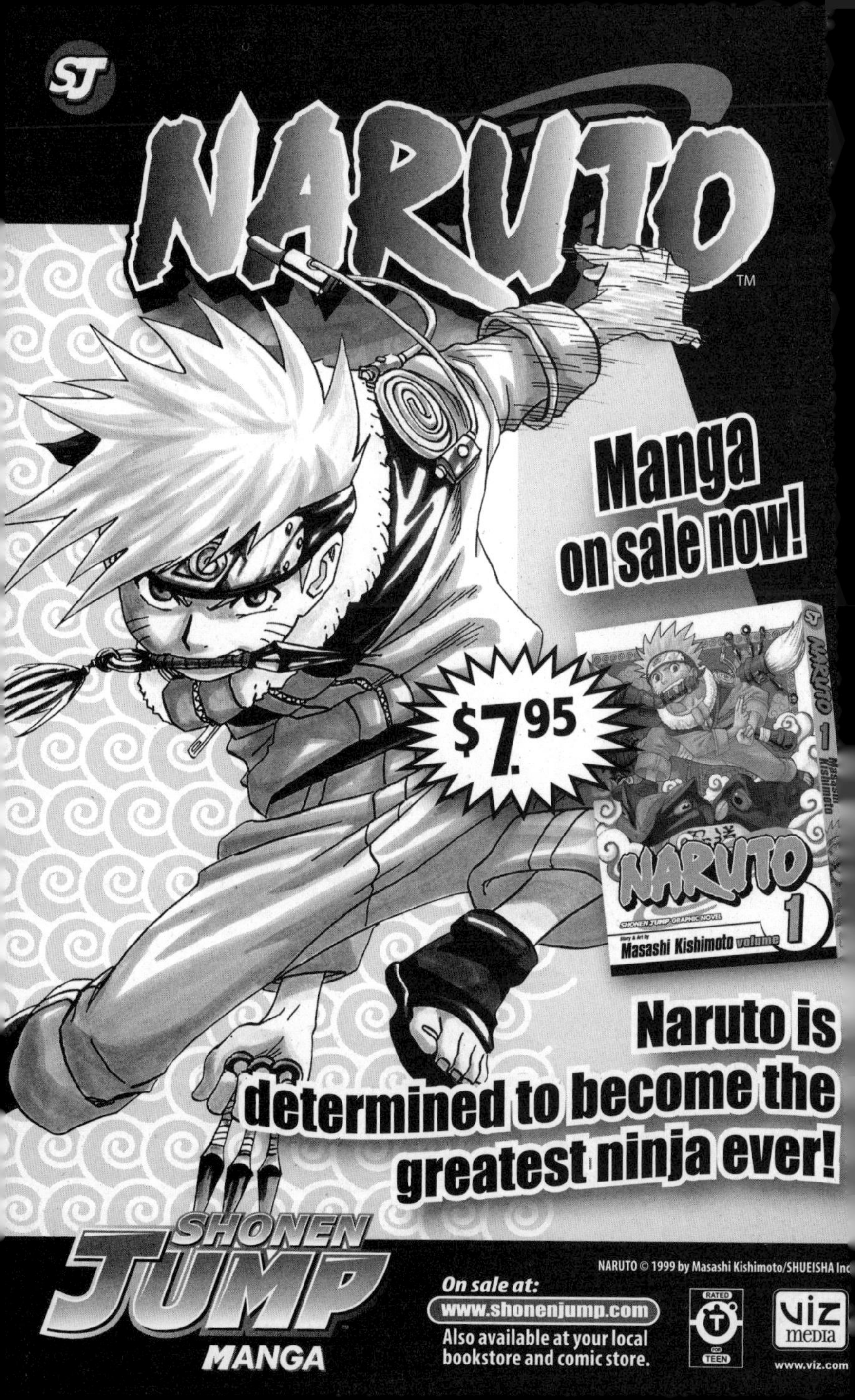
SJ
NARUTO™
Manga on sale now!
$7.95
NARUTO 1
SHONEN JUMP GRAPHIC NOVEL
Masashi Kishimoto volume 1
Naruto is determined to become the greatest ninja ever!
SHONEN JUMP MANGA
NARUTO © 1999 by Masashi Kishimoto/SHUEISHA Inc
On sale at:
www.shonenjump.com
Also available at your local bookstore and comic store.
RATED T FOR TEEN
viz media
www.viz.com

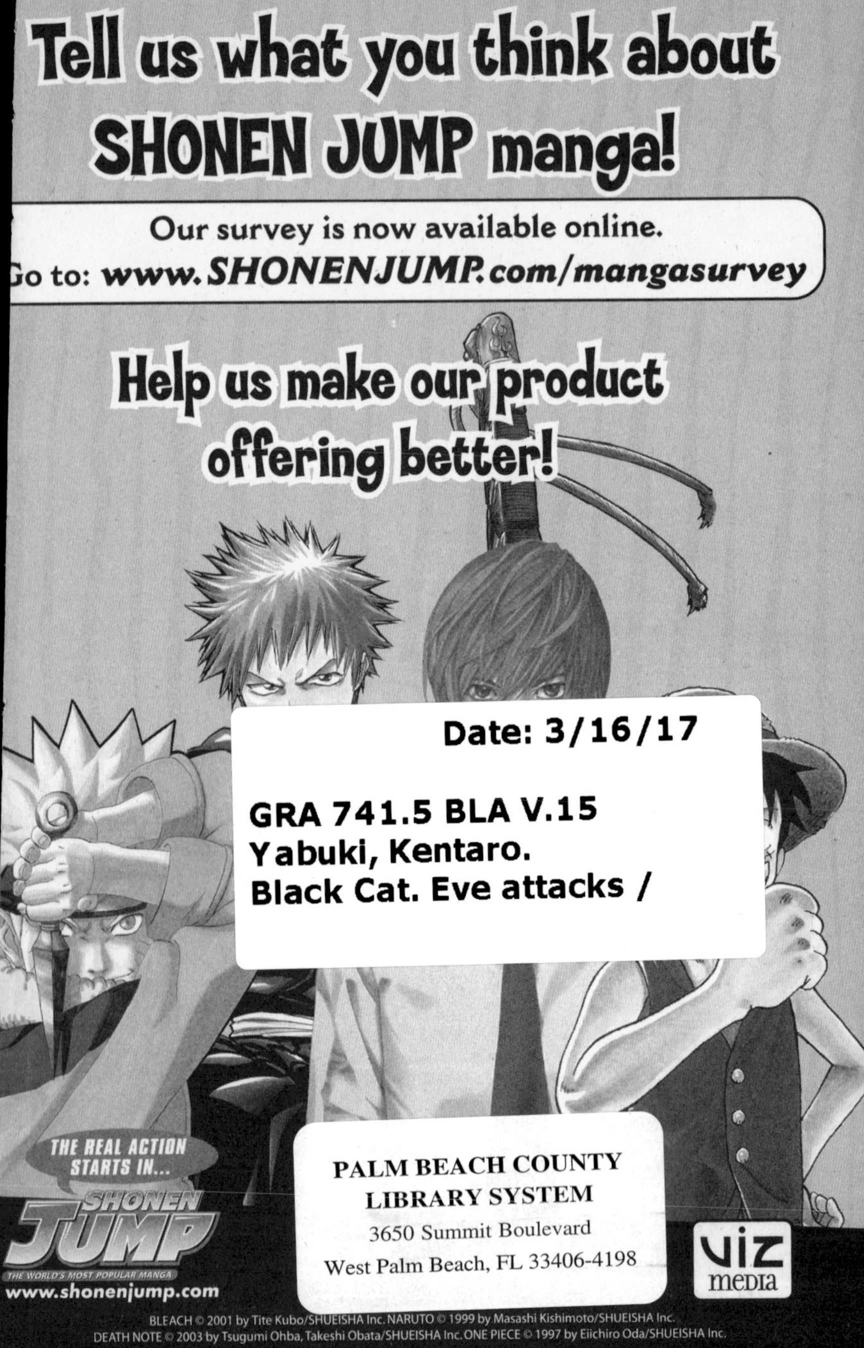
Tell us what you think about SHONEN JUMP manga!
Our survey is now available online.
Go to: www.SHONENJUMP.com/mangasurvey
Help us make our product offering better!
THE REAL ACTION STARTS IN...
SHONEN JUMP
THE WORLD'S MOST POPULAR MANGA
www.shonenjump.com
VIZ media
BLEACH © 2001 by Tite Kubo/SHUEISHA Inc. NARUTO © 1999 by Masashi Kishimoto/SHUEISHA Inc.
DEATH NOTE © 2003 by Tsugumi Ohba, Takeshi Obata/SHUEISHA Inc. ONE PIECE © 1997 by Eiichiro Oda/SHUEISHA Inc.

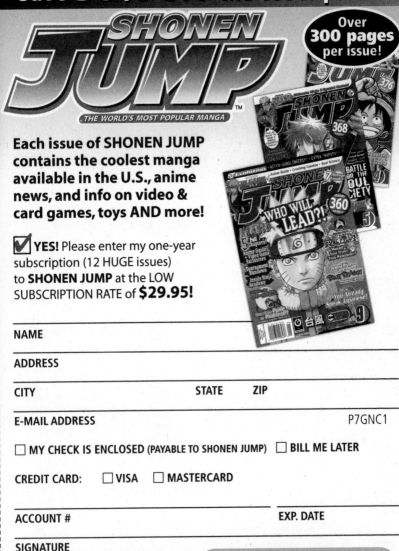